# THE BENEFITS OF FAMINE

---

# THE BENEFITS
# OF FAMINE

A POLITICAL ECONOMY OF FAMINE

AND RELIEF IN

SOUTHWESTERN SUDAN, 1983–1989

*David Keen*

PRINCETON UNIVERSITY PRESS   PRINCETON, NEW JERSEY

Copyright © 1994 by Princeton University Press
Published by Princeton University Press, 41 William Street,
Princeton, New Jersey 08540
In the United Kingdom: Princeton University Press,
Chichester, West Sussex

*Library of Congress Cataloging-in-Publication Data*
Keen, David, 1958–
The benefits of famine : a political economy of famine
and relief in southwestern Sudan, 1983–1989 / David Keen.
p.   cm.
Includes bibliographical references and index.
ISBN: 0–691–03423–0
1.  Famines—Political aspects—Sudan. 2.  Sudan—Politics
and government—1985– I.  Title.
HC835.Z9F3476    1994
363.8′09624—dc20    93-34900

This book has been composed in Adobe Caledonia

Princeton University Press books are printed on
acid-free paper and meet the guidelines
for permanence and durability of the Committee
on Production Guidelines for Book Longevity
of the Council on Library Resources

Printed in the United States of America

1   3   5   7   9   10   8   6   4   2

# Contents

# List of Illustrations

**Maps**

**Figures**

# List of Tables

MY FIRST field trip—to Khartoum and Darfur—was in June to August 1987. This self-funded research provided important background information on conditions in the north, and helped highlight the degree to which relief operations were vulnerable to political manipulation at the local level. I returned to Sudan in October to December 1988, close to the height of the famine. As a research consultant with Nexus Evaluations, UK, my main brief was to investigate the famine in southern Sudan, southern Darfur, and southern Kordofan and the effectiveness of international efforts to relieve it. I was also responsible for investigating the efficacy of aid to the west under the Western Relief Operation, something that yielded important insights about the relationship between the two sets of relief operations. I was able to interview a range of officials, aid staff, and "ordinary" Sudanese in southern Kordofan and southern Darfur, including many people from Bahr el Ghazal. I also conducted interviews with aid staff, government officials, and displaced people in Khartoum. I have drawn extensively on a wide range of secondary written materials available in England, as well as a range of aid agency documentation from British, Irish, and French Non-Governmental Organizations (NGOs) in particular. My research also benefited from a visit to UN headquarters in New York in the summer of 1990.

Famines accompanying civil war present particular obstacles to research. At the time when I visited camps in southern Kordofan in late 1988, people from Bahr el Ghazal were prepared to be interviewed only inside their huts (and sometimes only at night), where security guards could not see them. The killing of five people inside the Muglad camp in April 1989 was evidence that people's fears were justified. Those who spoke to me were nevertheless determined that their stories be heard. This book draws on their accounts and written evidence to document a human disaster that was never fully acknowledged at the time, and is already being forgotten.

Pointing out a number of specific massacres of Dinka in southwestern Sudan but downplaying the general devastation of the Dinka, a Sudan specialist at the U.S. Foreign Service Institute has written:

> A cynical observer might consider this situation an acceptable level of low-intensity violence because of the long-standing tradition of sporadic tribal warfare between the Dinka in southwest Sudan and the adjacent Rizeigat and Messiriyah tribes. In this context, even the occurrence of three unusually large massacres of Dinka in March, August and September [1987] was not entirely surprising, although they were dutifully deplored by both parties. The term

"acceptable level of violence" could not be used to characterize another event that left deep psychological scars among many [the writer then refers to the SPLA's shooting down of a civilian airliner at Malakal] (Bechtold 1990, 589–90).

It should hardly need to be said that there was nothing "acceptable" about the catastrophe that befell the Dinka in 1986–1988. The misinformation surrounding the famine at the time helped to make this catastrophe possible— and it is important, after the event, to recognize the enormity of what happened, to attempt a candid analysis of how this catastrophe was generated, and to wonder how similar catastrophes might be prevented. Sudan remains subject to human-made famine. Finding ways to address this continuing human rights disaster remains an urgent task.

# Acknowledgments

THE NATURE of this study is such that many, perhaps most, of those who helped me in Sudan would probably prefer not to be mentioned by name. They are warmly thanked just the same, especially those who were willing to relive their own suffering or who put themselves at risk in order to convey something of the suffering of others. Many aid agency staff in Sudan gave generously of their time.

At home, I have received funds for study from the Economic and Social Research Council, and thank them for this. I owe a big thank you to my friends at St. Antony's College, Oxford, who have sustained me with much encouragement when I was sorely in need of it: Elizabeth, Daniel W., Daniel B., Paula, Caroline, Matthew C., Matthew J., Joe, Klaus, Giti, Melissa, Melissa P., Minouche, Lucia, Fawaz, Nira, Lakshmi, Angela, Masa, and, especially, Paul and Gopal. I could not have survived without the rock-solid support of Andreas and Georgia in particular, something I will always remember. Georgia's technical help is also greatly appreciated. Neil and Ade helped me valiantly through my revisions. Away from St. Antony's, I owe special thanks to my friend James, as well as to Wendy, Martina, Pedro, Astier, Amir, Haro, Talia, Clive, Anne, Sara, Kelvin, Helen, Roy, Grandma, Ann, Angela, Matthew L., Simon M., Katherine, Sam B., and Andrew for their constant encouragement. I am also indebted to Andrew for his graphic contributions. I owe a great deal, also, to Anita for encouraging me to take on this task.

I would like to thank my former teachers, David Jones, Boyd Hilton, and Geoffrey Jones. This study has been greatly influenced by Amrita Rangasami and Alexander de Waal, both of whose work has been an inspiration for me. I am also grateful for their consistent encouragement. I have benefited greatly from the ideas, energy, and support of Peter Cutler. Valuable help and advice has been received from Barbara Harriss, Gavin Williams, Ann Waswo, John Ryle, Tony Vaux, Roger Winter, Andy Mawson, Bona Malwal, Ken Wilson, Tim Allen, Roger Hay, and, especially, Mark Duffield. Amartya Sen's work, although I have noted criticism, was a model of clarity. I am very grateful to Douglas Johnson and Wendy James for their expert guidance on many aspects of the southern Sudan. Most important, my supervisor, Megan Vaughan, has made an enormous effort in reading my work and earlier in helping to get the thesis into shape, and I am very grateful to her.

Cindy's love and encouragement has sustained me throughout the writing and revising process.

I would like to dedicate this study to my mother, who never wavered in her support, and to my late father. This work would not have been possible without their love and inspiration.

# List of Abbreviations

| | |
|---|---|
| ABS | Agricultural Bank of Sudan |
| AICF | Action Internationale Contre la Faim |
| CART | Combined Agencies Relief Team |
| CDC | Centers for Disease Control |
| DUP | Democratic Unionist Party |
| EC | European Community |
| EEC | European Economic Community |
| EWSB | Early Warning System Bulletin, RRC |
| FAO | Food and Agricultural Organization |
| FEWS | Famine Early Warning System, USAID |
| GOS | Government of Sudan |
| ICRC | International Committee of the Red Cross |
| ILO | International Labor Organization |
| JCA | Joint Church Aid |
| LRCRC | League of Red Cross and Red Crescent |
| MALT | Management and Logistics Team, RRC |
| MSF | Médecines Sans Frontières |
| NANS | National Alliance for National Salvation |
| NGO | Nongovernmental Organization |
| NIF | National Islamic Front |
| NPA | Norwegian People's Aid |
| ODA | Overseas Development Administration |
| OFDA | Office of Foreign and Disaster Assistance |
| OLS | Operation Lifeline Sudan |
| PDF | Popular Defense Forces |
| RRC | Relief and Rehabilitation Commission |
| RTO | Road Transport Operation |
| RTU | Road Transport Unit |
| SAC | Sudan African Congress |
| SCF | Save the Children Fund |
| SPLA | Sudan People's Liberation Army |
| SPLM | Sudan People's Liberation Movement |
| SRC | Sudan Railways Corporation |
| SRRA | Sudan Relief and Rehabilitation Association |
| SSPA | Southern Sudan Political Association |
| TCC | Technical Coordination Committee |
| TMC | Transitional Military Council |
| UNDP | United Nations Development Program |

| | |
|---|---|
| UNHCR | (Office of the) United Nations High Commissioner for Refugees |
| UNICEF | United Nations Children's Fund |
| UNOEA | United Nations Office for Emergencies in Africa |
| UNOEOS | United Nations Office for Emergency Operations in Sudan |
| USAID | United States Agency for International Development |
| USAP | Union of Sudan African Parties |
| WFP | World Food Program |
| WRO | Western Relief Operation |

# THE BENEFITS OF FAMINE

## CHAPTER 1

# Overview

A SEVERE FAMINE developed among the Dinka[1] of Sudan in 1985–1989, beginning in northern Bahr el Ghazal and spreading into southern Kordofan and southern Darfur as people were uprooted from their home areas (see Map 1). The study attempts to explain the causes of the famine, including the grave shortfalls in relief.

The famine—with deaths across the south in 1988 put at over 500,000, (U.S. Committee for Refugees, 1993)—promised, and to a large extent yielded, significant benefits (many of them economic) for a variety of powerful Sudanese interests, who helped to create the famine. The apparent "failure" of the Sudanese government and international donors to relieve this famine cannot be understood without comprehending how these "beneficiaries"—at the local level and in the central government—were able (and permitted) to manipulate famine relief for their own purposes. For the donors, although the famine itself was not functional, the pursuit of narrowly defined relief agendas served important functions, even as it tended to allow the creation and perpetuation of famine.

## CONCEPTIONS OF FAMINE: ITS NATURE AND CAUSES

Famine is routinely depicted in modern Western discourse as a short-term emergency, as "something simple, huge and apocalyptic,"[2] a terrible event that descends on particular societies from time to time and yields a number of unfortunate victims. Not unnaturally, famine is habitually referred to as a "disaster": indeed, it forms a regular focus—along with hurricanes, earthquakes, and floods—for the British journal *Disasters*. Amartya Sen has defined famine as "a particularly virulent form of [starvation] causing widespread death" (Sen 1981, 40), a conception widely adhered to in Western countries.[3] Allied with such conceptions is a commonly held view of famine as something every reasonable person would oppose. There are many texts on how to prevent famine, after all; very few on how to promote it.

For a long time, the "disaster" of famine was typically depicted as stemming from an inadequate food supply, arising perhaps from bad weather,[4] inappropriate agricultural practices (Ibrahim 1984), or population growth (Firth 1959). According to such portrayals, famine was nobody's "fault" (un-

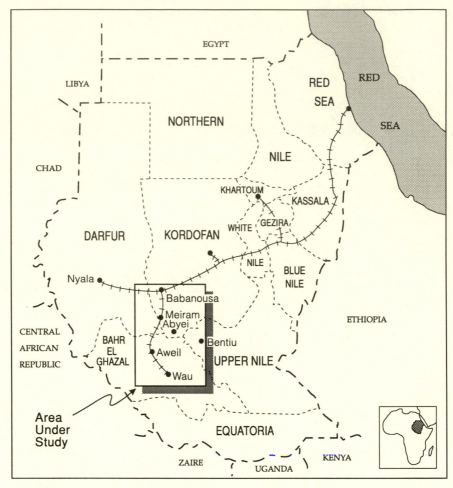

**Map 1**. Sudan, with Area under Study

less it was that of famine's "lazy," "incompetent," or "irreligious" victims),[5] and it conferred few, if any, benefits.[6]

While a concentration on food supply and natural disaster remains common in contemporary analyses of famine,[7] such approaches have been convincingly challenged by Sen, who argued in *Poverty and Famines* (1981) that the roots of famine lay not in aggregate food supply but in individual "entitlements" to food, with famine particulary likely when individuals were unable to afford whatever food was available.[8] Significantly, however, Sen's analysis shared important characteristics with the one he was rejecting. First, it was primarily an economic analysis of famine; the politics of famine and famine relief were little considered.[9] Second (a closely related point), Sen's emphasis on poverty and market forces as the root of famine and his rather cursory discussion of the role of the state implied a lack of attention to human responsibility: in his analysis, there were victims of famine, but few immediate culprits or beneficiaries. Indeed, "market forces" had in some sense taken over from previous nonhuman actors (God, the weather) as the principal author of famine: the lives of men and women were depicted as being at the mercy of Supply and Demand. Famine was still a "disaster"; in Sen's conception, it was now an "economic disaster" (Sen 1981, 162).

In their 1989 publication, *Hunger and Public Action*, Drèze and Sen turned their attention to the political sphere, to the role of public policy in protecting entitlements. Their model of famine incorporated both economic and political elements: where entitlements collapsed and states failed to take measures to protect entitlements, famines were likely. Particular types of state (lacking democratic forms of government or a free press) were seen as likely to be particularly neglectful of famine relief. And effective relief might be prevented by "negligence or smugness or callousness on the part of the non-responding authorities" (Drèze and Sen 1989, 262).

However, the possibility that states and politically powerful groups may actively promote famine and actively obstruct relief for rational purposes of their own is not addressed. Indeed, the Drèze and Sen conception of the state is essentially a liberal one, in which the failure to act in the public interest is perceived as a failure of public policy. A certain community of interest among "the public" is assumed: Sen and Drèze stress that although there is likely to be dispute about the division of the benefits, "public action for social security is in some sense beneficial for all groups" (ibid., 17).

The view that poverty and market forces lie at the root of famine is now widely advanced (World Bank 1986, 27; Independent Commission on International Humanitarian Issues 1985, 63–64; Fraser 1988, 247), as is the view of famine as a failure of public policy, or the result of relief "blunders."[10] Such portrayals tend to be relatively inoffensive to governments in famine-affected countries, governments with whom aid agencies and major international donors are often seeking good relations. Indeed, emphasizing official obstruction of relief may expose aid agencies to expulsion. Moreover, highlighting the fact that relief has not reached its intended beneficiaries may discourage contributions from the general public, and may be seen as reflecting badly on those who approved the operation (Davis 1974; Clark 1991). Meanwhile, journalists may be heavily dependent on aid agency sources. Even rebel groups may be reluctant to highlight the creation of famine if they themselves are being accused of contributing.

An alternative perspective to that of Sen and Drèze portrays famine not simply as a disastrous event but as a process, with beneficiaries. Amrita Rangasami has suggested that the famine process cannot be defined with reference to the victims of starvation alone. It is a process in which benefits accrue to one section of the community while losses flow to the other."[11]

Precisely the same trends in prices that are highlighted by Sen as creating victims of famine may also create a number of beneficiaries. This has been remarked on from time to time. Lenin spoke in 1918 about profiteering from high grain prices (Lenin [1918] 1945, 64) and saw semistarvation as functional for capitalism in that it ensured a supply of cheap labor (Lenin [1917] 1939, 138). Price movements during famine in northern Nigeria in 1973–1974 were observed to have certain beneficiaries (Watts 1983, 440).[12] The acquisition of land by certain groups during famine has been observed in Rajasthan, India (Jodha 1975, 1616), and in Bangladesh (Hartmann and Boyce 1979, 26).

Price movements during famine are likely to cause, and reflect, a loss of assets among the victims. And this process is not necessarily outside human control. Rangasami argues that famine is "a process during which pressure or force (economic, military, political, social, psychological) is exerted upon the victim community," progressively depriving it of assets (including, eventually, the ability to labor) (Rangasami 1985, 1749).

Drawing on local understandings of famine in India in particular, Rangasami challenges Sen's notion that famine necessarily involves mortality,[13] stressing that famine may, but need not culminate in mortality: famine victims, Rangasami argues, will die only if there is no early and effective intervention by the state to stop the process of asset depletion.[14] The "aimless wandering" of people, although deemed a "premonitory sign" of famine by officials in late nineteenth-century India, actually occurs only at the final stages of famine, Rangasami suggests (ibid., 1750). However, "in political systems such as India the state intervenes only to halt the starvation process but will not consider intervention in the economic process" (ibid., 1797).[15] This omission is seen as contributing to widespread pauperization and recurrent famine (ibid., 1797).

De Waal, too, has emphasized the distinction between "famine" and "famine mortality." Drawing on local perceptions of famine in western Sudan in the mid-1980s, he has suggested that "famine" should be understood to mean the disruption of a way of life, involving hunger and destitution (including loss of assets) and sometimes but not always involving death: there are "famines" and "famines that kill" (de Waal 1989a). De Waal emphasizes that proper relief is not simply a matter of providing food; also needed are water, medical services, and help with the economic strategies people employ in the face of famine. While many of these concerns were actively pursued by officials in colonial India (Government of India 1901), their importance has often been forgotten in more recent times. This study follows de Waal's and Rangasami's broader conception of the famine process.

As long as we continue to identify famine simply with starving to death, the idea that famine may confer economic benefits is hard to credit. But if we conceive of famine as an extended economic and political process, it becomes more plausible that there may be economic beneficiaries. The military functions of famine are more readily and commonly recognized, as when a besieged town is starved of food.

If famine is conferring certain benefits, it follows that the groups benefiting from famine are likely to have an interest in preventing effective relief. It is not difficult to find examples of the withholding of relief by those who stood to gain economically from so doing. The granting of alms and poor relief in medieval Europe was often akin to famine relief, given the desperate condition of many recipients (Mollat [1978] 1986). But withholding relief on the grounds that it promoted laziness and moral laxity was commonplace (ibid., 134). In England, the 1349 Statute of Labourers threatened the imprisonment of anyone providing alms to beggars capable of work, as landowners attempted to secure labor supplies in the aftermath of the Black Death (de Schweinitz 1961, 1–5). Restricting relief in order to "encourage" the poor to work remained a pressing concern right through to Victorian England and beyond (ibid.), spilling over into British officials' preoccupation with the "demoralizing" effects of gratuitous relief in imperial outposts from India (Government of India 1901) to Sudan (de Waal 1989b) to southern Africa. Indeed, when thousands of starving Xhosa entered Cape Colony after the religiously inspired killing of their own cattle in 1856–1857, the governor refused relief to the able-bodied unless they contracted to work for a European employer for three to five years; meanwhile private relief was sabotaged by the Cape government. One newspaper explained that such relief prevented the Xhosa "from becoming what we would find it so much to our and their interest for them to be—labourers" (Iliffe 1987, 101).

In addition to lowering labor costs, withholding relief is also likely to boost grain prices. There is evidence from a variety of historical contexts that grain merchants have attempted (often successfully) to restrict the provision of famine relief.[16]

The incentive for withholding relief may be military. Blocking of food supplies, including relief, has frequently been used as a weapon of war in both international and civil conflicts.[17] The use of hunger as a weapon for starving rebels into submission has been documented by a number of writers.[18]

A second "rational" reason for withholding relief should also be noted—the desire to minimize the unwanted side effects of famine. These side effects—for example, the perceived threat to the health and security of local people posed by famine migrants—can sometimes be reduced by withholding relief at particular locations, thereby discouraging the presence of such migrants.

Suspicion of outsiders and vagrants has discouraged relief in a wide vari-

ety of historical contexts.[19] A widespread fear of migrants in medieval
Europe has been documented by Michel Mollat. Mollat contrasted the charitable attitude to the "true pauper," who was known to his or her fellow
villagers, with widespread suspicion of the "transient pauper," or "vaga-
bond": "Next to nothing was known about the men and women who lived as
vagabonds. Since they had fled their rightful place in society, might they not
be rebels? Or disease carriers? . . . Hospices prudently offered shelter to
'transient paupers' for only a limited period, and in times of alarm access to
the city was denied."[20]

In relation to famine in Darfur, western Sudan—an area that was later to
absorb many Dinka famine migrants—de Waal has emphasized the critical
role in causing excess mortality that was played by the health crises accompanying drought, notably by unusual concentrations of people in areas with
inadequate sanitation and water (de Waal 1989a). This work has important
implications for the way that famine migrants are likely to be perceived by
local authorities. Hostility toward migrants and withholding of relief from
them in Darfur in 1985 have been documented (de Waal 1989a, 169; Keen
1991a, 195, 199).

A third "rational" reason for withholding relief from famine victims is simply that this may allow the appropriation of these resources by less needy,
but more politically influential, groups. For the latter, securing relief resources arising from famine may be one of famine's main benefits.

In the context of longer-term assistance, Peter Bauer has argued that "the
materially most backward groups are not reached by aid. As they are inartic-
ulate and politically ineffective, their presence affects neither the international flow of aid nor the domestic allocation of funds."[21]

The "diversion" of relief resources has been noted in a number of contexts,[22] as has the channeling of relief resources to relatively privileged
urban groups (Vaughan 1987, 111; de Waal 1989b, 23; Sobhan 1979). Bauer
has argued that international aid in general is likely to bolster oppressive
governments in relation to civil society (Bauer 1984, 46; Hancock 1989); the
same may sometimes be true of relief aid (Copans 1983, 87–94).

## "POLICY FAILURE": WHAT DOES IT MEAN?

A number of insights in the field of policy analysis call into question the idea
that "policy" and "good intentions" can be neatly separated from "what hap-
pens in practice." These ideas are particularly salient when we compare the
seemingly benevolent "official discourse" surrounding the famine with the
reality of abuse and neglect.

According to most discussions of relief and development by governments
and aid organizations, "policy" is conceived as the enunciation and pursuit
of benevolent, laudable aims (see, e.g., Gittinger 1984). Policy is "problem-

oriented": it seeks to remedy poverty, disease, underdevelopment, famine, or whatever. Discussion of how to achieve these shared and self-evidently desirable goals is the essence of what Clay and Schaffer have called the "mainstream" approach to the policy process (Clay and Schaffer 1984, 3–5). If such benevolent policies "fail" (for example, if aid interventions fail to make a dent in the poverty of the intended beneficiaries), then according to this mainstream approach, it is likely to be because "policy" was thwarted by a variety of "obstacles to implementation" (Schaffer 1984, 181–84).

An alternative perspective rejects the assumption that policy aims are necessarily benevolent, and questions the usefulness of this idea of policy failure. As Schaffer has argued: "The . . . important question is not why public policy 'fails.' It does not always necessarily or completely do so. The formulation expresses an odd reification. Public policy is, after all, what it does. The point is to explain what that is, and then see if that explanation can itself be an instrument for change and improvement."[23]

Even as policymakers "fail" to achieve stated goals, it is quite possible that they are achieving other, unstated goals. Indeed, Keith Griffin has suggested in relation to analysis of development policy: "Rather than criticising governments for failing to attain what they did not set out to attain, or offering advice on how to attain a non-goal, it would be instructive if more time were devoted to analysing what governments actually do and why."[24]

Schaffer and Clay were influenced by the work of the French philosopher Michel Foucault, who put forward the idea that even when particular policy practices do not appear to be achieving their avowed ends (for example, the prison system appeared ineffective in preventing crime), they may nevertheless be serving a number of other, often hidden, functions (for example, the prison system could be seen as creating a limited class of criminals who could be easily monitored by the police) (Foucault 1977, 1978, 1981). In this spirit, Foucault described the prison system as "the detestable solution which one seems unable to do without" (Foucault 1977, 232). He applied the same sort of analysis to the imprisonment of dissidents in the former Soviet Union (in opposition to those on the Left who wished to "explain it away"), suggesting that a proper investigation of "the Gulag question" involved

> [r]efusing to restrict one's questioning to the level of causes. If one begins by asking for the "cause" of the Gulag (Russia's retarded development, the transformation of the party into a bureaucracy, the specific economic difficulties of the USSR), one makes the Gulag appear as a sort of disease or abscess, an infection, degeneration or involution. This is to think of the Gulag only negatively, as an obstacle to be removed, a dysfunctioning to be rectified—a maternity illness of the country which is painfully giving birth to socialism. The Gulag question has to be posed in positive terms. The problem of causes must not be dissociated from that of function: what use in the Gulag, what functions does it assure, in what strategies is it integrated?[25]

One of the reasons why "policy failures" should not be taken at face value is that policy outcomes may be actively and successfully shaped by groups with goals that differ from those expressed by policymakers at the top. For example, Pressman and Wildavsky (1973) noted that a minority employment program in Oakland, California, had foundered after taking insufficient account of which groups might (or might not) have an interest in "implementing" it. They argued that the principal goals of the people who had designed the program had nevertheless been achieved. These were, first, to be seen to be taking vigorous action (to reassure Oakland's black citizens at a time of increasing urban unrest) and, second, to spend funds quickly while they were still available.[26] Pursuing this line of thought, Smith and Clarke emphasized the need to create and maintain implementing "coalitions" (Smith and Clarke 1985, 6–7, 173), and Barrett and Fudge pointed out that agencies charged with "implementation" will often be able to influence policy even at the "decisional" stage (Barrett and Fudge 1981, 26).

If we accept that policy outcomes are likely to be shaped by a range of interest groups, this creates potential problems for those who originally enunciated the "goals" of policy. As Clay and Schaffer put it, when the expressed goals of policymakers do not work out in practice, by what means can this apparent "failure" be accommodated? And does maintaining an appearance of good policy outcomes militate against achieving good outcomes in practice?

Clay and Schaffer suggest that one way policymakers can escape responsibility for poor policy outcomes is through a rigid distinction between "policy" and (subsequent) "implementation." Policymakers can always blame "the other side of things"—implementation (Schaffer 1984, 168–69). The distinction may prevent improvements in policy, for lists of "obstacles to implementation" (perhaps including a "lack of political will" among the would-be implementers) are likely to discourage adequate thought about what decisionmakers might have done differently, what they might do differently in the future, or how the varied goals of those who were able to shape policy outcomes might have been allowed for in advance (ibid., 181–84). Declining to take responsibility for "implementation" may serve other functions, as Barrett and Fudge point out: any real attempt at intervention to cajole "implementing" agencies into doing the will of others might upset powerful groups; it might also reveal the powerlessness of the group doing the cajoling (Barrett and Fudge 1981, 276).

Clay and Schaffer argued that another escape route for officials seeking to avoid responsibility lies in shaping agendas. Their investigation of how agendas are shaped drew heavily, once again, on Foucault. Foucault set himself the task of "eventalization," something he defined as "rediscovering the connections, encounters, supports, blockages, plays of forces, strategies and so on which at a given moment establish what counts as being self-evident, universal and necessary." He stressed the importance of "shaking [the] false self-evidence" of particular practices (Foucault 1981, 5–6).

Clay and Schaffer stressed that only a limited range of issues, and a limited range of data, are likely to be considered by policymakers. Given the issues considered, and given the data taken into consideration, policy could be presented as remarkably unobjectionable. To the extent that the existence of alternatives could be suppressed, to the extent that decisions could be presented as springing automatically from the data available, few opportunities for blame would arise. "Paradoxically enough it always tends to appear that 'there was no choice' while, at the same time, what is done conveniently seems both therapeutic and axiomatic" (Schaffer 1984, 152). Choices always exist, however, Clay and Schaffer stressed. There are always other possible issues and agendas, other data that might be taken into consideration. They advocated a method of enquiry that seeks to highlight these choices, and to consider what "room for maneuver" there might have been (and might still be) to do things differently (Clay and Schaffer 1984, 1–12; Schaffer 1984, 142–93).

The shaping of agendas is not always an active, calculating process on the part of officials, Clay and Schaffer elaborated. Indeed, while officials may manipulate data and definitions, the existing data and prevailing definitions may in some sense manipulate officials.[27] In this connection, Geof Wood has argued that widely used labels often encourage a damaging focus on "cases" rather than on people with stories. A concentration on the "landless" in Bangladesh, for example, might appear uncontroversial and benevolent, but it risks ignoring the processes through which people lose their land, an omission that would not be encouraged by the use of a word such as "dispossessed" (Wood 1985, 5–13).

A third bureaucratic escape route highlighted by Clay and Schaffer is a lack of openness and a lack of proper evaluation of policy outcomes, including a frequent failure to consult the intended beneficiaries (Schaffer 1984, 177). "Without any revelations responsibility scarcely arises," Clay and Schaffer note.[28] Weber had emphasized that even producing accurate information on the surrounding world might be unnecessary for bureaucratic survival, in contrast to a business enterprise (Gerth and Wright Mills 1948, 235).

## THE USES OF FAMINE: AN ANALYTIC FRAMEWORK

The analysis of famine and relief in this study takes seriously the possibility that famine can serve important functions, as well as the possibility that those influencing policy may, in some sense, be succeeding even when the expressed aims of policy remain unrealized. When famine occurs, we may hear a great deal about "market failure" and "policy failure." But who exactly is failing (and who succeeding) when markets behave in particular ways, or when the expressed policy of relieving famine does not work out in practice?

Following Foucault's questions on the Gulag, this study asks: What use is famine, what functions does it assure, in what strategies is it integrated?

The priorities of those suffering from famine have received a degree of welcome attention (Jodha 1975; de Waal 1989a). But despite frequent references to corruption (Kent 1987, 19; Fraser 1988, 214–19) and to the use of food shortages as a weapon of war, relatively few writers have investigated the priorities of those who may not be suffering from famine but who may nevertheless be in a position to influence its course (two exceptions are Harrell-Bond [1986] and Kent [1987]).

In analyzing the local forces shaping famine and relief, this study seeks to follow Foucault's injunction to examine the exercise of power "concretely and in detail" (Foucault 1988, 115–16) at a variety of levels, avoiding the simplistic assumption that power is "possessed" and manipulated by a unitary body called "the state" (Foucault 1988, 156; Dreyfus and Rabinow 1982; Smart 1985, 78–79, 122–27).

The role of war has to a large extent been marginalized in the theoretical literature on famine,[29] which for the most part addresses itself to peacetime famines. It is noteworthy that three out of four of Sen's case studies for his seminal work on famines took place in time of peace (Sen 1981). In the fourth, it was a wartime economic boom, rather than any direct effect of conflict that was presented as the main engine of famine. In the later contribution by Sen and Drèze, just as discussion of the role of political variables (democratic governments are seen as more likely to relieve famine) is essentially tacked on to Sen's fundamentally economic analysis of the causes of famine, discussion of the role of war is essentially tacked on to the rest of the book (Drèze and Sen 1989, 274–75). Indeed, Drèze and Sen explicitly state, "It would be, particularly, a mistake to relate the *causation* of famines to violations of legality . . . the millions that die in a famine typically die in an astonishingly 'legal' and 'orderly' way" (ibid., 22). This statement, as we shall see, would make little sense to the Dinka of Sudan.

On the other hand, accounts that have addressed the impact of war on famine—often stressing the use of famine as a weapon of war and the subordination of relief to politics—have frequently been journalistic in approach, lacking any coherent theoretical framework. They have also tended to share with Sen and Drèze a tendency to consider politics in isolation from economics.

In contrast to studies depicting famine as a function of market forces (the economic approach) or as a weapon of war (the political approach), this study emphasizes the impact of political processes and inequalities on the way that markets (and other economic transactions) work, as well as the impact of economic processes on political decisions that shape patterns of relief. It also emphasizes the complexity of political processes. While it is one thing to condemn the "politics of famine" (see, e.g., Fraser 1988, 258), it is quite another to understand this "politics" in all its intricacy. And while it is one thing to urge that people behave better, it would probably be more helpful to suggest ways in which those who are concerned with improving relief might take into account—and counter—the priorities of those who are not.

Chapter 2 examines the historical roots of the 1985–1989 Sudanese famine, describing the interaction of economic and political factors. It is argued that the famine emerged from a long history of exploitative processes in the geographical area affected, processes that had created famine in the past, while conferring substantial benefits on groups with superior access to political power and the means of violence. Changing degrees of political protection against famine are traced. It is stressed that the Colonial government, like more recent governments in Khartoum, tended to regard the Dinka as unworthy of political protection so long as they were resisting central government control. Moreover, the British government, like more recent ones, sometimes directly promoted processes of famine in the south as a tool of state policy.

The 1980s famine arose from a combination of four processes: the loss of assets and production (primarily because of raiding); the failure of market strategies; the failure of nonmarket survival strategies; and the inadequacy of relief. Chapter 3 considers the first three processes, and chapter 4 examines the inadequacy of relief. All these processes, it is argued, yielded important benefits for a loose and shifting coalition of politically powerful groups within Sudan, who helped to promote these processes.

Notwithstanding Sen's emphasis on poverty as the root of famine (Sen 1981), it was, in a sense, precisely the wealth of victim groups that exposed them to famine. Processes of famine involved the forced transfer of assets from victim to beneficiary groups in a context of acute political powerlessness on the part of the victims.

Chapters 2 and 3 attempt to avoid a common tendency to dissociate war from economic and political relationships existing in "normal times." Commonly, war, even civil war, has been portrayed as something superimposed on society, rather than something that emerges from relationships and conflicts within society.[30] War has frequently been seen—in relation to Sudan and elsewhere—as an essentially senseless outbreak of violence with a number of innocent victims but no clear beneficiaries or functions.[31] The same misleading dissociation is found in many portrayals of famine, which sever famines from normal social relations and from the historical intervals between famines, while at the same time concentrating exclusively on the victims and ignoring the possibility that there may be beneficiaries.[32] In contrast to such portrayals, the civil wars in Sudan and associated famines can usefully be seen as a deepening of exploitative processes already existing in "normal" times, a continuation and exaggeration of long-standing conflicts over resources (ivory, slaves, cattle, grain, land, oil), and a means—for certain groups—of maximizing the benefits of economic transactions through the exercise of various kinds of force against groups depicted as fair game in the context of civil (or holy) war. Winning the war was not the sole, or even the most important, objective of many of those engaging in violence or blocking relief; and famine was more than a weapon of war. The primary goal for many was to manipulate war, violence, famine, and relief in ways that achieved economic goals. Attitudes and interests in relation to famine and the use of force were complex. Not only did they reflect a mixture of economic, political, and military goals, but there were also conflicts of interest among those who shaped famine and relief, and these interests often changed with the passing of time.

The accounts of southern Sudanese politicians who held power under President Nimeiri in the 1970s—Abel Alier, Bona Malwal, and especially Francis Deng—have tended to point an accusing finger at Nimeiri's "great betrayal" of the south in the late 1970s. This study attempts to avoid attributing famine simply to a transformation in the political climate in Khartoum, just as it steers clear of attributing famine to some problem of "evil" in northern Sudan, or to what Spaulding calls the attribution of "guilt by race" (Spaulding 1982, 18). While Nimeiri's volte-face was important and succeeding regimes in Khartoum were equally cruel in their policies towards the south, the conflict and famine had deep-rooted historical and local causes. No government of Sudan has ever been all-powerful. Indeed, successive regimes attempted to manipulate local conflicts and resentments that were always partially outside their control.

Central governments in nineteenth- and twentieth-century Sudan have repeatedly attempted to appease potentially disaffected elements in the north by tolerating or encouraging exploitation of the south. Famine among southern Sudanese cannot be understood without understanding the problems besetting people in northern Sudan. The 1985–1989 famine was the creation of a diverse coalition of interests that were themselves under intense political and economic pressures in the context of a shrinking resource base and significant environmental crisis in the north. Given Sudan's declining economy and mounting international debt, governments in Khartoum faced mounting pressure to secure access to oil in the south—by force if necessary. In the west, the peoples of Kordofan and Darfur (including the Baggara cattle herders, who played an important part in creating the famine) had for almost a century been marginalized—economically and, for the most part, politically—by Sudan's highly uneven pattern of development, and had themselves recently suffered severe famine, precipitated by drought. The Baggara were one of a number of groups in northern Sudan—including a range of marginalized ethnic groups, classes, and opposition elements—who might, in other circumstances, have successfully opposed the more autocratic and militaristic tendencies of successive Sudanese governments, based as these governments were on a narrow elite drawn mainly from central and eastern Sudan (especially the Nile valley north of Khartoum).

The famine cannot properly be seen as inflicted by "the north" on "the south," or by "Arab Sudan" on "African Sudan" as if these were wholly separate and homogenous entities with automatically conflicting interests. The distinguished Dinka historian and politician Francis Deng has pointed out that after generations of miscegenation, few northern Sudanese can claim to be homogeneously Arab (Deng 1990, 598). A more fundamental objection to the north/south paradigm is the importance of divisions within the north and within the south. Some southern Sudanese, not unnaturally, saw the famine and accompanying war as the latest chapter in their long experience of oppression by "the Arabs" and "the north." But it is important to disaggregate "the north," and to highlight some of the internal tensions, the complex economic and political pressures and conflicts, which would together undermine Sudan's reputation for political tolerance. It was the disunity of the north, as much as its unity, that created the conditions for famine.

The central government's encouragement of the Baggara militias and its continued pursuit of an apparently unwinnable war can be seen as an attempt by some elements (notably the Umma Party) to limit the continuing political influence of the Sudanese army. Meanwhile, the central government encouraged the economically deprived and politically disaffected Baggara to direct their discontent at the politically marginal southern Sudanese. Although the central government (and some international observers) sought to portray this violence as the latest manifestation of natural tribal hostilities, there was nothing inevitable about such outright conflict, and Chapter 2 shows how the changing attitudes of central governments had a critical influence on "tribal" relations.

Divisions within the north are further evidenced by the existence of a range of opposition groups that lobbied for peace, by elements in the army that favored a political solution to the war, and by the opposition of many Baggara elders to raiding in both the first and second civil wars. However, at the central government level, groups favoring a political solution to the conflict found themselves increasingly marginalized (and sometimes even stigmatized as traitors) in the context of a deepening civil war and a growing jingoistic hysteria orchestrated by elements of the Islamic fundamentalist press. Sudan's traditions of tolerance were gravely eroded in this abrasive political environment. Groups favoring a political solution reemerged into prominence with the Democratic Unionist Party/Sudan People's Liberation Movement peace initiative in November 1988, only for the peace movement to be quashed by a military coup in June 1989. At the local level, Baggara elders were to a large extent undermined by their inability to deliver state resources to ordinary Baggara people, by the increasing availability of sophisticated weaponry in the hands of their followers, and by the climate of hostility towards the Dinka accompanying civil war.

In the south, the relatively cautious attitude of Dinka elders was also undermined, in part, by their inability to deliver state resources (development, education, employment) to a restless younger generation with more modern education and, secondly, by civil war itself. Seeking a military solution to problems in the south, the rebel Sudan People's Liberation Army (SPLA) contributed to hardship and famine in certain respects by blocking relief supplies to government garrison towns. The SPLA openly acknowledged using obstruction of food as a weapon of war. It also used violence (including the forcible appropriation of resources) against elements of the civilian population. On the other hand, the SPLA provided important, if belated, protection for the Bahr el Ghazal Dinka against northern militia raids during the dry season of 1987–1988. The Dinka were never simply passive victims of famine: they organized, when possible, for their own defense. The role of the SPLA in the famine is examined in Chapters 3 and 4, and a more general discussion of the SPLA is undertaken in Chapter 6.

A number of southern politicians and southern militias were willing to collaborate with the Sudanese government in organizing and carrying out damaging attacks against southern civilians deemed to be associated with the rebels, something that prompted SPLA retaliation against the civilian groups from whom these militias were drawn. Southern Sudanese soldiers also played their part in the government army. Divisions within the south, and the sometimes aggressive role of the SPLA in non-Dinka areas in particular, are discussed in more detail in Chapter 6.

The inadequacy of relief is documented in Chapter 4, which shows how "international" relief operations were actively shaped by powerful local actors, including merchants, army officers, local and central government officials, and the SPLA. It is suggested that relief "failures" served three important functions for a diverse and shifting coalition of northern Sudanese interests. First, the inadequacy of relief permitted the largely untrammelled extraction of famine's benefits (of which economic and military benefits were probably most significant). Second, in areas of northern Sudan, the inadequacy of relief in particular areas offered the prospect of discouraging unwanted migration to those areas. Third, shortcomings in relief effectively "released" relief resources for use by groups for whom they had not been designated: the benefits of famine included benefits extracted from relief operations. For the SPLA, certain kinds of relief inadequacy contributed to its military goal of starving the government garrison towns in the south.

Chapter 5 examines how patterns of relief were actively shaped by the priorities and agendas of international donors. It asks to what extent donors' main goals were fulfilled, despite severe famine. And it looks at the ways in which largely unhelpful policies were rendered surprisingly unobjectionable in official discourse. While there have been a number of attempts to point up the geopolitics of international relief, notably the withholding of relief from "unfriendly" governments,[33] this study is unusual in that it looks at the interaction of local and international priorities.

Chapter 6 summarizes the argument of the study and points up the continuing relevance of this kind of analysis, in Sudan and elsewhere. It also presents some comparisons with famines in other parts of the world, and considers the implications for relief operations.

## CHAPTER 2

# Famine and Exploitation in
# Historical Perspective

THE FAMINE that decimated the Dinka of southern Sudan in the late 1980s was not an isolated event that suddenly took hold in 1985. Rather, it emerged from a long history of exploitative processes in the geographical area affected by the famine. These processes were facilitated when the Dinka (and other southern groups) lacked significant political representation, and impeded when such representation was significant. Three distinct periods can be discerned: the divisions are somewhat artificial but nevertheless helpful. During the first period, from the 1820s to the mid-1920s, exploitative processes creating famine remained largely unchecked, and such famines were common. This was the period of Turko-Egyptian rule, of the Mahdia, and of the often-violent establishment of British colonial rule. Frequently, famine served important functions for groups who had some access to the means of force but who were themselves under a variety of economic and political pressures. Meanwhile—foreshadowing events in the 1980s—humanitarian initiatives (notably the campaign against slavery) were repeatedly stymied by powerful vested interests at the local level together with an unwillingness (and to some extent, an inability) on the part of more distant actors to confront these local interests. During the second period, from the mid-1920s to the early 1960s, the central government began to take seriously the need to woo collaborators, not only in northern but also in southern Sudan. Tribal leaders were encouraged to work together with the Condominium government to evolve a system that would limit conflict among tribal groups and provide some protection against processes of exploitation. Directly human-made famines were rare during this period.[1] During the final period, from the mid-1960s to the present, the established system of protection was eroded by a number of political and economic developments, which together revived the vulnerability of Dinka groups (and, more generally, of southern Sudanese) to processes of exploitation, while providing certain groups in the north with both the motive and the ability to deepen this exploitation through the use of force. Foremost among these northern groups were the economically marginalized Baggara cattle herders,[2] who had played an active role in exploitative processes during the first period. Once again, the central government was prepared to tolerate exploitation by powerful local interests. Indeed, the central government actively encouraged this exploitation in order to deflect the political threat of the Baggara, to defeat political rebellion in the south, and to gain access to resources in the south in the context of growing economic and environmental crisis in the north. Elements of the economically marginalized Baggara were encouraged by the central government to attack the politically marginalized Dinka to the south, and famine once more came to have important functions for a range of central government and local interests.

These divide-and-rule tactics were part of a long and inglorious tradition embracing the earlier years of British governance, when those trying to rule a large impoverished country on the basis of very limited central government resources resorted to the manipulation of conflicts in civil society in order to retain some semblance of control.

Famine—in Dinkaland and elsewhere—has involved a wide range of suffering arising from socioeconomic disruptions, and there is evidence that the Dinka, like the people of Darfur, Sudan, studied by de Waal (1989a), have sometimes valued the maintenance of their culture and economic independence more highly than they valued their own short-term consumption. Sometimes the Dinka appear to have put a higher value on their way of life (which is inextricably linked with the survival of the group) than on life itself.[3] Famine embraces the destruction of a way of life, not just of individual lives,[4] and starvation is seen as only the last stage in a long process of hunger (*chok*), with the state seen as having failed if this final stage arrives.

Sen, as noted, has drawn a strong causal connection between poverty and famines. And it is true that Dinkaland was severely "underdeveloped" right up until the 1985–1989 famine, with very little economic development of any kind having been actively fostered by the state. Nevertheless, the wealth of the Dinka was considerable. In 1971, Francis Deng noted, "With bridewealth sometimes going as high as 200 cows, the Dinka are probably the richest cattle-owners on the continent of Africa and certainly in the Sudan."[5] Deng's statement should be treated with caution: the wealth of individual Dinka could be quite low, outside the chiefly circles in which Deng moved. But Deng was right to stress that "[i]n the field of wealth, Dinkaland [was] among the richest in the country's natural resources, especially in livestock, forests, agricultural land, and water, including such riverain resources as fish."[6]

All this was before the discovery of major oil reserves under land occupied by the Dinka and the Nuer (Alier 1990, 216–17). It is argued here that it was precisely the resources of the Dinka that—in the context of political powerlessness and the proximity of relatively powerful northern groups—made them vulnerable to exploitative processes that threatened to destroy their way of life and remove their assets. In this sense, it was not the poverty of the Dinka, but their wealth, that exposed them to famine.

Although some famines affecting southern and western Sudan were largely created by natural disasters (Johnson 1989b; de Waal 1989a), many of the most severe famines were precipitated by human actions.[7] The 1985–1989 famine was of the latter type.

In a context of widespread exploitation of southerners, one method of protection was the forging of local links with northern groups. The Ngok Dinka[8] of southern Kordofan (sandwiched between northern Sudan and the other Dinka) were able to win a measure of protection through their relationships with Baggara groups and by defining themselves, in important respects, as part of the political community of the north. This also allowed Ngok leaders to attempt a bridging role between north and south. The Ngok, together with their northern neighbors, the Messiriya Baggara,[9] form a particular focus of this chapter. After a period of relative peace, it was within Ngok/Messiriya territory that some of the worst famine mortality occurred in the 1980s. The breakdown in Ngok relationships with Baggara groups reflected a wider breakdown between north and south; it also effectively deprived Dinka tribes[10] further south of a valuable buffer against northern aggression.

Conflict between the Ngok and their Baggara neighbors, while always possible, was by no means as inevitable, natural, or traditional as governments in Khartoum were later to imply.[11] The distinction between Arabs and Dinka, while meaningful to both groups, was only one of a range of possible ethnic distinctions, albeit one that was to become paramount during Sudan's second civil war. For example, fighting between the Messiriya Humr and Zurug was not uncommon.[12] Ethnicities were malleable, and to some extent constructed by Sudan's rulers as a means of governing. When the colonial combination of economic inertia and political governance through "traditional" tribal leaders began to fall apart, ethnic divisions were increasingly encouraged by independent governments in defense of their own power. Divide-and-rule tactics, in fact, became more blatant under independent than under colonial government.

## FROM THE MID-1820s TO THE MID-1920s: THE POLITICAL AND ECONOMIC ROOTS OF DIRECTLY HUMAN-MADE FAMINE

### *Famine: Causes and Functions*

After the conquest of much of the Sudanese provinces of Nubia, Darfur, Kordofan, and Sennar in 1820–1821 by the Egyptian ruler Mohamed Ali, the southern Sudan was effectively treated as the hinterland of the Turko-Egyptian state. A source of government revenue, plunder, and labor, and an outlet for the energies of potentially rebellious Egyptian groups, it was no more than a dependency of the Turko-Egyptian state, a "reservoir of outsid-

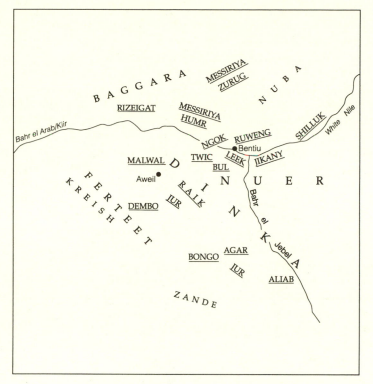

**Map 2**. Some Tribes (Underlined) and Peoples of Southwestern Sudan

ers" (James 1988, 133); its largely non-Muslim people had virtually no political rights or means of representation within the state apparatus. Indeed,
insofar as state power extended into the south, this was in many ways a
by-product of demand for tribute or slaves (Johnson 1988b, 148).

In the midnineteenth century, raiding and slaving from armed camps
(*zeribas*) created famine in Bahr el Ghazal on a huge scale, as previously
peaceful Muslim/non-Muslim relations gave way to violence. The raids
prompted large-scale flight among the peoples of Bahr el Ghazal, which in
turn led to major disruption of harvests and economic life in general
(Schweinfurth 1873, 260). The raids also deprived communities of grain and
cattle, and the taking of slaves deprived communities of labor (Gray 1961,
61–62).[13] Many of the militarily weaker groups, such as the Dengo, Jur, and
Bongo, were threatened with extinction (Collins 1971, 67; Cordell 1985,
30) (see Map 2). According to the German explorer Georg Schweinfurth,
who visited the zeriba areas in 1868–1871, "[s]carcely half the population
escaped slavery, and that only by emigrating" (Schweinfurth 1873, 238,
260; Gray 1961, 125; Cordell 1985, 30). Schweinfurth reckoned that the

overall population must have fallen by at least two-thirds, although his estimates will have been distorted by the fact that he traveled with the raiders, sticking to the main highways. One thing that particularly devastated the population was the enslaving of girls, who often commanded the highest prices (Schweinfurth 1873, 418). "I have myself seen whole tracts of Dar Ferteet turned into barren, uninhabited wilderness, simply because all the young girls have been carried out of the country," Schweinfurth commented (ibid., 437). Large numbers of Bongo were forced to quit their homes and live near the zeribas, where they could be more easily controlled and exploited (259). There was widespread recourse to wild foods, such as tubers, particularly by those who had been forcibly displaced (ibid., 259–60). So severe was the devastation that some of the Khartoum-based ivory companies began to worry that their trade might soon become impossible, since they would have no communities with which to deal (Gray 1961, 68). The Italian statesman Felix Gessi, who was governor of Bahr el Ghazal on behalf of the Turko-Egyptian administration between 1879 and 1881, found that the zeriba district had the "aspect of a country destroyed by fire" (Gray 1961, 125).

The Dinka, although somewhat better able to protect themselves than many peoples (through armed resistance and retreating into swampland), lost "hundreds of thousands of cattle," according to Major Titherington, who later worked among the Raik Dinka under the Anglo-Egyptian Condominium. Cattle were—and remain—the Dinka's principal insurance against famine, as well as the basis of their social interaction (Ryle 1989a; Deng 1971, 266–67).[14] Large numbers of Dinka were killed or enslaved. Many simply died of famine (Titherington 1927, 160). Schweinfurth describes how the Dinka were subject to annual cattle raids from the zeribas, with each zeriba typically requiring at least two thousand oxen a year (Schweinfurth 1873, 225). Dinka cattle were also raided on a large scale by traders making their way to their zeribas (Gray 1961, 157).

Dinka songs recall the raiding under the Turko-Egyptian regime and the Mahdia, which succeeded it, as a time when their land was "spoiled" by "Arabs." Chief Giirdit, of the Apuk branch of the Raik Dinka, who was in his nineties when interviewed by Francis Deng in 1972, said, "All the cattle of the Dinka, the Arab took. He took even the sheep and goats and the grain at home. People used holes in trees to hide seeds in the hope that in the right season they would try to cultivate again."[15]

These famines were clearly disasters for a great many people. But precisely the same processes that created and constituted famine[16] also bestowed important benefits on a range of politically powerful groups. Famine, considered as a process or combination of processes, was functional.

The Turko-Egyptian state was a direct beneficiary of the processes of asset transfer that created and, in part, constituted famine in the south. Understanding the roots of such famine is helped by understanding the pressures on its eventual beneficiaries. In particular, Mohamed Ali's regime in the 1810s was militarily weak, seeking to establish financial and political autonomy from the Ottoman sultan, and under threat at home both from insubordinate Albanian troops (who had installed him in power) and from the Mamluks, the governing elite of Egypt during the previous century. The conquest of Nilotic Sudan offered to provide a docile, loyal slave army and at the same time a means of distracting Mohamed Ali's Albanian troops from further insubordination at home (Holt and Daly 1988, 48). Slaves also came to provide one of the means of paying the Turko-Egyptian standing army (Spaulding 1982, 10). The use of raiding to distract politically dangerous groups with the promise of plunder in the south and to provide "payment" for the soldiers of a financially pressed state was to recur more than once, as governments repeatedly tried to buy loyalty by distributing the right to inflict violence.

The economic functions of raiding for the Turko-Egyptian state were also considerable. Sudan became a valuable provider of tribute in cattle, timber, gold, and ivory (Gray 1961, 3; Holt and Daly 1988, 54). Taxes on slave traders provided important revenue (Saeed 1982, 76–77). Meanwhile, slave labor came to underpin the social, agricultural, and commercial life of northern Sudan. Cultivation by slaves appears to have helped allow many northern Sudanese nomadic groups greater mobility than they were to enjoy when the twentieth century saw pastoralists increasingly tied to cultivation (Gray 1961, 5; Spaulding 1982, 11; O'Fahey 1980, 137). By the early 1880s, some two-thirds of the population of Khartoum were estimated to be slaves (around fifty thousand people) (Sanderson and Sanderson 1981, 10). Egypt also used many slaves as laborers (Gray 1961, 5).

Asset transfers also served important functions for traders, themselves under severe economic pressures by the 1860s. In the midnineteenth century, Syrian and Egyptian traders had penetrated the Bahr el Ghazal region by river (Holt and Daly 1988, 71). Their principal interest was in ivory, but by the early 1860s, the quantity of ivory available was rising only slowly in relation to a rapid rise in the number of traders competing for business. The stronger southern peoples, such as the Dinka and the Nuer, who could potentially supply traders with major quantities of ivory, were showing little interest in the goods the traders had to offer. Meanwhile, these traders were under pressure to secure quick returns: interest rates were high, and profit margins for traders in the south were being squeezed not only by competition but also by creditors and brokers in Khartoum (Gray 1961, 48–51).

Raiding cattle offered a solution to these problems. In particular, raiding the cattle of the weaker southern Sudanese peoples allowed merchants to obtain ivory and portering services from the Dinka and Nuer, who proved eager to exchange these goods and services for stolen cattle. By around 1870, raided cattle had become, in Gray's words, "the universal and indispensable medium of exchange" for traders, who carved out monopolies of trade and raiding in their respective geographical areas (Gray 1961, 48–51). Meanwhile, raiding of grain—though a significant cause of famine—helped to feed the large numbers of armed servants and other zeriba occupants who were necessary for this violent trade, and raiding for slaves and cattle allowed payment of these people without eating into the traders' profit margins. Eventually, slave troops comprised fully half of the armed forces of the Bahr el Ghazal traders (Schweinfurth 1873, 177, 226).

Petty traders from the north, who were known as *jellaba*, also supported and benefited from these exploitative processes. For the jellaba, too, the processes offered some relief from major economic pressures. Often from Dongola in the far north, the jellaba had been struggling to make a living before the advent of the zeribas. Turko-Egyptian encouragement of private land ownership and production of crops for export had tended to marginalize the poorer farmers and laborers in irrigated areas of Sudan, where cultivable land was scarce. Larger farms expanded at the expense of smaller farms, and traditional cultivators were often replaced by slaves. The losers in these processes were frequently propelled into the more dangerous southern slave catchment zone to seek their fortune as jellaba (Spaulding 1982, 1–20). Schweinfurth refers to those who came south to buy a small number of slaves as "speculative vagrants," suggesting that they had been experiencing considerable economic hardship in their home areas. Often they came with no more than a single donkey or bullock and a meager supply of tradable goods, perhaps including guns, which could be used in raiding (Schweinfurth 1873, 412–17).

The Baggara tribes of Darfur and Kordofan also benefited from, and supported, this system of exploitation in important respects. Many hired themselves to the major traders to accompany expeditions south (Schweinfurth 1873, 66). Others were able to exact a price for allowing these traders to move their slaves across Baggara territory. Some Baggara also made raids of their own, and slaveowning appears to have been widespread among the Baggara in the 1870s (O'Fahey 1973, 31–32).

Together, these diverse groups of beneficiaries wielded considerable political influence. The merchants in particular became, in effect, sovereign rulers of the territories surrounding their respective zeribas (Gray 1961; Schweinfurth 1873). But if the territories of the zeriba merchants were, in practice, miniature states, they were not states that offered any significant representation to the peoples they exploited. The indigenous peoples of Bahr el Ghazal enjoyed little or no representation at the local level or beyond, and were to a large extent placed outside relevant political and moral communities. As far as the Turko-Egyptian state was concerned, these groups were deemed to occupy not provinces but merely dependencies (Holt and Daly 1988, 45).

The question of the relationship between slavery and Islam is a difficult one, which arouses strong emotions in both northern and southern Sudan. In reading the historical material on relations between north and south in the nineteenth century, it is important to bear in mind that much of this history was written by Europeans, who were influenced by certain imperialist assumptions and agendas. In particular, as Carolyn Fluehr-Lobban (1990, 612–13) has pointed out, the "unquestioned assumption that Islam sanctioned slavery" served to legitimize British imperial ambitions in important ways, making the colonial conquest appear a kind of liberation.[17] The assumption also provided self-justification for Turko-Egyptian officials seeking religious sanction for their own slaving activities (Fluehr-Lobban 1990, 613). According to one strand of Islamic thought, which certain exploiting groups had an interest in emphasizing, the world could be divided into Dar al-Islam (the domain of Islam) and Dar al-Harb (the domain of war), with the taking of slaves in war permitted beyond the boundaries of Dar al-Islam (Gray 1961, 7; Fluehr-Lobban 1990). Stressing that the connection between Islam and slavery was in many ways a contrived one, Fluehr-Lobban notes a tradition attributed to the Prophet Mohammed, that "the wickedest people are those who sell people," and adds that "neither in the Quran nor the Sunna is there countenance for slavery."[18]

The drive to secure slaves from the south was clothed in a veil of religious justification; for example, the traders were generally known as *fakis* (priests) (Schweinfurth 1873, 413). Little attempt was made, however, to convert the south to Islam. Indeed, it seems likely that any widespread conversions would have created problems for the slavers by incorporating raided peoples into the Islamic community.

The peoples of the south were not completely without political protection. For one thing, local agreements and understandings between particular tribes could provide a degree of protection. During the turmoil of the Turko-Egyptian era, the Ngok Dinka chief, Kwoi Arob, established diplomatic relations with the chiefs of the Rizeigat of southern Darfur and the Messiriya Humr of southern Kordofan to protect his people against slave raids. According to Ngok history, he and the then-chief of the Humr, Azoza, ritually bled themselves and mixed their blood to seal the relationship (Deng 1986, 46). The protective role of Ngok leadership was apparently widely acknowledged by the Dinka, including southern leaders (ibid., 47). Dinka elders reported that Kwol's protection extended to the Twic Dinka (who had long sought refuge from floods in Ngokland) and elements of the Raik Dinka and the Nuer (Deng 1980, 207, 296; Deng 1978, 139).[19]

## Humanitarian Policy and Local Practice:
## The Power of Vested Interests

The other potential source of protection for southern Sudanese was the pinnacle of the Turko-Egyptian administration, where international pressure against slaving could be exerted. After Mohamed Ali, the humanitarian ideas that were gaining popularity in Europe found willing proponents in the viceroy Mohamed Sa'id and the khedive Isma'il (who ruled the Turko-Egyptian empire from 1863–1879); both men made attempts to suppress the slave trade. It appears that this action also served a more pragmatic purpose in legitimizing attempts to establish administrative control over areas dominated by the zeriba merchants (Holt and Daly 1988, 74–75), while at the same time promising to undermine the economic (and thereby the political) power of these merchants. An important landmark in efforts at suppression came in August 1877, when the khedive concluded the Anglo-Egyptian Slave Trade Convention, which promised an end to the selling of slaves in the Sudan by 1880 (ibid., 79).

Attempts to suppress the trade were repeatedly compromised by powerful vested interests, however. These groups tended to wield considerable influence within the administrative bureaucracy charged with suppression of the slave trade. An official inquiry of 1866 revealed that traders had quickly learned to bribe or elude the government's recently established river patrols, and that the river trade in slaves was continuing apace (ibid., 75). Government officials were generally poorly paid, and service in the south was often regarded by Egyptian administrators as a hardship made tolerable only by the prospect of kickbacks from wealthy traders. Confiscation of slaves by the Egyptian authorities in Khartoum was commonplace. It helped to impress the European consuls, anxious to see progress on the slavery issue. But it also created a new set of beneficiaries, and masked a deeper toleration of slaving. Confiscated slaves were commonly used as soldiers, and their children were divided among existing recruits. Former owners were always at liberty to buy (Schweinfurth 1873, 430). More generally, the continued importance of slaves for the Turko-Egyptian army was always likely to weaken humanitarian initiatives.

The expressed aim of relieving suffering in the south was largely subverted by the vested interests of government officials and local merchants, and the antislavery initiative itself became a chance for further profit. These dynamics were to find important echoes when humanitarian relief took the form of emergency food aid in the 1980s.

The appearance of suppression in the 1860s and 1870s was sustained to some extent by a geographical focus on the river trade. While the efforts to suppress the river trade were well publicized, the overland trade north from Bahr el Ghazal continued stronger than ever. Indeed, to the extent that the river trade was made more difficult by government interference, this only served to enhance the profits of the overland trade. At its height, the overland slave trade was perhaps six times as great as the river trade (Holt and Daly 1988, 71). Meanwhile, the government's inability to suppress the overland trade was underlined when the Turko-Egyptian regime, after an unsuccessful military campaign against the prime slaver el Zubayr Rahma Mansur, decided to recognize him as governor of Bahr el Ghazal (Gray 1961, 69).

In 1881, the Turko-Egyptian regime (its prestige weakened by the deposition of Khedive Ismail in 1879 and increasingly a puppet of the Western powers) was overturned in Sudan by the Mahdi, a charismatic religious leader called Mohamed Ahmed who said he had been chosen by God to restore the true Islamic community (Holt and Daly 1988, 86–87). From the point of view of many in southern Sudan, one oppressive government had merely been replaced by another. Slaves provided the nucleus of the Mahdist army (Johnson 1988b, 143). Indeed, it had been the threat posed to slave traders and to the Baggara raiding by renewed efforts at suppression that had, in large part, prompted the overthrow of the Turko-Egyptian government, with the Baggara playing a critical role among the conglomeration of supporters that the Mahdi called his Ansar (Holt and Daly, 80–88). The Rizeigat Baggara of southern Darfur had been hit by Egyptian interference in the slave trade after the independent Darfur sultanate was forcibly incorporated into the Turko-Egyptian empire in 1874 (Holt 1958, 43). This interference encouraged the Rizeigat to help overthrow the Egyptian administration in Darfur (ibid., 152). They were also resentful of Turko-Egyptian taxation, which was more onerous that under the independent sultanate of Ibrahim Mohamed (Holt and Daly 1988, 89). In 1884, the Mahdi carried out a full-scale invasion of Bahr el Ghazal, supported by a variety of groups with an interest in the slave trade, and the Baggara took the chance to acquire substantial booty (Holt 1958, 133). Meanwhile, Baggara groups took advantage of the Mahdi's regime to gain the upper hand in the critical grazing areas of the Bahr el Arab river, a long-standing source of dispute with the Dinka (Karam 1980, 64).

Again, those in the south had very little political protection against the Baggara, although some Shilluk and Dinka groups secured a degree of representation by aligning themselves with the Mahdi (Holt 1958, 8). When the Mahdi ousted the Turko-Egyptian government, the Ngok chief Arob traveled to meet him. Hoping to save the Ngok from raids such as those being carried out against the Malwal Dinka (Saeed 1982, 162), he registered his allegiance, and at the same time protested against those northern tribes still engaging in slave raiding and robbery. For the Ngok at least, Mahdist rule proved fairly peaceful (Deng 1986, 46–47).

Despite their booty in the south, the Baggara remained a potential threat to any government in Khartoum. In Darfur, the Rizeigat were particularly rebellious (de Waal 1989a, 63). Succeeding the Mahdi in 1885, the khalifa Abdallahi, who was of Baggara origin, sought to quell and to harness the power of the Baggara, in large part to defuse the threat of rebellion by them (Holt 1958, 160; de Waal 1989a, 63). Baggara were summoned to Khartoum, and widespread government requisitioning of food in western Sudan (to feed government troops, crush rebellion, and punish those who refused to move) led to terrible famine there in 1888–1892 (Holt and Daly 1988, 105–6; de Waal 1989a, 63). Meanwhile, a Baggara federation was formed, contributing to the construction of some common identity among the various Baggara tribes. Attempts to co-opt the Baggara included the increasing appointment of military governors from among the Baggara (Holt 1958, 246).

The attempt to quell the Baggara had only limited success, and it had important negative consequences for a number of other groups in Sudanese society. There was insufficient food for the Baggara who arrived in the capital. The heavily armed Ansar (consisting largely of Baggara owing religious commitment to the Mahdi) lurched out of the control of the khalifa (and to some extent even of the new military governors), ransacking the Nile north of Omdurman for grain, appropriating much of the Gezira cultivated areas, and contributing to widespread famine by the end of the 1880s. Holt refers to the khalifa's "weakness before the military monster he had created" (ibid., 254–55). Just under a century later, Khartoum was once again to court elements of the Baggara, in an only partially successful attempt to control them, with similar devastating effects among the victims of Baggara raids, which were this time concentrated on southern Sudan.

The khalifa's reliance on the undisciplined Baggara opened a rift between himself and the Awlad al-balad, the settled people of Sudan's ravaged riverain areas, who had supplied the governing elite under the Mahdi. The prolongation of government by plunder undermined the prospects of rebuilding Sudan's economy. And although the khalifa's forces put up substantial resistance to Britain's imperial ambitions, his increasingly precarious government fell to British and Egyptian forces at the battle of Omdurman in 1898 (Holt and Daly 1988, 99–113).

The gradual establishment of British colonial rule at the end of the nineteenth and beginning of the twentieth centuries saw a renewed commitment to suppressing slavery, at least in theory. In practice, slave raiding continued to be tolerated to a large extent, as did domestic slavery. Moreover, the British conducted their own raids on southern groups, which once again created famine.

The prime British concern in Sudan under the new Anglo-Egyptian Condominium was to suppress Sudanese discontent, thus protecting the Nile waters and encouraging political stability in Egypt itself. This, in turn, was seen as important in maintaining communications with India. At the same time, the British wanted to minimize expenditure (Collins 1971, 337). Their attempt to harness southern resources with forced labor and heavy livestock taxes, combined with an apparently slender return to southern peoples in social services, encouraged insurrection among many Dinka tribes and other southern groups (Alier 1990, 13–15). At this stage, the institutions of imperial rule gave scant formal representation to any Sudanese interests, let alone those of the only partially "pacified" south (Warburg 1971, 77; Deng and Oduho 1963, 13). British military and civilian staff were particularly thinly spread in the south, and the widespread use of terror in retaliation for insurrection appeared directly proportional to the insecurity of British officers in the country (Collins 1971, 91).

To give one example among many, after elements of the Agar Dinka rebelled in 1902, the land of the Agar was devastated by government troops, which burned villages, shot village leaders, destroyed sorghum, and confiscated so many cattle that the land was left virtually devoid of stock. Whole families died of hunger.[20] Charles Willis, who became director of intelligence in 1920, acknowledged that the government's policy for the south was "administration by raids," adding: "It is not surprising if the natives could detect but little difference between the old Turkish, the Dervishes and the Sudan Government [Condominium]. They all raided, but the last was not interested in slaves but took cattle only and was possibly more efficient in methods of getting them."[21]

In the Nuba Mountains area of southern Kordofan, local Baggara Arabs were commonly used by the British in punitive expeditions against rebel groups (Ibrahim 1988, 35). And one senior official, who began service in Kordofan in 1910, observed that the frequent use of "friendlies" (tribal militias) in punitive expeditions had led to indiscipline and fueled hostilities, and that the burning of villages and confiscating of cattle had punished the innocent (ibid., 154). As in the 1880s, the power of the sword was delegated to groups whom the central government could not fully control.

Significantly, British strategic concerns (notably, the protection of the Nile waters) dictated that priority be given to appeasing the northern interests behind the Mahdist regime to avoid the emergence of a powerful neo-Mahdist movement against imperial rule. This meant appeasing the Baggara and tolerating to a large extent their continued exploitation of the south. For two years after it broke out in 1881, the Mahdist revolt had centered on Kordofan (Holt and Daly 1988, 85), and the British were particularly concerned with appeasing the Baggara of this region. To this end, Kordofan was exempted from the decree that slaves be registered (Hargey 1981, 184–85; Warburg 1971, 170–74). The dangers of abolishing slavery became clear in the early 1900s, by which time a reduction in the number of slaves had combined with reviving agricultural production to create severe labor shortages in some areas (Warburg 1971, 176–88; Hargey 1981, 177; McLoughlin 1962, 365). In the event, in southwestern Kordofan at least, slaves were used for cotton production and cattle tending throughout the first two decades of the twentieth century (Warburg 1971, 170–77; Saeed 1982, 138). As late as the early 1920s, the slave population of Kordofan was estimated at fully 15 percent of the inhabitants (Hargey 1981, 381). This was *after* a significant drift of rural slaves to Kordofan towns during World War I, which had seriously jeopardized the nomadic and sedentary lifestyles of nonslaves, impoverishing the Messiriya Baggara in particular (ibid., 184). Meanwhile, domestic slavery continued to be tolerated throughout Sudan, and the Anglo-Egyptian army continued to recruit slave soldiers, often from "rebellious" tribes, during the first quarter of the twentieth century (Johnson 1988b, 143, 150). A system of military recruitment based on violence combined with government fear of the social and economic consequences of abolition to create what Gabriel Warburg has called a vast discrepancy between the official policy of abolition and its realization on the ground (Warburg 1971, 176–88; Johnson 1988b, 81). It was not the first time, or the last, that deference to powerful local vested interests effectively undermined an outwardly humanitarian policy.

In the meantime, Baggara raiding on the Malwal and Twic Dinka was not redressed by the British. It followed famines in the late 1880s and 1890s, which had caused widespread destitution among the Baggara (de Waal 1989a, 63–64). Presaging events in the 1980s in certain respects, this raiding was not only fueled by arms from Libya (Sikainga 1986, 60), but also appeared to be part of Baggara attempts to rebuild their herds in the wake of famine and to secure adequate grazing.[22] Access to water was a critical bone of contention, with the Rizeigat and Humr Messiriya claiming rights to wells around the Bahr el Arab river, as well as tribute from the Dinka (Collins 1971, 185–87). In 1906, the Humr delivered a crushing blow against the Twic. And in 1908, an exceptionally dry year, the Rizeigat raided the Malwal and Geringyang Dinka along the Lol River, in search of pasture, which was scarce along the more northerly Bahr el Arab in that year.

Significantly, British officials argued that such raids were to be tolerated since the Dinka were resisting the Anglo-Egyptian government (Henderson 1939, 71). The weak British military presence in Bahr el Ghazal was a further impediment to checking the raiding (Collins 1971, 187, 334; Collins 1983, 12). By the beginning of World War I, it was clear that the British had failed to check Baggara/Dinka hostility (Collins 1983, 5). Government raids on the Dinka, and government toleration of Baggara raids, suggested that, so long as elements of the Dinka continued to resist British rule and the Baggara remained a potent political threat, the Dinka peoples were considered to be largely outside the political community and largely undeserving of government protection.

Such protection as the Dinka did secure came primarily, once again, from their own initiatives. These included the deterrent of counterraids, such as those carried out in response to Rizeigat raids in 1908 (Collins 1971, 187). Not without significance were the initiatives of the Ngok Dinka chief Kwol Arob, who registered his loyalty to the Anglo-Egyptian government and apparently secured a promise from the Humr leader Ali Julla to the new government that he would suppress the slave trade (Henderson 1939, 71; Deng 1986, 46–48). However, Ngok elders report that Kwol's influence with the British was limited, and continued Humr raiding showed the limited value of any promise made.

## FROM THE EARLY 1920s TO THE LATE 1950s: THE CONSTRUCTION OF PROTECTION AGAINST FAMINE

Between the early 1920s and the late 1950s, the south was partially integrated into the Sudanese state, and tribal and central leaders together managed to construct some degree of protection against directly human-made famine. The Ngok Dinka played an important role in "sewing together" the south and the north, to use the image of Deng Majok, who was chief of the Ngok from 1942 to 1969 (Deng 1986, x).

Under the Turko-Egyptian regime, under the Mahdia, and during the early years of the Anglo-Egyptian Condominium, the peoples of southern Sudan had stood, in effect, outside the political community of the Sudan. Instead of the protection of the government, they had been subject to periodic raids by government-supported forces. In the early 1920s, this began to change. The Anglo-Egyptian administration became increasingly and explicitly concerned with how best to protect these peoples from exploitation by northern Sudanese interests, and with how to protect the weaker southern peoples against the militarily stronger ones, notably the Nuer (Sanderson and Sanderson 1981; Collins 1983; Johnson 1989b, 463–86).

What appears to have propelled this significant shift was the threat of wholesale rebellion by the Dinka of Bahr el Ghazal in 1922, when the apparent unity and numbers of rebellious Dinka had left British administrators severely shaken (Collins 1983, 33–37; Sanderson and Sanderson 1981, 121–22). The tolerance of a wide range of Dinka groups in Bahr el Ghazal for government impositions (including raiding), and for Baggara and Nuer raiding, was clearly reaching a limit (Sanderson and Sanderson 1981, 114–21). In addition, the Malwal Dinka, who were prominent in the 1922 disturbances, had been angered by the government's stipulation in 1918 that Darfur's southern boundary be fixed fully 40 miles south of the Bahr el Arab river, a measure that threatened Malwal access to grazing.

It began to become apparent to British administrators that the policy of quelling rebellious peoples in southern Sudan with punitive raids (including those that created famine), while capable of subduing particular groups for a period, was, in the longer run, simply not having the desired effect. Nor could a stable administration be built on forced recruitment of slave soldiers (Johnson 1988b, 150). As far as day-to-day administration was concerned, it was proving extremely difficult, in the context of oppressive British rule, to find influential southerners who were prepared to collaborate with the imperial power. Indeed, the very incorporation of a particular individual into the administration threatened to undermine whatever support he might command among his own people (Sanderson and Sanderson 1981, 114–22; Collins 1983, 33–37; Warburg 1971, 134). Meanwhile, as nationalism came to the boil in Egypt, threatening to spill over into the Sudan, British administrators became interested (as did President Jaafar Nimeiri at a later date) in the possibility of using a loyal south—and in particular a substantial southern military force founded on the Equatorian Corps—as a counterbalance to possible unrest in the north (Collins 1983, 166).

Whereas in the immediate aftermath of the Mahdia, British administrators had tended to tread softly on Islamic sensibilities, the passage of time encouraged the expression of a certain anti-Islamic bias among some British administrators. Some officials, particularly in the southern provinces, feared that northern religious leaders would spread their influence to the south through traders (Ibrahim 1988, 83; Sanderson and Sanderson 1981, 126; Alier 1990, 18).

The scarcity of British personnel in the vastness of southern Sudan had tended, in the 1900s and 1910s, to encourage strong retaliation in response to any sign of rebellion (Collins 1971, 88–91; Collins 1983, 12). By contrast, in the new political context of the 1920s, the scarcity of personnel underlined the importance of taking positive steps to woo collaborators. The British search for collaborators, in the south and the north, involved a search for the "traditional leaders" of Sudanese "tribal" society (Saeed 1982, 141). The hope was that these men would be able to secure the obedience of their followers to British rule. Such systems of indirect rule were held to be preferable to the creation of an indigenous educated class to swell the British bureaucracy. Experience of urban unrest in India and Egypt had instilled a deep suspicion of such groups (Collins 1983, 52).

The possibility of undermining local leaders by incorporating them into the administration was not the only difficulty with such a search for collaborators. The scarcity of British administrators meant it was necessary to find a relatively small number of "traditional leaders" with whom British officers could deal. Although executive and judicial authority had tended to be exercised at levels below the tribe (for example, by clan leaders among the Messiriya and by leaders of the various "sections" making up the Ngok tribe, the British concentrated executive and judicial authority in "tribal chiefs" (Saeed 1982, 169; Deng 1972, 141; Ryle 1982, 153). The British were thus attempting to create a type of local authority, as much as to confirm a type already in existence.

The "traditional leaders" co-opted by the British administration in the south, if not rejected out of hand by their own people, were often able to use their officially derived executive and judicial powers to build a loyal following, particularly in the new context of more benign British rule after the early 1920s. The Ngok chief Kwol Arob appears to have used his association with government to favor his own "Abyor" section of the Ngok, imposing his will on other sections (Howell 1951a, 265). His son, Deng Majok, who assumed full control of the Ngok in 1942, emerged as a powerful chief, his authority among the Ngok enhanced by selective use of his powers to tax and pass legal judgment. Meanwhile, Deng Majok appears to have won considerable favor among the British on account of his ability to command support not only from the Ngok but also from other Dinka groups (Deng 1986, 86) and to some extent from the Messiriya.

The system of indirect rule known as Native Administration—although built on a "tradition" that had to some extent been invented by administrative necessity—nevertheless came to provide the Ngok (and other Dinka tribes to the south) with a genuine political voice and with some degree of protection against famine.

Beginning in the 1920s, strong government security forces were recruited from both the Baggara and the Dinka, helping to reduce warfare in the Bahr el Arab area (Collins 1971, 189). Within two years of the threatened Dinka rising of 1922, effective protection for the Dinka from the Baggara (and the Nuer) had quickly quelled Dinka resistance to British rule (Sanderson and Sanderson 1981, 122). The newly powerful tribal chiefs, in conjunction with local authorities and security forces, created a system that carefully regulated grazing and minimized tribal disputes. In 1924, the southern boundary of Dar Rizeigat was fixed 12 miles south of the Bahr el Arab River.[23] From the 1940s to the early 1960s, the seasonal entry of Messiriya groups into northern Bahr el Ghazal and northern Upper Nile was closely monitored and regulated under the Native Administration system, as was the seasonal entry of Nuer and Dinka into southern Kordofan. Written entry permits would specify entry and exit dates, together with the permitted grazing areas. Annual conferences attended by tribal leaders and local officials from Kordofan, Bahr el Ghazal, and Upper Nile were held at the beginning of the rainy season, with a view to ironing out any differences before the various nomadic groups dispersed to their rainy season camping areas (Saeed 1982, 217). A similar system governed movement between Bahr el Ghazal and Darfur (Karam 1980, 10, 50). Each tribe had a designated homeland. Tribal conferences were held in the open, and representatives discussed grazing disputes, payment of compensation, and blood money in the presence of ordinary members of their tribes (ibid., 30; Deng 1982, 18–20).

Under this system, the tribal chiefs derived their judicial and executive powers (and hence their principal opportunities for capital accumulation) from their positions within the Native Administration (Saeed 1982, 169). They were valued by the British for their ability to control their own followers and to promote peaceful intertribal relations; the British even appointed salaried guards to protect them (ibid., 181). Hence, tribal chiefs had a strong incentive to seek to promote peaceful resolution of disputes, if only to maintain their own positions of privilege and power. Meanwhile, their followers could hope to avoid some measure of taxation and legal punishment by respecting the chiefs' authority (Deng 1986, 134–37).

Under the Native Administration system, the Ngok Dinka came to acquire a significant voice in the colonial administration. Although comprising only some 8 percent of the population of Messiriya District in southern Kordofan (Howell 1951a, 264), the Ngok wielded considerable influence (both with the British district commissioner, and in the Messiriya Rural Council, established in 1953) through the person of Chief Deng Majok. He enjoyed privileged status within Messiriya District, in that appeals from his court went straight to the district commissioner, while the appeals of other chiefs had to go to Babo Nimir, the paramount chief of the district since 1942 (when the Humr and Zurug branches of the Messiriya had been administratively merged under Babo's authority) (Deng 1982, 24; Saeed 1982, 120). Ngok representation reached a high point when Deng Majok, taking advantage of differences among rival Sudanese Arab groups, was elected president of the Messiriya Rural Council in 1965. Correspondingly, Babo Nimir owed his position in part to the support of the Ngok.

Relations between the Humr Messiriya and the Ngok Dinka were moderately friendly from the 1920s to the mid-1960s (Henderson 1939, 71; Cunnison 1954, 50). While there was certainly a legacy of ill-feeling stemming from the Humr's slave raiding in the nineteenth and early twentieth centuries, cooperation between the Humr and the Ngok was encouraged by a number of factors in addition to the Native Administration system, underlining the point that ethnic conflict along north/south lines was by no means inevitable.

First, the abundance of groups pressing in on the Humr and the Ngok meant that the two had at least a limited interest in assisting each other in the face of external threats. In the nineteenth century, when the Humr, on returning from service to the Mahdi, had been looted by the Zurug, the Ngok provided a place of refuge (Cunnison 1954, 50). Correspondingly, the Humr appear to have provided some respite for the Ngok from severe attacks by Nilotic groups who came to the Bahr el Arab in the 1920s (Saeed 1982, 164). Often, at the annual intertribal conferences, the Humr and Ngok would stand together as one bloc, in opposition to Dinka groups further south (Deng 1973, 53).

A second factor promoting Ngok-Humr cooperation was the skill of the Ngok leadership in using public affirmations of loyalty to the ruling government (whether Turko-Egyptian, Mahdist, British, or, later, Sudanese) to carve out a degree of government protection (see, e.g., Deng 1986, 47–48). This was complemented by a considerable willingness among the Ngok to adopt the appearance (though often not the reality) of cultural assimilation to the north. Such a willingness was expressed most forcefully in the charismatic and adaptable personality of Deng Majok, who endeared himself to many of his Arab neighbors by frequently dressing in *jellabia* (long smocks favored by northern Sudanese), by abstaining from drink, by celebrating Islamic customs, and by refusing to eat the meat of any animal not slaughtered according to Muslim requirements (ibid., 121). In addition, he provided generous hospitality when northern dignitaries came to visit (ibid., 234). In a context where to be seen as a non-Muslim carried important dangers, the adoption by prominent Ngok of certain elements of Arab culture appeared to provide a degree of protection.

A third factor tending to promote friendly relations (and one not unconnected with cultural assimilation) was the considerable intermarriage between the two groups. Importantly, these marriages nearly always involved Humr men and Ngok women, a common imbalance in Dinka-Arab relations and one noted with resentment by the Dinka (Deng 1978, 177–78; Deng 1980, 328–29). Generally, the Humr did not recognize full social ties with the families of their Dinka wives, nor did they regard such marriages as having full legal status (Howell 1951b, 445–46). The relatively dark complexion of many Baggara (in relation to other northerners)—to a large extent a result of sexual relations between the Baggara and the Dinka—was held by some Dinka to have encouraged a degree of insecurity among the Baggara about their "Arab" identity, and to have made the Baggara "among the quickest" to refer to southern Sudanese as "slaves" (Deng 1973, 49). Nevertheless, intermarriage did promote a limited understanding, and probably acted as a check on hostilities. One writer aptly described Humr-Ngok relations as characterized by an "intimate enmity" (Ryle 1989a, 19).

The Ngok's ties with the north, and with the Humr in particular, were seen by many Dinka elders as providing protection from raiding, not just for the Ngok but also for more southerly Dinka tribes, such as the Twic and the Raik (Deng 1980, 296). The Ngok's Kwol Arob had been recognized as leader of the Twic and Ruweng Dinka as well as the Ngok, and on occasion obtained release of members of these groups captured in raids (Deng 1986, 48, 230). Although leadership of the Twic appears to have diminished under Deng Majok, ties remained close, and Twic elders sacrificed a bull on Deng's grave, apparently because they regarded him as their own chief (ibid., p. 235). Twic elders said Deng would have been able to check the militia raids that began under Nimeiri in the early 1980s: "He would have asked Nimeiri: 'Why do these people go and kill people and you do not punish them?'" (ibid., 269).

If the Native Administration system provided important protection against famine by promoting peace and minimizing raiding, it also provided protection in another way: the chief of the Ngok was himself an important source of famine relief for those in distress. Deng Majok provided a range of services—including grain, cattle (for milk or meat), and, interestingly, cash—during times of famine (ibid., 133). At one time, chiefs had been supposed to receive a portion of the grain grown by each family, assuming thereby a responsibility for the poor, though this custom was defunct by the early 1970s (Deng 1971, 276). There was some feeling among tribal elders that Deng Majok may have favored non-Ngok, and that this was how he had built up his influence beyond the Ngok (Deng 1986, 133). The obligations of wealth were implied by the fact that the Dinka term for "wealthy" was the same as that for "generous" (ibid.). It would appear that there was some form of moral economy at work in traditional (or neotraditional) Dinka society, with some similarities to that discerned in precolonial Nigeria by Watts (1983, 125). This had been at least partially eroded by the 1970s.

## FROM THE LATE 1950s TO THE LATE 1980s:
## THE BREAKDOWN OF PROTECTION AGAINST FAMINE

In the late 1950s the system of protection against famine began to weaken. This was not a steady erosion: while the departure of the British and the coming of the first civil war left the Dinka increasingly exposed to famine and exploitation by the mid-1960s, the system of Native Administration continued to provide a measure of protection at local level. Moreover, the early years under Nimeiri helped restore some measure of protection for southern Sudanese at the center, as the south became an important power base for Nimeiri following his break with the Communists in 1970–1971.[24] However, protection for the peoples of southern Sudan was now dangerously dependent on Nimeiri's maneuverings in Khartoum. This system of protection fell apart in the late 1970s, when Nimeiri began, for a variety of economic and political reasons, to reconstruct his power base, turning away from the south and toward Islamic fundamentalist interests and the traditional sectarian parties, the Umma Party and the Democratic Unionist party (DUP).[25] Nimeiri's move toward the Umma Party in particular represented a recognition of the threat that the Baggara and Ansar posed to his rule. The Umma party had been formed in 1945 by supporters of the Mahdi's son, Sayyid 'Abd el Rahman, to press for independence (Holt and Daly 1988, 148). It drew

strong support from the Baggara and was closely linked with the Ansar organization that had originally fought on behalf of the Mahdi.[26] Nimeiri's reconciliation with the Umma Party was the beginning of a sustained attempt to
harness Baggara frustrations by turning them against the south.

At the economic level, meanwhile, the period starting in the late 1950s
saw significantly increased penetration by merchant capital into much of the
Sudanese countryside. This was encouraged by the removal of trading restrictions that had operated under British rule, by the rise of de facto individual land ownership with the decline of tribal homelands under Native
Administration, and by a major infusion of capital into Sudan from the newly
oil-rich Arab world. Significantly, both the Baggara and the Dinka were
largely excluded from the benefits of this pattern of economic development.
In the 1980s, the Baggara—enjoying greatly increased access to modern
weaponry and suddenly in favor with Khartoum at precisely the time when
the Dinka (and southern Sudanese peoples more generally) were losing virtually all political representation—turned, with encouragement from Khartoum, on the even more marginalized Dinka in a bid to ameliorate long-term
economic difficulties that had been exacerbated by drought in 1983–1985.
The resultant raiding and other forms of exploitation led, in large part, to the
very severe famine that reached its peak in 1988.

### From Cooperation to Conflict: The Reemergence
### of Directly Human-Made Famine

The Native Administration system had certainly provided some protection
for southerners in the short and medium term. However, in conjunction
with the neglect of southern development and education (Sanderson and
Sanderson 1981; Ibrahim 1988, 180), it tended to reinforce ethnically based
politics in a way that appears to have increased vulnerability to famine in the
long term. Reliance on traditional institutions, indeed, had in some sense
necessitated neglect of economic development and education, for such a
reliance could not have survived the emergence of a significant educated
elite (Sanderson and Sanderson 1981, 181). Although there was some missionary education, British rule largely neglected education in the south, and
British officials saw the solution to "the southern problem" in terms of continued British tutelage rather than the emergence of political self-help in the
south (ibid., 283). In large part as a result, the Dinka were generally poorly
placed to fill posts that became available under "Sudanization" in the early
1950s and then after independence in 1956 (Mawson 1989, 85).

With Egypt pressing a residual claim of sovereignty over Sudan and competing for the favor of northern Sudanese, the British carved out few safeguards for the south in hasty negotiations over independence (Alier 1990,

18–22). In 1955, southern members of the Sudanese parliament secured a promise from northern politicians, in return for southern support of independence, that a federal solution would be given due consideration. But the federal idea was quickly dropped once independence had been achieved (ibid., 23). British promises of continued protection for the south had helped to calm southern fears. More specifically, they had helped persuade the soldiers of the Sudanese army's Equatoria Corps to lay down their arms after they mutinied at the town of Torit in 1955, an action that is normally taken to signal the beginning of Sudan's first civil war. However, the British withdrew from Sudan without ensuring that political protection for southern Sudanese was in place (Deng 1990, 596–97).

For the south, independence brought a heightened threat of political (and economic) domination by the north, a threat against which the underdevelopment and sporadic paternalistic concern accompanying colonial rule provided little long-term protection. When the Sudanization of the administration began in 1955, the southern government positions previously occupied by the British were overwhelmingly filled by northern Sudanese (Deng 1986, 42). Northern sectarian parties dominated Sudan's first period of parliamentary government from 1956 to 1958, with the leaders of the Khatmiyya and Ansar sects maintaining and increasing the influence they had wielded behind the scenes under the British. The Arabization of southern bureaucracy continued, and in 1957 the government announced that missionary schools would be integrated into the national education system. Southern politicians, whose principal mouthpiece was the Southern Liberal Party (founded in 1953), were united in support of a federal solution for Sudan, but were weakened by tribal and personal differences, as well as by a degree of cynical opportunism. After the 1958 elections, the forty Southern Liberal members were divided between the ruling coalition (Umma and People's Democratic Party) and the opposition National Unionist Party (NUP) (Holt and Daly 1988, 170).

In November 1958, Sudan's first, brief experiment with parliamentary government came to an end in a military coup. General Abboud, who assumed power claiming to be saving the country from the chaos of politicians, was to rule until 1964. The coup did not mean an end to sectarian influence on Sudanese politics. Indeed, many of the leaders of the coup were of the Khatmiyya sect. The policy of Arabization and Islamization of the south was stepped up under military rule. Southern officials continued to be passed over or transferred to the north. Abboud imposed further, more severe restrictions on missionary activity in the south and ordered that the day of rest be changed from Sunday to Friday (Holt and Daly 1988, 178–79; Alier 1990, 24).

This campaign of Arabization and Islamization inevitably provoked resentment in the south. A new generation of Dinka increasingly favored resistance to the north, which they saw as progressively restricting educational and career opportunities for non-Muslims.

To the extent that education had been encouraged in the south, it tended (in a context of highly restricted career opportunities) to encourage resistance to northern rule rather than an active participation in government institutions on behalf of southern Sudanese. Indeed, education without opportunity encouraged divisions among the Dinka. In the years after independence, many younger Dinka with some modern (Christian) education began to confront the more conservative, "uneducated" chiefs. These chiefs' powers had often been artificially increased by the British: the British anthropologist and administrator Paul Howell had expressed his concern in the early 1950s that in enhancing the paramount chief's powers among the Ngok, the British had created "an effective autocracy in an essentially democratic society," storing up trouble for the future (Howell 1951a, 264).[27] Chieftainship, moreover, was losing some of its religious sanctity, and many Dinka now referred to the government, even that represented by the chief, as *jur* (foreigner) (Deng 1972, 142).

When Bahr el Ghazal moved to resistance in the late 1960s in a significant escalation of Sudan's first civil war, the educated younger Dinka were to form the leadership,[28] while the Nuer resisted in more "traditional" fashion, following "traditional" Nuer prophets (Sanderson and Sanderson 1981, 400, 427; Deng 1971, 67).

The Sudan government's lackluster response to a number of emergencies among the Dinka was also significant: the government's failure to relieve famine among the Dinka in Bahr el Ghazal in 1959 and three years of devastating floods in the Bor Dinka region in the early 1960s appear to have played a key role in propelling large sections of the Dinka toward identification with "southern" grievances and resistance, in contrast to their standing aloof in 1955 (Sanderson and Sanderson, 397). The first civil war, which lasted—on and off—from 1955 until 1971, reached a peak in the period 1961–1965, when the fight for southern secession spread to Bahr el Ghazal from its original epicenter in Equatoria.

In October 1964, General Abboud was replaced by a Transitional Government, dominated by an organization called the Professionals Front, which had played a key role in coordinating opposition to the Abboud regime. After demonstrations against this new government by the Ansar in Khartoum in February 1965, another new government was formed in that same month. Headed by Sirr el Khatim el Khalifa, this government was dominated by the Umma Party, the NUP, and the Muslim Brothers, an offshoot of the Egyptian Muslim Brotherhood founded in 1928. El Khalifa's government made a serious attempt to end the civil war, sponsoring the March 1965 Round Table Conference, attended by all the major political parties, the Professionals Front, and leading southern politicians. However, agreement could not be reached on the south's constitutional status, with southern control of the armed forces one of the sticking points (Holt and Daly 1988, 171–86).

A major opportunity had been missed. Elections in April–May 1965 ushered in a new coalition government consisting of the Umma Party and National Unionist Party. Significantly, southern representation in Khartoum was sharply reduced. Civil war had impeded elections in the south, exacerbating the political powerlessness that had helped generate southern resistance in the first place. The south had only twenty members of parliament elected in April–May 1965, and these were mostly northern merchants elected unopposed (Holt and Daly 1988, 186).

The new coalition, under the Umma Party's Mohamed Ahmed Mahgoub, stepped up repression in the south. Southern Front members and southern intellectuals were persecuted, leaving southern political parties virtually impotent. Sudan army soldiers carried out massacres in Juba and Wau. Many southern Sudanese fled in fear to neighboring countries. Political pressure from the south was increasingly confined to military action, in the form of the Anyanya, a loosely knit guerrilla army whose nucleus came from the soldiers who mutinied in Equatoria in 1955. The new government offensive and Anyanya reprisals narrowed the room for maneuver for southern and northern politicians still trying to negotiate a political solution. Sadiq el Mahdi became prime minister in July 1966. The Umma Party won more seats than any other party in the March 1967 elections, held in thirty-six southern constituencies; the elections were boycotted by the Southern Front, which supported the south's right of self-determination. El Mahdi's government established a Constitutional Draft Committee, which had only a small minority of southern members and was boycotted by the Sudan African National Union (which favored a federal solution for the south) and by the Southern Front. Sadiq el Mahdi favored an Islamic constitution for the south, something that may have helped his precarious position within the Umma Party, but virtually precluded any political agreement on the south (Gurdon 1984, 18–19; Holt and Daly 1988, 187–90).

Increasing numbers of southern Sudanese found their ability to secure state protection was under threat. Meanwhile, identification with the rebels threatened to renew their previous exclusion from relevant political and moral communities.

Even with the war spreading to Bahr el Ghazal, the Ngok had managed to steer clear of conflict for a long time. Deng Majok played a delicate balancing game, secretly sending cattle to the Anyanya rebels to appease them, while publicly assisting the government "hunting" parties that sought to root out the rebels. By the mid-1960s, however, it was becoming more and more difficult for the Ngok to avoid involvement in the conflict (Deng 1986, 238–42). And their increasingly close identification with the rebels, in the eyes of both the government forces and the Messiriya, tended, in practice if not in theory, to erode their rights to state protection. The fact that a son of Deng Majok himself was prominent in the Anyanya rebel movement made it particularly difficult to avoid such identification. The death of Deng Majok in 1969 was seen by the Messiriya paramount chief, Babo Nimir, as unleashing the disruptive aspirations of young missionary-educated Dinka (ibid., 269).

In the mid-1960s, Messiriya raids on Ngok Dinka villages became commonplace. The police and the army—both overwhelmingly commanded by northern Sudanese—took little action to prevent these raids, or to punish the perpetrators, sometimes arriving up to thirty days after the raids (Wai 1973, 106; Saeed 1982, 220). The army was itself involved in raids on southern Sudanese, including the Dinka (Deng 1972, 151). Raiding combined with declining veterinary services during the first civil war drastically to reduce Nilotic cattle populations (Johnson 1989b, 482). Attacks by the Anyanya also caused great hardship. There was widespread starvation, together with large-scale migration by Dinka and other southern groups to northern Sudan. Here, foreshadowing events in 1987–1988, they were generally less well treated than those who fled to neighboring countries (such as the Central African Republic and Ethiopia) (Deng 1972, 140, 161; Saeed 1982, 212–13).[29] Security restrictions on hunting, gathering, and fishing added to the severity of famine (Deng 1972, 161). Dinka songs record this time as a new "spoiling" of Dinkaland, only this time with more terrible weaponry:

> The Arabs have spoiled our land,
> Spoiled our land with bearded guns,
> Guns which thunder and then even sound beautiful,
> Like the ancient drums with which buffaloes were charmed,
> Until their horns were caught.[30]

Thus, after several decades in which those famines that had occurred in the south had been precipitated largely by natural disasters (see, e.g., Johnson 1989b), the 1960s saw the reemergence of directly human-made famine. As before, the processes of famine had important political and economic beneficiaries, who actively helped to create the famine. Raiding was used by both sides in the war to feed their troops and to win support through intimidation. Meanwhile, army officers profited significantly from the sale of captured cattle (Deng 1972, 151). A number of northern commercial interests benefited from cheap livestock and labor, while playing a part in facilitating the raids.

The human-made famine was accompanied by increasing abuse of those who had migrated to the north—equally indicative of the erosion of their rights to state protection. In southern Kordofani towns, such as Muglad, Babanousa, and El Fula, southern Sudanese were increasingly subjected to verbal and physical abuse from some of the (mostly Messiriya) residents. In 1965, seventy-two southern Sudanese (many of them Ngok), who had sought refuge at Babanousa police station, were burned to death by a crowd of local women and children, who entered the station and set fire to them while police, armed with rifles and teargas, stood by (Saeed 1982, 223–25).

Despite the growth of raiding and the widespread abuse of southerners, there were still some checks on exploitation, however. While there was often an imbalance of weaponry between north and south, it was not severe enough to render the southerners altogether helpless (and was considerably less severe than that which would be obtained in the early years of raiding in the 1980s). From around 1965, Rizeigat leaders actually paid a tribute to Malwal chiefs and Anyanya leaders for the use of grazing lands south of the Bahr el Arab river, underlining an interest in cooperation as well as conflict (which, despite central government encouragement of hostilities, would survive even the 1980s raiding and famine). The central government, though guilty of tolerating raiding and of conducting its own raids through the army, did not actively encourage Baggara raiding (as it would during the second civil war). The Messiriya (and the Baggara more generally) at this stage lacked close ties with Khartoum. Indeed, when the Messiriya appealed to the central government for arms, claiming that the Anyanya were launching attacks on them with firearms, support within the government administration was not substantial. Subsequent police reports stated clearly that the Messiriya were not being attacked with firearms and themselves regularly used illegal guns against Dinka armed only with spears. Therefore, the reports stated, they had no need of extra arms (Saeed 1982, 221–22).

A second factor limiting exploitation was that the mechanisms for conflict resolution under the Native Administration system remained largely in place. After the massacre at Babanousa, the paramount chief of the Messiriya, Babo Nimir, appears to have played an important role in soothing tensions (Deng 1982, 31–32). His close personal relations with Deng Majok were an important factor. Intertribal conferences continued to be held. Payment of compensation continued to be made. Although there were suspicions that some "traditional chiefs" had actually encouraged violence in order to prove to the central government that it had need of their reconciliatory role, this role remained a real one. In short, there were still some local mechanisms for limiting violence between potentially conflicting tribes (Deng 1982; Saeed 1982, 246). Despite these remaining checks on exploitation and violence, however, the civil war had clearly threatened, and partially undermined, the system of protection and conflict resolution under Native Administration.

The rise of General Nimeiri brought a greater threat to this system. Nimeiri's military regime regarded the Native Administration leadership as allies of the party politicians he had replaced in power in May 1969. In any case, the various Islamic factions were generally hostile toward him during his early years in power (Allen 1986, 9). In these circumstances, Nimeiri sought to create an alternative power base, drawn from "progressive" and "modern" forces (Karam 1980, 15). Under the new system of local government established in 1971, Native Administration was abolished in northern Sudan. At a stroke, the carefully bolstered "traditional leaders" were deprived of their official roles and their stake in resolving local conflicts; responsibility for local government was invested in a complicated system of local councils and local branches of the new Sudan Socialist Union (ibid., 15–39). Ethnic politics and conflicts could not be so easily abolished, however. Although intertribal conferences continued to be held (Mohamed Salih 1990, 127), many Dinka elders were to complain that when disputes emerged, there were now no recognized heads of the Baggara with whom they could negotiate.

Meanwhile, for the Ngok, still contained within northern Sudan, the abolition of Native Administration had removed an important means of representation. It threatened to swamp them in a provincial administration, where they would be vastly outnumbered by northern interests. As the center of political decisionmaking for Ngokland shifted upwards to the provincial level, the Ngok's ability to influence these decisions acquired a new fragility. As Francis Deng commented in 1971: "Local government within the tribe, once in the hands of a Dinka executive officer and his Dinka staff centred at Abyei, now consists of occasional visits by a Northern officer who is several hundred miles away and cut off for half the year because of inadequate communications."[31] Chieftainship was abolished among the Ngok in 1972, and political opponents of Deng Majok and his family were appointed to a council of elders and magistrates (Deng 1986, 262).

### A Fragile Peace

What protected the Ngok—for a time at least—was their relatively strong representation at the central government level.[32] In Khartoum, President Nimeiri was increasingly isolated. In March 1970, amid growing Ansar disaffection, there were serious riots in Omdurman. These prompted a direct government attack on the Ansar's stronghold of Aba Island on the White Nile, killing perhaps twelve thousand people (Holt and Daly 1988, 197). Nimeiri had also turned against his one-time Communist allies in 1971. In these circumstances, Nimeiri attempted to include in his new, secular power base not just the army, the educated, and a range of farmers and national capitalists, but also the south. This shift also reflected military developments in the south. Nimeiri's early alliance with the Communists and his forging of close relations with Eastern Bloc countries had encouraged Western assistance to those southern Sudanese displaced into neighboring countries. Indirectly, this strengthened the Anyanya movement, which by the late 1960s was also receiving increasing support from Israel, Uganda, and Ethiopia (Alier 1990, 68, 71). By 1971, it was clear that the government's attempts at a military solution to the rebellion were failing as Anyanya gained in strength (Holt and Daly 1988, 200–201). Some sort of agreement with southern forces now appeared desirable to Nimeiri. As under the old British plan, the south was to be a balance against powerful religious interests and possible rebellion in the north, including rebellion by the Baggara, whose religious and party loyalties jarred with loyalty to Nimeiri. The scheme was not without success, for southern politicians and soldiers were to play an important role in frustrating the Libyan-backed Ansar coup attempt of July 1976 (Allen 1986, 20). While the southern Communist Joseph Garang was executed, his fellow southerner Abel Alier was elevated to the vice presidency (ibid., 9). Critically, the Addis Ababa agreement of 1972 included a provision for the incorporation of elements of the Anyanya into the national army, and a provision that half the army's Southern Command be filled with southern Sudanese. These measures offered important protection for southern Sudanese, and by 1976 the Southern Command was under the full command of former Anyanya officers (Alier 1990, 66, 152).

Nimeiri's new strategy of wooing the south—not just through making peace but also subsequently—presented important opportunities for the Ngok, and particularly for the family of Deng Majok, whose son Francis Deng was influential in Khartoum, having risen to the position of minister of foreign affairs. In 1974, Kwol Adol (another son of Deng Majok) was appointed as head of the tribe's administrative and judicial hierarchy. Abyei was given special administrative status, and was raised to the "area council" level. Abyei was to benefit from a special development program. Ngok representation in the local police was stepped up (Deng 1986, 264–65). Abyei was to be Nimeiri's showpiece of north-south cooperation. The Ngok experienced a period of peace, with extra army and police patrols created to control herders' movements and minimize grazing disputes (ibid., 244–58).

Ngok elders recognized the fragility of this new peace, however, dependent as it was on the political whims of the central government and an increasingly powerful army. While the strengthening of army units (for example, at Babanousa and Abyei) was ostensibly intended largely to counter traditional tribal interests (Saeed 1982, 244; Davey et al. 1976, 1:28), the fortified Sudanese army was later to resume its role as an instrument against the south, when new groups gained favor in the capital.

The fragility of the Ngok's position was all the more worrying for Ngok elders since the Addis Ababa agreement, against the better judgment of many, had retained the Ngok within the Kordofan administrative region. Many elders felt their people had been sacrificed at Addis Ababa, retained in the north to symbolize north-south cooperation and to assuage Messiriya fears of loss of access to grazing in Ngokland, but deprived of the envisaged benefits of membership of the newly autonomous south (Deng 1980, 28, 223). Ngok elders were profoundly aware of the likelihood of local exploitation unless there was access to continued protection from sympathetic elements of the central government. One elder, pleading for an all-season road to be built to Abyei from the north and for more police to be stationed in the area, noted: "When the flow of words is broken with the breakdown of communications in the summer [that is, because of the rains], the man with the power of the Government becomes wild. He takes the thing of the man without a tongue to sustain himself. And in the dry season, all that is dodged to the other side of the mouth. That, we hate."[33]

Others felt that the temporary protection provided by the educated in Khartoum would not last. The Ngok elder Atem Moter warned Francis Deng in 1974: "You children do not know the truth, even though you are educated. I feel that this thing (Arab aggression) is going to finish off our people. The Arabs have now sharpened their claws and you will just sit and watch them mutilate our people. Unless Deng Majok rises from his grave, no good will come out of you."[34]

Although he documented such fears meticulously, Francis Deng largely discounted them. In this, he was probably influenced by his position as a government minister, as well as by a more general wave of optimism in what became known as Sudan's "decade of hope." In particular, Deng argued: "One must . . . distinguish between the chiefs' actual accounts of the past hostilities, their pessimistic subjectivities on the future, conditioned as they are by these hostilities, and a scientific prediction that places South-North relations in a broader context characterised by the dynamics of modern nation-building."[35]

Subsequent events were to show that these "pessimistic subjectivities" had more predictive power than the "science" of the educated. But for the moment, the Dinka enjoyed unusual political representation. For those elements of the Dinka (all but the Ngok) living in the south, there was now some kind of voice not only in Khartoum but also at the newly powerful regional government headquarters in Juba (Prunier 1986, 36; Allen 1986). Moreover, the new commissioners of each of the three provinces in the south (Bahr el Ghazal, Upper Nile, and Equatoria) were given the status of central government ministers. From 1972, local administration in Dinkaland was largely carried out by Dinka, with both educational and employment opportunities expanding significantly. It seemed possible that "government" might be appropriated and used to protect the interests of the Dinka (Mawson 1989, 87–88). Government revenues arising from commercial, agricultural, and industrial activities accrued to the regional treasury (Alier 1990, 223). In the Bahr el Arab region, the strong ex-Anyanya component in the southern army helped tilt the balance of power in favor of southern interests and against the Baggara. Abel Alier has commented: "For the first time in 73 years since the beginning of the condominium administration, Southerners were responsible for their own people."[36]

This fragile system of protection was not to last. In order to understand precisely why protection against famine dissolved in the late 1970s and early 1980s, it is necessary to look at the changing economies of the Dinka and Baggara, as well as changes in their access to political power.

### Partial Economic Integration among the Dinka

The costs and benefits for the Dinka of integration into market relationships are interwoven with the relationship between this integration and the use of force. In stressing the relationship between economic exploitation and violence, this analysis has certain similarities with a view put forward by Lenin and Hilferding: in newly opened-up countries, capitalism excites resistance (movements for national independence), "and European capital can maintain its domination only by continually increasing its means of exerting violence" (Lenin [1917] 1939, 248, quoting Hilferding).

Many Dinka resisted processes of economic integration, and force was used to overcome resistance to economic transactions perceived as disadvantageous. The partial economic integration of the south in turn gave further impetus to northern interest in continued exploitation. Partial economic integration meant that the prosperity of significant northern groups came to depend increasingly on their ability to exploit the resources of the south (whether these took the form of cheap labor, cheap livestock, or cash exchanged for northern grain). In the nineteenth century, as noted, southern Sudanese people's noncooperation with peaceful but exploitative trading had led to the use of armed servants, who acquired an interest in plunder and were paid by giving them a share. Somewhat similarly, northerners' defense of commercial interests in the south in the 1970s and early 1980s led to their enlisting the assistance of a variety of armed groups, who thereby gained a stake in expropriation and who could be paid, in effect, with a share in any plunder. In both cases, the resort to force had the effect of deepening economic exploitation, directly creating famine. Meanwhile, the south's new economic dependence on the north facilitated exploitation (and the creation of famine) via market mechanisms, as any restriction of supplies of grain from the north led to very high prices in the south. At the same time, it is reasonable to surmise that the exploitative economic relationships between the south and the north—including periodic raiding—played a role in preventing southern Sudanese peoples from turning their natural resources into the political power (including weaponry) with which they could defend themselves against famine and exploitation.

During the first half of the twentieth century, the degree to which the

Dinka were integrated economically into Sudan remained very limited. Partly, this was because the Dinka showed considerable resistance to such integration. Their reluctance to enter into the ivory trade or portering work in the nineteenth century has been mentioned, as has their reluctance to seek work outside their home areas, sometimes even to the point of choosing death as an alternative (Titherington 1927, 164). Selling of cattle was frequently regarded as shameful, and often cows could simply not be bought.[37] Wage labor was also seen as shameful and was associated with the forced labor of the recent past and with the neglect of obligations to kin:

> Money likes slavery,
> Slavery in which gentlemen are ordered.[38]

> The family has lost its value.
> Blood ties have been severed in the pockets . . .
> In the towns people dance to the drums in their pockets.
> If one has nothing, one goes with nothing.[39]

On top of a widespread Dinka suspicion of the market, British policy in relation to the south (in particular the Closed Districts policy of 1920–1956) had tended to discourage the economic integration of the south, leading some British officials to bemoan the lack of (taxable) sales of southern cattle (Sikainga 1986, 141; Abdel-Rahim 1968; Tosh 1981, 279). Among the various Dinka tribes, the Ngok were probably most exposed to integration into the Sudanese economy, as a result of their proximity to the north. As late as 1950, however, they had been largely shielded from outside influences by official restrictions and the lack of easy access by road or river (Howell 1951a, 263). Economic interaction between the Ngok and the Humr was for the most part limited to years of food shortage in Ngokland, with the Ngok apparently content to keep such interaction at a minimum (Howell 1951b, 443–47).

Significantly increased integration did nevertheless begin to occur with independence in 1956 and the end of the Closed Districts policy. The Addis Ababa peace agreement of 1972 gave an additional boost to such integration. For one thing, it became possible for northern Sudanese traders to travel in safety to remote parts of the south (Allen 1986, 12).

In Ngokland, Deng Majok (effectively chief from 1942 until 1969) promoted the development of a market economy, encouraging the sale of cattle (many of which he bought himself), and fining people cash instead of the traditional cattle fines (Deng 1971, 361; Deng 1986, xi, 130). On top of this, the government imposed taxes payable in cash, thereby successfully encouraging the sale of cattle (Deng 1972, 161). Cunnison, who worked in southwestern Kordofan in the early 1950s, noted that Abyei had a significant weekly cattle market (Cunnison 1966, 36). Although this market had become of marginal importance by the early 1970s after years of severe cattle loss in the south, it resumed its growth in the 1970s until by 1980 it had become a major link between the economies of north and south, with as many as twenty-five traders looking to buy cattle in Abyei in the period before the rains (Niamir, Huntington, and Cole 1983, 19, 27).

In Ngokland there was a significant dependence on northern grain by the early 1970s (Deng 1972, 161). And elsewhere in the south, the majority of towns outside western Equatoria became dependent on grain imports from the north. The inhabitants of many rural areas throughout the south came to depend on the availability of such grain from May through July, the months just before the harvest (Ryle 1989a, 7).

The spread of a money economy in both north and south led to new patterns of labor migration. Bahr el Ghazal became, in the 1960s and 1970s, an important source of laborers for southern Darfur and southern Kordofan (Shepherd 1984, 83). Young men would follow the planting of their own fields in border areas of Bahr el Ghazal with a move to the north, where they could take advantage of the later rains and earn money as agricultural laborers (Ryle 1989a, 13). The Malwal Dinka of Aweil area found work in Darfur, notably on commercial farms in the Ed Daien area. The Ngok found work in Kordofan, particularly on the commercial farms in the Muglad area (ibid., 19). Ngok Dinka girls and young women from Abyei obtained employment as domestic servants in Kordofan towns (ibid., 13). The migration of the Ngok and Malwal to southern Kordofan and southern Darfur was part of a wider trend. Many of the big agricultural producers preferred migrant labor to that of local people, who typically had to divide their time between their own fields and the land of the big farmers (Ahmed 1987, 274–75; Affan 1981, 179). Bahr el Ghazal and Upper Nile became important sources of migrant labor for the agricultural schemes in Renk and the central zone of Sudan (Ryle 1989a, 13; Duffield 1990a, 11). Meanwhile, there was a considerable exodus of Dinka to northern towns during the first civil war, an exodus that continued thereafter (Deng 1972, 152). Dinka and (more especially) Nuer came to provide a significant proportion of the construction workers in Khartoum (Ryle 1989a, 13).

For the most part, there was little investment of northern capital in southern agriculture. One significant development, however, was the creation of agricultural estates in the south in the late 1970s by wealthy oil magnates from the Middle East. Many of these were established near the Bahr el Arab River, which divided north and south (Prunier 1986, 32–33).

The south's increasing economic integration with the north did not necessarily mean increased vulnerability to famine. Indeed, the potential benefits of north-south trading were sharply illustrated in the 1920s and 1930s, when the Condominium government sought to minimize contact between tribal groups perceived as hostile toward each other. The separation of Bahr el

Ghazal and Darfur led to an acute shortage of grain and other supplies in Bahr el Ghazal, which had usually been brought through Darfur by the Baggara (Sikainga 1986, p. 141).[40] It was clear, moreover, that grain brought south by the Humr could play a role in mitigating shortages in Ngokland. One such shortage occurred during the rains of 1950, prompting many Humr to go south to barter grain for cattle (Cunnison 1966, 174). The Humr would sell either grain they had grown themselves or grain they had purchased from Dar Hamar to the north.

Another potential benefit of integration was that in times of crisis, many Dinka were able to find work in the north, with Muglad town a particular magnet (Howell 1951b, 444). Wage labor became an important survival strategy in lean years (Ryle 1989a, 13), and markedly so during the first civil war (Saeed 1982, 213). Even in normal times, temporary migration became an important means of earning money with which to buy cattle and marry. Cash wages were also used to buy manufactured goods that were unavailable or simply too expensive in the south (Ryle 1989a, 13). Partly because young Dinka women would sometimes think less of a young man they had observed working as a laborer, Dinka youths often welcomed the chance to earn money in areas far from their home villages (Deng 1971, 308; Deng 1972, 161–62).

Meanwhile, the livestock trade centered on Abyei had come, by 1980, to provide a significant source of income for many Dinka (Niamir, Huntington, and Cole 1983). Small-scale trade (for example, in chickens, beer, and dairy produce) was also a significant source of independent income for Dinka women, who had previously enjoyed few or no property rights (Deng 1971, 363).

If there were some positive effects of economic integration for southern Sudanese, there is nevertheless evidence that northern interests took the lion's share of the benefits. Moreover, the distribution of economic benefits on the north/south border was in practice inseparable from the exercise of various kinds of force, threatened or actual. As both the political representation of southerners (Dinka in particular) and the economic opportunities in northern Sudan declined steeply after the mid-1970s, the partial economic integration of the south proved damaging in a number of important respects.

North-south trading was dominated by northern traders, whose privileged access to trading networks and local monopolies or near-monopolies allowed them to buy cheap and sell dear, causing widespread resentment among southern Sudanese. Such resentment was evidenced by attacks on merchants,[41] which themselves sometimes provoked retaliation by Baggara militias.[42] Dinka resentment was also evident in the statements of Dinka chiefs, documented by Francis Deng at the end of the first civil war. The complaints of chief Stephen Thongok, chief of the Atuot Dinka of Bahr el Ghazal, were not untypical: "[The Arabs] are still controlling our economy.

They are the people who own the shops, and all the money is still in their hands" (Deng 1978, 178). He added that, while security had slightly improved, the Arabs "still have the voice and they still have the whip" (ibid.). As for the Ngok, it was clear that, even in the early 1950s, before the penetration of merchant capital had become marked, the prices at which Humr sold grain and bought cattle during food shortages among the Ngok were very favorable to the Humr (Cunnison 1966, 37).

The exercise of violence during the first civil war helped to deepen exploitation, and to overcome the traditional resistance of the Dinka to economic integration. Famine—created to a large extent by raiding—may have served, whether intentionally or not, an important "function" here by forcing sales of labor and livestock and purchases of grain.[43] Merchant involvement in the raiding suggested some commercial motivation: local merchants supplied commercial vehicles for the transport of Messiriya fighting squads from Muglad and surrounding areas to battlegrounds in the south (Saeed 1982, 221). There were also reports of the stealing of Ngok Dinka grain by large groups of Messiriya and merchants, who set out from Abyei or Muglad on trucks, sometimes preceded by army personnel; sometimes, this grain would be bought back by the Ngok from the merchants who took it (*The Vigilant*, July 8, 1965).[44]

By the end of the first civil war, the livestock population of the Ngok (and of other Dinka) had been markedly reduced by tax demands and an increasing resort to the sale of livestock in order to fund the purchase of desperately needed grain (Deng 1972, 161). Purchase of Dinka cattle at very low prices and selling of grain at very high prices became very common in the later years of the first civil war. In Ngokland and elsewhere, Dinka would frequently sell grain at harvesttime, in order to buy salt and other market goods, only to buy grain back at high prices before the following harvest (ibid., 161; Deng and Oduho 1963, 19). Dinka (including Ngok) elders reported that by 1973–1974 the numbers of cattle in the Abyei area had dwindled to the point where only four people had significant stock (Deng 1980, 294, 336). Wartime raiding, as well as market transactions influenced by this raiding, had played a significant part in this decline.[45]

At the same time, some elements among the Dinka could still derive a degree of protection from exploitation as a result of the exercise of political power at local level. Noting the sale of grain by Dinka at harvesttime, and the repurchase at high prices later, Chief Deng Majok imposed restrictions on the sale of grain (Deng 1971, 266). A desire to check the worst excesses of exploitation also led Deng Majok to outlaw trading outside Abyei town, and to set aside a single day of the week for trading in the town (Deng 1986, 130).

Before the advent of these grain and livestock markets, the Dinka had responded to food shortages by resorting to wild grains, by hunting and fishing, or simply by consuming the milk and meat of their own cattle (Deng 1972, 161). Loaning of cattle by the relatively wealthy was also an important buffer against famine (Deng 1971, 267). Such strategies did not simply disappear as market transactions became more common, but the new shortage of cattle after the first civil war must in itself have impinged on many of these economic strategies, probably adding to the new dependence on imported grain.

If the level of exploitation in Ngokland was often significant, it appears to have been worse among many Dinka tribes further south. One such was the Twic, neighbors of the Ngok. Traditionally subject to Humr raiding and still subject to exploitative market transactions, the Twic lacked the Ngok's marriage ties with the Humr. They also lacked the degree of political control over markets that was exercised by Deng Majok. In fact, some of the Twic would travel north to the market in Abyei to benefit from the more tightly regulated markets established there (Deng 1986, 234).

Turning to labor migration, while it did provide an additional option for Dinka tribes during hard times, its benefits should not be exaggerated.[46] There was apparently a strong "push" factor, with the abovementioned loss of livestock wealth providing a key stimulus to migration to the north (Deng 1972, 161). It seems likely that the distribution of benefits arising from such migration was conditioned to a large extent by the political developments (for example, government-facilitated raiding and government taxation) that helped determine its magnitude.

In the aftermath of the first civil war, northern commercial interest in Dinka cattle increased considerably. Significantly, by the late 1970s what one report referred to as the bonanza to be made from purchasing cattle in Abyei had created a powerful interest in maintaining, even expanding, this trade among the merchants involved. At the beginning of the 1980s, larger traders were making between Sud. £50,000 and £100,000 a year on the purchase of cattle in Abyei. Some would purchase as many as six hundred head of cattle in Abyei, reselling with profit margins of 200 to 300 percent. Meiram, in southern Kordofan, was also an important market. Cattle merchants enjoyed an oligopolistic position and came from a limited number of experienced northern Sudanese merchant families. Access to trading was also limited by the need for large amounts of capital. Meanwhile, the Dinka's own lack of capital, agents, and necessary family ties made it practically impossible for them to join the privileged ranks of those moving cattle to northern markets. A Harvard research team found that by 1980 a number of Ngok had managed to carve out a subsidiary trading role for themselves, buying heifers in Abyei and exchanging them for Twic bulls and oxen. But the profits here—perhaps 160 Sudanese pounds for a five-day round trip—were hardly comparable. The livestock trade, while bringing some additional cash into the south, was thus the focus of considerable resentment. By the 1980s, the trade had come under attack from elements of the Ngok. Significantly, army personnel began to acquire an increasing interest in the trade, as they were bribed into giving special protection to northern merchants (Niamir, Huntington, and Cole 1983, 1–33; El Khalifa et al. 1985, 213; Ateeg 1983). Meanwhile, in Darfur, similar interests in livestock trading had been created (see, e.g., Ryle 1989a, 18). The difficulties of securing continued profits from the trade in the context of the second civil war, together with the further erosion of Dinka representation in wartime, were to encourage a further increase in the application of force to livestock transactions, through raiding and physical intimidation in the marketplace. In processes that both created and constituted famine, army personnel and northern merchants were to work together to secure livestock (and other sources of profit) from the Dinka; this story is taken up in Chapter 3.

Another growing attraction for certain northern Sudanese interests in the 1970s was Dinka land. The new agricultural estates along the Bahr el Arab have been mentioned. These were subject to incursions by Dinka, resentful of the loss of land, and the owners found it necessary to guard the estates by arming nomadic groups, notably from among the Rizeigat. Many Dinka were killed by these guards in repeated conflicts over land (Prunier 1986, 32–33).[47] The protection of these unpopular commercial interests contributed to a wider process of arms acquisition among the Baggara, helping to create a severe imbalance of weaponry in relation to the Dinka. A similar, more devastating, process of arming militias was used to protect newly discovered oil fields against the southern rebels.

Land occupied by the Dinka may have been coveted for another reason. Government proposals for a Southern Stock Route, under which cattle would be driven from the west to the capital along a more southerly route than normal, promised to reduce the costs of taking cattle to markets by increasing the availability of grazing and water en route. The proposed route offered to stimulate production in areas through which it would pass. However, the proposed route went right through parts of southern Kordofan with a heavy Dinka presence, notably Meiram. And in the context of rising Dinka-Arab tension in the early 1980s, merchants feared that cattle on the route would be vulnerable to attack (El Khalifa et al. 1985, 46, 175).

The new (or, in view of previous slaving, renewed) reliance on southern labor among various northern groups was also dangerous in some respects. During the first civil war, migrant laborers had become, in the words of one police report, "an indispensable factor for the farmers and townspeople in places like Al Fula, Al Muglad and Babanousa" (Saeed 1982, 213). Meanwhile, the continued growth of commercial agriculture created increasing demand for southern labor. Farmers in Kordofan found it difficult to tempt people from within the region into paid employment in the context of a dramatic rise in labor migration from Messiriya areas to central Sudan in the

1960s, with many young men joining the army and many others going to neighboring countries (El Sammani 1985, 89). There also appeared to be some scorn for manual agricultural labor among the Baggara, something that had been encouraged by slavery, and which continued to encourage the use of southern Sudanese labor in the new context of a free (or at any rate, freer) labor market (Hargey 1981, 457; Ibrahim 1988, 100). Many wealthy Rizeigat families relied on southern (mostly Dinka) labor (El Khalifa et al. 1985, 35). Among settled Messiriya farmers, utilization of Dinka labour helped permit the growth of groundnut and sesame production, notably in the Muglad area (El Sammani 1985, 85, 158–59). At the same time, in the new political context of the 1980s, economic integration was to provide scant protection against famine; Chapter 3 explains how market prices (including labor rates) were shaped by the use of force or threatened force in ways that deepened famine, rather than protecting against it.

### Marginalization of the Baggara

The generation of this exploitative climate cannot be properly understood without considering the changing political and economic position of groups that were to benefit from famine among the Dinka in the 1980s, notably elements of the Baggara of southern Kordofan and southern Darfur. It was the economic and political marginalization of these "beneficiary" groups, followed by a sudden resurgence in their access to the means of exerting force (through weaponry, political protection, and political decisions on relief), that created the conditions in which the famine became possible. As with the jellaba in the nineteenth century, marginalization in the north bred violence and famine in the south. The Baggara's neglect in development policy was exacerbated by, and to some extent contributed to, the environmental crisis in the north. The most serious drought came in 1983–1985. Drought and environmental decline encouraged the Baggara to look toward the relatively fertile lands of the south for economic salvation.

Although the Baggara had gained substantial economic rewards from their political and military muscle in the 1880s, they were in many ways politically and economically marginalized as British rule was consolidated, as were many other pastoral groups.[48] Baggara interests could not be ignored altogether, as early toleration of raiding and the "go slow" policy on slavery abolition testified. However, increasing restrictions on movement into the south and tightening restrictions on slavery did place substantial economic pressures on the Baggara. Further, British administrators tended to draw sharp boundaries between potentially conflicting ethnic groups, and for the most part these were drawn to the disadvantage of Baggara groups (including the Messiriya). The British desire to "protect" and appease non-Muslims has been mentioned. There was also a pressing imperial need to expand cotton cultivation, with Egyptian nationalism posing a possible threat to supplies from Sudan's northern neighbor. In the 1920s and 1930s, much of the best land for expanding cotton cultivation in the Nuba Mountains area, southern Kordofan, was reserved for the sedentary Nuba (identified—wrongly, as it turned out—as much better equipped to grow cotton than the traditionally nomadic Messiriya) (Ibrahim 1988, 62–69).

Many Baggara groups could ill afford such discrimination. In particular, the Messiriya Zurug had, in any case, insufficient land for normal expansion, as a result of having been driven west by other tribes, including the Hawazma, and having lost the valued land around Muglad to the Humr. This constriction led to regular quarrels with neighboring tribes (MacMichael 1967, 142–43; Henderson 1939, 49).

Pressure on grazing among the Baggara had been significantly increased by a dramatic rise in the numbers of their cattle, from at least the 1950s. Improved veterinary services had helped boost the cattle population of Kordofan from some 1 million in 1953 to around 2.4 million in 1976, while numbers in Darfur had risen from around 1 million to more than 3.6 million in the same period (Karam 1980, 87). Increased remittances from rising migrant labor in the 1960s had been invested in animals, swelling the numbers in Messiriya areas (El Sammani 1985, 90). Together with a rapidly rising human population, the rise in livestock populations had contributed to considerable degradation of the land, including many areas occupied by the Humr (Karam 1980, 5, 37; Wilson 1977, 500–504; El Sammani 1985, 54, 76).

In the meantime, the total area available for grazing had been severely restricted by the growth of cultivation (notably for export) (Davey et al. 1976, 1:27; Karam 1980, 5; El Sammani 1985, 86, 99–100). A rise in the area cultivated by smallholders had been encouraged by a rapid increase in the number of wells. Even by the early 1950s, new wells and associated cultivation had caused a squeeze on Humr grazing in the traditional northerly wet-season grazing lands known as the Babanousa (Cunnison 1966, 41). Between 1967 and 1972, the number of wells in the Western District, in southern Kordofan, rose fourfold (Saeed 1982, 112). Messiriya nomads came increasingly into conflict with newly sedentary Messiriya, as well as with Nuba cultivators, on their northward migrations (ibid., 140–41). There were frequent complaints of Nuba cultivators burning grazing lands to deter nomads from coming near, and of attacks by cultivators on herders (ibid., 450).

Particularly damaging to the Baggara were the expanding mechanized farms in southern Kordofan and (to a lesser extent) southern Darfur. The growth of large farms had been greatly facilitated by changes in the law on land ownership. Under the Native Administration system, different tribes had been allocated their own domains (*dars*), over which they exerted considerable control. With the end of Native Administration, the state was granted rights of ownership over all land that was not registered as private property (ibid., 252; Karam 1980, 5). As under British rule, the state used the granting of cheap leases (and privileged access to cheap inputs) as a key strategy in winning political support (Ali 1988, 187; Ibrahim 1988, 187). Little or no compensation was paid to the previous users (Shepherd 1984, 89). The state-run Mechanised Farming Corporation, established in 1968, acted as the conduit for major World Bank loans to allow clearing and culti- vation of millions of acres of land (around 5 million by 1984). Together with loans from the state-owned Agricultural Bank of Sudan, this allowed mecha- nized farming to spread from Kassala and Blue Nile provinces to southern Kordofan, Upper Nile, and other areas of Sudan (ibid., 89; Ali 1988, 29).

The growth of cultivation in the Lagawa area posed a particular threat to the Messiriya nomads, many of whom were accustomed to spending the dry season in the area (Saeed 1982, 155). Their southerly migration routes were cut off by the new agricultural schemes (Ibrahim 1988, 120; Mohamed Salih 1993, 24–25). Nomadic delegations (including senior representatives of the Messiriya) complained bitterly that the fire lanes set by the Nuba Mountains Agricultural Corporation (cleared corridors for preventing the spread of fires) were severely restricting the nomads' opportunities for grazing (Saeed 1982, 450–54).

In his study of the Nuba Mountains region, H. Ibrahim, noted that no- madic routes had run for three hundred years from the belt of sandy soil in Kordofan through to the Bahr el Arab region, and added: "The location of the mechanized farming schemes amid this grazing zone has completely disturbed the fragile balance of Baggara transhumance, jeopardizing the liv- ing of thousands of nomads."[49]

The problem was exacerbated by the exhaustion of mechanized farming land (for example, the old Habila scheme in southern Kordofan) within some fifteen years of initial cultivation, because of lack of rotation and fertilizer, a pattern that characterized commercial agriculture in much of Sudan (Ibrahim 1988, 110). This fueled the land hunger of the mechanized farming sector.

Meanwhile, opportunities in the growing mechanized sector were domi- nated by jellaba from outside the region (who tended to move out of cotton as prices stagnated) and by government officials, both mostly from central Sudanese cities (ibid., 80, 102–3, 122, 187).

Another source of pressure on the Baggara was rapid inflation, and in particular the rising price of grain through the 1970s and 1980s, even before the drought-led famine of 1983–1985 (Ahmed 1987, 323–32; El Hassan 1985, 205–6; Keen 1986). The growth of large mechanized farms in southern Kordofan did not bring cheap grain to the area, since the food was largely exported from the area (Ibrahim 1988, 112, 191). The grain market in south- ern Kordofan was monopolized by a small number of major merchants cum mechanized-scheme owners from outside the area,[50] with the Agricultural Bank of Sudan playing a role in boosting the prices wealthy individuals could obtain by advancing loans to them to permit speculative storage (Ibrahim 1988, 80; El Hassan 1985, 1, 308–12). In southern Darfur, much of the trading was dominated by Zaghawa, a formerly nomadic tribe from northern Darfur, many of whom had migrated south during the drought in the late 1960s; opposition to Zaghawa merchants' price increases, and to growing class schisms in Ed Daien, helped fuel the emerging, aggressive Rizeigat ethnic identity that was to be channeled against the Dinka in raiding and other atrocities (Mahmud and Baldo 1987, 23–24). Meanwhile, economic pressures on the Rizeigat were increased by rising cash crop production in western Kordofan and eastern Darfur, which turned this area into one that regularly produced a grain deficit (Abdul-Jalil and Rabih 1986, 340). Combined with drought in the early 1970s and the growing pressure on grazing, rising prices encouraged large numbers of Messiriya to abandon their nomadic way of life, focusing more and more on cultivation in their home areas, or seeking work in towns or in Nile Valley agricultural schemes (Saeed 1982, 53, 316). The 1960s and 1970s saw a rise in unemployment among former pastoralists, as well as among the sedentary Nuba of southern Kordofan. By the beginning of the 1980s, the majority of wage workers in Babanousa, southern Kordofan's biggest town, were people who had abandoned a nomadic way of life at some point in the previous three decades (ibid., 224). The Baggara's increasing resort to grain cultivation (and retention of some of their herds) led to the abandonment of rotational grazing, contributing to the decline in the quality of grazing. Sedentarization—and consequent vulnerability to ecological degradation—affected the poorer Baggara most; those with larger herds were generally able to reap the benefits of keeping their cattle on the move (ILO/UNDP 1976, 247; Hunting Technical Services 1974; El Sammani 1985, 178).[51]

The price squeeze and land squeeze on Baggara groups were part of a wider process of increasing social and economic differentiation between large mechanized farmers on the one hand, and nomads and peasant farmers on the other; perhaps 90 percent of Sudan's marketable food surplus was controlled by less than 1 percent of the farmers by the end of the 1980s (Duffield 1990a, 10). The sedentarization of nomadic groups also extended well beyond the Baggara (see, e.g., Hales 1978).

If the Messiriya were largely marginalized, their leadership was nevertheless not completely without influence in Khartoum. The paramount chief, Babo Nimir, was able to use marriage ties with the Mahdi family to secure land for himself and his brother, Ali Nimir, in the Gedaref area (Saeed 1982, 159–60). And under the military regime of General Abboud (1958–1964), Babo Nimir was appointed to the forty-member military council (ibid., 160).[52] However, the great majority of ordinary Messiriya, like other pastoralists, remained marginalized by a pattern of development in which political and economic power was concentrated in the hands of a northern riverain elite from the areas that as of 1993 comprise Blue Nile, Northern, and Khartoum provinces. This elite, which had not had to mobilize large sections of the Sudanese population in any prolonged independence struggle, was able to manipulate traditional religious loyalties in order to maintain not only its hold on political power and but also a near-monopoly on the most profitable commercial enterprises (Niblock 1987, 204–32; Khalid 1990; Ibrahim 1985; Mahmoud 1984).[53] While the Umma Party elites dominated opportunities in the Gezira area, the Khatmiyya had a strong hold on urban commercial operations centered on Khartoum; private and public investment were heavily concentrated in these two areas (Warburg 1992, 129–30). One technique for which the Umma Party was criticized was nominating riverain politicians to stand for safe seats in Darfur (Woodward 1990, 114). Meanwhile, the Baggara's traditional leadership was to a significant extent co-opted by Sudan's riverain elite.

The 1958–1964 period saw the rise of a Messiriya Ethnic Union, based on urban Messiriya disgruntled with the status quo under Native Administration and what they saw as the neglect of Messiriya interests (Ibrahim 1988, 211, 216). A split between the Native Administration leadership and younger Messiriya men was evident during the raiding of Dinka in the mid-1960s, associated with the first civil war. After one raid on the Raik Dinka in 1965, Messiriya paramount chief, Babo Nimir, had managed to ease tensions by convincing the Raik Dinka that the raid had been the work of young men and not the elders (Deng 1982, 32). The Messiriya Ethnic Union was one of a number of urban-based ethnic organizations emerging at this time, with Arab ethnic organizations growing in large part as a response to the rise of an increasingly vociferous Nuba ethnicity. This ethnicity had itself been encouraged by the British with their sponsorship of a non-Muslim political pressure group, the so-called black bloc (Ibrahim 1988, 211, 261–62).

The emergence of ethnic politics was also stimulated by an expansion in the role of the state (for example in allocating mechanized schemes and government rations). In the absence of strongly competing ideologies under Nimeiri's single-party system, appeals to ethnicity were the easiest way for emerging educated elites to recruit support (ibid., 269, 278–79; Karam 1980, 6). Moreover, the neglect of non-Arab groups in economic and educational development encouraged these groups to organize along ethnic lines in order to "catch up" (Ibrahim 1988, 35, 83), while other groups organized to defend their relatively privileged position. Significantly, ethnic divisions (notably between the Baggara and the Nuba) appear to have consolidated the dominance of the jellaba merchants over district politics; these merchants were also able to use their access to rationed goods and agricultural schemes and licenses to recruit supporters from among rural council delegates. In general, ethnic groups who were excluded from the most important economic benefits wound up competing, rather than cooperating—as the rebel Sudan People's Liberation Army was to urge, at least on a military level—to reshape the political economy of Sudan in their own interests (ibid., 282–85). This competition for resources was to be expressed most dramatically and damagingly during the famine peaking in 1988.

In theory, under the parliamentary governments that followed the fall of General Abboud in 1964, the Baggara (including the Messiriya) secured representation at the center through their affiliation with the Umma Party. However, the leadership of the Umma Party was almost entirely drawn from the northern riverain provinces, and in practice, the party appeared to be less a modern political party than a way in which the Mahdi family organized its supporters, or Ansar, for its own purposes (Ibrahim 1985, 329; Vincent 1988, 234, citing Bona Malwal). Resources continued to be concentrated on central areas of Sudan, with local administration largely left to a "tribal" hierarchy, institutionalized under the Turko-Egyptian regime and comprising, in order of rank, local *nazirs* (paramount chiefs), *omdas*, and *shaikhs*, in conjunction with local government officers, while traditional religious affiliations helped keep the Baggara loyal to the Umma Party (Woodward 1990, 29–31, 109–23; A.R.A. Ibrahim 1985; H. Ibrahim 1988, 286).

If anything, the political representation of the Baggara was further diminished under Nimeiri, as the abolition of Native Administration resulted in severe underrepresentation of Baggara groups in the organs of the Sudanese state (Ibrahim 1988, 275). Nomads were identified with corrupt, traditional, party government, and an official ideology portrayed them as resistant to change and progress (Karam 1980, 33). Nomadic groups were allocated scant resources in the 1970 Ten Year Plan under Nimeiri, just as they had been in the 1960 Ten Year Plan under Abboud (ibid., 74; Ibrahim 1985, 284). The western regions of Sudan continued to be neglected in development plans (Ibrahim 1985, 345).

Nimeiri's new local government system invested all important powers, including the power to settle tribal disputes, in the new provincial councils. One third of the provincial council members were appointed, and the remainder indirectly elected. The elected members were sent from the various town and rural councils, whose members had been sent from the ward, market area, and industrial councils (in the case of town councils) and the village and nomadic camp councils (in the case of rural councils). Since the number of functioning nomads' camp councils was only 105 out of fully 4,675 lower-level councils in Sudan, nomadic groups had very little chance of gaining substantial representation at the provincial level. Some provincial councils, even in traditional Baggara strongholds, had no nomadic representatives at all. In addition, the nomads' tendency to choose leaders by consensus rather than by election was thought to have discouraged them from seeking representation in the various councils (Karam 1980, 15–18, 35–39). Competition between rival dynastic families was another factor limiting no-madic representation (Saeed 1982, 145).

The system of local councils had been designed as an instrument for im-plementing ideas formulated within the new single party apparatus, the Sudan Socialist Union (SSU), rather than as channels through which popular concerns could be voiced. The SSU was scarcely any better than the local councils as a vehicle for popular (and especially nomadic) concerns. Created as a power base to cement Nimeiri's new, secular alliance, and designed precisely to combat the power of the old religious and Native Administration leaders whose strongholds had been among the Baggara, the SSU was al-ways an unlikely vehicle for nomadic interests (Karam 1980, 15; Niblock 1987, 262–72).

Not only were the Messiriya poorly represented at the key provincial council level, they also often lacked representatives on the People's Local Courts that dealt with grazing disputes. In southern Kordofan, the critical, heavily cultivated Lagawa areas of Knor Al Butha and Wadi Durungas fell within a district where the nomads lacked any representation. The courts in these areas tended to impose fines for the mere act of entering cultivated plots, whether or not there had been damage, and even when cultivators had sometimes physically attacked "intruding" Messiriya (Saeed 1982, 451–52).[54]

Meanwhile, in the south, the Baggara found their access to grazing under threat from newly confident southern politicians, from southern army units (in which former Anyanya guerrillas were strongly represented), and from southern police units (now staffed largely with southern Sudanese). Dinka herds were recovering after the first civil war and competing for grazing south of the Bahr el Arab river (Karam 1980, 53). In some areas, additional pressure on grazing arose from a 250 percent increase in the area of perma-nent swamp and seasonal floodplain since around 1960 (Johnson 1989b, 482).

Beginning in 1974, the Rizeigat found they were being denied dry season grazing rights in Dinkaland, south of the Bahr el Arab river. Rizeigat who attempted to graze in this area were harassed by Dinka. The Rizeigat hit back, burning villages and killing a number of Dinka. This led to a peace conference in 1975, at which the Dinka argued that an overabundance of cattle and people in the area left no room for the Rizeigat. The Dinka were supported by Bahr el Ghazal politicians, with whom the Malwal Dinka para-mount chief Ring Lual was influential. The Rizeigat were ordered to pay compensation (Karam 1980, 52–55). Further hostilities in 1976 resulted in the intervention of an army unit from Aweil. Made up of former Anyanya fighters, it threw its weight behind the Dinka (de Waal 1990b, 4). Intertribal fighting again broke out in 1978 (Karam 1980, 56).

Dinka chiefs attributed the difficulty in finding a solution to Malwal/Ri-zeigat and other Dinka/Arab tensions to the absence of the old Native Administration leadership among the Baggara group and among the Ngok (ibid., 57; Deng 1982, 47–48). The emergence of electoral politics in the south appears to have further eroded chiefly authority there. In general, whereas under Native Administration the various Sudanese chiefs had derived their status within the government administration in large part from their ability to control their followers and to resolve tribal disputes, the demands of electoral politics in both the north and the south now encouraged attempts to promote "ethnic" interests at the expense of other groups. As Karam noted in 1980 in relation to the Rizeigat/Malwal dispute in particular, "Now politicians do not force their tribes to accept boundaries against their will because they will lose their political support" (Karam 1980, 50).

The Messiriya were also experiencing increasing restrictions on their movements in areas to the south. The potential for conflict with various Dinka tribes is clear from Map 3. In particular, the presence of various Dinka tribes forced the Messiriya Humr to detour to either side (east or west) of these groups on their southward migrations (Niamir, Huntington, and Cole 1983, 10–11). The regulation of grazing through the Native Administration system and tribal conferences had been replaced, after 1971, by a much greater reliance on mobile police patrols (Saeed 1982, 244–49), and the Messiriya's corridors for movements were increasingly restricted. After a mobile police unit was attacked by Messiriya in Bentiu District, Upper Nile, in May 1976, the police (who were southern Sudanese) retaliated with attacks on Messiriya camps in the summer. When the Messiriya's seasonal migration took them back to the same area in January 1977, they were attacked again, this time by a joint command of police and army troops. Three Messiriya were killed (ibid., 277–78).

By 1985, a Khartoum University study of southern Kordofan observed that the Messiriya Humr no longer practiced their traditional grazing south of the Bahr el Arab river because of rising tension between the Humr and the Dinka (El Khalifa et al. 1985, 36). A second study noted that the Humr homeland had contracted significantly along its southern boundaries as a result of persistent conflict with the Ngok Dinka. This had threatened Humr access to perennial water sources, and the arrival of Um Bororo herders from West Africa had forced the Humr to change the timing of their migrations (El Sammani 1985, 56, 82, 86–87). In addition, the Humr saw the prospect of increased Ngok Dinka cultivation under the Abyei Rural Development Project as a threat to Humr northern grazing lands (Mohamed Salih 1993, 24–25). On top of all this, the mid-1980s saw a reduced access to alternative sources of dry season water, as the motor-driven pumps in "nomad settlement schemes" in the Muglad area were frequently shut down because of

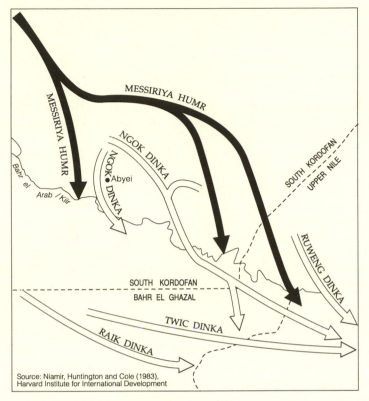

**Map 3**. Dry Season Migration Routes of Messiriya and Dinka. *Source:* Niamir, Huntington, and Cole 1983, 10.

growing fuel shortages, which were linked with Sudan's debt and a shortage of foreign exchange (ibid., 82–83).

The Messiriya were thus faced with a combination of pressures that severely restricted their freedom of movement and access to grazing and water at a time when numbers of cattle had risen rapidly and alternative economic opportunities were few. Because of their lack of influence in the organs of Nimeiri's state, in both the north and the south, they were virtually powerless to fight back against powerful agriculturalists or against the army and police units of the south. A crucial consequence, it would appear, was that the Messiriya turned in frustration (and were encouraged to turn) on their fellow herders and so-called "traditional tribal enemies" in the area, the Ngok Dinka. Meanwhile, the state was increasingly prone to blame conflicts and atrocities in which it had taken an active role on "traditional" tribal enmity (Saeed 1982, 228; Africa Watch 1990, 88).

In May–June 1977, the Messiriya—many of them angry and impotent in the face of attacks by army and police units in Bentiu District in 1976 and early 1977—raided the Ngok, killing 119 people, and stealing grain, goats, and more than 500 cattle (Saeed 1982, 278). As a result of state restrictions on their access to grazing land and their inability to stand up to the state, the Messiriya had come, in the course of the 1970s, to view the Ngok as their immediate antagonists (ibid., 387). Critically, this stance was to be encouraged by central government, in what appears to have been an attempt to divide and rule.[55]

In the 1980s, the economic pressures on the Baggara were exacerbated in important respects by drought and the beginnings of the second civil war. Cattle herds were severely reduced in the 1983–1985 drought, and this new impoverishment led to a further wave of migration by young men to urban areas (de Waal, n.d., 108; de Waal 1989a, 141–71; El Sammani 1985, 199–200; Africa Watch 1990, 81).[56] After the famine, it was very difficult to replenish herds in the market, as prices rocketed in late 1985 (de Waal 1990a, 16). The price of grain also rose significantly in 1986 in the Rizeigat and Messiriya areas, making it all the more difficult for herders to accumulate sufficient cash to permit restocking (ibid.). These problems were particularly severe for poorer herders. Meanwhile, although cattle mortality must have reduced pressure on grazing somewhat, this was offset by southward migration of non-Baggara tribes during the drought (El Sammani 1986, 70). The drought also exacerbated an environmental crisis that had long been developing in western Sudan. Drought also took an immediate toll on those Ansar (Mahdi family supporters) who had been settled on mechanized farming schemes at Habila, in southern Kordofan, and Um Hajaja, in southern Darfur, when they returned to Sudan after reconciliation with Nimeiri (de Waal 1990a, 17). These would-be agriculturalists were already suffering from shortages of fuel and spare parts, which reflected, in part, Sudan's gathering balance-of-payments crisis in the late 1970s (ibid., 17). The underlying economic crisis in western Sudan was exacerbated by falling groundnut prices, which had started declining in the mid-1970s, and by a drop in the numbers of migrant laborers from southern Sudan with the escalation of civil war after 1982 (de Waal 1989a, 107–9). Significantly, drought also drove many Baggara south into Dinka areas. Newly familiar with the territory, many were to return as raiders (interview with Ushari Mahmud, December 20, 1988, Khartoum).

The 1983–1985 famine had important beneficiaries, notably the owners of mechanized farms, because rising grain prices and falling labor costs helped stimulate an increase in the area occupied by these farms. In 1986, the area of Sudan occupied by mechanized farms rose sharply, from some 6 million feddans to about 9 million (de Waal 1990a, 18). This added to the squeeze on Baggara grazing.

The pressures on the Baggara were supplemented by a significant economic squeeze on traders (some of them from Baggara groups and some of them from outside the area), who were also to play a role in creating the famine of the late 1980s. In the famine of 1983–1985, traders withdrew to a large extent from selling grain and consumer goods and advancing sheil (loans against future crops), and concentrated on livestock trading, almost the only profitable activity for traders in Darfur and western Kordofan in 1983–1985. But this market collapsed in 1986. Between mid-1985 and mid-1986, cattle prices in Nyala, Darfur, rose from Sud. £100–150 to Sud. £800–1100, while numbers of cattle sold fell from more than ten thousand to three thousand a month, the lowest level for five years, as farmers and herders tried to rebuild their herds. At the same time, commercial flows of cattle from Chad and Bahr el Ghazal dried up, in both cases because of war, and local government enacted new restrictions on moving grain south from Darfur and Kordofan. Traders already operating in the south saw their rural markets disappear as a result of the war. In any case, Sudan's gathering economic crisis after 1978 made merchant capital investments less profitable and more risky (ibid., 19; Duffield 1990a, 16).

To trader discontent was added a threat to military involvement in trading, an involvement that had been encouraged during the military regime of Abboud and had continued thereafter (Woodward 1990, 125). Nimeiri's rule had seen the creation of special trading enterprises controlled by the military, giving officers privileged access to import licenses. Members of the military government both dispensed and obtained concessions and leases for mechanized farms during this period (de Waal 1990a, 19). These too came under threat in the 1980s, when special trading enterprises were disbanded or had their privileged status withdrawn.

### Baggara and Dinka: The Changing Balance of Power

Critically, while the economic pressures on the Baggara intensified, their links with the central government became closer in important respects during the late 1970s and early 1980s. At the same time, the fragile political representation of the Dinka collapsed. These political developments helped to make the famine of the late 1980s possible. They were intimately linked with a broader shift in the political orientation of governments in Khartoum. This shift involved embracing an increasingly aggressive Islamic agenda and turning progressively away from the south.

It is possible to isolate four main factors that propelled the changing balance of power at local and national level: a growing threat of rebellion by the Baggara; the rise of Islamic fundamentalism; the government's increasing interest in exploiting the economic resources of the south; and the advent of the second civil war. The resumption of formally democratic government in 1986 did not counteract this power shift; indeed, it may actually have exacerbated it. Democracy or no democracy, representation for the Dinka at the central government and local government levels was increasingly minimal. This removed the institutional checks on the crude exploitation of the Dinka, making human-made famine possible once again.

The growing threat of Baggara rebellion appears to have encouraged successive governments in Khartoum to bring Baggara interests inside the administration and, further, to attempt to channel Baggara discontent against even more marginalized groups—notably the Dinka. Whereas the Baggara's economic marginalization might in other circumstances have led them to contribute to a broadly based opposition to Sudan's riverain elites, their discontent was to a large extent deflected toward the south.

The renewed threat from the Baggara owed much to their acquisition of arms. The Baggara militias, or *murahaleen*, had obtained significant quantities of guns during the first civil war. After the war, the Baggara began to acquire increasing numbers of automatic weapons, both from Libya and from the arms markets created by wars in Uganda and Chad (de Waal 1990b, 5). Increasingly well armed, but still largely excluded from the organs of the Sudanese state, the Ansar, drawing critical support from the Baggara of Darfur and Kordofan, made repeated attempts to overthrow Nimeiri's secular government. In July 1976, the Ansar, backed by Libya, came close to overthrowing him. It was clear that despite—indeed, in part because of—Nimeiri's attempts to "modernize" Sudan, the religious affiliations of the Baggara, centered on the Ansar organization, remained a potent political threat. The narrowness of Nimeiri's escape appears to have prompted him to seek a reconciliation with Sadiq el Mahdi, leader of the Ansar, and Hassan el Turabi, leader of the modern fundamentalist Muslim Brothers. In July, the Ansar and the Muslim Brothers were brought into the Sudanese government, with both groups advocating an Islamic constitution, and both opposing southern autonomy (Allen 1986, 20). After this so-called National Reconciliation in 1977, many Ansar returned from exile in Ethiopia and Libya, having received extensive military training (de Waal 1990b, 6). As the Unionists, the Ansar and fundamentalist interests shared out government jobs among themselves, the two remaining southern Sudanese ministers (Francis Deng and Bona Malwal) were pushed aside. Bona Malwal resigned in 1978. Between 1978 and 1983, the cabinet did not include any southern Sudanese (Prunier 1986, 36; Malwal 1985, 32).

Meanwhile, Nimeiri was strengthening the representation of traditional Baggara interests at the regional level. The governor of Kordofan appointed in 1980, Bakri Adil, was from the Umma Party (Ibrahim 1988, 290). The new regional government of Kordofan, established through the reforms of 1981, was dominated by urban merchants and by the dynastic families that had formed the backbone of the Native Administration, including important representatives of the Baggara (Saeed 1982, 199).

These political developments at the central and regional levels, while improving the Baggara's access to political power, did not defuse the threat they posed. In 1978, the Ansar announced their dissatisfaction with the National Reconciliation. In Kordofan, Governor Adil proved to be no puppet for Nimeiri: in effect, he represented the opposition from within the government (Ibrahim 1988, 290). Nimeiri caused considerable resentment by refusing to allow the incorporation into the National Army of Ansar who had returned to Sudan after the National Reconciliation, in contrast to the incorporation of former Anyanya elements after the first civil war (de Waal 1990b, 7). The president's failure to relieve the 1983–1985 famine angered many Baggara and was one of the main reasons for his fall from power. Meanwhile, the control of the dynastic Baggara families over their followers appeared increasingly tenuous—another possible source of instability from the point of view of the government in Khartoum. Mention has been made of the co-optation of some Baggara leaders by Sudan's riverain elite amidst continuing economic neglect of the Baggara. The wide availability of arms among the Baggara offered an alternative source of authority—the gun—to the more traditional authority wielded by Baggara elders and political leaders. As late as May 1985, after the overthrow of Nimeiri, John Garang, leader of the SPLA, was appealing to the Baggara (and other groups in the north "who have always been neglected") to join the revolt against Sudan's privileged elite (Garang 1987, 61).

Clearly, the Baggara still required appeasing. And when Nimeiri was overthrown in May 1985, Baggara politicians were given prominence in the Transitional Military Council (TMC) that replaced him. Critically, Fadlallah Burma Nasser, a Messiri and a retired National Army major general, was appointed minister of state for defense (Ryle 1989a, 9). When the TMC relinquished power, as promised, after a year in office, the Baggara retained their influence in the formally democratic government led by the Ansar and Umma Party leader, Sadiq el Mahdi, with Burma Nasser keeping his ministerial position and another Messiri, Mahdi Babo Nimir, appointed as the army chief of staff (Mahmud and Baldo 1987, 17; Ryle 1989a, 9).

The prominence of these Messiri, as well as indicating the importance of accommodating Baggara interests and hinting at the important military role they were beginning to assume, also reflected the close links between the Baggara and the Umma Party. Baggara areas, as well as being strong supporters of the Mahdi family, constituted the Umma's main political constituency (ibid., 19). The 1986 election results had confirmed the continuing importance to the Umma Party of the Darfur and Kordofan regions after previous successes there in 1958 and 1964. The 1986 elections gave the Umma Party 100 of the 262 contested seats. Of these, 34 came from Darfur and 20 from Kordofan. The next most successful party (the DUP, with 63 seats) won only 2 seats in Darfur and 9 in Kordofan. The success of the Umma Party had been brought about in large part by the reformed Ansar organization, stretching down to the villages, something Sadiq el Mahdi had rebuilt on his return from exile after his National Reconciliation agreement with Nimeiri in 1977 (Chiriyankandath 1987, 98–99).

The second major factor tending to tilt the political balance to the detriment of southern Sudanese interests was the growing influence, on the national and international stages, of Islamic fundamentalists. Organized in the Muslim Brotherhood and the Islamic Charter Front (renamed National Islamic Front, or NIF), the Sudanese fundamentalists drew strength and funding from revivalist movements elsewhere in the Middle East, and were anxious to see Islam and Islamic law propagated throughout the country. They posed a potential threat to Sudanese governments that allowed themselves to appear too "secular," and were increasingly incorporated into government to deflect this threat (see, e.g., Woodward 1990, 210–11). Encouraged by the 1977 National Reconciliation, the new National Front coalition group (composed of Umma, DUP, and Islamic Charter Front representatives) appeared to regard the Addis Ababa agreement as a device with which Nimeiri had sought to perpetuate his leadership. This perception was probably accurate. In any case, they were determined to break up Nimeiri's alliance with the south. One way of doing this was by pushing Nimeiri to abrogate the Addis agreement (Alier 1990, 235–36). Nimeiri's ties with the south were further weakened in September 1983 when, under pressure from the fundamentalists, he introduced his "September laws," a version of Islamic *shari'a* law that was widely seen in the south as a threat to the region's cultural autonomy.

The Umma Party appeared to react to the rise of fundamentalist groups with a more moderate version of the NIF's revivalism. A growing danger was that the increasingly "Islamic" tone of government in Khartoum would exclude the largely non-Muslim south from the Sudanese political community. At the 1986 elections, the NIF won fifty-one seats, an achievement that reflected strong funding, good organization, and a significant following among graduates with their own reserved seats. Also significant, it appears, was a growing discontent with Western influence and conspicuous consumerism, particularly among poorer, uprooted urban groups, who were excluded from the benefits of modernization (Chiriyankandath 1987, 99–100). The NIF received some support at this stage from groups, such as the Fur of Darfur, who felt unrepresented by the two main parties. The NIF was to cement its new-found influence by entering the formally democratic government of Sadiq el Mahdi as a third coalition partner, along with the Umma Party and the Democratic Unionist Party. On an international level, Sudan's deepening need for international finance (with Arab countries and particularly Saudi Arabia an obvious source) may well have encouraged Nimeiri toward an overtly "Islamic" stance, and toward reconciliation with the Ansar and the Muslim Brotherhood (Warburg 1990, 626).

A third factor contributing to the Baggara-Dinka power shift was the government's renewed interest in exploiting the economic resources of the south: even as the Baggara and the NIF were gaining in political muscle, a number of economic developments were encouraging a new, hard-line attitude toward the south in Khartoum. In general, the shrinking resource base and gathering economic crisis in the north appear to have encouraged northern interests to seek to tap the abundant resources of the south—through increasingly violent means (see also Duffield 1990a, 22–23).

The growing resort to force to protect exploitative livestock trading centered on Abyei has been mentioned. But the most important resource to which Khartoum sought access was oil. The discovery of large oil deposits in the south in 1978 provided a major incentive to minimize the south's say in government and in the control of the region's resources. Oil offered some hope of reducing Sudan's mounting balance-of-payments crisis and reducing the country's increasingly heavy burden of international debt. Significantly, however, under the terms of the Addis Ababa agreement all taxes and government profits arising from the exploitation of oil resources would accrue to the regional government in Juba (Alier 1990, 223). In these circumstances, Nimeiri appeared increasingly determined to make fundamental political changes and to ensure that the central government would benefit from the oil. The government—ominously, from a southern point of view— planned a refinery in Kosti rather than in the south (Holt and Daly 1988, 204). A government bill presented in 1980 threatened to redraw the map of Sudan so that mineral-rich and fertile parts in northerly areas of the south (including the major oil fields and significant uranium deposits) would be included in the north (Malwal 1985, 32; Alier 1990, 182, 219). There was widespread talk in government circles of creating a so-called Unity Region, which would cover the area of major oil finds (Alier 1990, 216, 223). When the SPLA put a stop to attempts to extract the oil, the government attempted to secure access by force (Africa Watch 1990, 78–80, 88; Hutchinson 1988, viii). Getting oil back into production remained an important priority under Sadiq el Mahdi, who pressured the U.S. company Chevron to resume active operations (*Sudan Times*, November 4, 20, 1988). Oil was also discovered in an area fifty miles south and southwest of Babanousa (Saeed 1982, 224), another region that was vulnerable to possible SPLA disruption, particularly in view of the substantial (Ngok) Dinka presence in southwestern Kordofan.

Another incentive for reducing the south's say in the allocation of resources was the revived plan to increase the supply of Nile waters to northern Sudan and Egypt through the Jonglei Canal, widely seen in the south as conferring few benefits on the region and perhaps actively harmful (Allen 1986, 20; Holt and Daly 1988, 205).[57] As with the extraction of oil, the Jonglei Canal project was also halted by SPLA attacks.

Closely linked with the growing interest in securing southern resources, and with the increasing influence of Islamic interests in the central government, was Nimeiri's reversal of the Addis Ababa agreement, in particular the removal of the powers of autonomous rule he himself had established for the south. In June 1983, Nimeiri pushed through the redivision of the south in an attempt to exploit tensions between a number of disgruntled Equatorian groups and other southerners, notably the Dinka. In Equatoria, the Dinka were often seen as having taken an unfair proportion of regional government employment after Equatorians had borne the brunt of the first civil war (Allen 1986, 20–27; Prunier 1986, 55; Alier 1990, 189–90). Competition for jobs had been heightened by the return of many Equatorians from Uganda in 1979–1980 after the overthrow of Idi Amin. Migration of livestock from the Bor and Yirol areas into Equatoria during the flooding of the 1960s had also created some tensions between Dinka herders and Equatorian farmers (Alier 1990, 189). Corruption in the regional government was perceived to be a major problem (Holt and Daly 1988, 203). Some politicians in Equatoria saw an advantage in cooperating with Nimeiri's scheme, helping to make the division of the south possible.

The three regions of the south to which power was ostensibly devolved in 1983 were actually granted only very limited powers, and very limited sources of revenue. Critically, oil revenues were now to go to the central government. The heads of the new regions, now called governors, were appointed by the head of state, with the regional assemblies having no power to remove them. Whereas the Addis Ababa agreement had bestowed considerable responsibilities and powers on the southern president of the High Executive Council, these were transferred not to the new governors but to military commanders in the south. The military commanders were answerable directly to the minister of defense. Meanwhile, the governors were encouraged to defy the severely weakened regional government. In the context of stiffening southern resistance to northern attempts to extract economic resources from the south, Nimeiri's initiative proved deeply unpopular. He was seen by many to be undermining the institutions set up to represent southern interests (Alier 1990, 223–39).

The war itself constituted the fourth major reason for the central government's turning toward the Baggara and away from the Dinka, as Khartoum concerned itself with suppressing southern discontent rather than accommodating it. In 1982, government attempts to transfer potentially troublesome soldiers to the north were focused on Dinka areas, including Bor and Aweil, and on battalions that had been "absorbed" into the government army at the end of the first civil war. But Battalion 105 at Bor refused to move north and was on the verge of mutiny. For those in Khartoum who wanted to break the Addis Ababa agreement and to impose their authority on the "absorbed" forces, here was an important opportunity. On May 16, 1983, government forces launched an assault on the Bor battalion, which fled after a day of fighting. So far from quelling dissent, this incident sparked off widespread rebellion and was to usher in the second civil war (ibid., 240–47).

As the war intensified, the Dinka were increasingly identified by the government with the rebels, and stripped of their residual political representation within the Sudanese administration. Yet Sudan's heavily indebted government was ill equipped for suppressing rebellion. The Sudanese Armed Forces numbered only some sixty thousand men—not nearly enough to contain the insurgency. Nimeiri proposed conscription in September 1984, but the idea was quickly dropped because of its unpopularity in the north (de Waal 1990b, 2). Meanwhile, the government could ill afford to fund a protracted war (see, e.g., Brown 1988, 73–83). In these circumstances, the arming and encouragement of Baggara militias (as well as the largely Nuer Anyanya 2 militias in Upper Nile) offered the central government a cheap means of quelling southern opposition (Africa Watch 1990; Amnesty International 1989).

As civil war deepened and the conflict was increasingly projected as an Arab/African dispute, a range of groups that had identified themselves with a need for peace and a political solution found themselves increasingly marginalized and sometimes even labeled as traitors. In these circumstances, the widely renowned tolerance that had tended to characterize Sudanese political culture was severely eroded, and the remaining opponents of war became increasingly isolated.

Prominent among the groups favouring a political solution was the National Alliance for National Salvation (NANS), which had helped coordinate the opposition to Nimeiri. The NANS, which represented much of the Sudanese intelligentsia and a range of professional opinion, favored a kind of secular nationalism. The organization played a key role in securing the Koka Dam Declaration of March 1986, which was signed by the NANS, the SPLM and the Umma Party and called for a conference on the constitution and an end to the "September laws" (Woodward 1990, 204–5; Alier 1990, 269, 274). Other organizations that were party to the declaration included the Southern Sudan Political Association (SSPA), the Sudan African Congress (SAC), the Sudan Communist Party, the National Party, the National Unionist Party, and the Arab Baath Party. This declaration represented a broad swathe of opinion from both the north and the south, and constituted a significant source of hope for peace in Sudan.

However, the NIF was (unsurprisingly) not party to the Koka Dam Declaration, and neither was the DUP. Both the NIF and the DUP were often charged by the NANS, the Communist Party, and to a large extent the

Umma Party with having been too close to Nimeiri's regime. And the DUP appeared wary of the Umma–NANS–Communist Party alliance that had been at the forefront of both the revolt against Nimeiri and the Koka Dam peace initiative (Alier 1990, 269).

At the Koka Dam negotiations, the Umma Party leader, Sadiq el Mahdi, had been constrained in his ability to make concessions to the SPLM (notably on *shari'a*)by pressure from wavering Unionists, as well as from the NIF (Woodward 1990, 210). After the 1986 elections had brought about a coalition government composed of the Umma and DUP parties, the hopes attached to the Koka Dam negotiations were further eroded. Significantly, the Communist Party (which won only three seats) and the NANS (which lacked representation in the Assembly) were now virtually irrelevant to the struggle for power in Khartoum. The Umma Party began to take more notice of DUP views on the Koka Dam Declaration than of those of the NANS. Those parties favoring peace had lost their political usefulness to the Umma Party, and peace was accorded a diminishing priority (Alier 1990, 269–70).

Paradoxically, the end of military rule and the arrival of "democracy" appear to have accentuated the decline of southern representation, even as they reduced the political influence of northern groups lobbying for a political settlement. As in 1965, civil war impeded elections and damaged southern representation. No members of the Sudanese parliament, the Constituent Assembly, were returned in thirty-nine of the sixty-eight southern geographical constituencies in 1986, because of lack of polling in thirty-seven constituencies and assassination of candidates in the other two. Even in constituencies where elections were held, polling was low: the majority of southern members were elected with less than a thousand votes. The elections left the south with only thirty-six members of the Constituent Assembly out of a total of 262. Moreover, southern representation was fragmented, with important geographical imbalances. While Equatoria had twenty members (with two seats remaining vacant), Upper Nile had only seven (one of them Umma, with fifteen seats vacant) and Bahr el Ghazal had only nine (one Umma and one NIF, with fully twenty-two seats vacant). This gave the people of Upper Nile and Bahr el Ghazal only a very weak voice within the Constituent Assembly. And while the Dinka-led Southern Sudan Political Association (SSPA) gained a majority of the contested seats in Bahr el Ghazal, parties hostile to the SPLA and backing the 1983 division of the south won in Equatoria.[58] Moreover, as in 1968, tribal rivalries and a low level of electoral participation helped northern parties to win some seats. Northern soldiers made up a significant part of the electorate in the south (Chiriyankandath 1987, 98–99).

In addition to the more moderate elements in civilian political life, there were also elements in the Sudanese army that favored a peaceful, political settlement. For example, in 1985 and 1986, the minister of defense, Major

General Osman Abdullah, made missions—through the governments of Libya, South Yemen, and Ethiopia—to negotiate with the SPLA on behalf of the TMC (Alier 1990, 259). The support for a political settlement within some parts of the army was not as strange as it seemed: the most prolonged period of peace in postindependence Sudan had, after all, been ushered in by the military government of General Nimeiri, and the possibility remained that the south could once again be used to counter the power in the north of the traditional religious parties (as well as the increasingly powerful militias with which the Umma Party in particular was associated).[59] The army also knew only too well the destructiveness of war in the south, and the difficulties, in a context of limited government finances, of fighting a guerrilla movement on its own territory. (Indeed, in 1989 these difficulties were again to prompt some senior officers to call for peace—or for the resources to win the war).

However, there were also powerful elements in the army that favored a military solution to the problem of the SPLA; officers opposing a political settlement appear to have gained the upper hand over the group led by Osman Abdullah as early as July 1985 (Alier 1990, 260). The more the SPLA appeared to pose a threat to northern Sudan and the more it engaged in provocative actions, such as the downing of a Malakal civilian airliner in August 1986, the more the relatively moderate army officers were marginalized. Such actions by the SPLA, particularly when filtered through elements of the fundamentalist press, helped also to cement a degree of public support for a hard line in the war. At the same time, the more the bandwagon of NIF and *shari'a* gathered pace, the more the SPLA became alienated from the government and determined to seek its own military solution to the impasse (Woodward 1990, 220). Hardening attitudes on both sides helped narrow and constrain the middle ground in Sudanese politics. (Moderate elements in the north were not to reemerge until late in 1988, when, amid the growing unpopularity of the war, the NANS in particular was to play a key part in bringing together the DUP and the SPLM, a story taken up in Chapter 4.)

The concern of the SPLA and the Sudan government with negotiating from a position of (military) strength in itself helped to undermine the prospects for peace. Six of the southern Sudan parties were organized into the Union of Sudan African Parties, but even some of these drifted from the Koka Dam Declaration as the chasm between northern parties and the SPLA deepened (Woodward 1990, 213).

In December 1987, the SPLA temporarily captured Kurmuk on the Ethiopian border, provoking widespread fears that the war was coming "into the north." Woodward has observed: "There was thus a wave of jingoistic hysteria, which brought public condemnation as traitors on those who had been working for an accommodation with the SPLA, and even the threat of violence against the communities of southern origin living in the north."[60] Among those vilified as traitors were some representatives of the NANS.

On the international front, the Sudan government appealed to a number of Arab countries for military support, with SPLA attacks being widely presented as an Ethiopian-backed attack on the Arab world. Many Arab nations responded, including Saudi Arabia, Iraq, Jordan, Iran, and—perhaps most important in terms of immediate military help—Libya (Woodward 1990, 212; Lesch 1991, 62).

In the context of such hardening attitudes at the national and the international level, the vulnerability of the Dinka was heightened. They were increasingly labeled as "Garang's people" and as enemies of the government. Once again, they came to be excluded from the Sudanese state and the legal protection it was supposed to confer.

At the local level, the Ngok Dinka in southern Kordofan had for some time been suffering a loss of representation that matched the Dinka's progressive disenfranchisement in national politics. Indeed, shifts in the balance of power at higher levels of the administration dating from the mid-1970s had themselves begun to undermine the access to political power at lower levels that had been enjoyed by the Ngok within northern Sudan. This not only helped to erode the protection against human-made famine that the Ngok had previously enjoyed; it also removed the protection that the Ngok's presence and influence had previously provided for other Dinka tribes (notably those in northern Bahr el Ghazal).

As the central government increasingly turned away from seeking the support of the south and increasingly lined up with Baggara interests, and as the educated Dinka were marginalized in Khartoum (Deng 1986, 265), provincial government's hostility towards traditional Ngok leaders could no longer be checked at the center. The growing influence of Baggara interests at the Kordofan regional government level meant it was also increasingly unlikely to be checked at the regional level.

For its part, the provincial administration of South Kordofan regarded Abyei's special administrative status as a circumvention of provincial autonomy and a step toward annexation to the south (ibid., 265). Abyei lost its special administrative status in 1977, as its assistant commissioner, Justin Deng, was dismissed and never replaced (Saeed 1982, 282). Dinka officials in Abyei were progressively replaced by Sudanese Arab officials (Deng 1986, 265). The family of Deng Majok, which came from the Abyor section of the Ngok, began to press for separation from the north—covertly from around 1976 and overtly from 1980 (Saeed 1982, 268–69). Many Ngok claimed a right under the Addis Ababa agreement to a plebiscite to determine their regional affiliation (Mawson 1984, 522). Meanwhile, the South Kordofan authorities sought to work with those elements of the Ngok who advocated remaining in the north, something that further encouraged separatism among the influential Abyor. Abyei's development project collapsed amid implausible allegations that the Dinka were receiving arms from the project's sponsor, the Harvard Institute for International Development (Deng 1986, 265).

The political muscle of the Ngok at local level was limited not just by lack of numbers but also by lack of education. One Ngok elder said in 1974 that in the wake of serious conflicts with traditional chiefs, there were no educated youths left in Abyei: "It is we, the ignorant, who are left here. It is we who have remained exposed" (Deng 1980, 155, 292). Once Ngok representation at the center had collapsed, the shortage of educated Ngok in Ngokland made it all the more difficult to resist the hostile provincial and central administrations.

The diminishing local and national influence of the Ngok helped propel them toward outright opposition to the government and eventual civil war. War, in turn, exacerbated this loss of influence. When the second civil war broke out in 1983, the South Kordofan and national authorities moved quickly to get full control of Abyei.[61] Local control fell into Messiriya hands. The remaining educated men in Abyei were arrested and charged with treasonable offenses (Deng 1986, 266). Although they were subsequently released, the threat of repression remained. In 1986 a member of the Muslim Brotherhood was elected to the Constituent Assembly by the Abyei North constituency, centered on Muglad town, in polling heavily influenced by the large numbers of troops stationed in the area (Chiriyankandath 1987, 100). Also influential, it was widely alleged, were distributions of large sums of money to selected households.[62] Meanwhile, participation in local government (for example, town councils) was now confined to members of the ruling coalition parties (first, the Umma and DUP; later also the NIF).

As during the first civil war, the Ngok were not immediately drawn into the conflict. Along with other northern Dinka, the Malwal and Twic, they had resisted cattle raiding by the Raik Dinka, who had close links with the SPLA and had been given substantial arms at an early stage by the rebels. Baggara raiding played a key role in shifting northern Dinka loyalties in favor of the rebels (interview with Melvyn Almond, Oxfam-UK, Khartoum, November 10, 1988; Wilson 1989, 28).

The Ngok began to leave their home areas in large numbers following outright attacks by the Messiriya Humr beginning in 1985. There was now no buffer between the Messiriya and Dinka groups further south.

By the mid-1980s, there was no significant southern representation in northern Sudan, either at the central government level in Khartoum or at the local level in southern Kordofan. According to the Abyei Dinka Association, the Kordofan regional government dismissed Ngok Dinka protests against Messiriya raiding in March 1987, suggesting they should be more worried about the rebel leader John Garang (Abyei Dinka Association 1987,

2). For the south as a whole, while regional government was in theory restored by the Transitional Military Council government in 1985, the new High Executive Council was not allowed to function, or to move to the south. Khartoum continued to work directly with the three southern provincial governors (Alier 1990, 239). In the course of the second civil war, much of the civilian administration in the south retreated to Khartoum, as effective government collapsed (interview with Melvyn Almond, Oxfam-UK, November 10, 1988, Khartoum; *Heritage*, October 3, 1988). Meanwhile, the balance of power within the army had been shifting significantly, as southern Sudanese troops were transferred to the north (the Aweil battalion was transferred to Darfur in December 1982) and northern troops were transferred to the south, notably to the oil-rich Bentiu area (Alier 1990, 223–46). The safeguards against the abuse of military power agreed upon at Addis Ababa were thus being rapidly removed. Meanwhile, elements of the Baggara were increasingly willing and able—in conjunction with a newly aggressive national army—to exploit southern Sudanese, notably Dinka, through processes that created and constituted famine.

In a dynamic for which precedents had been set during the nineteenth century, exploitative peacetime arrangements had come under increasing physical attack by the early 1980s, prompting an increasing resort to force on the part of those seeking to defend and extend this exploitation. Meanwhile, as in the earlier nineteenth-century struggles, the instruments of force (in the form of soldiers and militiamen) themselves acquired an interest in economic exploitation. This was partly to secure their own subsistence in a context where the state lacked the resources to create a disciplined, well-rewarded military machine. The state's toleration and encouragement of such exploitation meant a partial loss of control by the central government. In a sense, the state was sponsoring the erosion of its own authority.

This chapter has pointed to the Dinka's long historical experience of exploitation and imposed famine at the hands of various northern Sudanese and imperial interests. At the same time, it has suggested that apparently "traditional" tribal hostilities were not inevitable. For a period, under later British colonial rule and in large part in response to the perceived threat of southern rebellion, a system was constructed that successfully prevented the worst excesses of exploitation and gave tribal leaders an interest in promoting peace among their peoples. However, the neglect of development and education in the south together with the colonial manipulation and encouragement of tribal identities and the failure to secure political safeguards for the south at independence left the south vulnerable to northern domination from the late 1950s on. The "traditional leadership" created among both the Baggara and the Dinka proved unable to control the younger, more discontented elements of their own followings in a context where the central government was neglecting both groups and neither set of leaders was able to secure significant state resources for their own people. While protection for the Dinka from Khartoum was temporarily revived with the Addis Ababa agreement (itself a response to southern rebellion), by the late 1970s ethnic hostilities were being actively encouraged by the central government in a bid to maintain power in a context of dwindling economic resources in the north and increasingly disaffected Baggara and Islamic elements. The fragile system of political protection for Dinka and other southern Sudanese groups was rapidly dissolving.

# Victims and Beneficiaries: A Case Study of Famine as a Combination of Exploitative Processes

*We were rich people. We have come down so far.*
(*Interview with Dinka famine migrant and
former herdsman, Meiram, southern
Kordofan, 1988*)

*Allah sent me the hunger.*
(*Leading northern Sudanese trader,
Muglad, southern Kordofan, 1989*)

ALTHOUGH the intensity of suffering varied from one area to another, it is clear that the people of southern Sudan suffered an extremely severe famine in the 1980s, and that the Dinka living in northern Bahr el Ghazal were particularly badly affected. The beginning of the famine cannot be neatly dated: the processes precipitating famine gathered force over an extended period from 1983 to 1988. At the peak of the suffering, in 1988, death rates among southern Sudanese famine victims were among the highest ever recorded anywhere in the world. In the camp at Meiram, in southern Kordofan, in just one week at the end of July, no less than 475 people died; on average, in a nine-week period from the end of June to mid-August, some 7.1 percent of the camp population were dying *every week*.[1] By comparison, in Korem, at the height of the Ethiopian famine, an average of about 1.6 percent of the total displaced were dying every week.[2] A little further south of Meiram, at Abyei, a total of some ten thousand civilians were reported by the Sudanese army commander Abbas Sadiq to have died between the beginning of the year and mid-October (*New York Times*, October 16, 1988).[3] Still further south, in the key government garrison town of Aweil, Bahr el Ghazal, there were 7,146 registered deaths between July and September 1988. Depending on which estimate of numbers of displaced is adopted, this represents between 5.6 and 7.7 percent of the total population of the town.[4]

These deaths were caused partly by increased vulnerability to disease due to malnutrition and partly by increased exposure to disease due to such factors as population concentration in government-held towns and inadequate sanitation.[5] Malnutrition rates were extremely severe at the peak of the famine, reaching levels that have been proven elsewhere to cause widespread disease and death (see Wilson 1991, 289–91). Local observers attached considerable importance to the lack of access to food, as well as lack of access to medicines and adequate sanitation, in precipitating morbidity and mortality.[6]

The famine did not simply bring about the deaths of individuals; it also involved the destruction—at least for a time—of a way of life. An estimated 30 percent of the south's population had been uprooted to northern Sudan or Ethiopia by mid-1989;[7] The economy of the Dinka was massively disrupted, with the Dinka suffering the loss of hundreds of thousands of their revered cattle. Slavery and sexual abuse were rife.

If this famine was a disaster for the Dinka and other southern Sudanese groups, it nevertheless conferred (and promised) substantial benefits for a variety of groups in northern Sudan, who promoted the processes of famine in a number of critical ways. The famine thus had functions as well as causes. While many in the north expressed opposition to the way in which the civil war was being fought and to the human rights abuses and exploitation accompanying it, these voices were marginalized within a Sudanese polity that found less and less room for toleration and moderation.

Probably the most important of these functions of famine were military and economic. The famine offered the prospect of relieving many of the pressures analyzed in Chapter 2. It offered a cheap counterinsurgency tactic. And it promised some remedy to the poverty of many among the politically resurgent Baggara. The famine involved a major transfer of resources from the south to the north, while offering the prospect of future economic transfers in the form of oil and other natural resources. *Pace* Sen, it was largely the wealth of victim groups that made them worth exploiting through processes leading to famine. Although people were reduced to poverty by these processes, their initial vulnerability arose as much through lack of political power as from lack of purchasing power or assets.

Of course, not every group that benefited from famine deliberately set out to create it. The question of intention is by no means easy to assess. Nevertheless, it is clear that a number of powerful groups actively promoted processes that would bring foreseeable benefits to themselves while bringing foreseeable suffering and even death to famine's victims. These processes were a decline in assets and production (mostly through raiding); changes in market prices; the restriction of survival strategies that bypassed market mechanisms; and finally, the inadequacy of relief (the subject of Chapter 4).

The concept of market forces is less helpful in understanding the famine than what I call forced markets, that is, markets that were actively shaped by various kinds of force. Once famine had developed (whether intentionally created or not), the "failure" to relieve it was influenced by the benefits it was yielding.

## DECLINE IN ASSETS AND PRODUCTION

The first process of famine, a sharp decline in assets and production, arose primarily from militia raiding. Drought and other natural adversities played a secondary role. This conclusion is drawn from four main types of evidence.

First, the loss of assets (notably cattle) as a result of raiding was extremely severe. Comparison of an International Committee of the Red Cross (ICRC) vaccination report of 1989 with estimates of cattle populations in 1977 suggests that the total cattle population in the flood region of Bahr el Ghazal (that is, the northeast, where the great bulk of cattle were) had fallen from close to 1 million to perhaps half this number (UN/SRRA 1990, 52).[8] Some put the losses even higher. By the summer of 1988, the executive officer of the Muglad District Council, in southern Kordofan, was estimating that at least 1 million stolen Dinka cattle had passed through Muglad District during the previous eighteen to twenty-four months.[9]

The importance of raiding is suggested, secondly, by the fact that famine and outmigration were strongly correlated with militia raids, both geographically and chronologically. By helping to concentrate people in government-held towns (and to keep them there), raiding added greatly to people's exposure to disease. Third, famine migrants and aid agencies emphasized the significance of raiding.

Fourth, although drought was sometimes stressed by the central government and by international donors, evidence suggests that the patchy incidence of drought would not on its own have created significant famine. Grain production in the south had often fluctuated widely, but this had rarely led to the kind of outmigration seen in 1986–1988 (see, e.g., Ministry of Agriculture 1974, 29, 35). Although drought played some role in the evolving famine, it was raiding that deprived people of the resources (grain stores and, especially, cattle) with which they had traditionally resisted natural adversity.[10] A Malwal Dinka chief, Deng Dang Wol, later explained this relationship: "Before, in a drought like this [he was referring to drought in 1989], we depended on our cattle for milk and meat. But today cattle and goats have been taken by murhaleen. Then came the drought. That is the source of hunger."[11]

Many cattle that were not raided were sent away as a precaution. The widespread loss of cattle made it more difficult to secure assistance through social ties: there were few cattle to lend; and those lucky enough to retain cattle were often reluctant to lend to those who had little prospect of returning the favor (interview with Melvyn Almond, Oxfam-UK, Khartoum, November 10, 1988). Elderly people left behind in Bahr el Ghazal were especially vulnerable to hunger as a result of the loss of cattle (UN/SRRA 1990, 51).

### From 1983 through Early 1986

The earliest manifestations of famine in rural areas of the south occurred in Upper Nile Province (de Waal 1990a, 2). Messiriya militias were active as early as 1983. The Messiriya and Anyanya 2, a mostly Nuer paramilitary force that split from the SPLA in October 1984, coordinated raids with the army (ibid., 8; Africa Watch 1990, 78, 88). In late 1984, the East Jikany Nuer and the Leek Nuer in the Bentiu area were overrun by an army of Messiriya. These Messiriya had been given machine guns and ammunition by the central government, and were apparently entrusted with depopulating the areas near Bentiu north of the Bahr el Ghazal river (de Waal 1990a, 3; Hutchinson 1988, viii). Raiding in Upper Nile caused widespread loss of cattle and other property. The stretch of country between Bentiu and Nasir was turned into a wasteland (de Waal 1990a, 3–9).

By 1986, many displaced people had gathered in the garrison town of Malakal. Others retreated to the bush, to more southerly areas, to northern Sudan, or to Ethiopia (ibid., 3–11; Sudan Council of Churches 1986). Meanwhile, food prices were rising rapidly, notably in Malakal (de Waal 1990a, 3). Famine had clearly been directly created by raiding.

In Equatoria, where the scale of raiding was significantly less than in Upper Nile or Bahr el Ghazal, famine was generally least severe. In late 1985, large-scale raiding spread to Bahr el Ghazal, bringing famine in its wake (ibid., 3–11).

Within Bahr el Ghazal, economic and social disruption (and eventually, starvation) was closely correlated with raiding. Late 1985 saw a marked increase in Humr Messiriya raiding on the Ngok Dinka in Abyei District, precipitating significant movements of Ngok to Abyei town as well as to other areas in northern Sudan, and to Gogrial District, in the south (Amnesty 1989, sec. 2.1). At the same time, there was a major escalation in Messiriya militia raiding on Malwal and Abiem Dinka in the densely populated Aweil District. There were also raids on the Twic Dinka, with 160,000 people reportedly rendered homeless; instances of death from starvation were reported even at this stage.[12] All these raids again caused massive disruption of people's way of life, including immediate displacement. In the spring of 1986, the Dinka military governor of Bahr el Ghazal Province, Brigadier Albino Akol said that since 1984, raiding in the eastern part of the province (the part in which Dinka groups predominated) had resulted in the theft of

340,000 head of cattle and the burning of countless granaries (*New York Times*, May 4, 1986). Some six hundred thousand people had been displaced by the raids, nearly half the local population (ibid.). The scale of cattle theft at this time is corroborated by police reports.[13] Twic elders claimed that raids in December 1985 and January 1986 had destroyed 48,000 metric tons of grain.[14] All this was *before* the worst of the raiding.

In early 1986, the Sudan Council of Churches estimated that 187,000 people in the Aweil and Gogrial Districts were affected by hunger. War and armed raiding from the north were cited as the principal causes (Sudan Council of Churches 1986). By the end of 1986, the UN was estimating that 690,000 people were at risk of famine in Bahr el Ghazal (USAID 1987a, 7–8, citing UNOEOS Technical Coordination Committee). This was 59 percent of those held to be at risk in all of southern Sudan, a proportion that appears to have reflected the particular severity of raiding in the province in the previous year and a half.

Resistance to the raiding was difficult or impossible. The northern Sudanese raiders had automatic weapons and rocket-propelled grenades. The villages they attacked were often inhabited largely by women and children, the men having already left the area. Where men were still resident, they were generally armed only with spears and a few old-fashioned rifles, at least before the SPLA advance in Bahr el Ghazal in the course of 1987 (Africa Watch 1990, 97).

In the aftermath of these northern militia raids, some people were displaced to rural areas lying between their villages and the government garrison town of Aweil (Amnesty 1989, sec. 2.1; UNDP 1988, annex 2, 1). Many gathered at railway stations within Bahr el Ghazal, north of Aweil (Oxfam-UK 1986f, 1). Others headed for northern Sudan, to the northern railway towns of Ed Daien, Nyala, Muglad, and Babanousa (Map 4) and to the cities of Khartoum and Omdurman (Amnesty 1989, sec. 2.1). Still others went to Aweil itself, seeking protection from the authorities and shelter from kin (Duffield 1990a, 27). Many of their makeshift homes were destroyed in a major fire on May 8, widely believed to have been started by the army (Oxfam-UK 1986f, 2). By May 1986, malnutrition among the displaced was already a major problem (ibid., 1).

Future grain production, as well as past production, was damaged in the raids. The prospect of further raids discouraged planting (interview with Mahmud Ushari, Khartoum, December 20, 1988). In any case, the burning of granaries in many areas meant that only families with buried seed corn could plant (Ryle 1989a, 20). Moreover, the necessary labor was often not available, as many women and children were taken captive and men very often fled to other areas (see, e.g., Aweil Rice Development Project 1987). Others, especially men, were simply killed. A 1990 UN/SRRA mission found that in northern areas of Bahr el Ghazal that had suffered militia raiding, the

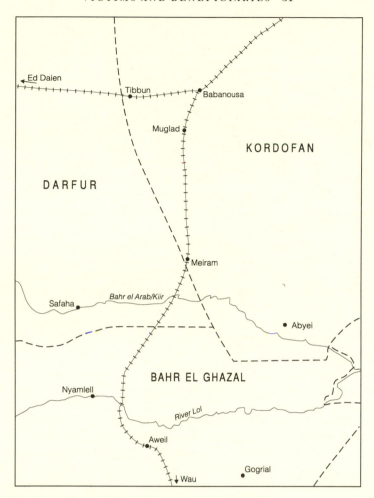

**Map 4**. Railway and Towns within the Famine Area

size of agricultural plots tended to be smaller than elsewhere; the report suggested that this may have reflected the preponderance of elderly people in these areas and the very small proportion of young men (UN/SRRA 1990, 59).

Drought was a minor factor in causing the outmigration of 1985–1986. The south is less vulnerable to drought than northern Sudan: Map 5 shows that the south enjoys relatively low yearly variation in what USAID calls the Normalized Vegetation Index, a satellite-derived measure of the intensity of plant growth. While there is evidence of drought in parts of southern Sudan in 1982–1984,[15] there was relatively little outmigration at this time, compared to 1986–1988. And while the 1985 harvest in the south was reported

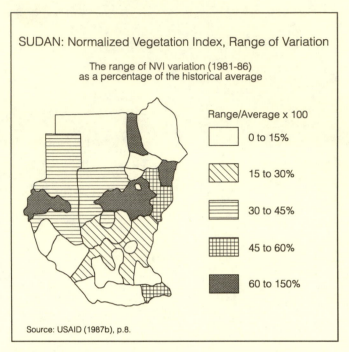

SUDAN: Normalized Vegetation Index, Range of Variation

The range of NVI variation (1981-86)
as a percentage of the historical average

Range/Average x 100

0 to 15%

15 to 30%

30 to 45%

45 to 60%

60 to 150%

Source: USAID (1987b), p.8.

**Map 5**. Normalized Vegetation Index for Sudan: Range of Variation as Percentage of Historical Average, 1981–1986. *Source:* USAID 1987b, 8.

as somewhat below normal, agency assessments in early 1986 nevertheless stressed war and armed raiding as the principal causes of famine in Bahr el Ghazal and Upper Nile. Pockets of drought were most significant in Equatoria, where famine was generally least severe (Sudan Council of Churches 1986).

### From Late 1986 through Early 1987

The dry season of October 1986 to April 1987 brought more raiding on northern Bahr el Ghazal, as the end of the 1986 rains once again made movement easy. As in 1985–1986, the militiamen had a largely free hand in northern Bahr el Ghazal, for the SPLA was preoccupied with fighting in Upper Nile[16] and, to a lesser extent, southern and central Bahr el Ghazal. The Malwal Dinka (Map 6) were devastated by raiding in January and February 1987 (Amnesty 1989, sec. 2.1). After the wave of renewed raiding during the dry season of 1986–1987, northern Aweil District, in which the Malwal resided, was practically denuded of cattle (Ryle 1989a, 12–13). Then the

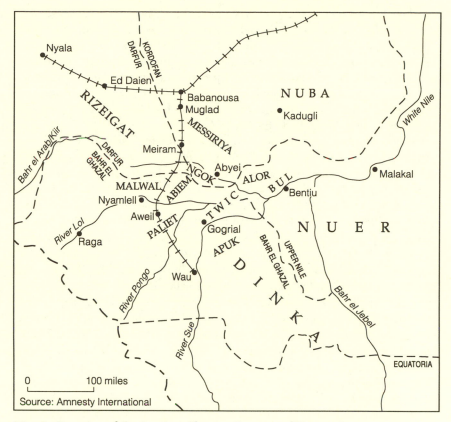

**Map 6**. Overview of Famine Area Showing Location of Various Groups. *Source:* Amnesty 1989.

Twic, Paliet, and Apuk Dinka, all living in the areas to the east of Aweil town, were badly hit by militia attacks. By May 1987, raiders had destroyed much of the area north of the River Pongo (Amnesty 1989, sec. 2.1).

Again, some of those attacked headed immediately for rural areas to the south of their home villages (UN/SSRA 1990, field notes, interviews with Twic chiefs, May 10). This contributed to a new and marked concentration of cattle in Apuk District, in eastern Gogrial, where people sought shelter for their herds (Ryle 1989a, 12–13). The Twic and Malwal both had marriage ties with the Apuk Dinka (UN/SRRA 1990, field notes, May 9). The new concentrations of cattle led to a damaging spread of cattle diseases between areas (UN/SRRA 1990, 52),[17] exacerbated by the collapse of veterinary services during the civil war (Almond, n.d., 39).

Aweil town was once again a magnet for those attacked, with deaths from hunger reported in the town by summer 1987.[18] Others headed for Wau, another government garrison town, where already severe needs were made worse by the fact that Ferteet peoples had been forced to flee SPLA attacks around the town (EC 1987c; Symonds 1987, 5; Ryle 1989a, 6). Ferteet civilians were deliberately killed by SPLA troops (Amnesty 1989, 110). Hardship in and around Wau was exacerbated by the use of Ferteet militias against the Dinka, with Dinka death squads formed to resist the Ferteet militias. In August 1987, there was widespread looting and burning of Dinka houses in the town (Africa Watch 1990, 68–69, 153).

Northern Sudan was also an important destination for the displaced— either directly, or indirectly via Wau or Aweil. Many took their remaining cattle with them. Some walked north along the railway line, with many settling in or near the southern Kordofan town of Meiram. The Malwal Dinka, subjected to militia attacks in the dry season of 1985–1986 and then devastated in 1986–1987, followed their traditional seasonal migration routes from eastern Aweil to southern Kordofan. This time the migration was one-way (Ryle 1989a, 12). The Twic, too, followed traditional seasonal routes, apparently responding to attacks that peaked in the spring of 1987. Many of the Twic walked from their home areas in northern Gogrial to Abyei, where they had traditionally sought markets and refuge from flooding. Again, the Twic migration was one-way. Malnutrition was a significant problem even at this stage (Oxfam-UK 1986e, 1). Meanwhile, in the course of 1987, the mounting food crisis in Aweil led many people to board trains there and head north. Others joined these trains at smaller towns in Bahr el Ghazal. Thousands of the new arrivals in northern Sudan were suffering from severe malnutrition (Amnesty 1989, sec. 2.2). In the autumn of 1987, an estimated thirteen thousand migrants from Bahr el Ghazal were camped in Meiram and Babanousa (letter from Mohed. Ali el Mardi, Governor, Kordofan Region, to Prime Minister Sadiq el Mahdi, undated). UNICEF surveys suggested moderate childhood malnutrition at 22 percent and severe malnutrition at 23 percent among the displaced in Meiram (AICF 1988, 7). Still others attempted the 600-kilometer trek east to Ethiopia.

While the pattern of outmigrations thus continued to correspond closely to the pattern of raiding, drought remained no more than a secondary factor. Rain fell strongly in most of the south in 1986.[19] Satellite pictures suggest that vegetation growth was abundant (Map 7). Further, 1986 grain production in traditional rain-fed areas of southern Sudan, compared to averages for the previous five years, was virtually unchanged (Ministry of Agriculture and Natural Resources 1987a, 4–5).[20] This was despite the escalating civil war, which was likely to reduce 1986 production by more than it had previously. Meanwhile, grain yields per unit of area cultivated—which give a better indication of natural adversity such as drought and pest infestation— had actually increased.[21]

In the administrative district of Aweil area council, a major departure

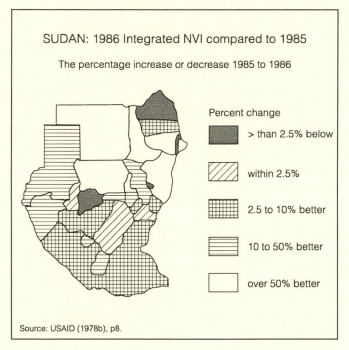

SUDAN: 1986 Integrated NVI compared to 1985

The percentage increase or decrease 1985 to 1986

Percent change

> than 2.5% below

within 2.5%

2.5 to 10% better

10 to 50% better

over 50% better

Source: USAID (1978b), p8.

**Map 7**. Normalized Vegetation Index for Sudan: Percentage Increase or Decrease, 1985 to 1986. *Source:* USAID 1987b, 8.

point for migrants in 1987, the 1986 harvest was estimated at only 35–50 percent of normal, but drought was not the most important factor. Northern Aweil in particular, while capable of producing a grain surplus in favorable years (UN/SRRA 1990, 46) had been heavily affected by militia raids since late 1985. An investigation by an agricultural project team funded by an international donor concluded that the bulk of the drop in production in Aweil area council had been due to a decline in area sown, which fell by some 50 percent as a result of rural people's having fled their homes because of raiding. Three additional factors causing the drop in harvest were isolated. First, there had been outright destruction and stealing of crops by raiding militiamen. Second, there had been minimal crop tending (poor weeding, scant bird scaring, etc.), partly because farmers were often too weak to perform their normal labors. Third, weather conditions had been unfavorable, with the rains falling late and then overabundantly (Aweil Rice Development Project 1987, 1). In addition, attempts by the army to prevent people from cultivating were said to have contributed to a poor harvest in 1986 in Bahr el Ghazal as a whole (Bona Malwal, personal communication).

Famine migrants themselves emphasized civil strife, rather than drought, as the key cause of outmigration in this period. Outsiders' access to famine migrants was severely restricted, something that helped the government to obscure the causes of the famine (Ryle 1989b, 67, 73). But some revealing information did become available. In a survey of southern Sudanese living in Khartoum shantytowns in February 1987, three-quarters of those from Bahr el Ghazal (and a similar proportion from Upper Nile) said it was insecurity that had prompted them to migrate (USAID 1987b, 1–2). Almost half of those from Bahr el Ghazal had been resident for less than twelve months, suggesting that they had left the province after the first major wave of raiding in the dry season of 1985–1986.

The primacy of conflict in shaping the famine is further evidenced by the gender and age composition of migrants. Young men headed overwhelmingly for Ethiopia, while women, children, and older men were more likely to head north (Ryle 1989a, 14; Interdonor Memo. 1988, 3; Interagency Situation Report 1988, 2, 4). It appears that young men feared for their lives if they headed for the areas from which the militiamen had come. There was considerable justification for such fears (see, e.g., reports of atrocities in Africa Watch [1990] and Amnesty [1989]).

### From Late 1987 through Early 1988

The 1987–1988 dry season saw outmigration at levels even greater than before. In the last quarter of 1987, there was a surge in migration to Ethiopia, with migrants arriving in Ethiopian camps at a rate of ten thousand a month (*Sudan Times*, June 19, 1988). This movement continued in 1988. In the three months from February to April 1988, about forty thousand people arrived in Ethiopia from Bahr el Ghazal, with many fewer from Upper Nile (*Sudan Times*, May 3, 1988; Interdonor Memo. 1988, 3). Perhaps a quarter of those who set off died before they reached the border.[22]

The first half of 1988 also saw a major new influx into Aweil town. In the spring and summer of 1988, some sixty-five thousand people arrived from the rural districts of Aweil and Gogrial. Aweil town's normal resident population of some twenty-eight thousand was now vastly outnumbered by displaced people (UNDP 1988, annex 2). Not all the displaced were registered, and some estimates put their number as high as one hundred thousand by mid-1988. Numbers peaked at the height of the wet season, when food supplies in rural areas tend to be lowest (Ryle 1989a, 15). Most of the displaced lived in the open, notably in the market area (UNDP 1988b, 8). Wau, too, experienced a major new influx. By the end of April, the local Catholic church estimated that the town harbored approximately 150,000 displaced people, and large numbers continued to arrive in May and June.[23] Whereas in 1989, when Bahr el Ghazal was relatively secure from militia attacks, the displaced population of Wau shrunk greatly during May as people left the town to plant,[24] this seasonal movement was largely absent in 1988. Raid-ing—and general insecurity—thus created famine not only by causing dis-placement to urban areas but also by keeping people there (often in very poor and insanitary living conditions). By the end of October, the number of displaced in Wau was put at one hundred thousand and their situation was described as "pathetic" (*Heritage*, October 31, 1988). In October, sixty-two people a day were reported to be dying in the town (*Sudan Times*, October 13, 1988).

There were also major new influxes into northern Sudan, with many peo-ple journeying from Wau and Aweil (Interdonor Memo. 1988, 1). In Abyei, the number of displaced people soared in the late spring of 1988. Slightly fewer than three thousand displaced people were in Abyei on April 14. By May 23, their numbers had swelled to some fifteen thousand to twenty-five thousand, with new arrivals at three hundred to four hundred a day (Inter-agency Situation Report 1988, 4–5). In June–July 1988, the town of Meiram, just north of Abyei, was the focus of a very large influx. At the beginning of June, some six thousand people were receiving grain at a general distribu-tion center (MSF-France 1988e). By August 4, fully twenty-six thousand displaced people were attending distributions.

To the west, many people from the northwestern part of Aweil district headed for the town of Safaha on the Bahr el Arab River, at the southern extreme of Darfur (Ryle 1989a, 12). In March–May 1988, over twenty thou-sand destitute Malwal and Abiem Dinka arrived in Safaha. They had run a gauntlet of ambushes by small groups of militia in a forest called Malek Mir a few miles to the south (Amnesty 1989, sec. 2.2).

Some of this migration in late 1987 and early 1988 was evidently a re-sponse to recent raiding, with militia raids continuing at significant levels (Amnesty 1989, sec. 2.1). Many of those who migrated in 1988 referred to such raids. One of those who migrated north from Bahr el Ghazal in early 1988 was Manut (name changed for security reasons), from Peth district, north of Aweil. He told me that northern militiamen had taken three of his daughters, burnt his house and sorghum, and stolen his cattle during the 1987–1988 dry season. After the attack, he had headed for Safaha with his wife, three sons, and three remaining daughters. Displaced people inter-viewed in late spring 1988 made frequent mention of a recent spate of militia attacks, during which recently planted crops had been destroyed (Inter-agency Situation Report, 1988, 4–6).

It is clear, nevertheless, that the dry season of 1987–1988 brought a re-duction in the frequency of militia attacks, compared with preceding dry seasons (Amnesty 1989, sec. 2.1). This appears to have reflected diminishing returns from raiding, combined with an increasing risk of encountering seri-ous military resistance from the SPLA, as the SPLA established a strong presence in Bahr el Ghazal (ibid., sec. 2.1). If it was militia raiding that was driving the outmigrations from rural Bahr el Ghazal in 1986–1988 (as is suggested here), then it would seem paradoxical that the most significant outmigrations to northern Sudan, to Aweil and Wau, and to Ethiopia should take place in late 1987 and early 1988, when the frequency of militia raids was declining.

However, as far as the migration to Ethiopia was concerned, the late 1987 surge was in large part due to a sharp reduction in the danger involved. The eclipse of the government-supported Anyanya 2 in Upper Nile in 1987 had removed the principal obstacle to such movement (Amnesty 1989, sec. 2.2; Ryle 1989a, 14).

Further, of those who migrated to garrison towns in Bahr el Ghazal or to northern Sudan in 1988, many, while not responding immediately to militia attacks, had nevertheless been severely affected by such attacks, clinging on in rural or urban areas of Bahr el Ghazal until they could hold out no longer. A report by the Aweil relief committee noted that most of those who flooded into Aweil in early 1988 were people who had hung on in rural areas, sometimes in their home villages, despite militia attacks on their villages. Many had fed on the leaves and roots of wild plants (UNDP 1988, annex 2, 1). When these people finally arrived in Aweil town, they had generally been without adequate food for many months. They were in very poor health and "in traumatic frame of mind and spirit." Some were described as "literally skeletons" (ibid., annex 2, 1). Among famine-affected people in Aweil in 1988, it was those whose villages lay in the northerly parts of Aweil and Gogrial area councils who had been most severely affected (Father Deng Rudolf 1988). These were also the areas that were most exposed to militia attacks from the north.

The very poor condition of new arrivals in Aweil and in the north itself suggested that they had suffered the onset of the famine process some considerable time previously. In most cases, this appears to have stemmed from militia attacks in the 1985–1986 and, more especially, 1986–1987 dry seasons. In contrast to the Ngok Dinka—who had better contacts in, and knowledge of, northern Sudan, encouraging them to evacuate the Abyei area before the worst of the 1988 famine (Ryle 1989a, 16)—the Dinka who arrived in garrison towns and the north in 1988 had clearly not left their homes until they were actually starving.[25] Many, as noted, arrived in the north from Aweil and Wau, where food shortages were extremely severe by the spring and summer of 1988.

The famine migrants arriving in Abyei were mostly Twic Dinka. Their severe malnutrition indicated that they were suffering the final stages of the famine process.[26] The Twic, as noted, had suffered badly from militia raiding in the dry seasons of 1985–1986 and 1986–1987. Those arriving in Meiram in spring 1988 were primarily Malwal Dinka from eastern Aweil and Twic Dinka from northern Gogrial (Ryle 1989a, 29). Many had previously mi-

grated to Aweil and begun their northward journey from there, often walking along the railway line (Amnesty 1989, sec. 2.2). Again, their physical
condition indicated that the famine process was far advanced among them.
Famine was similarly far advanced among those arriving in Safaha.[27] Many
were Abiem Dinka, and had been subject to heavy raiding in the dry season
of 1985–1986. The others were mostly Malwal Dinka who had been subject
to raiding in 1985–1986 and 1986–1987. The most severe cattle losses were
suffered by the Malwal and Twic, the two groups most strongly represented
among those who migrated to northern Sudan (UN/SRRA 1990, 52).[28]

Interviews with uprooted Dinka suggest a range of responses to militia
attacks, with migration to garrison towns or to the north often coming only
after other strategies had failed. One of those who walked to Safaha, in
southern Darfur, was Marial (name changed), a middle-aged man from the
Peth tribal section, north of Aweil. He told me how northern militiamen
attacked his village in the spring of 1987, burning his house and sorghum,
and stealing his forty-six cattle and other possessions. Like many victims of
militia attacks, his initial response was to head south, in his case to an area
near Aweil (UN/SRRA 1990, 45, 48).[29] To have headed immediately for the
area from which the militias had come would have made little sense. It was
only in the spring of 1988, after struggling for a year to survive without cattle
or seed, that he decided he had to walk north to the town of Safaha.

Further light is shed on the pattern of delayed migration when we consider that the majority of those who migrated to Aweil and Wau, and to
northern Sudan, in 1988 were women, children, and old men.[30] The frailty
of children and the old increased the risks of migration for them, apparently
encouraging them (and the women who cared for them) to remain in their
home areas for as long as possible. While raiding encouraged immediate
migration with cattle (either further south or to Ethiopia) to shield them
from further militia attacks, this was largely undertaken by young Dinka
men, for whom moving with cattle was a traditional responsibility (Duffield
1990a, 27). In the meantime, preserving a presence in home areas appears
to have offered some hope of holding on to traditional ways of life, often
including some form of agricultural cultivation.

Another clue to the delayed outmigration lay in patterns of relief. Until
1988, the near-absence of relief, either in garrison towns or the north, provided little incentive to undergo the hazards of migration.[31] When 1988
brought an increase in the promise (and in some parts of the north, the
availability) of relief, this appears to have played some role in encouraging
increased outmigration. Certainly, the governor of Bahr el Ghazal, Lawrence Lual Lual, attributed the major influx into Wau in 1988 to hopes of
ICRC food arrivals (*Sudan Times*, November 10, 1988). More important, the
uprooted Dinka themselves spoke of relief as something that could prompt
a decision to migrate. For example, Mabor (name changed) an Aweil Dinka,

from the village of Magondit, in the Peth area of Bahr el Ghazal, told me that
after spending a year to the south of Magondit in the wake of a militia attack
in the spring of 1987 that robbed him of his children and sixty cattle, he had
decided to walk north to Safaha on hearing of a relief operation run by
"white people." The importance of the new availability of relief in the north
was also stressed by Malwal chiefs (UN/SRRA 1990, field notes, May 11, 12).
The lure of relief is reflected in the songs of the displaced. A blind Dinka
woman in one of the southern Kordofan famine camps had a reputation for
composing songs on the spot. Told that I had come to talk with migrants, she
sang to the clapping of others:

> I heard there was an organization of white people
> Receiving the suffering in Meiram.
> Some people have been killed,
> And some people are dying because of hunger.
> That is why we decided to come and see the white people.
> When we came, we got what we heard:
> Food, treatment and plastic sheeting.

While militia raiding lay at the root even of late 1987 and early 1988
migrations, two additional hardships helped tip many people into leaving at
this time. One was SPLA requisitioning. The SPLA relied heavily on food
and military supplies from its bases along the Ethiopian border. When these
supply routes were impeded, this encouraged local SPLA units (and sometimes local bands loosely associated with the SPLA) to resort to forced requisitioning.[32] Until the reconciliation with the SPLA in 1987, the forces of
Anyanya 2 in Upper Nile posed a formidable obstacle to the SPLA's supply
routes from Ethiopia, encouraging problems of discipline among SPLA
forces. In 1986, with Ethiopian supply routes severed, some people in the
Aweil area compared the SPLA to locusts.

The increased presence of the SPLA in 1987–1988 created additional demand for food (Africa Watch 1990, 120), even though supply difficulties
from Ethiopia were easing. The arrival of the SPLA—too late to prevent
devastation by militia attacks—meant there were extra mouths to feed from
a poor 1987 crop (UNDP 1988, 6; de Waal 1990a, 10). One man, from near
Aweil, described how northern militiamen had taken sixty-five of his cattle,
leaving him with just five. When SPLA soldiers arrived in his area, they took
his rice. It was at this point, in the spring of 1988, that he had decided to
walk north. A woman from Aruk, near Aweil, complained that she had had
to give food not only to the SPLA and army but also the militiamen.

The other additional factor precipitating migration was the 1987 drought,
which, unlike the 1986 drought, appears to have been significant. In the
southern Sudan as a whole, it is clear that grain production was significantly

reduced from 1986 levels and from the 1981–1985 average. But while yields per unit of area cultivated were lower than in 1986, they were slightly higher than in 1981–1985.[33] Rainfall information is very patchy, but suggests some reduction in 1987.[34] A 1988 report by Father Deng M. Rudolf, the former chairman of the Relief Committee of Aweil, said famine in the Aweil area at that time had arisen from a combination of natural adversity and civil strife, adding that natural adversity had taken two principal forms in 1987: drought and a plague of locustlike insects (Father Deng Rudolf 1988; Interdonor Memo. 1988, 1). However, while the Dinka who left northwestern Aweil for Safaha in southern Darfur often gave drought as the reason they had left Bahr el Ghazal, they cited cattle-raiding much more frequently.[35]

### From Late 1988 through 1989

In late 1988 and 1989, the exposure of people in Bahr el Ghazal to both raiding and natural adversity diminished significantly. Although an excess of rainfall in 1988 had clearly damaged the harvest in some areas,[36] nevertheless the generally abundant rains in that year contributed to significant harvests in many areas. This appears to have played a part in the diminished severity of famine (including reduced outmigration) in 1989 (Amnesty 1989, sec. 2.2). Probably more important, at least in the Bahr el Ghazal area, was the improved security for rural people arising from the growing control exercised by the rebel SPLA, which allowed many displaced people to return to rural areas (UN/SRRA 1990). This control had been assisted by widespread flooding in 1988, which had helped to secure the Bahr el Arab border against militia raiding. By late 1988, the SPLA had a strong presence along the Bahr el Arab River, preventing further murahaleen raiding except in parts of eastern Bahr el Ghazal where the Twic Dinka border the Bul Nuer and where joint parties of Anyanya 2 forces and Messiriya murahaleen attacked civilians in December 1988 (Amnesty 1989, sec. 2.1). The SPLA has been accused by some in the south of being slow to protect the northern Bahr el Ghazal Dinka, of failing to encourage local militias while taking youths away to its bases in Ethiopia, and even of making political capital from the abuse of northern Bahr el Ghazal Dinka at the hands of northern murahaleen (*Southern Sudan Vision*, December 15, 1992). These are among a number of serious charges against Garang made by the SPLA breakaway Nasir faction. They cannot be verified, and it is fair to point out that the SPLA could not be everywhere at once. Even so, it does appear that the SPLA had more pressing priorities (the campaigns to take Rumbek and Juba, for example) while murahaleen attacks in the dry seasons of 1985–1986 and 1986–1987 were taking place virtually unopposed.

## Beneficiaries of the Loss of Assets and Production

A number of politically influential groups stood to benefit from the loss of assets and production on the part of famine victims (and from the population movements that followed and were in large part caused by that loss). These benefits—promised and to a large extent delivered—accrued to both the central government and local groups.

### CENTRAL GOVERNMENT INTERESTS

At the center in Khartoum, successive Sudanese governments were faced with a variety of economic and political pressures in the 1980s. These included economic recession; mounting international debt; insurrection in the south (which appeared likely to deepen economic crisis in the north by preventing access to oil deposits, by preventing the building of the Jonglei Canal, and by increasing government spending on security); and a need to accommodate a number of political interests, including both the Baggara (who were well armed, were discontented, and had shown in the 1970s that they remained a dangerous political force) and the growing body of influential Islamic fundamentalists.

In view of these pressures, the arming and encouragement of militia attacks, though it directly created famine, represented a solution rather than a problem for successive governments in Khartoum. Government support of the militias took the form of provision of arms, ammunition, and intelligence, as well as the effective provision of immunity from prosecution for theft, killings, and other violations of the law (Amnesty 1989, sec. 4.1; Africa Watch 1990, 78–97; Oxfam-UK 1986e, 1; Alier 1990, 256; *Sudan Times*, October 25, 1988). In Babanousa, the Messiriya militia were given guns (GM3's) and bullets by the army. Ties between the Humr Messiriya and the army were strong, with the Humr traditionally constituting a major force in the Sudanese army (Mohamed Salih, 1993, 20). The Messiriya were to reject a Dinka demand for Sud. £5 million in compensation for raiding on the ground that the army had asked them to attack the Dinka (Oxfam-UK 1986e, 1).

The militia strategy offered a way to win the war at minimum economic and political cost. Governments in Khartoum saw the Dinka south of the Bahr el Arab as the key supporters of the SPLA, providing soldiers, supplies, and information (Mahmud and Baldo 1987, 17). The provision of cattle, offering food on the hoof, was important in underpinning the mobility of the SPLA (Oxfam-UK 1986i, 3). Moreover, it was thought that the Dinka south of the Bahr el Arab could provide critical logistical support in bringing the war to areas north of the river (Mahmud and Baldo 1987, 17). Crucially, depopulating areas of the countryside (by militias and the army), while at the same time providing limited relief in garrison towns, offered a way to control a civilian population perceived as hostile.[37] Some observers held that the government's strategy was to persuade the SPLA to give up the fight on account of the hunger of its own people (Bona Malwal, personal communication). Nimeiri and subsequent governments found in the militia strategy an alternative to the more expensive strategy of relying on the army. In any case, the attacks on civilians, which were an integral part of the government's counterinsurgency strategy, were something the national army could not be seen to be carrying out (Oxfam-UK 1986i, 3).

For the central government, the militia strategy held out the promise not only of saving money but also of securing access to critical resources in the south. The strategy offered the prospect of harnessing southern oil and other resources by depopulating areas from which the SPLA drew critical support.[38] Following the discovery of oil in 1978, the idea of a so-called Unity Region was proposed in government circles: the region would embrace the major oil-rich areas of Bentiu and Gogrial area councils in the south and Abyei area council (where additional oil deposits had been discovered) and some other parts of southern Kordofan (Alier 1990, 216). It is striking that precisely these areas (together with the garrison towns of Aweil and Wau, which served as refuges for those displaced by militia attacks) were the most severely affected by famine in 1986–1988. This was more than a coincidence. The Bentiu area, with the richest oil reserves, was where the initial raiding had been concentrated and where both government and SPLA troops continued to be stationed in the greatest numbers. Nimeiri's use of Messiriya militias in 1983–1984 was designed to protect the Bentiu oil fields from SPLA attack. And in late 1984, Nimeiri—hoping to revive historical Nuer-Dinka animosities, in which the Dinka had generally been at a disadvantage—recruited the largely Nuer Anyanya 2, to cooperate with the army and the Messiriya militias in protecting these oil fields and attacking populations seen as hostile, notably the Dinka, the Shilluk, and also some groups among the Nuer.[39] Anyanya 2 was largely controlled by Daniel K. Mathews, who was governor of Upper Nile from 1983 through April 1985 (Alier 1990, 254). Cooperating closely with Nimeiri, Mathews was one of a number of southern politicians prepared to work with Khartoum in a way that exacerbated divisions in the south.

Officers of the Sudan army cooperated in planning raids and, moreover, increasingly directed their own attacks against civilians (de Waal 1990a, 8–9). In Abyei District, attacks on the Ngok Dinka were interpreted by the Ngok as an attempt to drive them away from a potentially oil-rich area, and to keep it from falling under southern control (Mawson 1984, 522). It has been commonly alleged that Chevron itself, which came under pressure to push ahead with extraction as Nimeiri signed an oil exploration deal with the rival National Oil Company of Sudan in December 1984 (*Africa Economic Digest*, December 14, 1984, 12), contributed to the arming of the militias to protect its oil interests (see, e.g., Alier 1990, 222). The oil fields were certainly important to Chevron, representing the company's largest exploration venture outside North America (Gurdon 1984, 85).

Another economic motive for depopulation in northern Upper Nile and northern Bahr el Ghazal was the land hunger generated by Sudan's pattern of horizontally expanding mechanized agriculture. The clay plain across which mechanized agriculture has spread in the north, damaging the soil and then of necessity moving on, extends into northern Upper Nile and Bahr el Ghazal. The beginnings of mechanized farming in these areas have already been mentioned. While the relationship between the central government, merchant interests, and the depopulation of this area remains unclear, nevertheless the further expansion of mechanized farming into this fertile belt was likely to be facilitated by famine and depopulation (Duffield 1990a, 31–32). Significantly, previous expansions of commercial agriculture (notably in the Gedaref area of Kassala Province and the Renk area of Upper Nile) had occurred to a large extent at the expense of the resident populations, and in the 1990s this process threatened to continue in the Nuba Mountains area and in southern Blue Nile.

From a political point of view, the militia strategy offered the prospect of avoiding unpopular conscription. Relying on the army to defeat the rebels would have entailed some form of conscription; instead, the army was to a large extent kept out of the firing line.[40] The use of militias to displace civilians associated with the SPLA also appeared to offer the prospect of significantly less diplomatic fallout than if the Sudanese armed forces had been the main instrument for such attacks.

Even more important, the militia strategy appears to have offered the prospect of appeasing the Baggara with booty and of defusing the growing threat of Islamic fundamentalism with an aggressively "Islamic" agenda in relation to the south.

The central government faced a persistent threat of unrest and rebellion from the Baggara. The militia strategy offered a way to channel the economic frustrations of the Baggara in ways that would help the central government to suppress another, more immediate source of dissent—in the south.[41] The Baggara, though economically marginalized in many respects, had experienced a resurgence in their political representation under Nimeiri after 1977, when the Ansar had come close to overthrowing the president. This resurgence had continued under the Transitional Military Council (TMC), which assumed power in May 1985, and under the prime ministership of Sadiq el Mahdi, facilitating a continuation of the militia strategy. This strategy was spearheaded, in particular, by General Burma Nasir, a Messiri and an outspoken supporter of the militias, who had been minister of state for defense under both the TMC and Sadiq el Mahdi. In addition, a number of Umma Party politicians had close connections with the Messiriya militias[42] and with the army. For its part, the National Islamic Front (NIF) set up and ran a Committee for the Defense of Islam and the Nation, which was essentially a political lobbying group on behalf of the Baggara militias (Africa Watch 1990, 91). The Baggara's strong connections in the central government, and the way that these encouraged the development of the militia strategy, contrasted markedly with the position in the mid-1960s, when the central government had largely turned a deaf ear to Messiriya requests for "assistance" against the southern rebels of that time.

The central government's interest in raiding was reflected in the increasingly close involvement of the national army. The army cooperated closely with the Messiriya militias in 1985, when the focus of militia raiding was switched to Bahr el Ghazal. Significantly, the occurrence of joint Rizeigat and Messiriya attacks south of Bahr el Arab in the dry season of 1985–1986 indicated an unusual degree of cooperation among groups who usually acted independently and sometimes in opposition to one another (Mahmud and Baldo 1987, 18). Dinka elders alleged that army officers had participated in militia raids, wearing civilian clothing.[43]

Islamic fundamentalism was another threat to governments in Khartoum. And the famine appears to have played a part in allowing Sudan's religiously based traditional parties to present themselves as truly Islamic in the face of this threat, while at the same time helping Sadiq el Mahdi in particular to establish his own Islamic credentials within the Ansar movement.[44]

Although el Mahdi had outwardly secularized the Umma Party, this was largely cosmetic (Vincent 1988, 185).[45] Indeed, the Umma Party remained formally committed to the establishment of an Islamic system based on the Koran and the Sunna. The directory of the Ansar movement, obtained by Vincent at the movement's headquarters in Omdurman, states clearly, "*Jihad* [holy war] is under way until the day of judgement" (cited in Vincent 1988, 266). Sadiq el Mahdi's desire to become Imam of the Ansar movement—and his desire to establish his Islamic credentials—was well known (ibid., 228). As prime minister, he had adamantly refused to revoke the Islamic laws he had once criticized as un-Islamic (Warburg 1990, 636). In a lecture given at the el Minhal Hotel, in Saudi Arabia, in October 1985, Sadiq el Mahdi was reported to have outlined "Five ways to Islamize and Arabize Southern Sudan"; one was "through settling a large number of southerners in the north so as to adapt themselves to the northern environment."[46]

The DUP's commitment to jihad was certainly not clear-cut. Indeed, the DUP leader, Mohamed Osman Mirghani, was eventually to play an important role in negotiating a possible peace settlement with the SPLA in late 1988, conceding that the DUP would not back the hated "September laws" (Warburg 1990, 635). Nevertheless, the DUP, like the Umma Party, was wary of the rising tide of Islamic fundamentalism, and lent some support to the Islamization of Sudan, as well as to measures that might weaken southern resistance to the northern power elite of which it formed a part.

A confidential DUP General Secretariat working paper on the south, obtained in Khartoum, suggested an intention among some elements of the DUP to use the impoverishment of the south as a tool for Islamization, including conversions carried out by organizations, such as the Islamic Relief Agency, involved in relieving famine:

> We support the continuation of the division of the Southern Region into three fragile regions without any economic viability and which shall remain dependent on the Central Government and the Islamic relief institutions such as the Islamic Da'wa Organization and the Islamic Relief Agency and others. In this regard we wish to correct the erroneous assumption that the division of the south in 1983 was the work of the deposed President Gaafar Nimeiri. The truth of the matter is that despite differences between our party and the butcher Nimeiri over his many tragic policies, the party leadership had endorsed Nimeiri's fragmentation of the Southern Region for the sake of Islam through his policy of divide and rule which at any rate is the ideal policy for the time being and a good step towards the creation of an Arab and Islamic state.

The document went on to affirm a desire to turn the south, "especially Equatoria, into an Arab Muslim enclave and a torch that shall illuminate the jungles of Africa south of the Sahara." The document also avowed DUP support for militias established in the south, notably in Equatoria.[47]

The hope that hardship in the south might provide the opportunity for religious conversions was sometimes expressed during the famine, though the importance of this is difficult to assess.[48] While religion appears to have been a relatively minor factor in encouraging the forcible displacement of populations, it may have lent a degree of legitimacy to the process in the eyes of some. A Red Crescent doctor working among famine migrants in southern Kordofan in 1988 voiced the hope that migration to the north would lead to wholesale conversions to Islam (Ryle 1989b, 93). Mahmud and Baldo mention a survey of famine migrants in Ed Daien in May 1986 by Islamic groups "for the purpose of Islamization and relief work" (Mahmud and Baldo 1987, 3).

The position of the army in relation to raiding was somewhat ambiguous. On the one hand, it is clear that the army operated in conjunction with the militias to organize and carry out raids on the south, that these raids had important strategic purposes, notably in Bentiu area, and that many army personnel benefited economically from the raiding and resultant famine.[49] On the other hand, elements of the army in the south had a lingering sympathy with the southern Sudanese, and there was a growing suspicion in some quarters that Prime Minister el Mahdi was seeking to boost his own position by channeling resources toward the militias at the expense of the national army. There were several documented instances of army personnel offering protection against the militias. For example, in December 1985, when joint Messiriya and Rizeigat militias attacked and killed Dinka officers and soldiers at Aryat, seventeen miles north along the rail line from Aweil, a small army unit chased away the attackers and returned the cattle stolen during the attack. The military governor of Bahr el Ghazal at that time was Albino Akol, himself a Dinka, and he appears to have had some influence on the army's stance, although it was not directly under his control (Mahmud and Baldo 1987, 18). In 1988, famine migrants in Meiram reported that they had been brought from Malwal by army truck, which had provided a degree of protection against the militias (interview with famine migrants at Meiram, November 1988). In Darfur in 1988, the garrison at Safaha—which had not cooperated closely with the Rizeigat militias in the same way that the southern Kordofan army had done with the Messiriya—not only offered some protection against local militias[50] but also played an important part in facilitating the movement of famine migrants by relief truck to more northerly parts of Darfur.[51] According to the testimony of famine migrants, the army was often more poorly armed than the militias, and government soldiers were afraid of militiamen. One woman said, "The murahaleen are stronger than the army, and the army are afraid of being shot by the murahaleen."

While the Addis Ababa agreement provided that half of southern garrisons be composed of southern Sudanese, nevertheless as southern representation in army units stationed in the south was increasingly eroded (Ryle 1989a, 8; Mawson 1984, 523), and as top government posts in the south were removed from Dinka control, the protection provided by the army appears to have become increasingly minimal. By early 1986, more than 75 percent of the army in Wau was composed of northern Sudanese. These were mostly from Darfur and Kordofan, including Messiriya (Oxfam-UK 1986d, 1). The remaining quarter of southern Sudanese soldiers was still regarded by the regional administration in Wau as critical in limiting the army's reprisals against villages said to be sympathetic to the SPLA (Oxfam-UK 1986a, 3). The Aweil garrison was almost exclusively northern (Oxfam-UK 1986f, 1).

Even the increasing "northernization" of the army in the south did not eliminate tensions between the army and the militias, however. In 1988, when the militias demanded protection against the increasingly powerful SPLA, the army refused (de Waal 1990a, 10). By 1989, it was becoming increasingly clear that important elements within the national army—though largely unsympathetic towards the south—were suspicious of the growing influence of the militias, and their apparently close ties with Prime

Minister Sadiq el Mahdi, the Umma Party, and Libya (Khalid 1990, 357). As government-held areas began to fall to the SPLA with some rapidity in 1988 and 1989, there was a feeling in some quarters that Sadiq was intent on building up the militias, while allowing the inadequately equipped army and the SPLA to exhaust each other in the south (ibid., 357; Alier 1990, 288). Many senior officers in the army were linked with the main rival to the Umma Party, the DUP, reflecting the concentration of schools and officer recruitment in the DUP's stronghold in northern riverain areas (Woodward 1990, 182).

## LOCAL INTERESTS

At the local level, the first process of famine offered important benefits to the Baggara of Kordofan and Darfur. The Baggara were under a variety of pressures, which together constituted, by the mid-1980s, a major economic crisis. These included the expansion of commercial farming in their grazing areas; increased restrictions on access to grazing in the south; rapidly rising consumer prices (including that of grain); and the famine of 1983–1985. The Nuer who joined the Anyanya 2 militias are not the focus of this discussion, although there are indications that some elements of the Nuer also found in raiding a release from their marginal status within the Sudanese political economy.[52]

For those who joined the Baggara militias, raiding offered the prospect of relief from economic pressures. For one thing, it allowed the direct acquisition of cattle, which, although unsuited to the ecology of northern Sudan, could be sold for cash. Very large numbers of cattle were acquired in raids; the routes to market (including Abyei and Safaha) for raided and distress-sales cattle are shown in Map 8.

As in the nineteenth century, exploitation of southerners was frequently the work of the more impoverished elements of the north. Young Baggara men were particularly severely hit by economic marginalization and drought, and they made up the bulk of the recruits to the Baggara Arab militias, with young Baggara in such towns as Ed Daien forming a particular focus of militia recruiting (Johnson 1988a, 10; Mahmud and Baldo 1987, 2). As in the first civil war, the raiding was often opposed by tribal elders (Mahmud and Baldo 1987, 23). But in the absence of the old Native Administration or any equivalent system to bolster the elders' prestige and influence, such opposition proved ineffective.

The Rizeigat raiding on Bahr el Ghazal has been investigated by a northern Sudanese linguist, Ushari Mahmud, whose pioneering human rights work with another northern Sudanese, Suleiman Baldo, highlighted the rebirth of slavery in Sudan. Mahmud was imprisoned by the Sudanese government as a result of his investigations. In December 1988, before he was

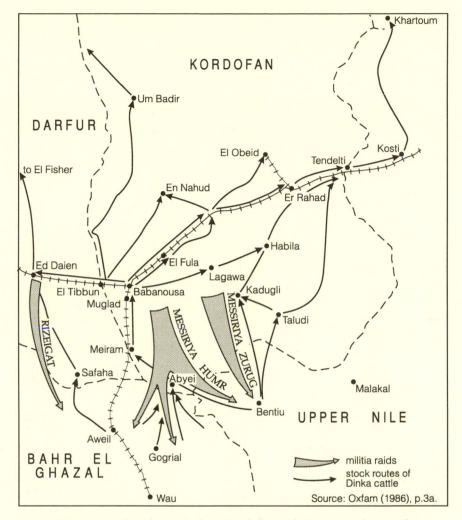

**Map 8**. Movement of Dinka Cattle from South to North. *Source:* Oxfam 1986l, 3a.

detained for the second time, he described the raids to me in a way that makes clear the precisely thought-out economic calculations that shaped the raids:

> The Rizeigat militia leadership would go to one (Rizeigat) village and start shooting in the air for two to three days. Rizeigat men would come there from different villages, on camels, on donkeys, on horses, with different kinds of guns. Then they would get their food supplies. Then they would go toward the Dinka area. They spread around a village very early in the morning and start burning around the village, burning the crops, and then they attack. The pat-

tern is that men run away. Hardly anyone puts up a fight. They get the wives and the children. They burn everything. They cut the fruit trees down. They want to make sure that nobody comes back to live in the area. Then they come back, and north of Safaha the distribution [of cattle and people] starts. This is done strictly according to your firepower and hierarchy and if you had a horse or donkey, your role in combat, how many people you captured—a very complex system of who gets what—women, children, and cattle. Only children who are being breast-fed are allowed to be with their mothers. You always find families dispersed.

The range of raided goods itself indicated a certain poverty on the part of some of the raiders. One Dinka man described how Rizeigat raiders, attacking his Bahr el Ghazal village of Maryal Bai in February 1987, had stolen sugar, his shirt, every good piece of cloth, mattresses, and even drinking cups (Mahmud and Baldo 1987, 20). Another said some of the raiders on his village of Majak Bai had been friends of his when he had worked in southern Darfur in 1974, trying to earn enough money to buy cattle and get married (interview with Garang Anai, acting chief, Adila settlement, December 3, 1988).

Raids provided much of the subsistence needed for the raids themselves. For example, in raids on the Twic in the dry season of 1985–1986, grain that was not burnt was fed to the horses, camels, and looted cattle of the raiders, Twic elders reported.[53]

If the benefits of famine included access to a range of assets, most notably cattle, they also included the prospect of improved access to grazing land and water for cattle already owned. More and more land had been coming under cultivation, increasingly restricting Baggara access to grazing land and water. Pressure from some Dinka groups was also restricting Baggara access in some areas. The famine offered a possible solution to their problem. In particular, the scorched earth tactics (burning of villages, crops, and trees) employed in the raids suggested an intention to depopulate much of northern Bahr el Ghazal and northern Upper Nile. A Minority Rights Group report stated: "Well-placed sources speak of a government policy to depopulate northern Bahr al-Ghazal through Arab militia activity, just as earlier raids tried to drive the Dinka out of Abyei. The outcome of such a plan, if successful, would be to place the crucial pastures of the Bahr al-Arab completely under Baggara control."[54]

Moreover, some of the raided Dinka themselves expressed the view that grazing ambitions lay behind the attacks. Alwel Bol Ater, a sixty-year-old woman from Achoro, who lost eleven members of her family and many head of cattle in raids by the Rizeigat, said the Rizeigat wanted to take over the Dinka's land, to bring their cattle to graze and bring their families to live in Dinkaland (Mahmud and Baldo 1987, 30).[55] While the strength of the SPLA has partially prevented Baggara access to this grazing land more recently, this strength was not an anticipated result of the raiding.

Another major benefit for Baggara groups that was promised (and in this case delivered) by the famine was improved access to southern labor. Increasing northern dependence on southern labor had been exacerbated by the drying up of supplies of this labor with the onset of the second civil war. Again, raiding brought direct and indirect benefits. The direct benefits came from the widespread capture of Dinka civilians during militia raids (Amnesty 1989; Ryle 1989b, 62; Alier 1990, 263–65). These captives were held in conditions of slavery, or something very close to it. Twic elders said some of their people, including children, had had their hands pierced and had been chained together before being led away.[56] In one day (January 12, 1986), more than seven hundred children and women were taken in raids by Rizeigat and Messiriya on Maryal Bai, Nyamlell, Ashana, and other villages. Others were captured once they had left their home villages. In 1988–1989, there was apparently a shift in the militia strategy: as growing risks and diminishing returns discouraged raiding into Bahr el Ghazal, there was increased emphasis on plundering (and killing) famine migrants as they headed north (Africa Watch 1990, 82).[57] As famine migrants headed for the southern Darfur town of Safaha, many children were captured in the forest of Malek Mir (Amnesty 1989, sec. 4.1).[58] To the east, displaced Dinka reported the capture of Twic children by the Messiriya as Twic famine migrants made their way through Abyei towards Muglad and other northern Sudanese towns (ibid., sec. 2.2).

Some two hundred to three hundred Dinka were enslaved in the southern Darfur village of Farhabil alone, according to Manjok Jieng Manjok, who helped several Dinka to escape (Mahmud and Baldo 1987, 28). There were persistent reports of a slave market at Tibbun (Ryle 1989b, 67; and reports to author). People were also sold in Safaha in 1988. Indeed, the resurgence of slavery was reflected in a sharp fall in the price of child slaves there, from UK £60 in February 1988 to UK £10 in April (Anti-Slavery Society for the Protection of Human Rights 1988, 5). The total number of those enslaved is unknown. One estimate, from a Swedish missionary, was that at least fifty thousand girls had been taken into slavery in the north (Sudan Times, May 11, 1988). A medical worker in Darfur interviewed fifty-five household representatives who had fled the south and found that, on average, one member of every household had been killed by militiamen and another captured.[59] With more than one hundred thousand people leaving the Dinka heartlands for the north in 1988 alone, this provides a further indication that very large numbers of people were captured.

Testimonies collected by the writer include sixteen first-hand accounts of Dinka who were subjected to some form of slavery.[60] Captured Dinka were used for a variety of unpaid herding, farming, and domestic work. Often, they were subjected to violence and sexual abuse. One boy, whose face was horribly burnt, said he was burnt while sleeping in the cattle byre. He believed he was burnt by somebody, but said his "masters" tried to convince him he had been burnt by the cows. Many reported that they had been addressed as *Abid*, or "Slave." Many were bought and sold, and knew their "price." Mahmud and Baldo present the testimonies of seven Dinka relating to the enslavement of themselves or friends and family (Mahmud and Baldo 1987, 20–33).

In addition to benefits from services extracted from those held in captivity, a number of benefits could be derived from the release of captives. Payment of a ransom was often demanded. And, as with the nineteenth-century practices described in Chapter 2, apparent attempts to remedy slavery actually created a new set of beneficiaries. The same Rizeigat subchiefs who had provided supplies for murahaleen raiders subsequently came to regulate the reclaiming of enslaved relatives, with Dinka paying between Sud. £400–500 to the subchiefs for each person reclaimed.[61] The practice, and the size of the ransom, are corroborated by Anti-Slavery Society findings (Anti-Slavery Society for the Protection of Human Rights 1988, 3).[62] Abu Matarig, in southern Darfur, was a notable center for such deals, as well as for the congregation of militiamen (interview with Ushari Mahmud, December 20, 1988, Khartoum; Ryle 1989b, 67). In addition to payments to local chiefs, the police often required payment if relatives were to be reclaimed.[63] The uprooted Dinka were extremely poor, with many unable to afford such sums.

The chronology and geographical focus of the raids suggest that economic motives were extremely important for the raiders. For one thing, the raids on Bahr el Ghazal were concentrated on one of the most cattle-rich parts of the south (Map 9). Further, the fact that the late 1985 raids south of the Bahr el Arab region came some two years before a major SPLA presence in the area suggested that the strictly economic motive for the raiding was more important, at least initially, than any counterinsurgency motive, although it is not always easy to separate the two (de Waal 1990a, 10; Oxfam-UK 1986i, 1).

It is true that small SPLA units had been observed south of the Bahr el Arab River in 1985 and that there were fears in the north that even a moderate SPLA presence south of the Bahr el Arab River would serve as a launching pad for insurrection in the north. Nevertheless, these units had not threatened groups of Rizeigat who had been propelled southward to Dinkaland by drought in the north (Mahmud and Baldo 1987, 17). It is clear, moreover, that the raids themselves prompted thousands of people to join the SPLA, including Dinka groups who had previously remained aloof (Mahmud and Baldo 1987, 19; Wilson 1989, 28; interview with Melvyn Almond, Oxfam-UK, Khartoum, November 10, 1988).[64] In this sense, the raids

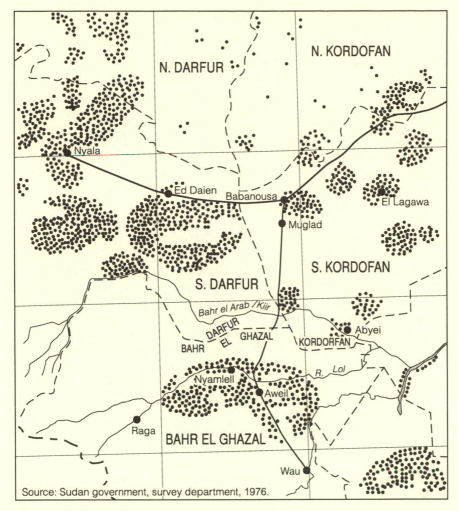

**Map 9**. Cattle Concentrations in Southwestern Sudan. *Source:* Sudanese government, survey department.

(for which economic motivation was critical) actually provided their own military justification, by stimulating the growth of the enemy.

Had the suppression of the SPLA been the only or even the most important motivation for the raids, the radicalizing effect of British raiding, and of militia raiding during the first civil war might reasonably have cautioned against raiding on groups that were maintaining a distance from the SPLA. Further, if combating the SPLA had been the main driving force behind the raiding, it might be expected that the SPLA's growing strength would have led to an increase in attempts to defeat it through raiding. The actual pattern—a diminution in raiding—reaffirms the importance of economic motives among the raiders.

A subsequent geographical shift in raiding away from Bahr el Ghazal is also suggestive of the importance of these economic motives. The diminution in raiding in 1988 has been noted, and by 1989 raiding in Bahr el Ghazal had almost ceased (Africa Watch 1990, 82). In mid-1988, with raiding opportunities drying up in Bahr el Ghazal, many Baggara Arabs from southern Darfur began to join a growing wave of raiding on the Fur of Darfur (*News from Africa Watch*, April 6, 1990, 1–9). The economic benefits from these raids were once again considerable. Many cattle were stolen (Africa Watch 1990, 85). The raids in Darfur gave further indications that securing land for settlement and grazing was an important priority for Sudanese Arab groups taking part, including the Baggara. The raids involved burning crops and villages and depopulating areas of Fur territory (*News from Africa Watch*, April 6, 1990). There were suspicions of a deliberate plan on the part of Sadiq el Mahdi and Colonel Qaddafi of Libya to "open up" the region for Arab control and settlement (Africa Watch 1990, 85; *News from Africa Watch*, April 6, 1990). Revealingly, the Fur were not only Muslims but had shown their loyalty to Khartoum and their religious affiliations by rejecting SPLA appeals for support and by returning fifteen Umma Party members to the Sudanese parliament in the 1986 election. There was no threat of insurrection from the Fur, but this did not protect them. Before long, the search for land and booty was to lead to severe raiding on, and displacement of, the Nuba in the Nuba Mountains region of southern Kordofan, something discussed in more detail in the conclusion.

Another important component of the "gains" reaped from raiding (and the famine it created) was sexual in nature. Sexual abuse of those captured in raids (including the rape of women and the castration of men) was widespread.[65]

Akol (name changed), a fifteen-year-old girl, said she was captured by an "Arab" man (name supplied) from a place called Battikh and was sold to someone in Dar Hamar. Her second "master" paid the first master Sud. £4,000 for Akol. She escaped within a period of twenty-four hours to Meiram. Akol said she walked for four nights, avoiding daylight out of fear that she would be caught again. During this time she ate nothing. "I used to walk at night, and in the daytime I climbed the tree in the bush to hide there until the sun set. Then I started again," she said. She said she was raped by her first "master" on the way to his home. "All the ladies who were captured with me faced the same problem. They were raped on the way. Even the underage girls were raped." When she and her "master" got to his house, she served as a maid and "a wife" to him. She said there were a lot of children enslaved at Sharif.

One young Dinka woman told me she had walked with her children from

Aweil towards Meiram, after her husband had refused to come with her out of fear that he would be killed by the murahaleen. She said that when she was nearing Meiram, she was captured by murahaleen and taken to Abyei. There she was made to do cleaning work, and planting of dura. She received no money. She was given enough food to feed her children. She said she was put into a hut, and "five men used me as a wife." She lived in these conditions in Abyei for a year, before she managed to escape one night. Another woman, who was twenty-one years old and from Malwal, said her "master's" wife had helped her to escape after her "master" tried to rape her several times.

In reemerging slave markets, the greatest demand, as in the nineteenth century, was for adolescent girls and young women, who might be sold for as much as fifty times the price of an elderly man or woman.[66] It was not only captives who were subject to sexual exploitation. The combination of army garrisons and impoverished famine migrants encouraged widespread male and female prostitution in army-occupied towns, notably in southern Kordofan (Interagency Situation Report 1988, 6). The long history of sexual exploitation of southern Sudanese is noted in Chapter 2; this complex element of the famine process cannot be adequately discussed within the confines of the present study. One thing that is at least suggestive, however, is that the sexual exploitation of southern Sudanese women accompanied a renewed Islamic drive to protect the purity of northern women. The tendency to "purify" one group of women while "sexualizing" a subordinated group has been notable in other historical contexts (Kovel [1970] 1988, 67–73), as has the widespread castration of males belonging to a rebellious subordinated group (ibid., 67–73), with sexual abuse serving to symbolize—perhaps for both "sides"—the domination of one group by another.

Sexual violence against men is illustrated by the experience of Makwac (name changed), a man around fifty-five years old, from Aweil. He was captured by murahaleen in May 1988 when he was heading for Meiram to buy food for his children and wives. His "master" sold him to another "Arab," from a place called Magoden. "It is this man who castrated me and branded me with an iron brand which they used for branding cows," he said. He added that many Dinka men had been castrated at Dar Sharif, and many were still enslaved.

As in Khartoum, there were those at the local level who claimed (and possibly believed) that the raiding served some kind of "religious" function, though quite how widespread this perception was is difficult to determine. The Humr, who formed the bulk of the fighters in the Messiriya militias that devastated the south in 1983–1988 (de Waal 1990b, 8), had been loyal supporters of the Mahdi in the late nineteenth century. They had been among the first to respond to the Mahdi's call to march to Omdurman when the Mahdia was established; had played a prominent part in the Baggara horse, the fighting force that had fought the Mahdi's battles in the name of Islam; and remained staunchly Mahdist in affiliation (Saeed 1982, 124; Cunnison 1966, 132). The Humr's new battles continued to be presented as a holy war: government radio called the raids a "jihad against the pagans" (*Sudan Times*, January 19, 1989). Similarly, the Rizeigat referred to their raids on the Dinka as *ghazwa*, a term that was used in the nineteenth century, implying a legitimate incursion into the land of the infidels (interview with Ushari Mahmud, Khartoum, December 20, 1988). The militias and the army between them were reported by Catholic bishops to have burned nine Catholic churches in the Nuba Mountains area of southern Kordofan in the course of 1987 (*Sudan Times*, January 19, 1989). The dangers in assuming that Islam sanctions slavery have already been stressed, as has the leading role of some northern Sudanese in publicizing and opposing the practice. However, it seems highly probable that religious divisions encouraged this abusive relationship. In the conclusion of his historical study on slavery in Sudan, Hargey noted that slavery is still sometimes seen as a divinely ordained institution (Hargey 1981, 456). Some Dinka spoke of having their Achilles tendons cut because they refused to become Muslims; others reportedly "converted" to avoid this fate (Jamal 1990, 3).

Religion, however, was often little more than a smokescreen for more pragmatic purposes. Even during the Mahdist uprising in the nineteenth century, the Baggara had quickly abandoned *jihad* when their immediate material desires had been satisfied.[67] To a large extent, religion continued to be used as a means of disguising and legitimizing more down-to-earth concerns, with the raids on the Muslim Fur confirming the importance of economic goals. One northern Sudanese poet, emphasizing the economic rewards reaped from conflict by merchants, wrote: "It is traders who are encouraging false strife / Dealing with religion as profitable goods."[68] Certainly, holy war was lucrative for a variety of northern Sudanese interests.

### Toleration of Raiding and Lack of Redress for Victims

The victims of raiding found little redress within the Sudanese political system, in either the north or the south. As in the nineteenth and early twentieth centuries, southerners were increasingly excluded from relevant political communities, and from the protection that membership of these communities conferred. Of critical importance was the collapse of the Dinka's ability to represent their interests in the north. This was intimately connected with the collapse of local mechanisms for resolving tribal disputes. There were no official investigations into the activities of the Messiriya militias, nor any attempts to disarm them or prosecute them for human rights violations (Africa Watch 1990, 91). Khartoum turned a similarly blind eye to atrocities carried out by elements of the Rizeigat and to a massacre of Dinka in Ed Daien in 1987 (ibid., 82–88; Mahmud and Baldo 1987). The absence of significant Dinka representation either in the parliament or at cabinet level allowed famine to progress amongst the Dinka without seriously undermining the political constituency or legitimacy of the government. Meanwhile, the Council of the South—created in October 1986 to represent southern interests in Khartoum—appeared to function more as a vehicle for the enrichment of southern politicians than as a genuine voice for the south (Khalid 1990, 391). For its part, the Sudanese press largely ignored the developing famine in the south and its underlying causes. Its readership was largely northern and urban. Most papers were owned by the NIF and its sympathizers. A lesser number were owned by the Umma Party and the DUP; few were independent (*News from Africa Watch*, August 30, 1990, 2–10).

Instances of the collusion of northern local government authorities in raiding (and the securing of a share in the spoils) are mentioned by Mahmud and Baldo (1987, 19) in relation to Darfur, and by Ryle (1989b, 62) in relation to southern Kordofan. Militiamen moved freely through areas of southwestern Kordofan once controlled by the Ngok. By 1983–1984, local government no longer promoted intertribal meetings to settle disputes between Dinka and Baggara, although it continued to do so for disputes among Sudanese Arab groups (Africa Watch 1990, 81, 96). Meanwhile, tribal elders—many of whom opposed the raiding and gave sanctuary to displaced Dinka—appeared to lack the authority to stop the raids. While the tribal leaders of the Humr and the Ngok met in February 1986 and reached agreement on compensation for victims, this compensation was never forthcoming and raiding continued (Oxfam-UK 1986l). Similarly, leaders of the Rizeigat Arabs and the Malwal Dinka met in January 1988 in Khartoum, but again the initiative proved unable to control the raiders. The growth of the militias had itself contributed to a longer-term decline in tribal leaders' authority (Amnesty 1989, sec. 4.1).

While there were some protests from the regional government of Bahr el Ghazal against the northern militia raiding, these fell on deaf ears (Republic of Sudan/UNDP 1984, 58). The protests were in any case severely muffled by the subsequent ousting of Albino Akol, a Dinka, from the position of military governor. There were reports in early 1986 that police and wildlife forces were being expanded as a means of channeling arms to the Dinka and countering the increasingly northern national army (Oxfam-UK 1986a, 3). But subsequently northern troops were flown into Wau, restoring the northern dominance (Oxfam-UK 1986b, 1). With the civilian governor, William Ajal Deng, among a number of Bahr el Ghazal officials staying in Khartoum, the acting governor in 1987 was Darious Beshir Ali, from the Ngogo tribe of the Ferteet tribal group, which was increasingly in conflict with the Dinka. While the Dinka were strongly represented in the Wau police, they appeared to have inferior resources in their repeated conflicts with the army in Wau. The army was used in conjunction with Ferteet militias to carry out a series of atrocities on civilian Dinka (Alier 1990, 255).

Dinka famine migrants emphasized that they had no practical means of redress against the raiders. Manut, who had three daughters taken by raiders, said: "Afterwards, I thought of coming to the town and asked whether this thing (the raids) is known by the government or not. But when I came to the town, I found Arabs in jellabia and I kept silent." Others reported that when they complained to local police about being held captive with no pay, the police asked for a fee to file the case—money the Dinka did not have.

It is worth noting that during the famine, Dinka were commonly excluded not only from relevant political communities but even sometimes from the human community. Under the Turko-Egyptian administration, slaves had been legally classified as livestock. And Mahmud and Baldo noted that the existence of slavery in Rizeigat areas had helped generate beliefs in some quarters that the Dinka were subhuman (Mahmud and Baldo 1987, 21). The accounts of southern famine migrants make it clear that such dehumanizing tendencies were commonplace. One woman said that in the course of a multiple rape by her captives, she had been called a "black donkey" (Whittaker 1988, 71). One young Dinka man I spoke with in Meiram said he feared he would be killed if he were found talking to me, and we arranged to speak inside a hut at night. He said he had been beaten and showed me scars on his knees. He said that if Dinka are hit in Meiram, they could not make a legal case: they had "no rights" and were treated "like dogs." Branding of Dinka captives with cattle irons has been mentioned.

Such dehumanizing tendencies have commonly played a part in facilitating widespread violence against particular groups (see, e.g., Kuper 1981, 84–100). Indeed, the extreme brutality that occurred is only explicable in the context of dehumanizing the victims.

Mabor, from the village of Magondit in the Peth area, in northern Bahr el Ghazal, of Dinka chief Edward Arop Kwot, gave this account of how he came to leave his village:

> One evening I was in my place, called Magondit, and I heard guns in Nyamlell, and when I asked I was told the Arab murahaleen came, and I ran to Akwac Ngamb, and the murahaleen came to my place and they took two of my children. . . . Then they took eight people—the wife of this old man [at this point Mabor gestured towards his half-brother, Deng (name changed)], his five children, and one other woman. They put them in a lwac [cattle hut]. Then they burnt the lwac. Everyone was killed. Deng was in Safaha. He had left the area.

Mowier (name changed), a boy about eleven years of age, from Matwec, described his capture by northern militiamen and the killings which accompanied it:

I and my family came to Malwal to sell cows, and on the way back to Matwec, near Ariath railway station, I was captured by Arab militiamen. We were fifty-three in number. Forty were killed, and there remained thirteen. Some people were tied up and then they were slaughtered with knives. When some of the murahaleen men were killed, they [the murahaleen] came and killed some of the captured because they wanted revenge.

And Makwac, the fifty-five-year-old man who was castrated by his captors, said:

With my own eyes I have seen them [murahaleen] shooting 18 people of our tribe. They tied them to a tree and then shot them and laughed gleefully. I don't know what is in their mind to the extent that they laughed at seeing human blood.

The loss of rights on the part of the Dinka was very extreme, "democracy" notwithstanding.

## FAILURE OF MARKET STRATEGIES

The second process of famine was the failure of the victims' market strategies. These included the purchase of grain, the sale of livestock and the sale of labor. An analysis of changing prices in all these markets allows important insights into the evolution of the famine process, and to this extent the analysis here takes a lead from Sen's work. Transport prices were also important, something not stressed by Sen. A more fundamental departure from Sen's approach lies in the argument advanced here that these economic phenomena cannot be properly understood unless we analyze not only the political context in which prices were created but also the ways in which certain groups (with superior access to state power) were able actively to shape markets and to benefit from the price changes that accompanied famine. More specifically, the relevant markets cannot be understood in isolation from structures of political power, from the structure of laws and lawlessness operating in Sudanese society, or from the actual or threatened use of force.[69] Four main types of force are identified: raiding; intimidation and collusion in markets; the restriction of nonmarket survival strategies (which provided an alternative to market transactions); and the obstruction of relief. The impact of the first three types of force on markets is illustrated in Figure 1. It is also emphasized that the behavior of prices in one market (for example, the cattle market) could be influenced by trends (themselves in large part a response to the exercise of force) in other, related

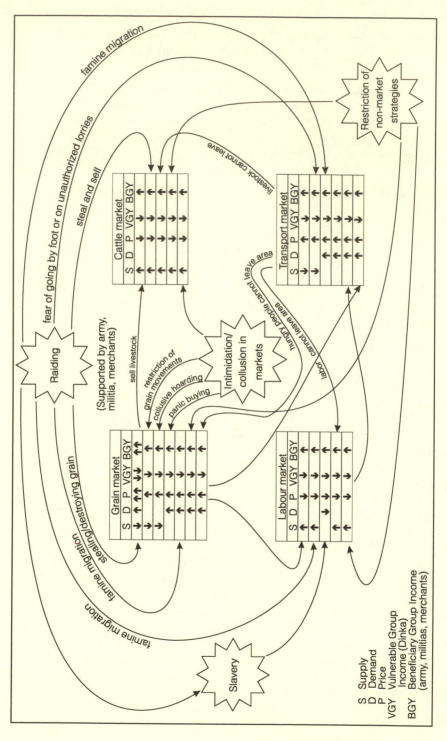

**Figure 1.** Forced Markets in Abyei Area Council

S   Supply
D   Demand
P   Price
VGY Vulnerable Group Income (Dinka)
BGY Beneficiary Group Income (army, militias, merchants)

markets (for example, the grain, labor, and transport markets). It is suggested that the concept of "market forces" is less helpful in understanding the famine than the concept of "forced markets." Foremost among the beneficiaries of these forced markets were merchants, army officers, and elements of the Baggara.

Not all the price movements accompanying famine were either anticipated or directly created by their beneficiaries. But such price movements did nevertheless constitute part of a complex exploitative system that was actively created by a variety of human actors who could reasonably have foreseen the profits—and the suffering—they would yield.

The use of force at one time also increased the opportunities for the subsequent use of force. In other words, as the processes of violence leading to famine deepened, as the "pressing down" of famine took effect,[70] it became progressively easier to exploit the victims of famine. In part, this was because people simply became physically weaker as famine deepened. Also important was the fact that raiding had tended to separate younger men from the rest of their families, creating a preponderance of women, young children, and older men among those migrating north (Interagency Situation Report 1988, 2). This can only have increased the vulnerability of migrants to the exercise of various kinds of force as they headed north. At the same time, as the famine's victims became poorer and weaker, they had increasingly little that was worth exploiting. It seems possible that this helped to facilitate the belated provision of relief, a point taken up in Chapter 4.

It is suggestive that, notwithstanding Sen's emphasis on market forces and the importance of a decline in demand for labor in particular, there was actually considerable demand for both the labor and the livestock of the Dinka in the areas to which they migrated in 1986–1988. This did not save them from deepening famine, however. This, in large part, was because labor and livestock markets were skewed by the exercise of various kinds of political force. One can go further: the substantial demand for Dinka labor and livestock (which tended to dry up in the initial phases of the second civil war) actually played a key role in driving the famine process in the first place. Famine helped renew the supply of labor and livestock, allowing the appropriation by a variety of relatively powerful groups of a greater share of the benefits of market transactions than was possible before the famine. While changes in market prices were an important cause of famine, they were also part of the function of famine.

These dynamics had also revealed themselves, although to a lesser extent, during the first civil war, when the exertion of force (including raiding) encouraged the Dinka and other southern Sudanese peoples to sell cattle and labor cheaply and to buy expensive grain. By contrast, from the 1920s, the British (and for a time in Ngokland, Deng Majok) had interfered in markets in a way that offered some protection for the Dinka against exploitation by northern merchants. A collapse of Dinka representation at the local and national levels, together with a developing alliance among herders, merchants, army personnel, and the central government, significantly altered the way these markets worked.

This analysis challenges neoclassical economic theory in important respects, in a context where the importance of "not interfering in the market" and the idea that markets somehow exist "outside politics" is still widely adhered to among international donors. In line with classical theory, merchant activities (buying cattle, selling grain) could mitigate famine in certain circumstances: as noted, drought-led food shortages in Bahr el Ghazal in the 1920s and 1930s were apparently exacerbated by political restrictions on northern traders. But critically, the profitability of famine for merchants—and their growing involvement in the grain and cattle trade (in association with army officers)—gave them an incentive to assist in the creation of famine in a number of ways. At the same time, the growing dependence of the south on northern grain increased the opportunities for creating famine in the south by restricting supplies of grain from the north.

Short-term economic benefits were derived from such price changes. The wider strategic and economic functions of debilitating the Dinka suggest that such price changes also contributed to a wider set of perceived benefits. Whether the manipulation of markets was intended as a weapon of war is not clear: sometimes, it was portrayed in this way, as when the Catholic bishop of Wau, Joseph Nyekindi, remarked in early 1989, "The market is the biggest gun in the war" (*Toronto Star*, March 25, 1989). The following discussion looks at the impact and genesis of price patterns in different (but related) markets, turning first to grain markets.

### Grain Markets

The intensity of the 1985–1989 famine appears to correlate strongly with high grain prices, both chronologically and geographically, although it is by no means easy to disentangle cause and effect. It seems likely that high grain prices tended to deepen famine (as grain was priced out of people's reach) and these high prices were also a consequence of famine (as influxes of famine migrants into particular towns boosted the demand for grain in those towns).

Although evidence of price patterns is somewhat sketchy, the pattern of grain prices during the famine appears to correspond in important respects to that predicted in a model developed by Peter Cutler in relation to Ethiopia. Cutler suggested that prices were likely to be highest at the epicenter of a famine, that is, where famine was most severe, and progressively lower as one moved away from this epicenter. Further, he suggested that, over time,

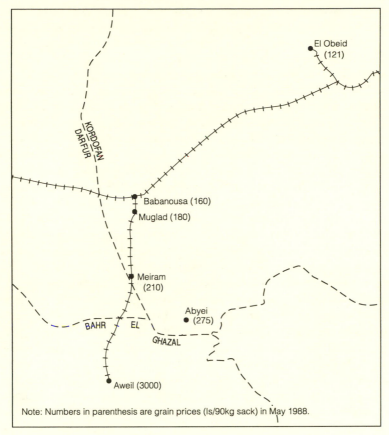

El Obeid
(121)

KORDOFAN
DARFUR

Babanousa (160)
Muglad (180)

Meiram
(210)

Abyei
(275)

BAHR    EL

GHAZAL

Aweil (3000)

Note: Numbers in parenthesis are grain prices (ls/90kg sack) in May 1988.

**Map 10**. Some Grain Prices in Kordofan and Bahr el Ghazal, May 1988
(Sud. £ ≠ 90-kilogram sack)

high prices were likely to spread outward from the epicenter, as grain was attracted to the area of severest famine while people moved away from this area, phenomena that would bring increased demand and reduced supply to an ever-wider area (Cutler 1984, 48–55).

In line with this model, prices in the south (where famine was far more severe) greatly exceeded those in the north. Further, these high prices in the south spread to some extent into southern Kordofan, notably in 1988, along with greatly increasing famine mortality and famine migration. Moreover, in 1988, grain prices within Kordofan were highest in the areas where famine mortality was most severe (Map 10). In May 1988, sorghum prices per sack in Abyei and Meiram were Sud. £250–300 and Sud. £210, respectively, while in more northerly Babanousa and Muglad (where famine mortality was lower), the prices were Sud. £160 and Sud. £180, respectively (Interagency Situation Report 1988, 7). In still more northerly El Obeid (where famine mortality was still lower), the price was only Sud. £121 (EWSB, June 15, 1988, 4). It is clear that the high price of grain in the south helped to raise prices in fringe areas, such as southern Kordofan—again, in line with Cutler's model. In the summer of 1988, grain was moving through the Meiram area, as merchants sought to take advantage of the Sud. £400/sack price in Malwal to the south (as well as much higher prices in some other parts of the south) (MSF-France 1988d). Further, prices in southern Kordofan also rose over time as famine intensified. Sorghum cost Sud. £110/sack in Meiram in September 1987 (UNICEF 1987a, 1). By August 1988, when famine mortality in Meiram was just past its peak, the price had reached Sud. £600/sack.[71] By September 18, 1988, when relief food had begun to arrive in Meiram and famine mortality had fallen significantly, the price of sorghum had fallen dramatically, to Sud. £120/sack.

It is important, nevertheless, to note that there were apparently substantial barriers to such ripple effects. In particular, the existence of sharply graded price-contours (see Map 10), together with the persistence of high prices in the south despite much lower prices in the north, suggested what many economists call "market failure" of some kind. It will be important to understand the causes of these persistent price differences.

Access to marketed grain was particularly important for those unable to obtain grain through exchange with nature. This included most of those living in government garrison towns and a great many of those who migrated to the north. People's dependence on army-controlled food supplies was exacerbated by the army's preventing people from moving outside the main towns of the south (Africa Watch 1990, 129–30) and from collecting wild foods. As grain prices escalated in urban centers, it became more and more difficult for the inhabitants to secure access to marketed grain. The acting governor of Bahr el Ghazal complained in early 1989: "The war is killing us with bullets and the merchants are killing us with their prices."[72]

Escalating grain prices accompanied growing famine mortality in southern garrison towns, with high grain prices appearing to reflect a combination of reduced supply and increased demand. There were serious food shortages in Aweil and Wau in 1986 (Aweil Rice Development Project 1987, 1). The food shortage in these towns grew more severe through 1987 and 1988. Many starved to death, while others fled north. Food shortages in Wau were becoming more and more acute in the spring of 1987,[73] and by March 1987 rice was priced at the equivalent of Sud. £720/sack. The gravity of the crisis in Wau came into sharp focus in the autumn of 1987: sorghum prices rose from Sud. £720/sack in October to Sud. £1,500 (if sorghum was available at all) in November, whereas the harvest would normally have caused a substantial price drop (RRC/EEC 1987; TCC meeting minutes, November 23, 1987, 2). On January 15, 1988, the acting governor of Bahr el Ghazal wrote to Prime Minister Sadiq el Mahdi: "We are alarmed by the gravity of famine situation in our Region. Right now, citizens are starving to death in the villages. Wau town has run out of essential items like grain. About this time last year over a thousand trucks loaded with food from production areas in the North had reached Wau. Until now there is not such a thing."[74]

It seems likely that raiding of areas north of Aweil had also helped raise prices in Wau: as noted, in favorable years this area's surplus regularly found markets in Wau. Prices in Wau remained high through the spring and summer.[75] Meanwhile, in Aweil in the summer of 1988, sorghum was priced as high as Sud. £3,000 per sack (TCC meeting minutes, September 5, 1988, 3).

Increased numbers of people in particular areas reflected to a large extent the impact of raiding. The loss of grain in raids inevitably increased demand for marketed grain. The reduction of supply stemmed to a large extent from the disruption of trade by civil war (combined with the south's growing dependence on northern grain). By the time of the famine, only a limited area of the south (including Renk and sometimes Kongor and Nasir and northern Aweil) produced a grain surplus, even in normal years, with most southern towns (and many rural areas in the preharvest period) depending on grain imports from the north. As southern towns were cut off from northern supply lines and in most cases from the surrounding rural areas, this disrupted both urban and rural economies (Ryle 1989a, 7; UN/SRRA 1990, field notes, interviews with Twic chiefs, May 10). Southern towns became unable to support their normal populations, irrespective of the displaced (Ryle 1989a, 16).

In part, the cutting off of southern garrison towns and the persistence of very high grain prices within Bahr el Ghazal were due to the SPLA, which attempted to place government-held garrison towns, such as Aweil and Wau, under siege. This meant blocking both commercial supplies and relief. For the SPLA, just as for the government, food was used as a weapon of war. The SPLA hoped to force surrender of the garrisons—not just Wau and Aweil but also Malakal in Upper Nile and Juba in Equatoria—and to force civilians in the towns to leave for the surrounding countryside.[76] In March 1984, the SPLA destroyed the railway bridge over the River Lol, between Aweil and Wau. The SPLA's shooting down of a civilian airliner at Malakal in 1986 brought an end to the ICRC airlift to Wau; no food was subsequently to be airlifted to southern towns other than Juba until December 1988 (Africa Watch 1990, 115–18). Increased SPLA control of Bahr el Ghazal in late 1987 added to the difficulty of getting food to Wau and Aweil.

Another major problem was the manipulation of supply by a variety of northern Sudanese interests profiting from exploitative trading. This strategy was facilitated by the south's dependence on northern grain. One of the main groups to benefit from high grain prices in the south was army officers. In many parts of the south, officers worked together with merchants to shape grain markets to their mutual advantage. The growing economic squeeze on army officers and merchants was noted in Chapter 2. Many officers and merchants found alternative profits in garrison town trading, using the army's control of movement in and out of these towns.[77] There were substantial opportunities for profit in grain and other foods (de Waal 1990a, 20).[78] The army was involved in the grain trade in all garrison towns, including Abyei, Wau, and Aweil (Africa Watch 1990, 130; *Independent*, March 3, 1989). In Aweil, the army enjoyed a monopoly of the sale of foodstuffs, and it was reported to be interested in maintaining a shortage of food for this reason (Aweil Rice Development Project 1987, 2). It was significant that trains from Babanousa to Aweil, which carried merchants' goods as well as some relief supplies, did not move from Babanousa without the consent and active cooperation of the army. In addition to profits made by army officers in Aweil, both soldiers and policemen profited from escort duties on trains carrying commercial goods from Babanousa to Aweil (Wannop 1989, 9). In Wau, too, the army was able to manipulate food prices to its own advantage, controlling at least some of the shops, levying a tax on all grain coming into the town, and a further tax on grain sold in Dinka parts of the town, where famine conditions were worst (*Toronto Star*, March 25, 1989; Africa Watch 1990, 119, 130; de Waal 1990a, 20). The army did little to facilitate commercial shipments into Wau, and when it did offer protection to commercial convoys, it charged a high price for the service (*Toronto Star*, March 25, 1989).[79] The threat of SPLA attack and the consequent need for military escorts for deliveries of grain and other supplies gave the army a great deal of influence in shaping the pattern of food deliveries, as well as providing army officers with a justification for the lack of deliveries that underpinned their own profits (Africa Watch 1990, 134). Meanwhile, the army and northern militias placed restrictions on traders (some from the south, some from the north) who tried to move food from northern Sudan into rural areas of Bahr el Ghazal (UN/SRRA 1990, 55). These various kinds of political influences help to explain why price differences between the south and the north were so extreme and persistent, notwithstanding a degree of demand failure in the south, of which starvation was graphic evidence. While this can be interpreted as evidence of "market failure," it should be noted that what represented failure from the point of view of famine victims (and perhaps of economists evaluating the benevolence of the market) nevertheless represented success for beneficiary groups.

Significantly, army measures that restricted the availability of grain in garrison towns did not threaten the army's own consumption.[80] It is clear that the military were able to feed themselves in the main southern towns (de Waal 1990a, 12).

The involvement of northern merchants in shaping, and benefiting from, high grain prices has been briefly mentioned. In theory, grain prices were limited by administrative controls.[81] In practice, merchants were often able to use their local political influence (and sometimes the threat of withholding stocks completely) to circumvent these regulations. Indeed, administrative controls on trading (such as licenses) had often in the past encouraged monopolistic trading, with local officials who granted licenses and favored traders sometimes able to share the benefits of such arrangements (Woodward 1990, 125). During the famine, merchants were able to use their influence over town authorities to regulate the movement of goods between one area and another. They were well connected with all the major political parties: Umma, DUP, and NIF (Woodward 1990, 209; Duffield 1990a, 16; Mahmoud 1984, 127–48). The strong local political connections of merchants in western Sudan, and their oligopolistic behavior, have been well documented (Abakr and Pool 1980, 185–98; see Chapter 2). In a sense, official collusion in the profiteering of merchants during the famine was an extension and distortion of previously existing practices: the benefits extracted by merchants and officials from forced markets were an extension of long-standing attempts to carve out a sphere of control in the marketplace.

Merchants were involved in delivering commercial goods to Aweil by train (see Chapter 4), and were able to maintain high prices by restricting the quantities delivered. The composition of the cargo carried by the trains from Babanousa was decided by a combination of local merchants, the town councils in Babanousa and Muglad, and the army. The railway trade had considerable political and economic barriers to entry: perhaps five or six merchants in Babanousa had sufficient funds, reported to me as Sud. £20,000, to be able to afford to pay the town councils for permission to take goods by train.[82] It is important to recognize that such restrictions did not bring benefits to all merchants, but rather tended to restrict the benefits of trading to a privileged and wealthy few. The very large and persistent price differences between Bahr el Ghazal garrison towns and northern Sudan thus appear to have reflected not simply transport and security difficulties but also the restriction of supply to Bahr el Ghazal by groups who stood to benefit from it.

At the end of May 1988, merchants with grain in Abyei were holding back most of their stocks (at least three hundred metric tons). Indeed, the Farmer's Association in Abyei, which controlled the grain stocks and in which merchants were heavily represented, was refusing to sell to the displaced (Africa Watch 1990, 130). Visiting aid agency staff reported that stocks were being held back in anticipation of an influx of cattle from Bahr el Ghazal (for which grain would be exchanged at rates favorable to northern merchants) (Interagency Situation Report 1988, 2). The higher the price of grain in Abyei, the more cattle famine migrants would have to sell to obtain their subsistence. It has been argued that grain storage may reflect traders' assumption of future price rises (and future scarcity) and that such storage may actually reduce famine by rationing current consumption (Ravallion 1985, 15). Given the extreme malnutrition and already high mortality rates in Abyei at this time, it is difficult to imagine that withholding grain from the market can have conferred any benefits on the Dinka. It seems likely, moreover, that withholding grain from the market was not simply a response to expected price increases but also a *cause* of such increases. Merchants' involvement in funding raiding and impeding relief also suggest that they were actively shaping price movements, rather than simply responding to them.[83]

To the north, Babanousa-based merchants with grain in Meiram were also reported to be reluctant to release grain from their stores (minutes of aid coordination meeting held at Concern office, May 27, 1988). It is clear that there were significant quantities of grain in private merchants' stores in Meiram during August 1988, notwithstanding the extremely high mortality in the town (ibid.). As noted above, merchants were able to exercise considerable control over the movement of grain by rail to Meiram from Babanousa. This was the only route open during the rainy season. During more normal years, small quantities of grain would be moved into Meiram from mechanized farming areas and El Obeid in March and April, allowing substantial profits (for Babanousa merchants with agents in Meiram) during the summer, when many small farmers begin to run out of their own grain. In 1988, with sorghum selling for Sud. £600/sack (more than seven times the price in December 1987), these profits must have been considerable. In September, there was still extraordinarily high mortality in Meiram, but grain actually moved away from the town in response to commercial considerations. Private grain moved north out of Meiram towards Muglad in September by train, as strong pressure from international donors led to the arrival of significant relief grain, prompting prices in Meiram to collapse from more than Sud. £600/sack in August to Sud. £120/sack on September 18 (a price lower than that in Muglad at this time) (MSF-France 1988j). A number of factors suggest oligopolistic behavior: the suddenness of the price collapse; the fact that merchants were clearly taken by surprise at the arrival of grain and falling prices in Meiram; the evident ability of merchants to respond quickly to price differences by shipping grain between Meiram and Muglad; and the relatively small numbers of merchants involved in the rail grain trade.

Meanwhile, in Babanousa, senior town officials reported that the summer of 1988 saw merchants speculating on grain price rises as famine migrants flooded into the town. Merchants would close their shops to stimulate panic buying, propelling prices higher (interview with Abdulla Arabi, administrative officer, Babanousa Town Council, Babanousa, November 30, 1988).

In contrast to northern merchants, southern famine migrants lacked any significant access to state power in the north, and their leverage in shaping prices was virtually nonexistent. They were not in a position to make payments to government officials, nor were they part of the constituency of local politicians in the north. They generally found very little government employment (see, e.g., Mahmud and Baldo 1987, 3).

Famine migrants' lack of political muscle was on occasion graphically illustrated by prohibitions on the purchase of grain. For example, Dinka were banned from buying grain in Aweil in early 1988 and in Meiram in mid-1988 (de Waal 1990, 23). It seems possible that these bans arose in large part from the fact that prices had risen to such high levels as to threaten the access to food of resident populations.[84] The bans on grain sales contrast with earlier bans effected by the Ngok chief Deng Majok, which had been designed to mitigate the suffering of Dinka forced to sell their grain to northern merchants. The susceptibility of markets in this area to political manipulation was not new. What was new was the way these markets were now manipulated exclusively for the benefit of non-Dinka groups.

### Cattle Markets

Another set of market transactions of critical importance in the famine process was the sale of cattle. As noted in Chapter 2, this was one of the principal ways in which the Dinka had, in the past, obtained grain during times of food shortage. For those trekking north, the towns of Safaha and Abyei became key centers for selling livestock. But just when grain prices were rising, livestock prices were declining.

In Abyei, the price of cattle in relation to the price of grain reached a nadir in 1987, when the numbers of cattle being taken out of the south (by raiders and famine migrants) peaked. In July and August of 1987, cattle were being exchanged for a single 90-kilogram bag of sorghum. By May 1988, as the flow of cattle from Bahr el Ghazal diminished somewhat, cattle were still being sold for the equivalent of only 0.8–2.4 sacks of sorghum, depending on the condition of the cattle. Agencies reported that cattle were fetching only 30 percent of their normal value in Abyei at this time (Interagency Situation Report 1988, 2–8). Prices were also considerably lower than elsewhere in the north. While livestock prices in Abyei were in the region of Sud. £220–660,[85] in El Obeid, to the north, prices were averaging Sud. £1,717.

Again, these price trends, though they helped to create famine, and indeed constituted a part of the famine process, yielded important benefits for groups who helped to create the price movements.[86] With cattle being exchanged in Abyei in July–August 1987 for no more than a single sack of grain, the potential profits for those able to sell grain and buy cattle (later sold for meat) were very great. The cattle/grain price ratio in El Obeid, the major livestock and grain market of Kordofan, was around 27:1 at this time.[87] Thus, the grain-purchasing power of those with cattle was a remarkable twenty-seven times better in El Obeid than in Abyei. In 1988, as the flow of livestock into Abyei dwindled and the 1987 drought in western Sudan boosted local grain prices, the contrast was less extreme, but still dramatic. In Abyei, as noted, cattle were being exchanged in May 1988 for something between 0.8 and 2.4 sacks of sorghum. Meanwhile, in El Obeid, the cattle/grain price ratio had diminished somewhat, to 14:1.[88] The ratio of cattle prices for El Obeid:Abyei was around 4:1.[89] Meanwhile, the costs of driving cattle north still allowed substantial profits: even in 1980, with cattle prices in Omdurman around three times cattle prices in Abyei, a small-scale trader could realize a net profit (after losses en route and expenses) representing 200 percent of his original investment, and large-scale traders could realize profits between 200 and 300 percent (Niamir, Huntington, and Cole 1983, 27–28). Both merchants (Baggara and non-Baggara) and army personnel benefited from this trade, an alliance originally fostered by Dinka resistance to livestock trading in the late 1970s.

Even before the second civil war, it was virtually impossible for Dinka to break into the lucrative business of driving cattle north from Abyei. In particular, they lacked the financing to do so, and they lacked the necessary connections and government support (including army support). Thus, the substantial peacetime profits from this trade were reserved for Sudanese Arab traders. With the increased army involvement in livestock trading, increased militia activity, and diminished resources among the Dinka, the moving of large numbers of cattle by Dinka to El Obeid or other northern markets to take advantage of the high interregional price variations was now all the more impractical. A system of commerce that was exploitative even in normal times had now become still more exploitative. Benefits that were described as a bonanza in 1980 had now escalated further, and they were still reserved for northern traders.

Just as with grain, the livestock price changes that were contributing to famine among the Dinka cannot be adequately explained by reference to "market forces." Livestock markets were skewed by the exercise of force, or threatened force, at a number of different levels.

Of prime importance here was raiding. This had helped to create the major outpouring of people and livestock in the first place, and had helped reduce famine migrants to a state where they were desperate to sell livestock in order to buy grain. Raiding had also led to the sale of raided cattle in markets where Dinka were trying to sell their remaining cattle, helping to lower the price the Dinka could obtain. Police action against the sale of raided cattle, although promoted by Dinka policemen, was generally weak (Oxfam-UK 1986l). Significantly, the chief beneficiaries of livestock price changes had contributed to the raiding. It is clear that livestock traders provided financing for the murahaleen raids. For example, merchants in Ed Daien—one of the two biggest cattle markets in Darfur and an important market for stolen cattle—provided money for guns and ammunition for Rizeigat militias (Oxfam-UK 1986j, 5; Mahmud and Baldo 1987, 2).[90] Meanwhile, the benefits reaped by army personnel were matched by army involvement in the raiding. A second major set of political influences on live-stock markets were the abovementioned barriers to the movement of cattle to markets further north, in particular, the necessity of gaining the coopera-tion both of local authorities (in which merchants were influential) and of the army. A third set of influences was the use of intimidation in towns where livestock were sold. In the early days of raiding, Abyei and Safaha served primarily as centers for the resale of raided cattle; later, they were the focus of cattle sales by Dinka, with soldiers and merchants forcing such sales at below-market rates. One practice was that a soldier would force a Dinka migrant to write to a relative in Bahr el Ghazal, encouraging the relative to bring cattle to Abyei for sale. These cattle would then be bought cheaply under coercion, or simply confiscated (de Waal 1990a, 17–23).

As noted in Chapter 2, merchants were under pressure from the loss of trade to the south, from attacks on trade (for example, in the Abyei area), from the drying up of supplies of southern labor, and from high interest rates. The famine appears to have played a part in relieving these pressures.

Livestock markets were influenced by other (manipulable) markets as well as by degrees of access to nonmarket strategies (again, manipulable). For example, the higher the price of grain in Abyei, and the greater the difficulty of leaving Abyei by foot (because of militia activities and restric-tions on taking grain out of the town, to cite two factors), the more livestock the famine migrants would be forced to sell in order to escape from Abyei.

### Markets for Other Assets

Other forms of asset selling were of potential significance for famine victims. For example, the displaced in Safaha made and sold grass mats to try to raise money that would permit them to continue their journey north by truck. Even in such small-scale enterprises, however, the terms of trade were highly exploitative. Grass mats sold in Safaha to Rizeigat agents for Sud. £1 were resold further north for Sud. £4.50 (Sudanaid 1988, 4). Similarly, cheaply priced wood, hides, and handicrafts in Aweil, while providing a limited income for impoverished people in Aweil, offered an important source of profit for soldiers and policemen bringing them north on return train trips to Babanousa (Wannop 1989, 9).

### Labor Markets

By the mid-1980s migrant labor had become an increasingly important strat-egy for combating famine among the Dinka—but during the famine it was difficult to secure subsistence through selling labor. An important reason was that in 1987 and 1988, labor markets were distorted (and labor rates diminished) as raiding and resultant famine sent large numbers of migrants north into southern Darfur and southern Kordofan (de Waal 1990a, 24). The threat of attack or capture for those attempting to move on further north (and the restricted transport market) boosted the local supplies of labor and inevitably reduced its price. Labor markets were further distorted by the threat of violence to many Dinka workers held in conditions of slavery or near-slavery. Even where there were no such threats, the availability of slave labor must have tended to depress labor rates.

One significant focus of laboring was the southern Kordofan town of Meiram, where various forms of employment had been traditionally available to migrant Dinka. In October 1987, some eight thousand to ten thousand displaced people were living in Meiram, mostly working as sharecroppers or wage workers on the groundnut farms of local people. The rewards of such work, however, were clearly insufficient for their welfare. Despite the availability of work during the harvest, the condition of these people was evidently poor: between four hundred and five hundred patients a day were attending the UNICEF health center in Meiram for various kinds of treatment.[91]

Farm labor was again available around Meiram in 1988. A seasonal movement of the displaced to and from outlying farms was reported (Ryle 1989a, 16). But many of these workers received no wages: there were numerous reports of displaced people getting only food, and of poor working conditions. At the beginning of November 1988, a steady succession of sick Dinka were arriving back in the camp from surrounding farms, where illness had rendered them of no further use to the farmers for whom they were working (MSF-France 1988l). Farm work was similarly available around Muglad and Babanousa, but in November 1988, some fifty people a day were arriving in Muglad camp, many of them reporting that they had fled from mistreatment on local farms (Concern 1988f). Many families were unable to secure farm labor in the first place because they were families headed by women committed to staying with young children (CARE 1988; SCF-UK 1988; Ryle 1989a, 27). This, in turn, reflected the substantial risk of violence and death faced by any younger men who headed north from Bahr el Ghazal.

Meanwhile, the potential earning power of older children often counted for little. In southern Kordofan, many desperate parents had given away their children—or sold them, as cow and goat tenders or domestic help (Ryle 1989b, 67; Amnesty 1989, sec. 2.2). Similar transactions took place in Safaha, Darfur, as famine migrants tried to raise the money to escape Safaha by truck (interview with Aloung Jereboum Macour, SCF-UK, Adila, December 3, 1988; Sudanaid 1988, 5; Oxfam-UK 1988a). One report suggested that Sud. £37 was a typical price paid in such sales.[92] The political context of this famine thus shaped not only the price at which commodities were sold but also conceptions of what might legitimately count as a "commodity."

Clearly, as with livestock prices, reduced and low wages were only detrimental for some people. In fact, while they contributed to the severity of famine, they provided substantial benefits for those who were able to mobilize this cheap labor, serving to relieve a number of economic pressures on these groups. Moreover, many of the groups who benefited were also involved in creating famine and in actively distorting markets to their own advantage.

Many in the north had become increasingly dependent on continuing supplies of southern labor, but the early stages of the second civil war had resulted in a drying up of supplies of migrant labor from the south. In the Meiram area in 1988, local farmers complained of a labor shortage. This was apparently made worse by widespread malaria, which debilitated local people at a time when they needed to be working their fields. Local people expressed the importance to them of obtaining Dinka labor, and these concerns were echoed by farmers elsewhere in some of the major production areas.[93] An additional problem was that cash crop farmers were under pressure to grow more because of rising grain prices, while those growing peanuts—a key crop in the Meiram area and throughout much of southern Kordofan and southern Darfur—found the price of their product was stagnant between 1987 and 1988 (SCF-UK/Oxfam-UK 1988b; el Khalifa et al. 1985, 36).

The cheap labor of famine migrants and captured Dinka offered a partial solution to these problems, although the extent to which large-scale famine migration to northern Sudan was specifically intended remains a moot point. Nevertheless, the presence of Dinka famine migrants appears to have helped relieve certain economic pressures by reducing outlays for portering, wood collecting, and other low-status tasks.[94] There were reports that many groundnut farmers made use of forced labor/slavery. These farmers appear not to have been much involved in sponsoring raiding, although there were reports of Berti involvement in raiding near Aweil (de Waal 1990a, 17; interview with Garang Anai, acting chief, Adila settlement, southern Darfur, December 3, 1988). The potential value of the famine migrants to resident farmers was underlined by Dinka reports that they had been told by Sudanese Arab farmers not to try to return to Bahr el Ghazal (Ryle 1989a, 10).

The resurgence of slavery during the famine reflected northerners' perceived need for cheap southern labor. It is clear from the accounts of those held in captivity that the threat and use of physical force underpinned arrangements in which work was performed for no pay. One elderly woman, thin and painfully fragile-looking, told me that after she had been captured and taken to Meiram, her "master" threatened to kill her if she did not do housework sufficiently quickly. After finishing this unpaid work, she would go every day to Meiram market to beg for peanuts.

Famine migrants were sometimes forcibly removed from camps in southern Kordofan, often to work for no money. One woman told me three of her children—aged nine, five, and three-and-a-half—had been taken from Meiram camp in this way. She said she did not know where they were, but added, "If I knew, I would go there and get them back, or be killed myself."

Another woman said she had refused to be taken away from Meiram camp to work, since her previous mistreatment by northern captors had convinced her to stay in the camp. On November 2, 1988, when many of the inhabitants of the Meiram camp were beginning to regain their strength, soldiers of the Sudanese army came to the camp and took away several hundred relatively healthy Dinka to work on farms in the area (MSF-France 1988l). In theory, the police were supposed to supervise contracts of employment between the Dinka and the respective farmers, but no such contracts were made. In Muglad town, with the army pressing for the approximately five hundred men in the camp to work, a group of armed farmers came to the camp to obtain laborers from among the famine migrants. Agency staff reported that those who left the camp to work were not being paid (interview with Bridgette Quirk, Concern, Muglad, November 27, 1988; interview with Roland Roome, CARE, Muglad, November 28, 1988).

In the political and security context of southern Kordofan in 1988, wages could even be negative. One Sudanese Arab farmer took on a Dinka man from Aweil with the understanding that he should work for him once they reached the farmer's home area. However, it was the Dinka who paid his employer (Sud. £20)—for protection en route.

### *Transport Markets*

Another survival strategy involving market transactions was the attempt to purchase transportation to regions with superior security and access to food (and other necessities). The importance of entitlement to transportation is not mentioned by Sen, a silence in keeping with his tendency to play down the importance of local as well as national food availability declines in causing famine.[95] However, while a lack of money and assets increased the vulnerability of some famine migrants in relation to others (in line with Sen's analysis), this was very often because it prevented some famine migrants from moving to better-provisioned (and also safer) areas.

Many of the displaced in Safaha, Abyei, and Meiram were without money and unable to afford fares for truck or train rides north. Truck fares from these areas rose during the famine (Interagency Situation Report 1988, 3). Rail fares were supposed to be fixed by the state, yet these also rose to unusually high levels, affecting those trying to get out of Aweil and Meiram.[96] Others could afford train and truck fares, and were able to pass quickly through Abyei and/or Meiram to Muglad and cities in northern Sudan, or through Safaha to Ed Daien.[97]

Trends in transport prices, though they helped exacerbate famine, were actually beneficial for some groups. And again, it was not simply "market forces" that raised these prices beyond what many famine migrants could afford. The supply of such transportation was artificially restricted, as only certain trucks were "authorized" for the transport of famine migrants. Demand for such transportation had been initially boosted by raiding and consequent hardship. It was further artificially increased by the high grain prices in Abyei and by restrictions on the purchase of grain other than that for consumption within Abyei town itself (Interagency Situation Report 1988, 6). This made it more difficult for people to make their own way from Abyei. The likelihood of experiencing further militia attacks was a further disincentive to travel on foot, and hence a further incentive to travel by truck. Those on unprotected trucks were very vulnerable to attack (Africa Watch 1990, 89).

Both merchants and army officers profited from the high price of travel on "authorized" trucks (de Waal 1990a, 23). Meanwhile, policemen and soldiers made substantial profits from famine migrants seeking a train ride north from Aweil to Babanousa (Wannop 1989, 9).

## FAILURE OF NONMARKET STRATEGIES

The failure of nonmarket survival strategies was another critical element in the evolution of the famine process. These strategies included securing access to nonmarket foods and walking to safer, better-provisioned areas.

Deng's study of the Dinka makes clear the traditional role of nonmarket survival strategies, as well as the increasing shift from reliance on wild foods, milk, and meat in times of shortage to reliance on bought grain. To a limited extent, nonmarket strategies still offered valuable protection during the famine. There was widespread resort to lalob leaves and wild grain in response to raids in northern Bahr el Ghazal (Ryle 1989a, 20; UNDP 1988b, annex 2). And once people had been uprooted to Abyei, catching fish was reported to be more important in saving people's lives during the rains of 1988 than famine relief (Ryle 1989b, 84). People in Abyei also ate the boiled leaves of the baoab and hejlij (Interagency Situation Report 1988, 7). Seeking assistance from kin or tribes with whom there had been intermarriage was also an important strategy (UN/SRRA 1990). Many Dinka leaving Bahr el Ghazal for Darfur attached themselves to small communities of Dinka permanent migrants who had moved to Darfur villages before 1984. The number outside displaced settlements probably exceeded the number in them (Ryle 1989a, 22).

However, the usefulness of these strategies was severely constrained in the context of the famine, notably by the use of force on the part of famine's beneficiaries. This, as discussed in Chapter 2, had also been the case to some extent during the first civil war.

The negative impact of cattle raiding on such nonmarket strategies as borrowing cattle and consuming milk and meat has been mentioned. In addition, there were a number of impediments to fishing and gathering wild foods. For example, military permission for collecting wild foods around Abyei was withheld, and wild foods had to be bought in the market (Interagency Situation Report 1988, 7–8). In parts of Darfur, local Rizeigat people banned Dinka migrants from collecting wild foods and from cutting and selling firewood; sometimes wood was confiscated by armed locals (de Waal 1990a, 23–24; testimony of displaced Dinka). Fishing among the Twic—who traditionally had exchanged the fish they caught for grain from western Bahr el Ghazal—was restricted by the physical dangers of going to the Bahr el Arab River (UN/SRRA 1990, 54, 57). Meanwhile, the potential value of fish in Abyei was reduced by the theft of Dinka nets by Nuer boys (Ryle 1989b, 88). Fish in a seasonal lake 3 miles from Aweil could not be caught because of security restrictions on movement outside the town (UNDP 1988, 6).

Further, during the famine, moving by foot was very hazardous, and subject to considerable official control. This made it more difficult for people to reach places where food, cash, and/or relatives were more plentiful. Anyanya 2 militiamen killed Dinka migrants crossing Zeraf Island on their way to Ethiopia. Dinka migrants, especially men, were often killed attempting to leave Wau and Aweil; the area east of Wau was declared a free fire zone, and the army cleared trees and shrubs around the town so that the soldiers could see any SPLA units, as well as any townspeople, who were trying to leave (Africa Watch 1990, 130; de Waal 1990a, 23).[98]

In northern Sudan, many of the famine migrants trapped in Abyei and Meiram in 1988 were deterred from walking north by the threat of militia attacks en route, or by the army itself. Seven people were shot by the army and fifty arrested while trying to take food out of Abyei (Interagency Situation Report 1988, 2, 7). When the Catholic church in Abyei tried to help people leave the town with grants of money, it was accused of helping SPLA saboteurs (Africa Watch 1990, 129). In the summer of 1988, as the numbers of famine migrants in Muglad mounted, the Babanousa-based first executive officer for the Abyei area council, Salah Ahmed Nasser, refused a request by the Muglad town council to transport these people to Babanousa (Concern 1988c; MSF-France 1988b). When relief trains belatedly arrived in Meiram in early September, famine migrants were barred from taking the empty trains returning to Babanousa, despite pressure from the Meiram relief committee (MSF-France 1988i).[99] When one train arrived in Meiram, more than three thousand people attempted to board it in the hope of obtaining a ride to the north. In the end, only three hundred were allowed to board. Of these, twenty were found dead on the train when it arrived in Muglad (*Sudan Times*, September 6, 1988). Allegations that the police had taken people off trains were confirmed to the writer by famine migrants, who said some of those removed had already paid the fare.

Again, the "failure" of nonmarket survival strategies conferred important benefits. There were important military benefits in restricting these non-market strategies, notably the control of Dinka movements and the deepening of the process of debilitation among the Dinka. Of particular importance were the perceived security gains in restricting the movement of people between government-controlled towns and surrounding rural areas, where the rebels exerted greater control. This common antiinsurgency tactic echoed similar practices during the first civil war (Wai 1973, 103). It also represented an attempt by the government to ensure that substantial civilian populations remained under its control, just as part of the aim of the SPLA was to drive populations into areas under *its* control by blockading garrison towns. The government's control of civilian populations also created the possibility of using them as a human shield against SPLA attack. Some Dinka expressed the fear that those in camps or settlements would be subject to violence in revenge for any killings of northern Sudanese by the SPLA further south (interview with Garang Anai, settlement leader, Adila, southern Darfur, December 1988).[100] It is quite possible that restricting movement served a function in creating a "hostage" population.

There were also political gains from the prevention of the movement of hungry people to places where they would be more visible to the foreign press and international donors. Strict controls on movements of the displaced by train date from the arrival in Khartoum, on April 24, 1988, of a train from Aweil with seven thousand displaced people. Six children had died at Khartoum railway station, and the publicity surrounding the train embarrassed the government (*Sudan Times*, May 11, 1988). No further trains left Aweil until 1989.

Restricting the movement of famine migrants also promised to keep them away from major towns, where they were likely to put pressure on the scarce resources of local people and to pose a significant health threat to residents.[101] The refusal by the executive officer in Babanousa to grant permission for people to move from Muglad to Babanousa should be seen in the context of widespread fears that the resources of Babanousa would be stretched to breaking point if the famine migrants were allowed to come (interview with Abdulla Arabi, administrative officer, Babanousa Town Council, Babanousa, November 30, 1988).

Finally, there were also significant economic benefits: the more that nonmarket strategies were constricted, the more necessary it became for famine migrants to enter into (exploitative) market transactions (whether in grain, livestock, labor, or transport markets). Although the intentions behind constricting nonmarket strategies appear to have been complex, one of the foreseeable effects was to increase the profits from market transactions (see Figure 1). Army personnel, who played the key role in enforcing restrictions on nonmarket strategies, were benefiting from these market transactions, as we have seen.

## Survival Strategies: A Comparison

The influence of political factors on the success or failure of market and nonmarket strategies (as well as on vulnerability to asset theft in the north) is brought into sharp focus by comparing the experience of the Dinka with that of Nuer groups who were affiliated to the government-backed Anyanya 2 in Upper Nile and who were driven into southern Kordofan by the SPLA. In the summer and autumn of 1988, the Nuer were generally in a much better state of health than were other southern Sudanese, notably the Dinka (Ryle 1989b, 88). Moreover, the Nuer continued to keep hold of cattle in the Abyei area (indeed, they often increased their stock), again in sharp contrast to the Dinka (Ryle 1989b, 88; *New York Times*, October 16, 1988). One factor that appears to have helped the Nuer was the fact that their family units were largely maintained through their northward migration, with younger men not shying away from southern Kordofan out of fear of death, as was to a large extent the case among the Dinka (interview with Bridgette Quirk, Concern, Muglad, November 27, 1988). This helped insulate the Nuer to some extent from the exploitation (and accompanying lack of access to wage work) that was frequently the lot of female-headed Dinka families. Importantly, Nuer family members were also protected by safe passes from the government, and many of them were armed (ibid.; Ryle 1989b, 88). In Abyei, indeed, young Nuer men had a machine gun emplacement pointing directly into the Abyei marketplace, a graphic illustration of the fact that markets were not governed by "market forces" alone. Nuer boys exploited their access to arms and government support to loot Dinka in Abyei. This included the theft of the Dinka's fishing nets (Ryle 1989b, 88; *New York Times*, October 16, 1988). It was, thus, not the fact of displacement that determined famine migrants' fate but, to a large extent, their political status in the north, and particularly their perceived relationship to the SPLA.

## CHAPTER 4

# The Inadequacy of Relief:
# A "Policy Success" for Powerful
# Groups in Sudan?

THE FOURTH process creating famine was the "failure" of famine relief—a "failure" that actually served important functions for politically powerful groups in Sudan.[1] Sen has stressed that market mechanisms cannot be relied upon to distribute even abundant food resources in ways that prevent famine. Evidence presented here suggests that the same is true of institutional mechanisms. The inability of particular groups to command food reflected not simply a lack of purchasing power within the market but also a lack of lobbying power within local institutions, particularly in relation to the beneficiaries of famine.

## THE INADEQUACY OF RELIEF

Relief provision to those suffering from the famine was gravely insufficient, contributing to very high malnutrition and mortality. By the time of the famine, traditional local systems of famine relief had been to some extent eroded by long-term political and economic developments. For the most part, these traditional systems were not replaced by significant international or state relief. Although the famine evolved over a period of several years, relief distributions began to approach substantial levels only after the worst of the famine (that is, after the summer and autumn of 1988, when extraordinary death rates were recorded in Meiram, Abyei and Aweil).[2] Not only did this directly deprive people of food; it also meant that the market processes creating famine were allowed to proceed virtually unchecked. In addition, since the lack of relief forced many to leave their home areas, the ability of famine victims to maintain their assets and production was greatly impeded. The fact that the limited supplies of relief were concentrated on government-held towns, neglecting rural areas, not only helped to undermine rural economic life but also added greatly to people's exposure to disease in overcrowded urban areas. This can only have greatly exacerbated famine mortality (cf. deWaal 1989a; African Rights 1993, 17, 49).

**TABLE 1**
Relief to Bahr el Ghazal, 1986–1989 (mt)

| Year | Relief | Year | Relief |
|------|--------|------|--------|
| 1986 | 2,140[a] | 1988 | 1,298[c] |
| 1987 | 4,000[b] | 1989 (up to June 21) | 13,514[d] |

*Sources:*1986: Minear 1991, 8. 1987: EC 1987f; Symonds 1987; TCC meeting minutes, November 9, 1987, 2. 1988: EWSB, September 15, 1988; Bonner 1989, 89; Wannop 1989, 5. 1989: USAID 1989, 6; Minear 1991, 7.

[a]This quantity represents 2,000 metric tons delivered to Wau plus 140 metric tons of confirmed relief food to Aweil. There may have been other small quantities, but the figure is approximately correct.

[b]Although 8,843 metric tons were delivered to Raga, most of this was stolen or destroyed. The TCC figure for relief to Bahr el Ghazal was 3,000 metric tons (plus the grain in Raga).

[c]This quantity represents deliveries up to September 18. Only very small amounts were delivered subsequently, in small-scale airlifts in December.

[d]Some 111,654 metric tons were delivered to the south as a whole by the end of 1989.

Table 1 shows approximate quantities of emergency food aid delivered to Bahr el Ghazal between 1986 and 1989. Before 1986, there were no significant international relief efforts to the south.[3] Levels of need in 1986–1988 in particular far exceeded deliveries. In early 1986, the Sudan Council of Churches estimated that 187,000 people in the Aweil and Gogrial districts alone were affected by hunger (Sudan Council of Churches 1986). At a standard ration of 500 grams of grain a day, such a population would need 34,128 metric tons to survive for a year. This compares with just over 2,000 metric tons administered to the whole of Bahr el Ghazal.

The discussion in this chapter concentrates on relief to government-held areas. But it is important to record that, for the most part, international relief to rebel-held areas was simply not attempted. Within Bahr el Ghazal, relief deliveries were concentrated on the government garrison towns of Aweil and Wau,[4] but even deliveries to these towns proved small in relation to needs.

Trains to Aweil were dispatched from Babanousa, in southern Kordofan, but little grain reached Aweil in 1986.[5] As for Wau, an operation by the agency World Vision aimed to provide the town with some 2,000 metric tons of relief (Minear 1991, 8). However, much of the relief arriving in Wau did not reach the intended beneficiaries (de Waal 1990a, 21).

Relief deliveries to Bahr el Ghazal in 1987 were extremely inadequate in relation to an increasing need. With the United Nations estimating that

690,000 people were at risk of famine in Bahr el Ghazal at the end of 1986, an aid agency/UN team[6] estimated that 38,250 metric tons would be required for Bahr el Ghazal to cover just the first six months of 1987 (EWSB, March 15, 1987, 3). This figure dwarfs the 4,000 metric tons of relief administered in the whole of 1987.

In 1987, Aweil town was again a key focus of relief operations, with some fifty thousand displaced people in the town by August. Despite this level of need, transport by air was deemed impossible,[7] and deliveries by rail to Aweil were once again extremely low. The total relief grain arriving in and purchased in Aweil was only 690 metric tons—enough to feed the estimated fifty thousand displaced people for less than a month.[8]

The second main focus of Bahr el Ghazal relief operations in 1987 was again Wau. With five thousand people in Wau reported to be in "extremely poor condition" by August 1987, and another forty thousand "seriously affected by food shortages," the major international relief effort[9] had delivered only some 200 metric tons to Wau by November 1987, out of a shipment of 8,843 metric tons channeled through the western Bahr el Ghazal town of Raga (TCC meeting minutes, November 16, 1987; Symonds 1987, 2). This quantity in Wau would have fed forty-five thousand people for less than nine days.

As famine intensified in 1988, relief deliveries diminished. Only some 1,298 metric tons of relief grain were delivered to the whole of Bahr el Ghazal between the beginning of the year and September 18, 1988. Negotiations between the ICRC, the government, and the SPLA over possible relief operations to government- and SPLA-held areas of the south began in February 1988 but yielded no deliveries until small quantities were airlifted in December (Bonner 1989, 89).

In 1988, the trains from Babanousa to Aweil brought a total of sixteen wagonloads of relief rice (some 480 metric tons), plus one wagonload of oil. As a result, the Aweil relief committee had, in the spring and summer of 1988, only about 598 metric tons of cereals (mostly rice) for distribution to displaced people in very poor condition. Around seventy thousand displaced people were registered at one point, with many more unregistered. This quantity of cereals would have been sufficient to feed even the registered population for only seventeen days. The Aweil relief committee decided, shortly after the arrival of the March trains from Babanousa, to distribute 3.2 kilograms per person to some sixty-five thousand displaced people, using up almost half the total available grain. This distribution was described by a local relief worker as "a drop of water in an ocean of abject poverty" (Father Deng Rudolf 1988). Meanwhile, medical drugs were extremely scarce in Aweil, and immunization programs had not been undertaken (UNDP 1988b, 4 and annex 2; TCC meeting minutes, February 15, 1988).[10] The lack of relief food appears to have combined with these medical deficiencies and a lack of adequate shelter to produce the extraordinarily high mortality in Aweil in 1988 (UNDP 1988b, 4–6).[11]

Deliveries to Wau remained at very low levels in the winter of 1987–1988 and through 1988. Back in November 1987, the NGO World Vision had estimated delivery needs for the coming twelve months at 36,000 metric tons, but between January and November 1988, only some 200 metric tons of relief food (rice) were delivered to Wau (EC 1988f, 2). Taking a conservative estimate of 150,000 displaced people in Wau by the end of April, this quantity would have been enough to provide a ration of 500 grams per day for less than three days. In fact, when feeding camps for the displaced were established in June, they could accommodate and feed only some 6,700 people.[12] The high death rates in Wau in 1988 were noted in Chapter 3.

By the time the much-publicized but small-scale airlift relief operation to Aweil began in December 1988, the crisis in Aweil town was well past its peak. By the end of November, the numbers of displaced people had fallen dramatically, with a UNDP mission reporting that the remaining population of twenty-eight thousand in Aweil included very few displaced people (UNDP 1988b, 3). Many had returned to rural areas, which were not covered by the relief operation. While large numbers of the displaced again congregated in southern towns in 1989, it is clear that the famine had significantly lessened in severity (USAID 1989, 9, 11; *New York Times*, March 14, July 19, 1989). Meanwhile, relief deliveries picked up significantly. In May 1989, under the UN's Operation Lifeline Sudan (OLS), a total of forty-eight freight cars delivered 1,440 metric tons of emergency supplies: sixteen wagonloads to Malwal, sixteen to Mabior, and sixteen to Aweil (Wannop 1989, annex 1). This was more relief than had been delivered to Bahr el Ghazal by rail in the entire period 1987–1988. Further relief followed, bringing the total delivered by rail under Operation Lifeline close to 4,500 metric tons.[13] Wau and rural areas of Bahr el Ghazal also received substantial relief under Operation Lifeline in 1989 (Minear 1991, 42; Wannop 1989). And by the end of June, over 13,500 metric tons had been delivered to Bahr el Ghazal.

If relief to Bahr el Ghazal was minimal until after the worst of the famine, this was also true of relief directed at those who had fled into northern Sudan. Relief for those moving north from Bahr el Ghazal in 1987 was minimal. The peak of the 1987 influx into southern Kordofan came in July–August (EC 1988c, 1), but a proposal for supplementary and therapeutic feeding (to be handled by UNICEF) and general distribution (to be handled by regional government, the central government Relief and Rehabilitation Commission [RRC], and WFP) was not made until September 10 (UNICEF 1987a, 1). Nor did these distributions last for long; distributions of free grain in Abyei, for example, were stopped in November.[14]

Again in 1988, the displaced in southern Kordofan received relief only in very inadequate quantities. There were fifteen thousand to twenty-five thousand displaced people in Abyei by the end of May, among whom levels of malnutrition were extremely high. Abyei was supposed to receive relief grain under the donor/government Western Relief Operation (WRO), which had been initiated in late 1987 and aimed at the whole of Kordofan and Darfur. However, by the end of April 1988, just 18 metric tons of WRO grain had reached Abyei (Interdonor Memo. 1988, 1). With local purchases from merchants in Babanousa and Muglad, food stocks in Abyei for free distribution amounted to a maximum of 350 metric tons at the beginning of June. The rains had begun, threatening to cut off Abyei from further relief until November at the earliest (minutes of aid coordination meeting held at Concern office, May 27, 1988; Interagency Situation Report 1988, 2). Even assuming no further migration into Abyei during the June–October period, a total of 350 metric tons would have been sufficient to provide a ration of only 132 grams per day.[15] In fact, at the end of May, ration distributions in Abyei amounted at most to about 145 grams per person per day, with the local church and the local council providing rations in alternate weeks (Interagency Situation Report 1988, 7–8). Moreover, all the emergency drugs delivered by UNICEF in April had run out by this time.[16]

By the end of June, after intense efforts on the part of a nongovernmental Irish aid agency, Concern, and further local purchases, the total relief grain stocks in Abyei amounted to 600 metric tons. This amount would have been sufficient to provide only 246 grams per day over the four months until November, even if the number of displaced people had remained at twenty thousand (Concern 1988a). In fact, the number of displaced in the town escalated to something nearer forty thousand by October 1988,[17] and much of the relief food—as we shall see—was distributed to those not suffering from famine. The extreme scarcity in Abyei was accompanied by severe malnutrition and very high death rates. An anthropologist who visited Abyei in the autumn after the worst of the crisis reported, as noted, that locally caught fish had very probably done more to keep people alive than the very limited distributions of relief food (Ryle 1989b, 84).

In mid-October, a U.S.-funded airlift was launched to bring some 90 metric tons of relief food to Abyei (*Sudan Times*, October 16, 1988). In addition, Concern arranged for relief to be taken to Abyei on donkeys (TCC meeting minutes, November 7, 1988). Yet rations remained insufficient in October. Stronger children were reported to have fought successfully for limited supplies of the UN's Unimix food, leaving the weaker children with nothing (*New York Times*, October 13, 1988). Distributions to the displaced were no more than 2.2 kilograms of sorghum every ten days—about half of subsistence level. There were no oils or beans (TCC meeting minutes, November 7, 1988). There was, moreover, no provision for those in rural areas around Abyei.[18]

Relief provisions for Babanousa and Muglad in 1988 were better than those for Abyei, but still inadequate (Concern 1988d). Relief administered to displaced people in Meiram in 1988 was insufficient to prevent some of the highest mortality rates recorded anywhere in the world. The displaced were not receiving any food from government sources (TCC meeting minutes, May 9, 1988). Special feeding programs were established by MSF and, briefly, UNICEF (MSF-France 1988c). Alongside these, the major international donors were to have provided a general ration. But this ration proved very inadequate in relation to need, as low relief deliveries combined with a soaring displaced population.

While those displaced people living outside the camp (in and around the town of Meiram) received adequate or near-adequate rations from the start of distributions at the beginning of June 1988 until mid-July, they received quite inadequate rations thereafter. After July 18th, these people received only a half-ration on August 3, and then virtually nothing until September 2. Further, while those inside the Meiram camp were given more relief than were those outside, even the camp population received only one full ration in the period July 28–August 29.[19] The camp population, moreover, consumed only a proportion of the grain distributed there, because of "leakage" of grain from the camp. In early September, receipt of grain by people residing in the camp was estimated at about 1.7 kilograms per week—roughly half of what people were supposed to receive (SCF-UK/Oxfam-UK 1988). One Dinka man in the camp said this was also the amount the camp population had been getting in June and July, with people coming from outside the camp to collect distributions.

Special feeding programs made little sense where the general ration was so low, and these programs were ended by MSF-France at the beginning of August in favor of a mass distribution of cooked food to as many children as possible. At the end of August, MSF-France described its own work in Meiram in this context as an "ugly charade" (MSF-France 1988g, 2–3).

Low rations were only part of the problem at Meiram. MSF-France had insufficient facilities to establish adequate sanitation or provide enough water. And the displaced Dinka, generally lacking the money and containers that would have allowed them to take water from the local pump, resorted to taking water from the stagnant pools around the camp. These pools were contaminated with human feces, because of the lack of adequate sanitation. Diarrhea was widespread in the camp, and poor sanitation was reported as a key cause of death (MSF-France 1988a, 1988e, 1988f).[20] Indeed, water contaminated in this way had previously been used in suicide attempts among the Dinka (Deng 1986, 253).

Still more common than diarrhea within the camp were respiratory throat infections, to which a lack of clothes and blankets had contributed (MSF-France 1988f).[21] The next most common condition in the camp in August was malaria. It was not until the end of August that badly needed malaria and diarrhea drugs arrived by train (interview with Natalie Isouard, MSF-France nurse, Meiram, November 25, 1988).

There was one significant exception to this pattern of inadequate relief provision. This was the relief given to those who moved from northern Bahr el Ghazal to southern Darfur in 1988. As the 1988 rains approached, threatening to cut off relief to some 15,800 people in Safaha, these people were moved by a consortium involving Oxfam-UK, SCF-UK, and MSF-Belgium to seven resettlement sites around Ed Daien and Nyala to the north. Here, they received largely adequate relief (RRC/EC 1988j, 1–2). Rates of malnutrition and mortality among these people fell rapidly, in sharp contrast to very high mortality and malnutrition in southern Kordofan, where death rates rose until the end of July of 1988.[22] It should be noted that the terrible condition of those in Safaha had reflected an earlier failure to deliver relief to Bahr el Ghazal and that there was no Western Relief Operation food in Safaha in March when severe food shortages were experienced.[23] Nevertheless, the evacuation of Safaha was a quick and effective response to the emergency there.

## CAUSES AND FUNCTIONS OF INADEQUATE RELIEF

### Relief Resources: Shortage or Maldistribution?

Could it be that the inadequacy of relief reflected wider problems of scarcity within Sudan? The Sudanese government argued that relief was constrained by poverty and economic crisis, adding that this was why outside help was needed.[24] It is true that Sudan is one of the poorest countries in the world, and has suffered major economic crisis since the late 1970s. Nonetheless, resources that might have been used for the relief of the famine were actually abundant. The real problem lay in the uses to which these resources were put.

As famine in the south deepened, very large quantities of grain were exported from Sudan. According to Food and Agriculture Organization (FAO) figures, exports of cereals totaled 237,000 metric tons in 1988 (FAO 1989b, 118). However, at the offices of the Agricultural Bank of Sudan in Khartoum in December 1988, I was shown figures indicating that in 1988 Sudan exported fully 466,000 metric tons of sorghum to Europe (mostly to traders in the Netherlands), as well as 34,000 metric tons to Saudi Arabia. The great bulk of Sudan's sorghum exports routinely went to Western Europe and the Middle East (see, for example, USAID 1987a, 2). Although Prime Minister el Mahdi had promised during the resumption of exports in 1986 that grain was being sent to "people in worse situations," most of the exports were eaten by animals.[25]

In addition to raising market prices within Sudan in ways that can only have exacerbated famine, such exports reduced the stocks available for relief.[26] At the same time, they clearly served important functions for powerful interests inside (as well as outside) Sudan. For the small but influential group of Sudanese merchant-farmers engaged in large-scale sorghum production, exports provided important income, as well as support for domestic prices. The benefits of exports were boosted by Saudi Arabia's willingness to pay an above-market price. For the government itself (urged on by international creditors, such as the World Bank and the IMF), permitting and encouraging the export of sorghum promised an easing of Sudan's acute balance-of-trade and -payments problems (Shepherd 1988, 60–63). The continued high levels of exports during gathering famine in the south compare unfavorably with events in 1984, when exports of sorghum had been severely, if belatedly, curtailed as famine escalated in parts of northern Sudan (ibid., 63).

Despite these high levels of exports, there were still very large stocks of grain within Sudan; yet these were not used for the relief of the famine. In August 1988, at the height of the famine, the total quantity of sorghum being held in stock by the Agricultural Bank of Sudan (ABS) was 365,984 metric tons (EWSB, August 15, 1988, 5). This in itself suggested a low priority for relief. Moreover, ABS was implicated in specific relief holdups. The 1988 harvest in Sudan turned out to be one of the largest in recent memory (FAO 1989a, 113). This did not mean the end of the famine, however.

A further abundant source of food—which might, given different political priorities, have been used for famine relief—was the ongoing food aid programs. Sudan remained a major recipient of Western food aid throughout the famine. A total of 661,400 metric tons of wheat and other grains were made available to Sudan in 1987, most of it under the U.S. scheme known as PL480 (Bickersteth 1990, 223). This total compares with the 82,000 metric tons of grain administered as relief to the whole of Sudan in 1987, and the 4,000 metric tons administered to Bahr el Ghazal. Thus, relief administered to Bahr el Ghazal amounted to only around 0.6 percent of the total food aid made available to Sudan. The percentage that actually reached famine victims in Bahr el Ghazal will have been significantly lower. Most of the aid grain went to urban areas in the north, with 70 percent of wheat imports reaching the Khartoum market (USAID 1987a, 3). The political importance of these distributions became clear whenever attempts were made to cut the wheat subsidy, something that typically led to politically damaging riots, as for example, in January 1989 (Bickersteth 1990, 225). In 1988, food aid concessional imports totaled 379,000 metric tons[27]—still clearly sufficient to tackle the famine, had this been made a priority.

Even the resources made available for emergency aid could have significantly relieved the famine, had they been channeled to those most in need

**TABLE 2**
Relief by Region, 1986–1987 (mt)

|  | 1986 | 1987 |
|---|---|---|
| Equatoria | 5,000 | 12,000 |
| Upper Nile | 1,000 | 3,000 |
| Bahr el Ghazal | 2,000 | 4,000[a] |
| Darfur | 51,000 | — |
| Kordofan | 107,000 | 20,000[b] |
| Eastern | 35,000 | 35,000 |
| Northern | 2,400 | 1,000 |
| Central | 18,000 | 6,000 |
| Khartoum | 2,000 | 1,000 |
| Total | 223,400 | 82,000 |

Sources: 1986, Bahr el Ghazal: Minear 1991, 8.
Ec 1987f.

[a] Most of the 8,843 metric tons of grain delivered to Raga were stolen or destroyed.

[b] In July–September 1987, 20,000 metric tons of sorghum from the national government were distributed in Kordofan (letter from M. A. el Mahdi, governor of Kordofan Region, to Prime Minister Sadiq el Mahdi, autumn 1987).

of them. However, relief distributions did not correspond to need. Notably, while the severity of famine was far greater in the south than in the north in the period 1986–1988, the pattern of relief grain deliveries favored the north. All indicators of famine showed much more strongly in the south than the north. Levels of outmigration, grain prices, hunger, and mortality were far greater in the south; so, too, was the disruption of people's way of life.[28]

Table 2 shows the approximate quantities of relief administered to the various regions of Sudan in 1986 and 1987 (EC 1987f; Minear 1991, 8), and Table 3 indicates regional distributions of internationally-donated relief in 1988 (EWSB, September 15, 1988, 5). These tables show clearly that the Darfur, Kordofan, and Eastern regions received the bulk of relief grain administered in 1986–1988, while the southern regions of Equatoria, Upper Nile, and Bahr el Ghazal—although far more severely affected by famine—received far less. Between them, the three southern regions possessed perhaps 26 percent of the population, and a much higher percentage of the very needy;[29] yet they received only 3.6 percent of recorded grain deliveries in 1986, only 23 percent in 1987, and only 12.1 percent in 1988.

Neither were the most needy regions given priority within the south. Equatoria was generally less affected by the second civil war than Bahr el Ghazal and Upper Nile (New York Times, January 3, 1988). And a significantly smaller percentage of its people were affected by famine than in Bahr

**TABLE 3**
Relief by Region, January 1–
September 8, 1988 (mt)

| Region | Relief |
|--------|--------|
| Equatoria | 7,874 |
| Upper Nile | 3,119 |
| Bahr el Ghazal | 1,298 |
| Darfur | 13,599 |
| Kordofan | 34,143 |
| Eastern | 41,600 |
| Total | 101,633 |

*Source:* EWSB, September 15, 1988, 5.

el Ghazal.[30] Yet it was Equatoria Region that consistently received the bulk of the relief given to the south. Possessing only some 26 percent of the southern population (Otor 1984, 6), Equatoria received fully 62.5 percent of the south's relief grain in 1986, 63 percent in 1987, and 64 percent in 1988. Bahr el Ghazal itself, with perhaps 40 percent of the south's population (ibid., 6), received 0.9 percent of relief administered in 1986, 4.9 percent in 1987, and just 1.3 percent in 1988. The apparent lesser intensity of civil war (and hence of "security obstacles") in Equatoria may partially account for its privileged receipt of relief. However, major population centers in Bahr el Ghazal were themselves accessible, given sufficient determination, as we shall see. The strong suspicion is that the Sudan government attached greater (though still inadequate) priority to relieving Equatoria: the government had for some time been cultivating support in Equatoria, first for the division of the south into three units and later as a counterweight to what the government and many Equatorians saw as the Dinka-dominated SPLA. This had included supporting various militias in opposition to the SPLA. Meanwhile, in the areas of the north to which famine victims migrated, distributions corresponded no more closely with need: the very small amounts of relief received by the Dinka in southern Kordofan were accompanied by substantial distributions in northern Kordofan, where needs were much less severe (Ministry of Finance and Economic Planning/EC/Masdar 1988).

In addition to the government's argument about resources, both donors and the Sudanese government argued that a vital obstacle to famine relief was the problem of access. The various obstacles said to be impeding relief were summarized by Walter Bollinger, deputy assistant administrator of the USAID Bureau for Africa in statements before the U.S. Congress in July 1988. First of all, he said, there were important security obstacles (U.S. Congress 1988b, 7)—a theme the Department of State was to reiterate in October 1988, when it emphasized the disruption of relief by SPLA attacks (Bonner 1989, 95). The government's apparent slowness in distributing relief had been further encouraged, Bollinger told Congress, by: "the country's vast size; the lack of accurate data on conditions; the depressed state of the economy . . . ; the very low level of development, particularly in logistics; the inexperienced and thinly staffed bureaucracy and the primitive and unreliable means of communication."[31]

The UN also placed great emphasis on logistical obstacles. For example, the 1988 UN appeal dealing with famine relief gave primacy to resource problems on the railways, and infrastructure deficiencies at Babanousa (UNOEA 1988, 39–46). Inaccessibility was also commonly cited by government officials as a prime reason for the lack of relief. Frequently, the SPLA was blamed, with poor security held to have impeded relief to areas bordering southern Sudan (for example, Meiram and Abyei) as well as areas within Bahr el Ghazal itself. Also blamed were heavy rains and mechanical breakdowns on the railways (letter from Dr. el Hag el Tayeb el Tahir, acting commissioner, RRC, in *Sudan Times*, July 19, 1988; de Waal 1990a, 11–12; *Le Monde*, November 3, 1988; RRC/EC 1988g; *Guiding Star*, November 3, 1988, citing acting commissioner, RRC). When I asked the first executive officer of Babanousa why famine migrants had not been transported north from Abyei and Meiram before the 1988 rains, he replied that there were "no trucks available" (interview with Salah Ahmed Nasser, first executive officer, Babanousa, November 30, 1988).

However, while problems of access were often significant (notably in relation to Bahr el Ghazal), the most fundamental cause of the lack of relief distributions was the low priority attached to relieving famine by various levels of the Sudanese administration. Blaming problems of "access" provided a classic "escape route," by means of which government and international donor officials were able partially to avoid blame from potentially critical elements of Sudanese and international opinion; at the same time, blaming "access" problems appears to have narrowed the "room for maneuver" toward improving these relief outcomes.

### Relief to Bahr el Ghazal

It would be foolish to dismiss the security or logistical obstacles facing relief efforts to Bahr el Ghazal in the context of civil war.[32] The SPLA repeatedly showed hostility to government-controlled shipments destined for the south. For example, in 1984, the SPLA destroyed a bridge on the rail line from Aweil to Wau, cutting off rail links between Wau and the north. It threatened and sometimes attacked the trains to Aweil. It attacked river convoys and shot down several aircraft flying between north and south (Africa Watch 1990, 116–17, 125; *Sudan Times*, January 23, 1989).

However, access difficulties were far from insuperable. In 1988, while international donors were still citing security reasons for not providing relief to most of the south, a Norwegian relief organization, Norwegian People's Aid (NPA), showed that it was possible to work successfully in at least some parts of the SPLA-held zone, administering a successful aid program in eastern Equatoria. In Bahr el Ghazal, despite the security constraints that existed, trains and trucks were able to get through to major government garrison towns in Bahr el Ghazal, both before and after the SPLA established a major presence there; the principal problems were the infrequency of such shipments, the shortage of escorts, and the composition of the shipments. Moreover, the security situation in Bahr el Ghazal was itself dependent to a large extent on government (and donor) decisions relating to the content, control, and destination of "relief" shipments. Given a different and more equitable set of relief priorities in 1989, it became possible to reach not only garrison towns but also rebel-held areas of rural Bahr el Ghazal. The SPLA's attitude to 1989 operations suggested that it was not averse to relief per se, but rather to relief (or, very often, shipments masquerading as relief) that was directed almost exclusively at government-held areas.

It is revealing of the government's priorities in 1986–1988 in particular that the low levels of distribution of relief in Bahr el Ghazal were matched by low assessments of need and low allocations. At an aid coordination meeting in December 1986 (chaired by the RRC), the government rejected an assessment by the NGO consortium CART (Combined Agencies Relief Team) that the south required 71,000 metric tons for the first six months of 1987. CART's estimate had actually been substantially lower than one by indigenous NGOs.[33] Accepting even the CART estimates would almost certainly have meant declaring a famine; in the event, there was to be no such declaration by the government thenceforth (Africa Watch 1990, 109).[34] The needs estimate passed to the World Food Program (WFP) in Rome did not have the status of a government appeal, and no government appeal was to be forthcoming until the summer of 1988 (*Sudan Times*, June 30, 1988). Despite a clear statement from CART that relief was needed immediately, it was decided that there was no need for relief until April 1987, with (erroneous) reports of recent relief arrivals seen as providing "breathing space" (Oxfam-UK 1986q, 2).

At the end of 1987, inadequate needs assessment was further encouraged, when the government expelled four aid agencies active in the south, including World Vision and the Lutheran World Federation (Africa Watch 1990, 110). For 1988, according to the RRC's assessments, Bahr el Ghazal would require only 11,000 metric tons; by contrast, Kordofan would need 71,000 metric tons (EWSB, September 5, 1988, 5). While the argument was advanced, by both the Sudanese government and international donors, that needs assessments and allocations should be "realistic" (that is, they should reflect likely problems with delivery), these low assessments and allocations clearly risked legitimizing and encouraging a weak response. Significantly, even the ICRC, which sought to get around problems of access by agreeing on relief flights with the government and the SPLA, produced a plan in which the neediest areas of southern Sudan (including the area around Aweil) were neglected.[35]

Considerable light is thrown on the issue of "access" by investigating the movement of trains from Babanousa, in southern Kordofan, to Aweil, in Bahr el Ghazal. Original evidence on the frequency and composition of these trains was obtained by the writer at Babanousa railway station.

The small amounts of relief delivered to Aweil by train in 1986 have been noted. This was despite the fact that the SPLA was at that time a very weak force in Bahr el Ghazal and the security obstacles to getting grain by train to Aweil were minor (Africa Watch 1990, 82–84). Significantly, a train arrived in Aweil in August 1986 carrying no relief food (Oxfam-UK 1986m). The SPLA continued to have only a weak presence in Bahr el Ghazal for most of 1987 (Africa Watch 1990, 82–84), and the accessibility of Aweil was demonstrated by the passage of trains at various points throughout the year. Nevertheless, the frequency of relief trains was low, notably in relation to levels promised by the Sudanese government. In the spring of 1987, the government had promised three trains a month.[36] There were subsequently only ten trains with relief in the entire period from the spring of 1987 until the end of 1988. It is true that when the SPLA gained substantial control over rural Bahr el Ghazal in late 1987, the difficulty of getting trains to Aweil increased significantly. Nonetheless, the journey was still possible with military escorts, as the arrival of three trains in March 1988 demonstrated. Such escorts, however, were generally not forthcoming. After the three March trains, there were no further trains until January 1989.

The trains that did run to Aweil, moreover, carried only very small quantities of relief supplies. Table 4 shows quantities of relief carried by the trains to Aweil from February 1987 through December 1988. According to the accounts of major bilateral and multilateral aid donors, the Sudanese government had promised them in May 1987 that three trains a month would each have 108 freight cars and that the majority of freight cars would be used for relief.[37] On this basis, the fourteen wagonloads of relief actually delivered between the late May promise and the end of 1987 constituted only 1.2 percent of the minimum pledged.[38] Further, considering that the average train had thirty freight cars, the twenty-three cars carrying relief dispatched in all of 1987 represent something less than 10 percent of all freight cars dispatched. Despite government promises of substantial relief, the dispatching of such small quantities of relief did not represent a deviation from central government policy by provincial officials. There is evidence that it was fully intended by senior officials in Khartoum. In particular, on June 17,

**TABLE 4**
Relief by Train to Aweil, 1987–1988

| Date of Leaving Babanousa | Total Relief Food Carried (wagonloads) |
| --- | --- |
| February, 17 1987 | 4 oil |
| April, 29 1987 | 4 oil and 1 rice |
| June, 20 1987 | 1 rice |
| June, 27 1987 | 2 rice |
| September, 20 1987 | 3 rice |
| September, 30 1987 | 1 rice[a] |
| October, 2 1987 | 6 rice and 1 oil[a] |
| March, 2 1988 | 1 oil and 4 rice |
| March, 2 1988 | 9 rice |
| March, 2 1988 | 3 rice |
| December, 25 1988 | 6 relief or 13 relief |

Sources: Through March 2, 1988: Babanousa railway station records. December 25, 1988: six wagonloads—Sudan Times, January 23, 1989; thirteen wagonloads—interview with Bryan Wannop, UNDP, New York, August 24, 1990.

[a] MALT reported that four trains left Babanousa for Aweil on October 2, carrying eight wagonloads of relief (TCC meeting minutes, October 12, 1987). It appears that one of these was recorded at Babanousa station as having left on September 30.

1987, as UN officials subsequently reminded Prime Minister el Mahdi, the Steering Committee of the state-controlled Sudan Railways Corporation had stated its intention that less than 7 percent of wagons would carry relief supplies.[39] Actual proportions did not deviate far from this stated intention.

Meanwhile, at the height of the famine in the summer of 1988, twenty-three wagonloads of grain consigned to Aweil were "discovered" in Babanousa railyard by NGO staff. Ten had been waiting there for a year, and eight for two or more years (Concern 1988b; interview with Mark Cunningham, Concern, Khartoum, November 2, 1988).[40]

If trains to Aweil were used for delivering only very small amounts of relief, what then was their primary purpose? An important insight is supplied by information from a Sudan Railways Corporation worker, who provided the writer with a detailed breakdown of the contents of the three March 1988 trains to Aweil and whose information tallies broadly with more aggregated information given at aid coordination meetings.[41] There were seventy-one freight cars, excluding an unspecified number carrying merchants' goods on the second train. Less than a quarter (seventeen) carried relief for the citizens of Aweil. Fifteen of the freight cars carried grain for the army; twenty-one carried soldiers and military goods; and a further eighteen (plus the unspecified number on the second train) carried merchants' goods. Eight of the eighteen merchandise cars also carried a small number of railway workers[42]; railway workers were typically eight to a car, leaving considerable space for the sorghum, sugar, salt, oil, clothes, onions, and dates that merchants paid them to take on board. It should be stressed that the March 1988 trains carried significantly greater quantities of relief food than did any other trains to Aweil between March 1986 and April 1989 (see Table 4). The proportions allocated to military and merchants' goods could be expected to be significantly higher on the other trains from Babanousa to Aweil in this period.[43]

Information is also available on the contents of the much-publicized January 1989 "relief" trains. Reports from Aweil said that out of sixty freight cars arriving in the town, fully fifty-four were loaded with some 1,600 metric tons of supplies for the army (leaving six carrying relief). The UNDP resident representative put the number of freight cars carrying relief at thirteen, acknowledging that the rest were used for military and commercial goods (interview with Bryan Wannop, UNDP, New York, August 24, 1990). Much of the relief food loaded onto these trains had never moved beyond Meiram rail station in southern Kordofan (*Sudan Times*, January 23, 1989). Meanwhile, the government continued to promise much more relief than was delivered: in September 1988, it had promised four relief trains, with one hundred freight cars per train (interview with Bryan Wannop, UNDP, New York, August 24, 1990).

Even if we take the most conservative estimate of the number of merchants' freight cars on the March 1988 trains, and the most liberal estimate of the number of relief freight cars on the January 1989 trains, relief freight cars constituted only some 23 percent of the total arriving in Aweil in the period March 1988–January 1989.[44] It seems clear that during the period March 1986–January 1989, military and commercial aims took precedence over the delivery of relief to Aweil.

As with Aweil, the inaccessibility of Wau was more apparent than real. Twenty-two merchants' trucks reached Wau from the north on March 19, 1986 (Oxfam-UK 1986c, 1). Virtually a whole convoy of relief food arrived in 1986 but was taken by the army in Wau (de Waal 1990a, 21). Subsequently, relief shipments from the north via the Bahr el Ghazal town of Raga were persistently held up by the failure to provide military escorts.[45] In 1987, when a major relief operation aimed at Wau was staged, the army did not provide escorts either for trucks from Raga to Wau or for UN-donated RTU (Road Transport Unit) trucks that were stuck in Wau and might have been used to fetch relief from Raga (TCC meeting minutes, February 15, 1988; Symonds 1987, 11). In any case, RTU was dragging its feet on the issue of transporting relief for RRC, while apparently allowing truck use for military purposes (TCC meeting minutes, Aug. 10, 1987).[46] There was thus a hollow ring to the statement of RTU's director, Aldo Barone, in June 1987, that the organization (which had just been renamed from Road Transport Operation and split from RRC): "will continue to be an operative support of any emergency relief and development programmes organized by the Relief [and] Rehabilitation [Commission], in conjunction with donor agencies and government departments in the Sudan."[47]

When it came to relief approaching Wau from the south, the army similarly neglected to provide escorts.[48] Further, when a bridge on the Raga-Wau road collapsed in the rains, army personnel dismantled the approach to the bridge and the central pillar, allowing the immediate passage of troops over a causeway built with these materials but at the same time precluding speedy repair. A large stock of relief grain accumulated in Raga, and most was subsequently stolen or left unusable because of the theft of protective sheeting (Symonds 1987, 3, 10).

During the subsequent dry season, commercial and military goods moved frequently from Raga to Wau. The commercial shipments included a 180-truck convoy in November 1987, with no relief food represented (TCC, November 23, 1987). This appears to have been one of at least four convoys that moved from Raga to Wau in the 1987–1988 dry season, without relief food. Shipment of military goods to Wau was also common, and military goods were often interspersed with food products (U.S. Congress 1988b, 13). The advent of the 1987–1988 dry season created the possibility of moving substantial relief supplies from Nyala, in southern Darfur. to Wau via Raga (TCC meeting minutes, November 23, 1987). But relief shipments to Wau from Raga remained at very low levels (EC 1988a). Another possibility was bringing in relief by air. But while the Sudan military regularly flew food into Wau to feed its troops, relief was not carried by this means (*Sudan Times*, December 16, 1988).

The pattern of relief operations to the south helped to create the security obstacles that were then cited by the government to excuse the inadequacy of relief. In particular, the direction of relief exclusively at government-held areas, and the use of "relief" trains for military and commercial purposes, encouraged the SPLA to view "relief" shipments with maximum hostility, just as the mixing of military and relief goods and discrimination against areas of rebel strength were encouraging rebel attacks in Ethiopia (cf. Africa Watch 1991, 188–90). It is true that the SPLA expressed the goal of stopping food shipments to garrison towns, whether or not these contained military supplies. In a remarkable statement, considering that the suffering Dinka constituted the backbone of SPLA support, John Garang wrote, "[The government's] garrison towns in the South are famine-stricken and are real disaster areas, and this is good; our military strategy is working" (Garang 1987, 71). However, by mixing military and relief goods, the government removed any possibility of shaming the SPLA into allowing relief deliveries, while creating maximum opportunities publicly to blame the SPLA for blocking relief. At the same time, the bias of relief efforts toward government-held zones, in conjunction with government-sponsored devastation of rural areas, inevitably created a perception within the SPLA that "relief" was an arm of the government's military strategy—that it was being used to bolster the government's attempts to control civilian populations and to keep the garrison towns afloat.[49]

Significantly, some local elements of the SPLA, who were witnessing Dinka suffering at first hand, looked with more favor on relief than did Garang, creating at least the possibility of local agreements with SPLA units,[50] and SPLA sympathies in Aweil were strong. Significantly also, the SPLA had agreed to relief distributions to civilians in a number of government-held towns under Operation Rainbow in 1986 (Africa Watch 1990, 108). The SPLA justified its threat to the Aweil trains on the ground that they were being used to carry military supplies, rather than food for civilians (*Sudan Times*, November 29, 1988, January 12, 23, 1989; *New York Times*, October 10, 1988). U.S. State Department officials reported that it was the mixing of military goods and food products on truck convoys to Wau that attracted SPLA attention to these shipments (U.S. Congress 1988b, 13). After a shift in the SPLA's stance, the organization agreed to the passage of the January 1989 shipments to Aweil (and subsequent shipments under Operation Lifeline) on the understanding that these would be used only for relief.[51]

Both the government (notably in Bahr el Ghazal and Upper Nile) and the SPLA (notably in Equatoria) attempted to undermine the subsistence base of hostile or indifferent populations, apparently hoping that people would be attracted to areas under their respective control (Oxfam-UK 1986i, 2). In this context, the channeling of (largely unmonitored) international relief efforts toward government-held rather than rebel-held areas inevitably appeared to the SPLA as something likely to strengthen the government's hand in the battle for civilian support. Channeling relief-only shipments to government garrison towns would at least have made it more difficult for the SPLA to be seen to be attacking them.

In July 1986, it had been proposed that a consortium of relief agencies should handle distribution of relief food for Bahr el Ghazal, along the lines of distributions by the CART aid agency consortium, which had carried out fairly far-reaching relief operations in Equatoria in 1986 (TCC meeting minutes, July 29, 1986).[52] This proposal was expanded at an aid coordination meeting in December 1986 (chaired by the head of the RRC, Kamil Shawgi), when relief agencies put forward a plan that all aid to the south should be neutral and accountable on the lines of CART (Africa Watch 1990, 109). These proposals might have formed the basis for relief operations with some semblance of neutrality. An informal pact between the SPLA and the Bahr el Ghazal regional administration facilitating the work of UNICEF and veterinary teams in rural areas suggested some scope for preserving neutrality (Oxfam-UK 1986a, 11). The Relief Committee in Wau had informal links with the SPLA, which it hoped might permit food distributions in surrounding rural areas (Oxfam-UK 1986c, 3). However, spurred by the SPLA's shooting down of a civilian aircraft in August 1986, the recently established government of Sadiq el Mahdi appeared determined to block any relief that was not closely under its own control, and the December 1986 neutrality proposal was rejected by the government, which insisted that all relief had military escorts (Africa Watch 1990, 108–9). Meanwhile, even in Equatoria, attempts at a wide-ranging relief operation were being narrowed by government hostility. In late 1986, CART's operations came under severe pressure from the governor, Peter Cirillo. After two of CART's members were expelled, the consortium abandoned the use of the word "neutrality." In other compromises, a government representative was allowed onto the CART steering committee, and CART accepted the provision of military escorts for its trucks. In a remark that highlights the malleable quality of "security" constraints in the south, one Oxfam worker with many years of experience in the south commented in August 1987 that since December 1986, "CART has thrown away any pretence of being neutral and has now decided to 'toe the government line.' This must surely be the perception of the SPLA. We are now likely to be regarded by them as under the control of the government and we must therefore expect to be treated accordingly."[53]

At the same time that the government was precluding the possibility of "neutral" relief shipments, it was also punishing attempts to cooperate with the SPLA for relief purposes. This, too, played a key role in rendering large areas of the south (including most of rural Bahr el Ghazal from late 1987 on) "inaccessible" to relief. Of particular significance was the government's expulsion of Winston Prattley, the head of the UN Office for Emergency Operations in Sudan (UNOEOS) and UN resident representative, on October 30, 1986, after Prattley had negotiated with both the government and the SPLA to provide a limited quantity of relief to civilians in government-held towns, principally Juba, under Operation Rainbow (Africa Watch 1990, 108). The government claimed that Prattley had violated diplomatic norms by even speaking with the SPLA. Meanwhile in Juba, Governor Cirillo fiercely suppressed any attempt by relief agencies to cooperate with the SPLA (Clark 1987, 70). In between the failed Operation Rainbow of 1986 and the ICRC operation that began in December 1988 (with Operation Lifeline following closely in 1989), there were no agreements between the government and the SPLA on relief. This rendered huge areas of (SPLA-held) southern Sudan "inaccessible."

In 1988, a long-running attempt by the ICRC to get relief to government-

and rebel-held areas in the south was blocked first by the government and then by the SPLA. The ICRC proposed an airlift, initially to three government-held and three SPLA-held towns in the south. The idea was mooted in January 1988. The SPLA agreed to the plan in March. However, delays in government approval meant there was no progress until August. Some of the delays were caused by the central government, such as a two-month wait for a response to ICRC's initial proposals. Some were due to local army commanders' obstructing travel permission for surveys. After August, the SPLA began to cause delays. In addition, the government obstructed a crucial survey of the town of Akon until November. Only on December 4, 1988, did the airlift begin. It did not reach as many as six southern towns until February 1989 (Africa Watch 1990, 111).

If the "inaccessibility" of famine victims was more apparent than real, it is important to look for other explanations of the inadequacy of relief. One factor, clearly, was the desire to use "relief" trains for delivering military and commercial goods. Not only did these take priority over relief; the relief designation also provided useful cover for other goods, and the SPLA risked bad publicity if it attacked the shipments.[54] The inadequacy of relief also appears to have served important military and commercial functions by directly fostering famine in Bahr el Ghazal. The depopulation of large areas of Bahr el Ghazal—and the debilitation of those that remained—offered the prospect of weakening the SPLA's main support, the Dinka, while bringing large numbers of southern Sudanese civilians directly under government control in southern garrison towns. The provision of adequate relief would have greatly stemmed the tide of outmigration, helping the Dinka to remain in their traditional lands.[55] Indirectly, the deprivation of relief may also have boosted outmigration by forcing the army and southern militias (both the government- and the SPLA-supported ones) to resort to plundering civilians. While the government, unsurprisingly, did not explicitly state an intention to starve the Dinka from their homelands, the deprivation of relief to rebel-held areas (which came to include most of the lands of the Dinka by 1988) was explicitly justified by the government on military grounds (*Sudan Times*, May 8, 1988).

Certainly, the Sudanese government's principal military actors were well placed to restrict relief. The army's effective veto on shipments to Aweil and Wau, which required military escorts, has been mentioned. There was, moreover, a direct personal link between the militia strategy and the restriction of relief from Babanousa to Aweil. General Fadlalla Burma Nasser, a Messiri, had been one of the principal architects of the militia attacks (Wannop 1989, 11). And as minister of state for defense in May 1987, it was he who made the promises to donors (never remotely fulfilled) that there would be substantial relief for Aweil. Later, as minister of state for transport (under the minister for transport) and then as minister for transport, he attempted to obstruct the proposed Operation Lifeline delivery of grain by rail to Aweil (ibid., 6; interview with Bryan Wannop, UNDP, New York, August 24, 1990).

The military's control over deliveries was matched by considerable control over distributions once relief had arrived. At the December 1986 aid coordination meeting mentioned above, the government had insisted that relief be consigned to local authorities, rather than to aid agencies as had been the case with CART's operations in Equatoria. In the war zone, consigning grain to the local authorities meant consigning it to the army (Africa Watch 1990, 109).

The commercial benefits of famine contributed to the inadequacy of relief in Bahr el Ghazal. The impact of relief obstruction on various markets is illustrated in Figure 2. This was the final major way in which the exercise of force at the political level (and withholding of food is clearly a kind of violence) helped shape markets in ways that yielded benefits to some, even as it deepened processes of famine.

The benefits derived from high grain prices were dependent on the absence of effective relief.[56] Indeed, on the rare occasions when relief deliveries were substantial, they were capable of bringing grain prices in famine areas dramatically lower.[57] This was the case in Wau, where ICRC relief arrivals beginning in December 1988 had reduced grain prices significantly by February 1989.[58] Part of the price-reducing effect appeared to come from release of private stocks.[59]

The control over commodity flows to garrison towns that was exerted by merchants and army personnel—both profiting from high prices in the towns—extended also to relief. The large proportion of "relief" shipments devoted to military and commercial goods was itself evidence of this control. The collapse of southern representation within the army in the early 1980s can only have increased the military's willingness to profit economically, as well as militarily, from famine among the Dinka. Relief deliveries to Wau were held up in early 1986 as merchants with trucks in Ed Daien (the northern town from which World Vision was dispatching grain) delayed the departure of their trucks until the commercial sorghum that had recently arrived in Wau had been sold (Oxfam-UK 1986c, 2). And the rebel leader, John Garang, alleged that northern merchants bribed railway workers not to load relief onto trains at Babanousa (Africa Report, July–August 1989, 47). Certainly, the use of bribes to delay rail deliveries and create local shortages of particular highly priced products (as well as to speed delivery) has been reported in other parts of Sudan (Abdel-Aziz 1979, 278; Ibrahim 1985, 239). It is clear also that soldiers, policemen, and railway workers profited from nonrelief goods they took with them to Aweil, and that they were often paid by merchants to take such goods. Irrespective of bribes or payments, they stood to gain in important respects from restricting relief supplies and boost-

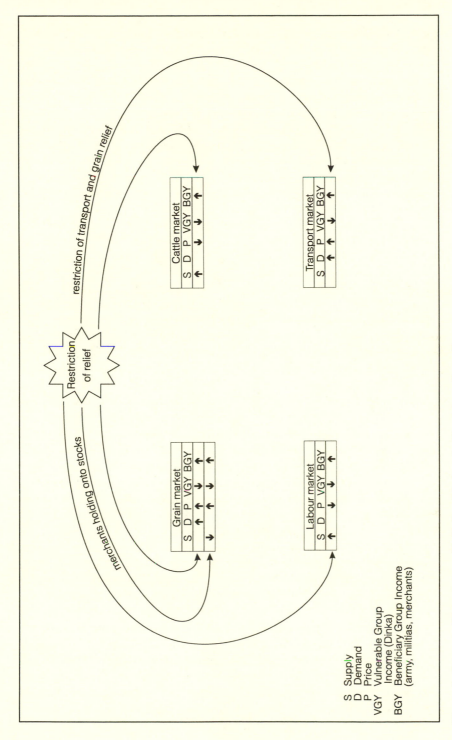

**Figure 2.** Impact of Restriction of Relief on Markets in Abyei Area Council

ing prices (Wannop 1989, 9; interview with Sudan Railways Corporation worker, 1988).

As a rule, international donor representatives were reluctant to highlight or counteract the vested interests opposing relief, markedly so in the period 1985–1988. Nevertheless, in 1989 donors became less reticent on problems affecting relief operations. Bryan Wannop, the resident representative of the UNDP and UN special coordinator for emergency and relief operations, played an active role in trying to get unescorted relief-only trains to Aweil under Operation Lifeline, and his account provides an important insight into the systems of profit and exploitation that were threatened by relief operations, not only in 1989 but also in preceding years:

> We were aware that we were stepping on toes by pushing through an unarmed and unescorted train which would carry relief goods only. The local policemen and soldiers who generally profit from their escort duties by carrying with them large amounts of commercial goods which they then dispose of at a significant profit in Aweil stood to be adversely affected by the concept of a successful unescorted train. Similarly, their opportunity to purchase wood, hides and handicrafts in Aweil to sell on their return was being eliminated as was the money they made from 'allowing' the displaced to travel on the train to 'sanctuary' in northern Sudan. Of course, the commercial traders were also not keen to see increased tonnages of relief food going in that would depress the usually high prices in Aweil, especially when the train would not carry commercial goods for them. We were introducing a pattern which was dangerous to the traditional groups involved because it eliminated profiteering.[60]

Wannop emphasized the strength of both military and economic objections to a relief train: "The strength of the forces opposed to a dedicated relief train, especially one carrying food into SPLA-controlled territory, had not been fully realized and it seemed to us that the more determined we became to get the train to move, the more determined the forces opposed to it became."[61]

The inadequacy of relief also increased the benefits to be derived by merchants and army officers from Dinka cattle, through both market and non-market channels. Had relief supplies to northern Bahr el Ghazal been sufficient, this would have greatly reduced the Dinkas' exposure to looting as they headed north, as well as removing the need to sell cattle at "desperation" prices.

Adequate relief (and reduced outmigration) would also have reduced the benefits from exploiting Dinka labor, something from which merchants and army officers also benefited. The depopulation of much of northern Bahr el Ghazal (and Upper Nile) also offered the prospect of access to valuable grazing and farming land there. Critically, it also offered the prospect of access to the abundant oil reserves in the area.

**TABLE 5**
Relief and Political Representation by Region, 1986–1987

| | 1986 Relief (mt) | 1987 Relief (mt) | Number of Seats in Sudanese Constituent Assembly |
|---|---|---|---|
| Equatoria | 5,000 | 12,000 | 20 |
| Upper Nile | 1,000 | 3,000 | 7 |
| Bahr el Ghazal | 2,000 | 4,000 | 9 |
| Darfur | 51,000 | — | 43 |
| Kordofan | 107,000 | 20,000 | 43 |
| Eastern | 35,000 | 35,000 | 31 |
| Northern | 2,400 | 1,000 | 20 |
| Central | 18,000 | 6,000 | 55 |
| Khartoum | 2,000 | 1,000 | 34 |
| Total | 223,400 | 82,000 | 262 |

Sources: 1986, Bahr el Ghazal: Minear 1991, 8. Rest: EC 1987f; Chiriyankandath (1987, 99).

In southern Kordofan, the obstruction of relief to Bahr el Ghazal appears to have been sanctioned and encouraged by a number of religious leaders in the north. Islamic mullahs in the Meiram-Muglad area were reported to be preaching, during May 1989, that the planned train was part of a foreign-inspired conspiracy to provide food to the enemy, the SPLA (Wannop 1989, 10). It is reasonable to surmise that such objections were of long standing.

The considerable political influence of groups who stood to benefit from a lack of relief to Bahr el Ghazal was matched by an extreme underrepresentation of victim groups within the formally democratic Sudanese administration. The collapse in Dinka representation from already low levels—in both the south and the north—was noted in Chapter 2. Victim groups were weak not only in relation to those directly benefiting from famine but also in relation to many other nonvictim groups seeking to obtain a large share of relief distributions.

Table 5 compares approximate quantities of relief administered to the various regions of Sudan in 1986 and 1987 with the regional distribution of members of Sudan's Constituent Assembly (Chiriyankandath 1987, 99). In 1988, Darfur, Kordofan, and Eastern regions continued to get a large share of relief, with southern regions (notably Bahr el Ghazal and Upper Nile) receiving only small quantities by comparison (see Table 3). While this kind of analysis is inevitably somewhat crude and the number of elected representatives was clearly not the only factor influencing distribution of relief, the low representation for Bahr el Ghazal and Upper Nile in particular does appear to have handicapped these regions in competing for relief resources with regions where needs were less acute. The relatively high representation of Equatoria in relation to the rest of the south, and its relatively high receipt of relief, is particularly suggestive.[62] Significantly, the underrepresentation of the south and the overrepresentation of Equatoria within the south were mirrored in the higher echelons of government.[63]

A further handicap was that many of the Assembly members representing Bahr el Ghazal and Upper Nile, being sympathetic to the SPLM/SPLA, were unlikely to command the ear of the government in Khartoum. Of the nine Bahr el Ghazal members, four belonged to the Dinka-led South Sudan Political Association, which was sympathetic to the SPLM. Of the seven Upper Nile members, four were sympathetic to the SPLM (Chiriyankandath 1987, 99–101). Kordofan appears to have benefited from its heavy Umma Party representation, and from demands that voters who had helped the Umma Party to make major gains in the region at the expense of the DUP in 1986 receive some reward (Oxfam-UK 1987b, 2). The sale of relief could provide useful revenue for underfunded regional governments, which favored selling relief food rather than distributing it free (Agricultural Planning Unit 1987, 2; Heads of Mission, n.d.).

In 1985 and 1986, the Bahr el Ghazal provincial government, under its military governor, a former Anyanya commander and apparently an SPLA supporter, struggled to obtain relief for Aweil.[64] For example, in May and June of 1985 the Bahr el Ghazal administration paid Sud. £26,000 to the Sudan Railways Corporation to bring sorghum from Babanousa. However, the military governor, a Dinka, had no operational command over the mostly northern army in his province (Oxfam-UK 1986a, 3). Moreover, he was later replaced by Abu Gurun, who became infamous for his brutal hostility to the Dinka (Africa Watch 1990, 68–70).

Within the cabinet, southern representatives were marginalized. Generally, southern Sudanese ministers got lower-ranked posts, with the real power lying in the major ministries such as Defense and Finance (*Sudan Times*, May 30, 1988). The Minister of Transport, Aldo Ajou Deng, was from Aweil, but his voice appeared to carry little authority within the cabinet (*Sudan Times*, September 26, 1988). Meanwhile, governors in the south, appointed directly by the prime minister, were ineffective advocates for their people (*Sudan Times*, December 20, 1988). This appears to have been particularly the case for Bahr el Ghazal and Upper Nile, where even requests for food aid were low, notably in comparison to Equatoria (EC 1986a, 1987f). For its part, the press was largely dominated by interests hostile to the south and to relief efforts, with the NIF having the support of half Khartoum's ten daily newspapers (*Guardian*, March 21, 1988; *Sudan Times*, July 8, 1988).

The weak political position of southern famine victims was exacerbated by the weakness of the RRC, which had a brief to represent them after taking over the relief coordinating role of UNOEOS upon the expulsion of Prattley

in October 1986 (Africa Watch 1990, 109). In practice, the RRC commissioner—lacking ministerial status and at the same time appointed directly
by the prime minister—was largely subordinate not only to the prime minister but also (increasingly) to the minister of social welfare, zakat (an Islamic
tax) and the displaced, who claimed responsibility for displaced famine victims and who had close ties with both the prime minister and the NIF
leader, Hassan el Turabi. With the prime minister concerned to play down
the severity of the famine,[65] the RRC's ability and willingness to publicize
famine or relief holdups was very limited. To give one example of the RRC's
limitations, the RRC commissioner announced—erroneously—in November 1986 that news of famine was exaggerated and relief was arriving in the
south in substantial quantities (*Sudan Times*, November 14, 1986).

Inequalities at the political level were also influential in determining the
fate of the relief grain that did arrive in Bahr el Ghazal. More often than not,
such grain did not reach the designated beneficiaries. While it is possible
to regard such diversion as evidence that relief efforts were undermined by
corruption, the practice typically received official sanction of some kind.
It is more usefully seen as a manifestation of policy than as one of policy
failure.

In Aweil, the military and traders reportedly took a large proportion of
relief distributions that reached the town (Africa Watch 1990, 127; EC
1987g, 1). Government departments also pressed for a share (UNDP 1988,
10). As late as April 1989, the commissioner of Aweil misappropriated 750
metric tons of relief (Africa Watch 1990, 127; van Voorhis 1989, 8).

In the case of relief earmarked for Wau, the position was worse. In December 1986, a convoy of Italian relief food to Wau (the first relief that year)
was taken by the army (de Waal 1990a, 8–9). In 1987, the army used its
control over relief supplies stored within its own compound at Raga, in Bahr
el Ghazal, to organize large-scale looting of relief intended for the people of
Wau to the east. By August 21, 1987, of 5,659 metric tons originally stored
at the army compound, only 590 metric tons were left. By February 1988, it
was reported that only 35.5 metric tons of relief food were left in Raga, out
of a total originally stored in the compound and elsewhere of almost 9,000
metric tons (TCC meeting minutes, February 15, 1987).

On Saturday June 27, 1987, in the presence of the donors' relief coordinator, Paul Symonds, army personnel had told a large group of Raga residents
that Symonds had come to take the food to the SPLA in Wau, and that they
should come to the compound on the following Monday and take the food
themselves. At this time, there was significant hardship among the people in
Raga, many of whom were from a variety of non-Dinka tribes and had been
displaced to Raga as a result of raiding by the SPLA (Symonds 1987, 4–5).
Thus, the relief was portrayed as heading for the very group that had created
suffering in Raga. Large-scale looting of the relief sorghum stored in the

army compound subsequently occurred on precisely the day stipulated by army staff—Monday, June 29. Symonds described the scene: "The stacks were alive with people. Dura [sorghum] was being dragged away as fast as people could move. About 700 persons, men, women and children were involved. The army personnel sat and laughed at our attempts to stop the stealing" (ibid., 6).

Looting by local people provided a cover for the army's own looting (ibid., 4–7). Army staff gained direct commercial benefits: officers sold much of the looted grain to merchants who had come from Wau to buy it (and were later to resell it at a substantial profit in Wau);[66] and the army in Raga used stolen sorghum to pay women to work on its farm and to clean the military compound.[67] Indirect benefits arose from the elimination of free relief grain from local markets. This inevitably helped to sustain high grain prices in Wau, from which army officers were profiting. There was little redress against the army's extraction of these benefits in the context of civil war. A state of emergency had been declared in the south, so there was no local or civilian control of army activities and no recourse to law to investigate the theft (ibid., 4). The regional government of Bahr el Ghazal disclaimed any responsibility on the ground that it could not control the army (TCC meeting minutes, February 15, 1988). Meanwhile, death threats prompted the local RRC representative to leave, precluding any redress through this organization (Symonds 1987, 7).

In 1988, the army continued to take a share of relief earmarked for Wau. Between January and November of 1988, only about 200 metric tons of relief food (rice) was delivered to Wau, and the army was reported to have exacted a heavy price—a substantial share of the produce carried—in return for protecting commercial and relief trucks (EC 1988f; TCC meeting minutes, February 15, 1988). When relief distributions under ICRC eventually began in the winter of 1988–1989, merchants in Wau successfully lobbied for restriction of relief distributions to accredited displaced people, a strategy that was likely to keep the impact of relief on prices to a minimum.[68] Bryan Wannop, of UNDP, pointed to the power of "the military/commercial coalition" in Wau as a substantial threat to relief operations there (interview with Bryan Wannop, UNDP, New York, September 6, 1990).

The extensive local diversion of relief was matched at the central government level by a more subtle and routinized diversion of relief resources. This was the manipulation of exchange rates by the government, allowing the government to "cream off" a large proportion of international resources devoted to relief (Duffield 1992, 10). It is difficult to put a figure on this form of diversion, but in 1989 when a preferential exchange rate was granted for relief operations to the south, the Sudanese government reckoned this cost it some Sud. £90 million (Deng and Minear 1992, 94). Heavy import taxes were another means of siphoning off relief resources.

Another factor discouraging effective relief was the Islamic agenda of some elements in the north. The fact that several international NGOs involved in the south had overtly Christian affiliations inevitably fed into the Sudanese government's suspicions of relief to the south, with these NGOs sometimes seen as successors to imperial missionaries. Fears that famine would be used by "Christian" aid agencies to promote Christianity were significant in some quarters.[69] These fears encouraged the expulsion of a number of agencies with Christian affiliations that were working in the south, including World Vision and the Lutheran World Federation.

### Relief to Southern Famine Migrants in the North

While donor and government officials stressed the access difficulties impeding relief to famine migrants in southern Kordofan,[70] these difficulties were, again, not insuperable. In fact, there were no significant security obstacles here. Again, a fundamental cause of the inadequacy of relief lay in the uneven distribution of political power at various levels of the Sudanese administration, and the consequent low priority attached to relief. Disenfranchised by long-term political changes, the Dinka were further disenfranchised by their movement into areas where they did not form part of the constituency of local politicians. Indeed, when the commissioner of Eastern Bahr el Ghazal lobbied on behalf of those displaced from his region into southern Kordofan, the RRC asked the Governor of Bahr el Ghazal to stop interference in affairs that were not his responsibility (TCC meeting minutes, November 2, 1987, 5). By contrast, when a number of Fur people were displaced from the Jebel Marra area of Darfur in 1988 by the raiding of rival Sudanese Arab groups, the prime minister pushed for an immediate response and the governor of Darfur acted quickly to get relief to the displaced (interview with Peter Strachan, Oxfam-UK, Nyala, December 6, 1988). The Fur had voted en bloc for the prime minister's Umma Party in 1986.

The "inaccessibility" of Abyei town was far from absolute. The town was readily accessible by truck during the dry season, and in 1988 it could be reached overland as late as June. Certainly, the rains eventually cut off this overland route. But even then, helicopters were replenishing the town garrison: the soldiers at least were well fed (*Le Monde*, November 3, 1988; *Heritage*, October 31, 1988). There was, moreover, a landing strip for planes at Abyei, yet the possibility of using it was ruled out at an aid coordination meeting with RRC in May 1988.[71] Airdrops were another neglected option.

Meiram town was accessible by both rail and truck during the dry season, and remained reachable by rail throughout the rains of 1988. In the summer of 1988, the government blamed a six-week delay in the dispatch from Babanousa of a train carrying relief on the lack of a military escort, but there had

**TABLE 6**
Western Relief Operation Allocations within
Kordofan, Late 1987–Early 1988 (mt)

| Area Council | Tranche 1 | Tranche 2 |
|---|---|---|
| Soderi | 4,000 | 3,500 |
| Bara | 3,000 | 2,500 |
| En Nahud | 2,500 | 3,000 |
| Um Ruwaba | 2,250 | 3,000 |
| El Obeid | 1,800 | 3,800 |
| Dilling | 683 | 1,536 |
| Rashad | 617 | 1,109 |
| Kadugli | 506 | 1,359 |
| El Fula | 756 | 1,250 |
| Abyei | 78 | 745 |

*Sources:* Food Aid Administration 1988a; RRC/
EC 1988a.

actually been no SPLA activity within one hundred miles of the town (de
Waal 1990a, 11–12). Moreover, trains with a military mission were moving
freely to Meiram and beyond: for example, at the beginning of August, a
train was reported traveling through Meiram on its way to Bahr el Arab to
fetch some soldiers.[72] Such shipments could be organized very rapidly, in
contrast to the delays affecting relief. A Sudan Railways Corporation worker,
with direct experience of the patterns of train movements on the line from
Babanousa to Aweil, told the writer that soldiers from Meiram and Bahr el
Arab (both on the rail line to Aweil) would send messages to the Babanousa
railway authorities that they required bullets and food. He added, "If they
[the railway authorities] receive a message at eveningtime, the train will start
at nighttime." It was widely rumored that Meiram was one of the centers at
which the Messiriya militias' obtained arms, and that much of the ammunition for these arms came by train from Babanousa.

Significantly, and in line with patterns of relief to Bahr el Ghazal, the low
level of relief delivered to southern Kordofan was matched by low allocations. In late 1987, the district known as Abyei area council, which was to
experience some of the highest famine mortality rates ever recorded anywhere, received no grain at all in the original allocation (the first "tranche")
of Western Relief Operation (WRO) grain. This was subsequently increased
to 78 metric tons. When the influx from Bahr el Ghazal increased in the
course of early 1988, only modest increases were made, giving Abyei just
3.68 percent of the total. Table 6 shows allocations of WRO grain within
Kordofan region under the two "tranches" (Food Aid Administration 1988a;
RRC/EC 1988a).

These allocations were made jointly by the Kordofan regional govern-

**TABLE 7**

Government Relief Allocations within Kordofan, 1988 (mt)

| Area Council | Allocation | Area Council | Allocation |
|---|---|---|---|
| Bara | 3,000 | El Fula | 610 |
| Soderi | 2,000 | Rashad | 380 |
| Um Ruwaba | 2,000 | Dilling | 300 |
| El Obeid | 2,000 | Kadugli | 0 |
| En Nahud | 1,500 | Abyei | 0 |

*Sources:* Food Aid Administration 1988b.

ment, the RRC, and international donors. It is difficult to know the precise role played by each party in the decisions, or the precise rationale(s). The greater severity of drought in the north in 1987 was clearly a factor.

That the low allocation to Abyei mirrored Sudanese government priorities is strongly suggested by Table 7, which shows allocations in a separate Ministry of Finance–funded operation, also in 1988 (Food Aid Administration 1988b). The two area councils with substantial influxes of southern famine migrants, Abyei and Kadugli, were the only two that were allocated no Ministry of Finance sorghum.

A similar pattern of low allocations to areas taking famine migrants from the south was visible in Darfur. Only very meager allocations were made to Buram area council (containing Safaha) (Technical Committee for Relief and Rehabilitation, n.d.). And the influx into Safaha in early 1988 led to only modest and tardy modifications. In particular, when donors reacted to the arrival of malnourished people in Safaha with a request that the South Darfur provincial government divert 1,500 metric tons of Western Relief Operation grain to the displaced, the provincial government proved very reluctant to do so.[73]

After the extreme famine mortality in southern Kordofan, donors argued that the WRO had not originally been intended to meet the needs of displaced people. Yet the need for relief in this area could reasonably have been anticipated by all parties concerned. After all, there had already been famine in Abyei area council in 1987, as evidenced by large-scale sales of livestock, malnutrition, and disease among the displaced. Donors and aid agencies had sent a team to assess the situation in Abyei area council at this time (Minear 1991, 9). Meanwhile, the inadequacy of relief to Bahr el Ghazal in 1987 was well known, and might reasonably have been expected to lead to increased northward migrations as people ran out of food. Indeed, the severity of the crisis in Bahr el Ghazal had been brought into clear focus as tens of thousands moved east to Ethiopia, a migration peaking in late 1987. If relief of famine had been an important priority for Sudanese government authorities, moreover, there were arguably good reasons for actively encouraging migration to the north: substantial distributions in relatively secure areas within walking distance of Bahr el Ghazal offered one way of overcoming the much-emphasized security obstacles to relief within Bahr el Ghazal.

The pattern of widespread holdups in dispatch and delivery also suggested government obstruction of relief, as well as a desire to manipulate resources that might have been used for relief for a variety of other purposes. At the outset of the WRO program, in late 1987, estimates of Agricultural Bank of Sudan (ABS) stocks within Kordofan itself were more than 140,000 metric tons (RRC/donors 1987, 10). These stocks diminished in the course of 1988, but sorghum stocks held by the Agricultural Bank of Sudan (ABS) totaled some 366,000 metric tons as late as August 1988. Despite these stocks, at the beginning of May 1988, supplies from ABS for the WRO were at a standstill.[74] Such delays undoubtedly exacerbated the famine, not only because the WRO was the vehicle for supplying displaced southerners but also because the lack of WRO deliveries to local people in southern Kordofan and southern Darfur added to the political difficulties of channeling relief to the displaced.[75] The standstill in supplies had arisen from the insistence of the Ministry of Finance that donors buy grain from the ABS (a semiautonomous department of the ministry) at Sud. £65/sack, rather than the Sud. £45/sack originally agreed with donors in December 1988.[76] While in theory the ABS had a brief for promoting food security in Sudan, in practice this was largely undermined by its position within the Ministry of Finance (to which it was reported to owe Sud. £80 million in 1988) and by a pressing need for revenue, whether from donors or exports (Woldegabriel 1991, 10).[77] Even beyond the confines of relief operations, the longer-term development strategies of the ABS had suggested that food security was never more than a secondary concern.[78]

Insofar as ABS did give priority to food security, it was to the food security of urban areas. Donors themselves privately recognized that this was a higher priority for ABS than supplying famine relief under the WRO, with stocks seen by donors as unlikely to be released at all once they fell to near 300,000 metric tons (Interdonor Memo. 1988, 4). Ensuring adequate food supplies to urban areas had long been a priority for governments in Sudan, including the Anglo-Egyptian Condominium government (de Waal 1989b, 23). ABS also helped undermine relief operations by supplying underweight bags and by offering sorghum that was unfit for human consumption.[79]

Another factor delaying the WRO was government reluctance to release funds to cover transport costs. While the minister of finance had agreed to the use of counterpart funds (raised from government sales of ongoing program food aid) to cover WRO transport costs, release of these funds by the minister was very sluggish.[80] Yet in the spring of 1988, it was clear that poor performance by transporters was related to low payment for WRO delivery (in relation to other available work): deliveries picked up when payments were significantly increased (interview with Alfred Van Ginkel, Financial Administration/Operations, RRC, MALT, Khartoum, October 25, 1988).

Whereas in 1986 relief deliveries had been speeded by the use of RTU (then RTO) trucks (which served as a bargaining tool in relation to private contractors), these trucks—estimated at 560[81]—were not made available as a government resource for the WRO, despite a recommendation that they should be from USAID's monitoring company (Hassabo and Co. 1988, 15). By contrast, RTU was reported by the head of the donors' logistics agency in charge of the WRO to have bid successfully, as a private company, for WRO delivery work (interview with Alfred Van Ginkel, Financial Administration/ Operations, RRC, MALT, Khartoum, October 25, 1988).

Transport of WRO grain for southern famine victims was also disrupted by widespread diversion en route, part of a much wider pattern of diversion of relief supplies intended for the south.[82] Many government officials and army officers were reported to have collaborated with merchants to control a thriving black market, stocked largely with misappropriated commodities that had been officially earmarked for the south (*Guardian*, February 9, 1988; Duffield 1990a, 21). The regional governments of the south were widely accused of colluding in such activities (see, e.g., *Sudan Times*, November 29, 1988, January 19, 1989).

The appropriation of relief should be understood in the context of widespread manipulation of government supplies of sugar, edible oil, and fuel for private gain before the famine, as well as what Mark Duffield has called the "growing use of public office to further private gain" (Davey et al. 1976, paper no. 17; Ibrahim 1985, 236; de Waal 1989a, 106; Ibrahim 1988, 280; Duffield 1990a, 21; Brown 1992, 212–13). Given the diminishing resources in local government and the civil service, given the sharply falling real earnings of government officials,[83] and given the otherwise limited opportunities for merchants in a context of economic downturn, high inflation, high interest rates, and a need for a quick return on investments, the temptation to profit from sales of relief goods was considerable (Shepherd 1988, 64; de Waal 1989b, 53; Republic of Sudan/UNDP/ODA 1984, 71; Minear 1991, 19; Duffield 1990a, 22). Indeed, the selling of official supplies was reported to be sometimes the only way that provincial government officials could subsist (*Sudan Times*, July 18, 1988). Civil war provided a fertile soil for an increase in the private use of public goods. In particular, the disruption of trade helped to create severe shortages in southern Sudan and neighboring areas, encouraging abuses by officials who had access to very highly priced goods distributed through government channels (as well as to "international" relief). It is clear also that civil war could give an appearance of legitimacy to the appropriation of commodities earmarked for southerners (Symonds 1987). It would be a mistake, then, to regard such corruption as a matter of individual aberration or even as simply a breakdown in normal administrative procedures. Rather, it represented one way in which the state apparatus could continue to function despite—even to some extent at the expense of—a breakdown in civil society.

A low priority attached to relief of famine migrants in southern Kordofan is also suggested by the absence of any attempt to evacuate famine migrants from Abyei (or, indeed, from Meiram) before the rains of 1988. The feasibility of such an operation was demonstrated by the successful evacuation from Safaha, in southern Darfur. In southern Kordofan, government officials blamed a shortage of trucks (interview with Salah Ahmed Nasser, first executive officer, Babanousa Area Council, November 30, 1988). Yet the Oxfam operation in Safaha had employed local trucks, and the supply of trucks was considerably higher in Kordofan than in Darfur (Hassabo and Co. 1988, 15). Critically, the connections among the militias, local government authorities, and the army appear to have been closer in Kordofan, where both the South Kordofan commissioner and the governor were Messiriya in the autumn of 1988 and where some Messiriya militiamen were reported to have uniforms and ranks. In Darfur, the largely non-Rizeigat regional authorities gave NGOs a tacit go-ahead to move the Dinka from Safaha, fearing another massacre like the one that had taken place at Ed Daien, in Darfur, in 1987 (Oxfam-UK 1988h, 2; Mahmud and Baldo 1987).[84]

Neither the RRC nor the RTU trucks were made available for moving the displaced, in either Darfur or Kordofan (TCC meeting minutes, April 12, 1988). Significantly, when the central government undertook to resettle famine migrants from Khartoum (where they were seen as a health and security threat) to Bahr el Ghazal in late 1989 and 1990, it provided train transport from Khartoum to Babanousa and Muglad, where trucks were provided to take them further south to Abyei (UN/SRRA 1990, 57).[85] The "transport constraint" appeared to have largely disappeared.

Importantly, the inadequacy of relief to southern famine migrants in the north also allowed the relatively unrestricted extraction of benefits from famine itself (see Figure 2). The desire in some quarters to debilitate the Dinka—as the principal supporters of the SPLA—has been noted. Given the perceived threat to security constituted by Dinka migration to the north, the severe weakening—or outright elimination—of this group may have been perceived as all the more "necessary." It bode ill for relief that Abyei, Meiram, Muglad, and Babanousa—sites of the main famine camps in southern Kordofan—were also the principal militia bases in the area (UN/SRRA 1990, field notes, May 12).

The commercial benefits of famine, often neglected in famine studies, were substantial in southern Kordofan and southern Darfur (see Figure 2). The profits of army officers and merchants from the grain trade on the edge of the war zone have been noted. In Abyei, the belated arrival of relief in

October after an absence of deliveries since June proved damaging for those selling grain: the price of sorghum fell by more than half (Africa Watch 1990, 130). Meanwhile in Meiram, the rapid price falls when relief arrived in September and the shipping of grain back north out of the town suggest that the intervention of international donors upset the calculations of merchants who had felt confident that the town and railway authorities would not dispatch significant relief to Meiram in the autumn of 1988. Sales of grain in Meiram were made by agents of merchants based in Babanousa, so the beneficiaries of high grain prices in Meiram were geographically well placed to influence rail dispatches from Babanousa (until heavy donor pressure for delivery, via the governor of Kordofan). The alleged bribing of rail workers by merchants has been mentioned. Army officers also appear to have been involved in profiting from the sale of expensive grain in Meiram, an involvement matched by the army's effective veto over rail shipments from Babanousa (including those to Meiram). Adequate relief in such centers as Abyei and Safaha in the form of emergency supplies or transport would also have reduced the profits of those merchants and army personnel who bought cattle and handicrafts from Dinka desperate to escape.

Relief was also a threat to the exploitation of labor. Before NGOs began working in Adila (where one of the seven NGO Darfur settlements was established in the spring of 1988), many of the displaced in the surrounding rural areas were reported to have been working against their will for no money. The coming of the NGOs prompted local people, of the Ma'aliya ethnic group, to improve their treatment of displaced people working for them, with the displaced now having the option of fleeing to the relief settlements (Ryle 1989a, 25; interview with Garang Anai, acting chief at Adila settlement, Darfur, December 3, 1988). In this respect, the settlements appear to have served a function analogous to that of the sanctuaries for escaped slaves that were established under Condominium rule as part of the government's antislavery campaign (Hargey 1981, 385). The acting Dinka chief at Adila said he feared that any NGO departure would prompt local people to come to the settlement to reclaim Dinka children; indeed, even with the NGO presence, local people did sometimes come to settlements looking for Dinka children who had escaped from them (interview with Garang Anai, acting chief at Adila settlement, Darfur, December 3, 1988; minutes of aid coordination meeting, Khartoum, August 2, 1988). In Kordofan, too, the relief camps were regarded by some of the displaced as a place where they could shelter from the severe economic and sexual exploitation that was common in the surrounding areas. It is reasonable to surmise that the exclusion of NGOs from certain areas, in Bahr el Ghazal as well as in southern Kordofan, facilitated exploitation and human rights abuses in these areas, including raiding.

In 1988, relief agencies were frequently criticized for creating labor shortages by distributing relief to displaced people. Oxfam experienced significant criticism on these lines for its work in Darfur (interview with Marcus Thompson, Oxfam-UK, Oxford, October 20, 1988).[86] There were similar criticisms in southern Kordofan. In the autumn of 1987, the manager of the El Fuda state farm, southern Kordofan, complained of a shortage of labor caused by provision of relief at nearby Meiram (UNICEF 1987b, 2). In November 1988, the army came to the Meiram camp for the displaced and took away a large number of Dinka for harvest work on the El Fuda farm. Meanwhile, farmers in Meiram complained that the Dinka constituted their sole potential laborers, and that ever since the relief distributions began, the Dinka had not wanted to work (interviews with farmers in Meiram market, November 1988). North of Meiram, in Muglad, NGOs were criticized by army personnel for creating "dependency" among the displaced and discouraging them from working (interview with Mike McDonagh, Concern, Muglad, November 24, 1988).

Although there was much talk of the importance of making the displaced "self-reliant,"[87] such self-reliance would actually have run counter to the interests of many influential local employers. In Kordofan, the displaced were given no land to cultivate. In Darfur, only some of the settlements provided land for the displaced, and even then in inadequate quantities (Oxfam-UK 1988c).

A final set of benefits threatened by relief were those arising from unusually high transport prices. Any adequate provision of relief transport for famine migrants would have threatened the profits made by merchants and army officers from provision of expensive "authorized" truck transport for migrants seeking to escape from Abyei. Provision of adequate relief within Abyei and Meiram would also have reduced the desperation that encouraged large payments by those attempting to leave.

As in the south, the distribution of political power at local level generated a particular pattern of local distributions, which is not usefully conceptualized as corruption. When relief did arrive at its designated destination, the overriding influence of the army and local Messiriya, together with the absence of effective registration or monitoring by outside agencies, encouraged the widespread, officially sanctioned diversion of relief away from the intended beneficiaries. Again, such diversion yielded direct benefits through appropriating relief and indirect benefits arising from unchecked famine. It seems likely that the significant economic crisis among many local people in the Abyei/Meiram/Babanousa area encouraged such practices.

Monitoring distributions was especially difficult in Abyei town, where western NGOs were repeatedly refused permission to work (Africa Watch 1990, 128).[88] For much of 1988, responsibility for local distributions was jointly held by the Abyei relief committee and the Comboni Fathers, of the Italian Catholic Church. The relief committee was very close to the military:

it was chaired alternately by the Abyei executive officer and the army colonel, and it contained essentially the same people who served on the Security Committee, with overlapping responsibilities (ibid., 128). The concentration of power in the hands of groups benefiting from famine was increased in early October 1988 when the Comboni Fathers were stripped of their relief responsibilities by the (Messiriya) Kordofan governor, Abdel Rasoul el Nur (Oxfam-UK 1988h, 2). The Sudanese Red Crescent became the lead agency in the town. Although it "coordinated" with western NGOs, nevertheless SCF and Oxfam were not represented on the relief committee (eventually withdrawing in February 1989). The Sudanese Red Crescent, moveover, was reported to be "under tremendous political, social, and psychological pressure to cooperate closely with the local Misiriya authorities" (Africa Watch 1990, 128). There were implausible charges—conveyed by the Red Crescent medical coordinator in Abyei, an Umma Party stalwart—that Oxfam had been proselytizing in Abyei. This contributed to the expulsion of an Oxfam nurse from the town (Oxfam-UK 1988h, 4).

In 1986, Messiriya militiamen took food direct from the NGO CARE in the region of Abyei, and from local Dinka subchiefs, or *omdas*, to whom relief had been distributed.[89] In 1987, less than 50 percent of food for displaced people in southern Kordofan reached its target, according to estimates from MSF-France staff.[90] And according to information from Western church officials in Abyei, in both 1987 and 1988 government officials permitted the use of food aid for the displaced as fodder for cattle owned by northern Sudanese (U.S. Congress 1989, 77). John Garang claimed to have good evidence that relief food to Abyei was handed to the army and the local Messiriya-dominated relief committee, whence it disappeared into the market (interview with Garang in *Sudan Times*, November 29, 1988). Certainly, from early October 1988, when Abyei began to become accessible by land again, the first groups to receive relief whenever a consignment arrived were the army and the local Messiriya (Africa Watch 1990, 127–28). Officials of the Sudanese Red Crescent admitted they were unable to prevent this: at the beginning of November 1988, a Red Crescent official, Beshir Mohammed Ali, acknowledged that the continued suffering in southern Kordofan was due to a pattern of relief distributions that channeled relief to local inhabitants as well as to the displaced (*Guiding Star*, November 3, 1988).

In Meiram to the north, "leakage" of grain was institutionalized in 1988: 20 percent of the amount allocated to the displaced was given to the town authorities under an agreement between the RRC and the Meiram food distribution committee (consisting of local Messiriya merchants and representatives of the army, police, and MSF-France) (Oxfam-UK 1988d, 3). The allocation was seen as a pragmatic step toward obtaining the goodwill of the town authorities, who had originally asked for 50 percent and who were in a position to block relief efforts altogether if they so chose (MSF-France

1988c). There is no indication, however, that the amounts originally allocated to the displaced in Meiram took account of such an agreement.

In the absence of adequate general distributions, distributions in the camp for the displaced were sometimes the only ones to take place, and many Dinka who were not registered in the camp were sent there to bring grain away. Visiting aid workers at the beginning of September reported:

> Recently the following pattern has emerged at distribution times. At 4 A.M. the army surrounds the camp and then proceeds to supervise the distribution. However, on more than one occasion, following the 'distribution' there is hardly any food to be found in the camp. It is understood that children are sent into the camp by the army and other Arabs to collect food during the distribution.[91]

According to one MSF-France report, before the RRC representative arrived in Meiram in September, "entire columns of grain-carrying Dinka could be seen leaving the camp for the Arab town or the Army headquarters" (MSF-France 1988j). In Meiram, Dinka reported to me that much of the grain that left the camp in this way ended up in Meiram market.

A third opportunity for officially organized diversion in Meiram lay in local farmers' sending Dinka to the general distributions, a practice that became increasingly common through the summer of 1988 (MSF-France 1988c, 1988m). "Since there is no system of registration, this is excessively easy," an MSF-France report commented (MSF-France 1988m). Indeed, the Meiram relief committee and the army refused to accept a system of registration, perhaps for this reason. Many of the laborers sent to distributions clearly needed food themselves: an MSF field report of July 26, 1988, observed, "The fact is that these workers and their families who live in the area around Meiram seem to be in scarcely better condition than those staying in the town." However, it is not clear that the grain received by these Dinka served actually to supplement their incomes: the widespread intimidation of Dinka laborers and the local opposition to registration suggest that much of the grain distributed in this way would have found its way into non-Dinka hands; and according to the *Sudan Times*, some of the "leaked" food in Meiram was used to underwrite slave labor on local farms (*Sudan Times*, September 11, 1988). Together with the rapid influx of new arrivals from the south, such distributions to all comers helped swell the numbers of Dinka seeking relief distributions in Meiram to well in excess of the food available, encouraging major interruptions of distributions.

There was no effective counter to such abuses in Meiram. In particular, there were no Dinka on the Meiram relief committee. The need for local RRC representation had been noted in October 1987 (UNICEF 1987). But there was to be no RRC representative in Meiram until one arrived with the donor delegation in September 1988 (interview with Christopher Carr, MSF-France, Khartoum, November 20, 1988).

Another major function of relief "failures" lay in the prospect of minimizing the unwanted side effects of famine. Famine migration gave rise to a number of fears in northern Sudan, and there was a common perception that relief would attract more migrants, with attendant economic, health, and security risks. Attempts to block the northward movement of migrants were evidence of these fears.[92] Since any economic benefits arising from migration would themselves have been threatened by adequate relief, in practice both the fear of migrants and the desire to make use of them once they arrived appear to have militated against the provision of proper relief.

Aid agency staff perceived that local authorities' desire to avoid the various problems arising from large numbers of famine migrants in their respective areas had tended to discourage the provision of relief supplies in southern Kordofan in the hope that migrants would pass quickly through (interview with Marc Lejars, MSF-France, Khartoum, October 25, 1988). Also significant among northern officials was a desire not to attract migrants from the south. This became particularly clear in southern Darfur at the end of 1988, when the South Darfur provincial government was very reluctant to invite aid agencies to Safaha, for fear of attracting a further influx of southern Sudanese into Darfur in 1989 (interview with Wim Van Damme, MSF-Belgium, Nyala, December 7, 1988). Provincial officials said any provision for future waves of migration should be supplied within the borders of Bahr el Ghazal.[93] Aid agency staff felt that an NGO presence in Safaha would have attracted more migrants, and the evidence of Dinka's being attracted north by the provision of even limited relief (see Chapter 3) supports this judgment (interview with Wim Van Damme, MSF-Belgium, Nyala, December 7, 1988).

Economic fears surrounding famine migrants included the fear of high grain prices, which would be likely to harm poorly paid local officials, as well as others on low incomes (although it was to the advantage of merchants). Cutler's point about high prices spreading out from a famine epicenter—as food moves in and people move out—was borne out to some extent. In Babanousa, townspeople were reported to have bought stocks of sorghum in the early summer of 1988, fearing further influxes of displaced people, while merchants closed their shops to encourage panic buying. Rising grain prices meant that local people experienced considerable hardship (interview with Abdulla Arabi, administrative officer, Babanousa Town Council, November 30, 1988). In Meiram, there were reports that local people, as well as the displaced, were suffering significant nutritional problems (TCC meeting minutes, May 9, 1988, 4). Poor harvests in 1987 (USAID 1988a, 23) and the weak WRO relief effort added to the vulnerability of local people.

Another potential threat posed by famine migrants was the threat to the health of local people arising from unusual concentrations of migrants, who were often sick. The disease-ridden environment produced by large-scale migration had added greatly to famine mortality in Darfur in 1984–1985 (de Waal 1989a; see also Sen 1981, 205). And hostility toward migrants during this famine had encouraged withholding of relief from them (Keen 1991a).

During the late 1980s famine, perceptions of a health threat from famine migrants were common. In 1988, residents of Meiram accused Dinka famine migrants of bringing disease to the town and of straining the town's water resources. By the summer of 1988, water had became an important source of tension between the Dinka and local people, who were reluctant to provide the displaced with water (MSF-France 1988j, 4).[94] Similar concerns arose in Babanousa, where the town council administrative officer (in charge of the displaced) complained to me that the displaced were poorly educated and "polluted the environment," while exacerbating water shortages (interview with Abdulla Arabi, administrative officer, Babanousa Town Council, November 30, 1988). In Darfur, too, there were tensions between local people and the displaced over limited supplies of water (interview with Pierre Poivre, MSF-Belgium, Khartoum, November 10, 1988; interview with Garang Anai, acting chief, Adila settlement, December 3, 1988).

The perception of famine migrants as a security risk also appears to have discouraged relief. For example, the town authorities in Muglad, in southern Kordofan, who placed a number of obstacles in the path of NGOs providing for the displaced, feared that provision of relief would attract Dinka migrants and thereby threaten security (interview with Mike McDonagh, Concern, Muglad, November 24, 1988). A common association between outsiders and criminal activity acquired special force in wartime (Davey et al. 1976, 31).

Bishop Macram Max Gassis, of the diocese of El Obeid, referred in July 1988 to migrants from the south (of whom one hundred thousand had come to El Obeid, and then continued north): "The government is not interested to offer them any service. On the contrary, the government sees in them [a] security risk and expects them to go back to their area by denying them vital services."[95]

Security fears (and the obstacle to relief they constituted) were dramatically illustrated when the governor of Kordofan, in May 1988, objected to the Catholic church's assistance to people displaced from the south, claiming that these people were providing cover for SPLA terrorists in league with the Roman Catholic church, which he said was transferring southern Sudanese citizens from Abyei to Khartoum as part of a plan of sabotage (*Sudan Times*, May 29, 30, 1988). Since the displaced in question were primarily women and children in very weak physical condition, the charge of terrorism was not a very credible one.[96] Nonetheless, despite the strong element of paranoia involved, accusations such as the governor's reflected real fears. The SPLA's rapid gains in the south in 1987–1988 can have done little to allay fears that SPLA activity would spread to the north via the displaced.

When I asked the first executive officer of Babanousa why no provision had been made in 1988 to move starving people in the far south of Kordofan to the safer and better-provisioned Babanousa area, his choice of words suggested that the displaced were far from welcome, as well as implying a lack of interest in helping them to avoid the twin threat of famine and militiamen: "We did not prevent anyone who *dared* to come to Babanousa from Abyei or Meiram. It is up to them. They are free" (my emphasis). Political obstacles to any trucking operation in southern Kordofan were stressed by aid agency staff (interview with Mark Cunningham, Concern, Khartoum, November 11, 1988). As noted, these obstacles were less significant in Darfur.

### Changing Relief Patterns: The Domestic Context

The above analysis prompts an important question: if the benefits of relief "failures" for politically powerful groups were so important, both in maximizing the benefits of famine and in minimizing the unwanted side effects, how was it that significantly increased relief to the famine area became possible in 1989? Three factors played a part in this important shift: political realignments in the central government, side effects that threatened both the government and the rebels, and a change in donors' attitudes. For a time at least, these factors worked together to soften the stance of the Sudan government, in part by enhancing the position of elements in the north that had long been ambivalent about the war.[97]

First, political realignments in Khartoum were altering the interest of a number of northern groups in pursuing the war and blocking relief. The most important of these were the DUP and elements of the army. In many ways, late 1988 and early 1989 saw the partial reemergence of an alliance that had helped underpin the Nimeiri regime. This alliance brought together important elements of the Unionists, the army, and the south as a counterweight to the Umma Party (and the Baggara militias with which the Umma in particular had close ties).

The position of the DUP in Khartoum had been severely weakened by the incorporation into the coalition government of the NIF, with Prime Minister el Mahdi ejecting senior DUP ministers from his government in early 1988. While the DUP was being progressively marginalized in Khartoum, its principal foreign backer, Egypt, was increasingly interested in pressing for peace in Sudan. This shift in Egypt's stance apparently reflected an increasing fear of Islamic fundamentalism in Cairo, together with a growing recognition of Egypt's need to secure and improve the flow of water in the Nile, notably through the suspended Jonglei Canal project (Woodward 1990, 225). In these circumstances, the DUP was more inclined to seek new allies in the south, as well as a political settlement to the war. It pursued closer relations with the SPLM and mended its relations with the National Alliance for National Salvation (NANS) and the Union of Sudan African Parties (USAP), both of which favored a political settlement (Alier 1990, 271).

Having reached an accord with the SPLM in November 1988 (something that became known as the Sudanese Peace Initiative), the DUP found little support from the Umma Party. The DUP left the government at the end of December, but continued to press strongly for peace. The party was strongly in favor of the proposed Operation Lifeline trains from southern Kordofan to Bahr el Ghazal. The DUP minister of social welfare, Ohaj Mohamed Musa, gave vigorous support to the train (Wannop 1989, 2, 9–10). The DUP recognized that the success or failure of the peace process was intimately linked with the success or failure of the relief trains.[98] In particular, if anything had gone wrong with the trains, opponents of the peace process could have used this to prove the SPLA was intractable and a negotiated settlement impossible.

The DUP's newfound support for relief was matched by an increasingly powerful lobby within the army. SPLA advances had made Sudan's civil war look increasingly unwinnable from the government's point of view. The government's policy of famine had apparently bred more resistance than compliance. Some officers feared that the Umma Party was seeking subtly to undermine the army, by embroiling it in an unwinnable war while strengthening the Baggara militias in the Umma's traditional heartlands in western Sudan. The DUP's strong ties with army officers have been mentioned, as has the memorandum by army officers to the prime minister, demanding peace or the means to win the war. Senior army officials in these circumstances were increasingly supportive of relief efforts and of the possibility of a limited reprieve from military setbacks. Back in December 1988, the belated launch of ICRC relief efforts was widely credited to pressure from the defense minister, the retired general Abd el Majid Hamid Khalil (Minear 1991, 136). In relation to the 1989 Operation Lifeline, UNDP's Bryan Wannop noted in 1989:

> The military authorities in Khartoum were consistently supportive. . . . Problems such as obtaining military clearances for some areas involved in the relief operation which had been difficult earlier, from November [1988] onwards were granted most promptly. Furthermore, while a number of senior people in the Government continually cited the military's need for a train to Aweil to restock the garrison as a reason why the unescorted relief train concept could not be implemented, in our discussions with the military they repeatedly made clear they had sufficient stocks in hand and if we were able to move quickly enough we could dispatch several relief trains before they would need the rail line to carry military supplies.[99]

For its part, the Umma Party—previously largely hostile to relief—was now ambivalent, particularly in the context of growing international pressures. Some Umma members of the Sudanese parliament were influenced by the strong drift of public opinion in favor of peace (Wannop 1987, 10). On the other hand, some elements were still seeking to maintain a strong Islamic image that would rival that of the NIF and were hoping to discredit the DUP initiative, seen as an Egyptian move and one that might diminish Umma influence (Alier 1990, 271–72).

The changing political climate in Khartoum gave renewed opportunities for the previously marginalized groups who favored peace. The NANS in particular had been consistent in looking for a political settlement. The NANS had maintained contact with both the Umma Party and the SPLM, and in 1988 the NANS had established an amicable relationship with the DUP, playing a major role in bringing the DUP and SPLM together for the Sudanese Peace Initiative (Alier 1990, 274).

A second major (and related) change by 1989 was that the side effects of famine had become increasingly threatening both to the Sudan government and, in different ways, to the SPLA/SPLM. By the end of 1988, the SPLA/SPLM appeared ready to welcome an opportunity to consolidate its new, tenuous governance of much of the south (Minear 1991, 67). To do this— and to stem the tide of population loss, which threatened its ability to operate as an effective guerrilla force—it needed relief. In the north, it is reasonable to surmise that during the raiding that in large part created the famine, the possible future side effects of famine were of minor importance in relation to the more immediate economic and military motivations for raiding, especially as the primary initial response of those raided was to head south, away from their attackers. When large numbers did begin to move northwards, while this did bring significant economic benefits to some groups (such as those using Dinka labor), nevertheless the various side effects of famine became an increasingly pressing concern for politically powerful groups in northern Sudan.

For a long time, these anxieties tended to discourage relief in the north without encouraging relief in the south. Indeed, the fact that the Sudanese government did not want the Dinka in either the south or the north goes a long way toward explaining why so many people died in this famine.

In Khartoum, there was a long record of hostility to western and (especially) southern famine migrants, and this appears to have been exacerbated by growing security fears with the SPLA capture of the town of Kurmuk in late 1987 (Chiriyankandath 1987, 101; Oxfam-UK 1987d). The war was increasingly seen as encroaching on the north. At the end of 1987, the commissioner of Khartoum had made it clear that he saw the southern Sudanese newly arrived in Khartoum as a security and health threat, and suggested that general distributions of relief should be handled in such a way as to attract people away from Khartoum (RRC 1987, 1).[100] Destruction of shanty dwellings in Khartoum was noted by donor officials in 1987 and 1988 (EC 1987d, 6–7; *Guiding Star*, November 17, 1988). The rapid influx of southern Sudanese into Khartoum severely strained local services and resources (Alier 1990, 289). International donor representatives noted in October 1987 that tensions between residents and the displaced were running high in Khartoum, and aid activities in Khartoum in 1988 were kept at a low level partly for this reason (EC 1987d; Interdonor Memo. 1988, 6–7). (Large-scale forced movements of the displaced away from Khartoum were later to be carried out under the military regime of Lieutenant-General Omer el Beshir, who took power in June 1989.) In Darfur and Kordofan, many local officials were reluctant to provide relief for displaced southerners.

Eventually, when famine migrants in Khartoum emerged as a major threat to the legitimacy and popularity of the Sudanese government in late 1988, this threat appears to have prompted some groups in the capital to press for more provision of relief in the south and in southerly parts of the north in a bid to keep migrants away from the capital. There were reported to be more than 1 million southerners in Khartoum by 1989 and some feeling among senior government officials that the capital's "Arab character" was under threat, with the migrants polluting its religious purity (U.S. Committee for Refugees 1990, 16–17). In September 1988, the minister of social welfare called for the "establishment of reception centres at the internal frontiers to care for the displaced so as to stop their movement to capitals and urban areas" (Ministry of Social Welfare 1988, 1). Such reception centers were seen by some agency staff as likely to serve military functions— more people from Bahr el Ghazal would be attracted to the centers, where they could be policed by Messiriya—even as they helped keep migrants away from the capital (Oxfam-UK 1988e, 3). In October 1988, the RRC advised the commissioner of South Kordofan that government policy was to discourage movement to Khartoum by assisting the displaced in "settlement sites" in places such as southern Kordofan.[101] In late 1988, the central government was pressing for adequate preparations for a future influx of displaced people into Darfur, apparently anxious that these people remain in Darfur (interview with Wim van Damme, MSF-Belgium, Nyala, December 7, 1988).

Officials in Khartoum wanting to stem, perhaps even reverse, the influx of southerners constituted one source of support for the 1989 relief trains to Aweil (interview with Bryan Wannop, UNDP, New York, August 24, 1990). Significantly, the Khartoum displaced were not included in the 1989 Operation Lifeline effort (U.S. Committee for Refugees 1990, 20).

A significant element in the perceived threat posed by southern migrants was a perceived electoral threat. This grew in importance as the numbers with substantial periods of residence in Khartoum increased and the 1990 elections approached. The prime minister's Umma Party cannot but have been aware of the potential political significance of such migration, for migration to Khartoum from western Sudan had played an important part in his coming to power in 1986 (Chiriyankandath 1987, 98). Migrants from the south threatened a possible reversal of such benefits, for their loyalties lay elsewhere. The political dangers posed by such migrants had been emphasized in 1986, when the Reverend Philip Abbas Ghabboush, of the radical Sudanese National Party, was elected from a poor constituency in the north of the capital with southern as well as Nuba votes (ibid., 101).

Another threat posed by famine migrants in Khartoum was the threat to the legitimacy of government: their presence was visible evidence of massive upheaval in the south, and they were readily accessible to the international media, who gave increasing publicity to famine in the autumn of 1988.

On top of the specific threats posed by famine migrants, the war in the south was increasingly seen by many as undermining the economy of the north. The war had pressured the government into increasing taxes and postponing development projects. Prices of essential commodities were rising rapidly in Khartoum, and unemployment was also increasing (Alier 1990, 268, 274). In December crowds marched through the capital demanding "the overthrow of the government of famine and high cost of living" and protesting the rejection of the peace accord (*Sudan Times*, December 28, 30, 1988). A number of elements within the northern Sudanese political fabric—the nonfundamentalist press, the NANS and associated professional, workers', and farmers' trade unions, the Arab Baath party, the Communist Party, and the Union of Sudan Africa Parties—expressed their preference for talking with the SPLM/SPLA to secure some kind of political settlement (Alier 1990, 268, 273). Popular support for peace was helping to create a political climate favorable to a relief agreement with the SPLA.

Despite these developments, very significant obstacles to relief remained in 1989. Famine relief still threatened to interfere with profiteering. It was still vulnerable to theft. The army's support for peace could not be relied upon. And there remained significant hostility toward the SPLA from the NIF and assorted government-supported militias. As noted, in southern Kordofan the strength of opposition to relief for Bahr el Ghazal appeared to grow stronger as the departure of relief-only trains grew imminent. It appeared that the NIF was anxious to wreck the trains (interview with Bryan Wannop, UNDP, New York, September 6, 1990). A successful relief train would have dramatically illustrated the feasibility of negotiating with the SPLA, a move the NIF had consistently opposed, notably in relation to the DUP/SPLA peace initiative (Wannop 1989, 10; Alier 1990, 271). UN officials had information that the NIF had paid Sud. £1 million to stop the train, using local militias. A militia attack was made on the first Operation Lifeline train, although whether the NIF was behind it remains unclear (Wannop 1989, 11–16).

It took a third major change to overcome such obstacles. This was the significant change in donors' attitudes toward the relief issue. This shift helped produce a notable improvement in the efficacy of relief in 1989, although many problems with relief remained, and obstructionism was subsequently to reassert itself. It is to the actions and agendas of donors that we now turn.

## CHAPTER 5

# The Inadequacy of Relief: The Role
# of International Donors

We have consistently wanted to believe that
whatever government was in place was going
to do the right thing; was going to cooperate with
the delivery of food and assistance to people
desperately in need. In every instance, we have
been disappointed in those expectations.
(*U.S. Congressman Howard Wolpe,*
*October 25, 1990*)

THE ROLE of international donors in relation to the famine is best examined
by focusing on three of the most significant: the European Community (EC),
the United States (in particular, the agency responsible for emergency relief,
the U.S. Agency for International Development [USAID]), and the UN.[1]
The UN, while it occupied a rather different position from other donors, was
still a major source of funds for relief and development, and a potential
source of diplomatic pressure. Although these donors had considerably
greater political leverage than did NGOs and Sudanese relief organizations,
they failed to respond vigorously to the famine until it was past its peak,
deferring to a very large extent to the priorities of Sudanese government
officials, who were largely hostile to relief. Donors' underreaction appears to
have served important strategic and bureaucratic goals for the donors.

Meanwhile, the large gap between needs in the south and levels of assistance was obscured by the way donors presented information on the famine
and by the (related) ways in which they constructed their relief agendas.
Donors' policies retained a remarkably "unobjectionable" quality, even as
they left escalating famine largely untouched. This narrowed the room for
maneuver toward improved policy outcomes.

Unfortunately, this shaping of relief agendas, together with the lack of
clear responsibilities for donor organizations and officials in relation to Sudanese famine victims, produced a lack of accountability among the donors,
which matched the lack of accountability to famine victims within the Sudanese administration. Until the end of 1988, the lobbying power of the Dinka
within donor organizations was scarcely greater than their lobbying power

within Sudanese institutions. Donors' responsibility for halting what one Dinka elder had called the "flow of words" from famine regions requires careful consideration.

Only after severe famine among the Dinka in particular had been brought directly to the attention of Western publics by media exposure in the autumn of 1988 did donors' relief agendas begin to broaden significantly, considerably improving the efficacy of relief, albeit temporarily and albeit after the worst of the famine had passed. As Cutler (1989) emphasized in his study of relief to Ethiopia in 1983–1985, increased media coverage meant that the risks for donors of not taking vigorous action came to outweigh the risks of action.[2] In addition to coverage of the famine, donors faced a growing threat of public exposure from NGOs, which also helped to change the donors' stance. However, once media publicity died down in the course of 1989 and 1990, donors once again allowed themselves to be manipulated by Khartoum.

## THE STRATEGIC CONTEXT

Since the early 1970s and President Nimeiri's break with the Communists, Sudan had been an important ally for Western governments, notably the United States. It offered access to the Red Sea, a key channel for Middle Eastern oil supplies, and a base for the United States's rapid deployment force. It was seen as the only "Arab" government to support Egypt and the Camp David agreement. Like Nimeiri's regime, both the succeeding Transitional Military Council government and that of Sadiq el Mahdi offered Western countries (most importantly, the United States) and the conservative Arab states (notably Saudi Arabia) the prospect of keeping Egypt's strategic neighbor free from the twin threats of Communism and Islamic fundamentalism. The SPLA was persistently presented as having dangerous links with Communism, via its ties with Ethiopia.[3] U.S. worries about the Communist threat in Sudan, already fed by the Communists' having obtained a share in power in 1969–1971, were reinforced from 1982 on by the receipt of arms in the south from Ethiopia. Meanwhile, Libya, an alternative source of support for Sudan if Western aid were to be reduced, was often seen as embodying the threat of Islamic fundamentalism (*Times* [London], January 16, 1987), notwithstanding a certain unease on Gadaffi's part with fundamentalism itself. The specter of a hostile alliance among a transformed Sudanese government, Ethiopia, and Libya was underlined by the 1981 Aden Treaty among Ethiopia, Libya, and South Yemen (Woodward 1990, 170).

Sudan's strategic importance was reflected in very substantial economic support from Western donors. The "friendly" government of President Nimeiri had been repeatedly propped up by Western aid and loans. But amid gathering economic chaos and escalating debt in 1984, Nimeiri fell from Western favor and became increasingly unpopular at home. He was toppled in April 1985 in an uprising that was closely linked with USAID's insistence on harsh austerity measures as a precondition for release of frozen aid monies (Brown 1988, 81; Brown 1992, 178). Sadiq el Mahdi, too, relied heavily on Western assistance: before the last months of his administration, Sudan was the largest recipient of U.S. foreign aid in sub-Saharan Africa (Africa Watch 1990, 165). U.S. foreign aid assistance to Sudan totaled some $109 million in financial year 1986, $82 million in financial year 1987, and $73 million in financial year 1988 (U.S. Congress 1988b, 88).[4] Wheat food aid helped underpin Sudan's balance of payments and played a key role in placating the politically volatile urban areas: some 79 percent of Sudan's wheat supplies in 1987 came from food aid (Bickersteth 1990, 222–24). Despite some diminution in aid from the United States in particular (largely for domestic reasons), Western donors were still providing roughly half the recurrent government expenditure in Sudan in the winter of 1988–1989 (*Financial Times*, February 24, 1989). Meanwhile, Western investment in Sudan gave the West a considerable economic reason to maintain ties with the Sudanese government. In early 1984, Sudan's foreign debt amounted to U.S. $8 billion (Brown 1988, 76). Western investment in Sudanese oil (the extraction of which had been prevented by the SPLA) was also substantial. By 1984, Chevron had invested over $1 billion in Sudan (*Times* [London], January 16, 1987).

The donors' strategic interests provided critical context for their actions in relation to the famine. Donors' actions were unhelpful in three main ways: the donors allowed the Sudanese government to define the relief problem, they failed adequately to monitor the delivery of relief or to ensure it reached the intended beneficiaries, and they avoided addressing the underlying conflict.

## DONORS' UNWILLINGNESS TO MOVE BEYOND GOVERNMENT DEFINITIONS OF THE RELIEF PROBLEM

As the famine evolved, donors proved largely unwilling to move beyond government definitions of when and where relief distributions were acceptable and possible. The strategic reasons for this deference were clearly important: in March 1989, after the height of the famine, the *New York Times* reported: "American diplomats acknowledge that the lack of public criticism of [Sadiq el Mahdi's] . . . failure last year to provide food to famine victims stemmed from a desire not to push him into the arms of next-door Libya."[5]

The Sudanese administration was largely hostile to relief for southern Sudanese (notably the Dinka). The absence of a government appeal for relief until the summer of 1988 proved a particular obstacle to vigorous action by the UN (interview with Bryan Wannop, UNDP, New York, August 24, 1990). Moreover, donors' neglect of rebel-held areas, and the south more generally, largely reflected a deference to the sensitivities of the Sudanese government. In the context of government hostility to relief to the south, donors tended to devolve responsibility for needs assessment and the channeling of relief to the south onto other organizations (ICRC, NGOs, and the government's own RRC), offering little support to these organizations when they came into conflict with powerful elements within the Sudanese government. This appears to have allowed donors to avoid outright conflict with the Sudanese government, while at the same time providing them with a way of minimizing their own accountability for the lack of assistance reaching the south.

In the summer of 1986, NGOs had been hopeful of support from the UN (specifically, UNOEOS) for their advocacy of wide-ranging, neutral, accountable relief operations in the south. The EC had established contacts with the SPLM's relief arm, the Sudan Relief and Rehabilitation Association (SRRA) (Oxfam-UK 1986o, 1). However, by the end of August, hopes of reaching all parts of the south with international aid were dwindling, as the UN appeared to be directing its efforts toward relieving government-held areas, apparently with a view to leaving relief aimed at rebel-held areas to the ICRC (Oxfam-UK 1986n, 1).

When the Sudanese government expelled the UN's special representative, Winston Prattley, at the end of 1986, this was a major blow to hopes of reaching all parts of the south. It virtually put an end to donor/NGO attempts to reach beyond the government garrison towns. Prattley's expulsion drew scant protest from the major donors, such as the United States and the EC (Bonner 1989, 88). Nor was there any penalty imposed by the UN itself (interview with Bryan Wannop, UNDP, New York, August 24, 1990). The incident helped convince most NGOs that channeling relief to rebel-held areas of the Sudan would not be tolerated by the Sudanese government or supported by donors.[6] Norwegian People's Aid delivered significant relief to SPLA-held areas of eastern Equatoria in 1988, which had a significant impact on the then-limited civilian population there (Roger Winter, personal communication, 1992). But apart from this, there was to be no significant relief to rebel-held areas until 1989—after the worst of the famine. Donors argued that a concern with Sudanese "sovereignty" precluded such operations, apparently forgetting the major relief operation into Eritrea from Sudan that was carried out in the face of opposition from the Ethiopian government (Africa Watch 1991, 177–210). The precedent of relief to Biafra during the Nigerian civil war was also ignored (Wiseberg 1974, 73). The donors' frequent assertion that the rural southern Sudan was "inaccessible" not only reflected a lack of political will; it also failed to explain how it was possible for Norwegian People's Aid to work there.[7]

At least until Operation Lifeline Sudan in 1989, UN officials and bilateral donors typically regarded relief to rebel-held areas as off limits. Indeed, Prattley's successor at UNDP, Bryan Wannop, told me, "When I replaced Prattley, I made clear I wouldn't talk with the SPLA" (interview with Bryan Wannop, UNDP, New York, August 24, 1990). SPLA-held areas remained a taboo subject in UN relief discussions throughout 1988.[8] Even as late as November 1988, there was no reference to the SPLA in the UN's 164-page famine appeal document, and no plan for sending food to rebel-held areas (UNOEA 1988). One EC official summed up the lesson drawn by aid officials of all kinds from Prattley's expulsion: "If you want to stay in this country, you don't be seen to be helping people behind the lines."

USAID, for its part, was extremely cautious. Right up until January 1989—when Julia Taft, director of USAID's Office of Foreign Disaster Assistance (OFDA), angered U.S. diplomats by meeting with representatives of the SPLM/SPLA—officials of USAID would not set foot in SPLA territory. USAID's stance appeared to be linked with State Department fears of a Sudanese government backlash against U.S. interests if assistance were to be given to rebel-held areas (Minear 1991, 115–17). It was the lack of such a relief effort that did so much to encourage the SPLA to see relief operations as biased and to attack relief shipments that seemed to be aimed only at supporting the government and at encourging the depopulation of large areas of rural Bahr el Ghazal and Upper Nile.

Avoiding relief to rebel-held areas meant avoiding the risk, first, of visibly failed operations, such as Operation Rainbow, and, second, of possible expulsion from Sudan. There was also a significant risk that good accounts would not be provided of any relief channeled to rebel-held areas (John Ryle, personal communication, 1990). Donor officials in Khartoum were under pressure from national headquarters to be able to show that money spent on relief had not been wasted (EC 1986b, 1989). The risk that good accounts could not be provided also applied to government-held areas, however. Some observers charged that donors applied higher standards of accountability to SPLA-held areas than to government-held areas, and that the inability to ensure such accountability, while not discouraging relief to government-held zones, was used as a further reason for withholding assistance to SPLA areas.[9]

Another factor discouraging relief to rebel-held areas was the risk of retaliation by the Sudanese government against existing development projects in northern Sudan,[10] something that appears to have inhibited NGOs as well as donors. While inaction in relation to the south was defended on the "humanitarian" grounds that it helped preserve such development projects,[11] the severity of unmet suffering in the south casts doubt on the validity of this argument. The context of often-intense competition among donors (notably the EC and the UN) for government favor and for a major role in development initiatives appears to have helped to underwrite the general pattern of deference to Sudanese government priorities (Duffield 1990a, 41).

Donors' deference to government priorities was also evident in a damaging lack of support for the NGO consortium CART during its attempt to secure significant relief for the south. By late 1986, CART was coming under increasing pressure from the Sudanese government to surrender control of relief operations to the government. CART's 1986 distributions in the south had provided a possible springboard for relief operations that could reach government-held, rebel-held, and indeterminate "gray" areas in the south. At the same time, CART was attempting to galvanize a major relief effort to the south as a whole by securing government support for its considerable estimates of need. Donor support of CART at this critical stage would have been extremely valuable, and CART staff recalled that when Governor Peter Cirillo of Equatoria expelled two CART workers in November 1986, the consortium was "looking for a great deal of support from the EEC," which had previously played a critical and constructive role in establishing and funding the consortium (interview with Anthony Nedley, Oxfam-UK, Khartoum, November 6, 1988). But the EC announced at the beginning of 1987 that it would commit itself to the funding of CART for only the month of January. The CART chairman told the EC: "This will effectively mean the end of the only relief distribution system in Equatoria. . . . In order to work effectively CART requires a minimum of 6 months funding commitment."[12] The EC did not speak out in support of CART's assessments of needs, which were actually lower than estimates by Sudanaid and the Sudan Council of Churches. Instead, in a context where precise needs assessment was very difficult,[13] the EC echoed the skepticism of the government. At the end of January 1987, Oxfam staff in Sudan were told by the EC office in Khartoum that EC staff in Brussels were not prepared to accept CART's assessment of needs. EC food in Kenya would not be released, pending a further investigation by EC staff (Oxfam-UK 1987a). The pursuit of this investigation, which delayed relief operations significantly, inevitably weakened CART's attempt to raise the alarm in the winter of 1986–1987. Meanwhile, donors committed only a small proportion of the 23,000 metric tons requested for Equatoria by CART.[14] CART's attempts to highlight problems in the south cannot have been assisted by USAID's Famine Early Warning System: its January 1987 report calculated relief needs for Sudan on the basis that southerners required only 92 kilograms per person per year, whereas northerners needed 146 kilograms per person per year, a government guideline uncritically accepted by USAID (USAID 1987a, 2).[15]

While EC officials later stressed their behind-the-scenes lobbying on behalf of CART and their desire that other donors take on some of the burden of supporting CART,[16] Oxfam staff felt EC's support for them had been very weak and suspected the EC was giving top priority to preserving close relations with the Sudanese government (interview with Mark Duffield, Oxfam-UK, November 2, 1988; interview with Anthony Nedley, Oxfam-UK, November 6, 1988). Oxfam's country representative commented: "It was just too hot for them. The EEC was backing the government" (interview with Mark Duffield, Oxfam-UK, November 2, 1988).

CART's assessments of needs were effectively ignored by the Sudan government. And CART progressively abandoned the concept of neutral relief shipments, confining its relief operations to government-held areas. Meanwhile, the possibility of neutral, agency-controlled distributions in Bahr el Ghazal was also abandoned.

Within the UN bureaucracy, no agency had a clear responsibility or mandate for providing assistance to Sudanese famine victims, unless they had crossed international borders and become "refugees" (in which case there was a responsibility to provide "protection" but still no responsibility to provide "assistance") (Keen 1992, 27–35). UNICEF figures show that although in 1987 the total amount of international aid money spent on foreign refugees in Sudan—mostly Ethiopians—was U.S. $558 a head (with international responsibilities for refugees being more clearly delineated), by contrast the aid community spent only U.S. $2.15 a head on displaced southern Sudanese (*Guardian*, August 18, 1988). Significantly, the northern Bahr el Ghazal Dinka were not close to any international border.

UNICEF made some attempt to facilitate relief to rebel-held areas, but its efforts were on a small scale and they eventually succumbed to Sudanese government pressure. UNICEF enjoyed a reputation as the most adventurous and independent of the UN agencies, a role facilitated by its independent sources of revenue. The organization opened a Coordinating Office in Nairobi in June 1988 to facilitate the work of private relief agencies wanting to work in SPLA-held areas.[17] During the Nigerian civil war, UNICEF had supported the Joint Church Aid airlift to Biafra, thus placing itself at odds with the UN Secretary General's pronouncements and policy (Wiseberg 1974, 73; Okpoko 1986, 38). It had played a relief role in many other civil wars. For a time in the summer of 1988, from its Nairobi office, UNICEF provided private relief agencies with drugs, food, and a light plane. However, the office was closed on October 9, after Prime Minister Sadiq el Mahdi expressed his disapproval (Africa Watch 1990, 112). Shortly afterwards, in January 1989, UNICEF's director in Khartoum, Cole Dodge, left Sudan, apparently because of pressure from the government (Bonner 1989, 101).

In the absence of major donor or NGO relief efforts to rebel-held areas, responsibility for attempting to reach these areas was left to the ICRC. The

ICRC's previous experience elsewhere had suggested it was likely to require strong support from donors in order to be effective. During the Nigerian civil war, the ICRC had exhibited a cautious approach to relief negotiations, and the organization appears to have been hampered at that time by a strong concern with protocol and with not alienating the government in Lagos (Wiseberg 1974, 72–73). The U.S. and British governments were reported to have pressured the ICRC not to send help to Biafra—pressure the ICRC appeared ill-equipped to resist (Okpoko 1986, 2).

The ICRC began Sudan relief negotiations in February 1988. But as a result of obstruction—by the government until August 1988, and then by the SPLA—the ICRC, as noted, proved unable to deliver any relief until small quantities were airlifted in December 1988. Its activities in the field were confined to confidential surveys (*Sudan Times*, October 14, 1988). Again, donors stressed the strength of their behind-the-scenes support: they said lobbying on the ICRC's behalf had been a key element of the meetings between the donor food aid group and Prime Minister Sadiq el Mahdi, which had taken place every six weeks in 1988 (EC 1989a; interview with Bryan Wannop, UNDP, New York, September 6, 1990).[18] The exact nature of donors' pressure on the ICRC's behalf is unclear. However, any such pressures were largely ineffective, and donors' *public* pressure on the Sudanese government on behalf of the ICRC was very little. Indeed, the Sudanese government was depicted as generally cooperative, with the U.S. State Department in particular tending to project misplaced optimism that the ICRC negotiations were about to bear fruit. In July, a State Department official informed Congress: "We are . . . pleased to report that efforts to involve the International Committee of the Red Cross in feeding operations on both sides of the battle lines, at long last, appear to be coming to fruition."[19]

He said he expected ICRC operations to commence by the beginning of August (U.S. Congress 1988b, 49). Yet at the same time, a U.S. Embassy cable from Khartoum to Washington was noting: "International Red Cross operations are at a standstill, reflecting an appalling lack of concern on the part of the Government of Sudan's military authorities toward the suffering of the people considering the ICRC reports of starvation in Wau."[20]

Devolving relief responsibilities to the ICRC appeared to be one of the most important "escape routes," or means of avoiding responsibility, employed by donor officials. After relief to rebel-held areas in 1988 had proved extremely meager, one key UN official said the ICRC had not pushed through negotiations with the zeal donors had wanted (interview with Bryan Wannop, UNDP, New York, September 6, 1990). At the same time, donors excused themselves from launching their own operations on the ground that this would interfere with the ICRC's negotiations. Thus, at the beginning of

November 1988, the U.S. Embassy, hearing that the Sudanese government had given permission for a survey of Akon town, said it would not push for an airlift to Aweil, because this might interfere with the ICRC negotiations (Bonner 1989, 100). However, on the same day, the head of the ICRC delegation in Khartoum, Pierre Pont, made clear that he did not feel donor initiatives would hamper ICRC negotiations. Meanwhile, the U.S. had been restraining UNICEF relief initiatives in the south, urging that relief be channeled through the ICRC (Minear 1991, 115).

Donors failed to counter government obstruction of relief not only in rebel-held but also in government-held areas. The very small quantities of relief supplied to all areas in and adjoining Bahr el Ghazal in 1986, 1987, and 1988 were documented in Chapter 4, as was the minimal relief for those who migrated north.

Within the government-controlled areas of the south, the concentration of relief efforts on Equatoria (in general, less needy than Bahr el Ghazal) has been noted. This pattern of relief offered certain advantages for donors. It is reasonable to surmise that Bahr el Ghazal's critical role as a Dinka stronghold, together with its severe political underrepresentation, even in relation to Equatoria, spelled substantial political risks for those attempting to arrange relief there. Further, the substantial NGO presence in Equatoria offered greater prospects for a proper, "accountable" distribution, something that was also attractive to NGOs themselves (interview with Bryan Wannop, UNDP, New York, September 6, 1988).

NGO reports of extremely severe malnutrition among famine migrants in southern Darfur and southern Kordofan in the spring of 1988 did not prompt donors to speak out publicly about the evolving famine, or to push strongly for an improved relief response. Donors, relying largely on indicators of drought supplied by the NGO CARE, sanctioned the low allocations to Abyei and Kadugli area councils under the Western Relief Operation. Indeed, donors actually wanted lower allocations to southern Kordofan than did the regional government, with donors not taking the relatively high population of southern Kordofan into account. Arguments over this issue led to a two-month delay in relief operations to southern Kordofan, with donors demanding a further survey of needs there (interview with Peter Jobber, WFP, Khartoum, November 2, 1988; RRC/EC 1988f). When donors did react to the increasing severity of famine (for example, by increasing the allocations to Abyei area council, and later by organizing airlifts), it was already too late to prevent very high mortality. The manifold political obstacles ensured that already tardy efforts were subject to further damaging delays. The rapid influx of displaced people into such towns as Abyei and Meiram, a common feature of famines, exposed donors' collective failure to anticipate the final stage of famine—despite the long-evolving crisis in Bahr el Ghazal—and to provide sufficient relief in advance. Meanwhile, donors did little to alleviate restrictions on migrants' freedom of movement, or on their ability to gather wild foods.[21]

In line with a tendency highlighted by Kent in his general study of relief, unwelcome information on famine was often discounted (Kent 1987, 133). One key UN official later acknowledged that NGO reports of famine were treated with some skepticism by donors for much of 1988 (interview with Bryan Wannop, UNDP, New York, September 6, 1990). As the famine was deepening in the early summer of 1988, one EC-funded official commented: "New staff [of European NGOs in Sudan] have never before been confronted with sights unacceptable in the Western World. Consequently relatively small crises have prompted large cries of assistance."[22]

Such doubts contributed to twofold cuts in NGOs' proposed budgets under the EC's emergency program and delays in approval, causing unfavorable reaction from NGOs (EC 1988d). Roger Winter of the U.S. Committee for Refugees was one of those trying to mobilize support for relief to the south. He reported: "In mid-1988 when I returned from the SPLA zone with video and photos of starving people in that sector, I was told flatly by a key AID official that their position was that the areas I visited were 'the empty quarter—there is no-one there.'"[23] Many aid officials were angry that their reports of evolving famine in southern Kordofan in particular had not prompted the donors into speaking out about famine, or getting more directly involved in improving relief performance. The senior MSF-France representative in Sudan complained that donors had not reacted to evidence of severe malnutrition and ration shortfalls in Meiram until press coverage at the end of August and in September. "There was a phase of complete and utter indifference. Nobody gave a damn. All our reports went to WFP," he told me (interview with Christopher Carr, MSF-France, Khartoum, November 17, 1988).

There was also a feeling that NGO information was not circulating among the various donors as much as it should. The UNDP resident representative commented: "Donors weren't sharing information among themselves. I had the impression they knew far more than they were saying." Specifically, he mentioned information the EC was receiving from Concern and the British were receiving from Oxfam (interview with Bryan Wannop, UNDP, New York, September 6, 1990). The apparent competition between donors cannot have helped in this respect.

The shaping of relief agendas helped underpin donors' underreaction to famine in three main ways. First, the existence of famine was often played down, even denied. Donors tended to define famine (sometimes implicitly, sometimes explicitly) in terms of nutritional crises and famine mortality. Such definitions were in line with some elements of contemporary academic discussion of famine. Since malnutrition and mortality became severe only in the final stages of evolving famine, such definitions tended to encourage and justify a lack of significant interventions during the earlier stages of famine. The reports of USAID's Famine Early Warning System (FEWS) used a methodology in which "[f]our stages of vulnerability [to famine] are identified: vulnerable, at-risk, nutritional emergency, and famine" (USAID 1989, 3). Thus, by definition, famine could occur only after a nutritional emergency. Crucially, only the very final stages of the famine were deemed to be "famine," according to this methodology.

Migration, in particular, was not seen as constituting a part of famine. The great exodus of people from Bahr el Ghazal and other parts of the south to Ethiopia, peaking in late 1987, indicated that famine, by this time, was sufficiently far advanced for people to abandon their homes and risk the severe hazards of the journey east. The terrible condition of those arriving in Ethiopia also indicated that the famine process was already far advanced. Yet this migration was taken by USAID as an indicator of forthcoming rather than present famine. Thus, the June 1988 Famine Early Warning System report noted: "Of great concern are the increasing numbers (from southern Sudan) seeking refuge in Ethiopia. This is a sign of stress previously identified as the one indicator that might *foretell* true famine in the south" (my emphasis).[24]

Since this report was issued in June 1988, and the outmigrations in question peaked in late 1987, this "warning," in any case, could not reasonably be described as "early." Outmigrations, indeed, were significant even in 1985–1986, and these were regarded by indigenous NGOs more as a consequence of previous failure to relieve famine than as a sign that famine might be about to happen. Thus, the Sudan Council of Churches noted in early 1986 that it viewed "with great and mounting concern the lack of assistance reaching the South from the international community and the consequent dislocation and migration of those affected from their homes and villages in search of food."[25]

The very significant security threats faced by those moving east or north from Bahr el Ghazal were powerful reasons for delaying outmigration until famine was far advanced. If this security threat (which came primarily from government-supported groups) had been more openly recognized by international donors, they might not have made the mistake of seeing outmigration as a sign of impending instead of present famine.

All this suggests that an "early warning system" may actually play some part in delaying response to a famine, by locating the famine in a perpetual future. The usefulness of having an information system with this designation (especially once a famine is far advanced) is to be doubted.

Donors' discourses on famine echoed those in official reports of the British colonial administration in India in the late nineteenth century, wherein the "aimless wandering" of migrants was generally seen as a precursor of distress and famine, rather than as a sign that famine was far advanced. This

view persisted in relation to relief in independent India (with many continuing to argue that famine relief became necessary at the point of nutritional
crisis), but has been convincingly challenged by Jodha and Rangasami, who
have argued that relief is needed to counter processes of asset loss in advance of the final stages of famine signaled by mass outmigration (Jodha
1975; Rangasami 1985).

In Sudan, the widespread equation of famine with mortality allowed the
presentation of a belated response as an early one. Julia Taft, the director of
the Office of U.S. Foreign Disaster Assistance and one of those who pressed
hardest for vigorous relief, gave evidence to Congress in March 1989 on
relief operations to Abyei in the previous autumn. She noted: "Daily death
rates were very high. . . . When word reached Khartoum the donors were
galvanized to act unilaterally. The Office of U.S. Foreign Disaster Assistance
quickly mounted a large-scale relief operation."[26]

Response to news of starvation deaths in Aweil had been similarly
prompt, according to Taft's account (U.S. Congress 1989, 110–11). Yet even
in terms of a quick response to mortality, this presentation was inaccurate.
The U.S. Embassy in Khartoum reported in July 1988 that eight hundred
people a week were dying in Aweil (U.S. Congress 1988b, 11), prompting
little reaction.

In a similar vein, an EC press release of November 17, 1988, noted:
"When reports reached Khartoum of food shortages in El Meiram, the EEC
delegation immediately arranged for the release of 300 mt." Yet there had
been food shortages in Meiram since at least 1987.[27]

Allied with the conception of famine as a nutritional crisis was a donor
focus on "numbers in need": their routine procedures appeared geared to
producing this kind of data. In line with Wood's general observation that
donors tended to focus on cases rather than stories, there was little attention
to the processes by which people had become and were becoming needy, or
to how these processes might be slowed or reversed.

The EC appeared to judge the severity of famine by nutritional indicators
rather than by asset loss; some NGOs felt donors regarded such asset loss as
in some respects a sign of progress. When Oxfam was lobbying the EC for
a substantial relief response in the spring of 1987, Oxfam's country representative noted:

> When tackled on the question of nutritional indicators not being helpful in
> relation to pastoralists, [the EC official] replied that to make good a claimed
> food deficit when people still have livestock could cause dependency. . . . In his
> view, pastoralism was, in any case, non-viable and in decline all over the re-
> gion. . . . It is important to note that USAID, UNICEF and EEC have all re-
> cently expressed similar views concerning pastoralism in the South, that it is on
> the way out and in twenty years would have disappeared anyway.[28]

Similar views had been expressed by Food and Agricultural Organization (FAO) officials during famine in the Sahel in the early 1970s, prompting Jean Copans to observe: "The FAO experts seem on the whole pleased at the disappearance of the cattle of the Sahelian nomads. They see these people as not producing enough meat for the market."[29]

The second main element of the shaping of relief agendas lay in the discounting of needs in areas of the south deemed to be "inaccessible." This helped to legitimize the near-absence of relief to such areas (notably rebel-held areas), contributing to policy's "unobjectionable" air. From 1987 until late in 1988, the presentation of "needs" in the south by international donors (and by the RRC, with whom they cooperated closely) did not reflect actual needs in the south, but rather those needs that might "realistically" be met, given a set of constraints that donors were unwilling to challenge. For example, the following assessment of relief quantities needed appeared in RRC's Early Warning System Bulletin of September 15, 1988:[30]

| | |
|---|---|
| Kordofan | 71,000 |
| Darfur | 51,000 |
| Upper Nile | 9,600 |
| Bahr el Ghazal | 11,000 |
| Equatoria | 11,280 |
| Eastern | 46,000 |
| Total | 199,880 |

According to these figures, the "needs" in the south were far outweighed by those in the north. In reality, the reverse was true. What appears to have happened is that the assessment of "needs" was conflated with assessments of who was "reachable" and who was not. Donors sometimes acknowledged that these figures for "needs" were contaminated by assessments of accessibility (TCC meeting minutes, November 9, 1987, 1). But this qualification was frequently omitted.

Given the apparent constraints of "inaccessibility," the numbers requiring relief could be—and were—presented as surprisingly small. Such discourses appeared to illustrate a point made by Wood in his more general discussion of donative policy: that there is likely to be "a constant endeavour to legitimise a small rather than large category of worthy recipients" (Wood 1985, 16–17). At close to the height of a famine in which perhaps 500,000 died, and at a time when NGOs were seeking major financial support from the EC, an EC-funded official expressed strongly his view that the numbers of "unacceptably malnourished that we are able to reach is limited to small groups, possibly totalling several hundred only" (RRC/EC 1988h). It is clear that the political sensitivity of highlighting famine in the south had influenced this assessment, for the official added: "Please do not think I am happy with the status quo but such are the sensitivities of the Sudan that an ill-conceived programme could do more damage than save people in the Sudan" (ibid.). The subsequent delays in approving NGO budgets (and cuts in these budgets) have been noted.

The construction of relief agendas in this way was not confined to the EC or the RRC. In April 1988, a joint donors' report on the displaced said the number of displaced people "in need and reachable . . . is restricted to the displaced populations (including the displaced refugee populations) of Juba and Yei" (Interdonor Memo. 1988, 4). The report mentioned the difficulty of getting food to Aweil, and Aweil was clearly classed among the unreachable areas.

Revealingly, the concept of the "unreachable" was invoked even in relation to hundreds of thousands of impoverished people displaced from the south who were living on the donors' doorstep in Khartoum. It was impossible to argue that security problems or logistical problems prevented access to these people. Yet the Sudanese government was particularly anxious not to encourage migration to the capital, and relief for those displaced to Khartoum was minimal. The joint donors' report of April 1988 had a new subheading, which appeared to offer a more hopeful prospect. It said: "People in need—and reachable." However, the report continued: "Only those newly arrived [in Khartoum] are in extreme need and are currently being helped by several NGOs. . . . Difficulties in reaching or in targeting needy people for food distribution limits scope for such actions."[31]

Who was "reachable" and who was not, however, was to a significant extent in donors' hands—and not just in Khartoum. Abyei, although deemed inaccessible during the summer of 1988, had an airstrip, which, when widespread publicity had given the donors new resolve in the autumn, was used to deliver relief supplies. Airlifts—expensive but nevertheless possible— were also organized to Meiram and Aweil, *after* the worst of the famine mortality in these towns. Meanwhile, although the possibility of SPLA attacks allowed the government to point to very real problems of access (notably in relation to Aweil), the degree to which such attacks were encouraged by the carrying of military supplies on "relief" shipments was obscured by both donors and the Sudanese government. The potential accessibility of Aweil—evidenced by the passage of trains from Babanousa to Aweil throughout 1987 and in March 1988—has been noted.

Discounting needs in "inaccessible" areas embraced the idea that needs could not be known because areas were "inaccessible" to aid officials. When USAID officials were challenged in Congress in July 1988 over their quietude in relation to the developing famine, they argued that the absence of donor representatives in the south had severely limited their access to information.[32] One senior official referred to "a total lack of information" on rural areas in southern Sudan (U.S. Congress 1989a, 35). Yet it was open to USAID to place representatives in the south, if it so chose. Indeed, USAID officials were repeatedly lobbied by the director of the U.S. Committee for Refugees, for one, to accompany him to SPLA-held areas to witness the famine themselves (Roger Winter, personal communication, 1992).

A third way in which donors' relief agendas helped legitimize and encourage under reaction to the famine was the importance attached by donors to avoiding the creation of "dependency"[33]—an argument that had helped limit relief under the Anglo-Egyptian administration and that had been used to justify the sale of relief grain during the drought-led famine of 1983–1985 (de Waal 1989b, 9; Deloitte, Haskins and Sells 1985).

The sale of Western Relief Operation grain was widely advocated on the ground that it would prevent "dependency" (RRC/EC 1988i, 1; Hassabo and Co. 1988, 5). Generous free distributions, it was thought, would "discourage the people from working and planting grain crops" (EC 1987e). Subsequent evaluations continued to stress the potentially harmful effects of relief distributions on "self-reliance and self-help" (Ministry of Finance and Economic Planning/EEC/Masdar [UK] 1988, 55; Deng and Minear 1992, 66). Much of the early WRO grain to arrive in Abyei town in 1988 was earmarked for sale (EC 1988c, 2). Yet the extreme poverty of displaced Dinka in the town meant they were ill-equipped to buy relief. We have seen that the concept of a "free market" was unhelpful in understanding economic trends during the famine: markets were profoundly shaped by the exercise of force at the political level. Nevertheless, donors sometimes presented relief as if it were a unique and potentially damaging intrusion of the political into the economic sphere, and the perceived importance of not interfering in the "free market" appears to have influenced (and inhibited) donors' reactions to the famine.[34] The need for a third "tranche" of relief under the WRO was questioned by EC officials on the ground that it would contribute to labor shortages and undermine incentives for normal commercial trade (EC 1988b). The full amount of WRO grain allocated was never delivered (Ministry of Finance and Economic Planning/EEC/Masdar [UK] 1988).

## DONORS' LACK OF ATTENTION TO IMPLEMENTATION OF RELIEF PROGRAMS, ONCE INITIATED

The many problems besetting distribution of relief, once operations had been initiated, were closely related to the various benefits of famine. Yet donors, for the most part, left responsibility for the politically sensitive tasks of monitoring relief distributions and overcoming official obstruction to NGOs and the RRC, just as they had left responsibility for reaching rebel-held areas to the ICRC. Again, this pattern was damaging to the victims of famine, since NGOs and the RRC generally lacked the political muscle to sway powerful obstructionist elements of the Sudanese government, whereas donors potentially wielded much more influence. At the same time, the division of responsibilities apparently served important functions for donors. First, it helped further to minimize direct conflict between donors and the Sudanese government. Second, it allowed donor officials to avoid responsibility when relief operations ran into problems: problems befalling relief were often simply ignored; alternatively, donors were able to argue that relief problems lay not so much in "policy" (their own responsibility, in association with government) but in "problems of implementation" (conceived as the responsibility of NGOs and low-level government officials).

Blaming "implementation" took many forms. After the worst of the famine, one official who had been working with USAID in Khartoum concluded that NGOs had to a large extent failed to provide USAID with the information it required to operate effectively. It was stressed that "AID is not an implementing agency," lacking the infrastructure and staff to find out information for itself, and that "[AID's] primary task is to disburse funds for various development and emergency programs and to monitor and evaluate the use of those funds." Significantly, if AID staff saw their task as simply giving money and then evaluating *other people*, no question of responsibility for policy outcomes would arise. In line with the "mainstream" model of policymaking highlighted by Clay and Schaffer, policy was explicitly seen as a response to information on "needs," with implementation following later, as a separate responsibility (Curtis 1991, 5–17).

For its part, the EC Commission reacted to criticisms of its procedures with a suggestion that evaluators should have paid more attention to assessing NGO performance. After the exceptional mortality in Meiram in 1988, EC officials said it had been RRC's responsibility to cover needs there, rather than a direct donor responsibility. "This was always on our minds," a senior Khartoum official subsequently explained.

Donors' apparent lack of concern with pushing relief through to famine victims had four main manifestations. First, donors rejected the idea proposed in some NGO circles that nonemergency aid to Sudan be linked with progress in relief distributions. There was a perception among many NGO staff that such "conditionality" had been rejected by donors for fear that it would increase Libyan and other Arab countries' influence in Sudan (interview with Mark Duffield, Oxfam-UK, Khartoum, November 2, 1988). Improved performance on relief was not linked to continuing aid until 1989— after the peak of the famine. Yet the relatively rare examples of substantial donor pressure for improved relief during the phase of underreaction, as well as the more substantial pressures in 1989 during Operation Lifeline, suggested donor pressure could bring results. In the summer of 1988, USAID threats to cancel delivery of wheat if ABS did not speed up release of sorghum appear to have borne fruit (Heads of Mission 1988; John Borton, personal communication, 1988).

Donor officials tended to argue that "conditionality"—like channeling relief to rebel-held areas—would constitute unwarranted interference in Sudanese sovereignty.[35] Yet donors were prepared to link continued nonemergency aid with reforms in the Sudanese government's *economic* policies, and donor references to "sovereignty" were less common in this context. The favored economic reforms were in line with the kinds of "structural adjustment" packages promoted by the World Bank and the IMF. One such package had been linked with aid by the U.S. government in 1983–1985 (Brown 1988, 73–83). A July 1988 letter from the USAID mission director to the Sudanese Ministry of Finance reveals explicit links that were made between future aid provision and the Sudanese government's willingness to pursue favored economic reforms. To give one example, a vigorous pursuit of structural adjustment would lead to a granting of $60 million under the PL 480 food program (an ongoing program aimed mainly at urban areas), whereas "in the absence of reform," this figure would be set at $25 million in 1989 and nothing at all in 1990.[36] Such a reduction would have been a major threat to the survival of the regime, just as the freezing of US aid monies had helped bring down Nimeiri.

A second manifestation of donors' lack of concern with ensuring receipt of relief by famine victims was the lack of adequate monitoring or supervision of relief deliveries and distributions. Apart from the use of CART in Equatoria, donors devolved the main responsibilities for local distribution and monitoring of relief onto government authorities. After the expulsion of Prattley in the autumn of 1986, the EC began to hand over its relief to the military authorities within Bahr el Ghazal, with the military commissioner given responsibility for deciding what proportion should be handed over to the Aweil and Wau relief committees (Oxfam-UK 1986p, 1). The donors' lack of adequate monitoring of deliveries was strikingly illustrated by events at Babanousa, in southern Kordofan, where, as noted, twenty-six missing freight cars carrying EC/USAID food aid intended for Bahr el Ghazal were "discovered" by NGO staff in Babanousa station in June 1988, with some having been there for more than two years.

Donors' tendency to divorce themselves from responsibility for finding out what happened to their relief was stressed by staff of foreign and indigenous NGOs (e.g., interview with Mark Cunningham, Concern, Khartoum, November 2, 1988; interview with Marc Lejars, MSF-France, Khartoum, October 25, 1988). The Darfur regional director of the indigenous Sudanese Red Crescent said of the Western Relief Operation: "The donors didn't take any responsibility except buying the grain and sending it out—because there was no monitoring" (interview with El Hadi Ahmed, Sudanese Red Crescent, El Fasher, December 10, 1988).

While some valuable information on the fate of donated food did become available to donors as a result of investigations by NGO staff in particular, these investigations were ad hoc and often belated.[37] There were suggestions from senior agency personnel, moreover, that donors showed a lack of interest in information on relief distributions that came through private channels. The Sudan representative of MSF-France went so far as to suggest that neither the EC nor the RRC was interested in what happened to their food unless news of abuses leaked out into the public domain (interview with Christopher Carr, MSF-France, Khartoum, November 20, 1988). Certainly, publicity was to be of critical importance in radically altering donors' agendas and actions in relation to the famine in late 1988.

The ability of NGOs adequately to monitor or supervise distributions naturally depended on their ability to gain access to famine areas. But NGO staff complained that while donors gave them money, they were generally reluctant to provide diplomatic support when the Sudanese government denied travel permits or permission to work in particular areas (Duffield 1990a, 41–42).[38] Further, when agencies were actually expelled, donor protests were muted. In the winter of 1987–1988, the Sudanese government expelled four agencies working in the south (including World Vision, the main channel for U.S. aid to the south). Roy Stacey, the deputy assistant secretary of the Bureau of African Affairs, U.S. Department of State, said of the expulsions: "We very much regret this decision. These views have been made known to the Prime Minister very forcefully, that we think this is a *mistake*" (my emphasis) (U.S. Congress 1988a, 58). Meanwhile, UNICEF and MSF were pressured by the government into pulling representatives out of the southern towns of Juba and Wau (*Atlanta Journal and Atlanta Constitution*, June 27, 1988). The expulsion of NGOs inevitably increased the control of government authorities, notably the army, over relief distributions in the south.

NGOs' ability to monitor relief was also a problem in the north. Access to Abyei town was limited in 1988. In southern Kordofan, NGOs played very little role in general distributions, which were largely left to local committees, in which army officers were particularly influential (Africa Watch 1990, 123–28).[39]

In addition to NGOs, another possible source of information on relief operations was the RRC. However, even some junior officials within donor organizations felt that donors devolved responsibility for relief onto RRC, but then failed adequately to support it. This charge appears to have had some validity. When the RRC took over relief responsibilities from UNOEOS after the expulsion of Prattley, the donors largely neglected to build up its administrative strength. Instead, there was what one key UN official described as a "short-sighted" emphasis on giving food and money (interview with Bryan Wannop, UNDP, New York, August 24, 1990). RRC staff were largely temporary, on secondment from other government departments. And whereas there had been more than sixty expatriate managers and advisers involved in relief before the RRC took over responsibilities from UNOEOS, by April 1988 there were less than ten. The RRC was described by donors at this time as "overstretched with limited staff and insufficient operational resources" (Interdonor Memo. 1988, 8). By contrast, after the worst of the famine, fully 175 staff from the UN alone were assigned to Operation Lifeline in 1989, with the United States providing significant resources to strengthen the RRC (Minear 1991, 37, 117).

In the context of hostility to relief on the part of many elements of the Sudanese government, the meager resources allocated to the RRC during the phase of underreaction inevitably reduced its ability to ensure receipt of relief by famine victims. In particular, the RRC was poorly equipped to stand up to the Ministry of Social Welfare. Meanwhile, divisions among the donors cannot have helped in organizing a coherent lobby on behalf of the displaced. The UN tended to support the Ministry of Social Welfare. It experienced a number of problems in its relationship with the RRC (interview with Bryan Wannop, UNDP, New York, August 24, 1990).

The RRC was also poorly equipped to monitor or supervise distribution of relief at the local level, a role that NGOs were often denied. RRC representation in the field was weak. For example, it was not until September 8, 1988, that an RRC representative began supervising grain distribution in Meiram. This belated supervision appears to have helped reduce abuses that had previously been the norm, including the "leakage" of grain from the camp to the town (MSF-France 1988j, 2–3).

Donors' devolving of responsibilities to the RRC was well illustrated in August 1988. At a meeting of the donor/government/NGO Technical Coordination Committee (TCC) on August 15, donors were reminded by the chairman (from the RRC) that the RRC had written to them asking for help to arrange an airlift to Aweil, and that there had been no response so far. A USAID official replied that the RRC should arrange the airlift and the donors would pick up the cost (TCC meeting minutes, August 15, 1988). Yet with RRC no more than a weak force in relation to government interests opposing relief, there was to be no airlift to Aweil until donors themselves pushed through an operation in December.

The devolving of relief responsibilities onto an ill-equipped RRC is also well illustrated by relief operations aimed at southern Kordofan in 1988. In areas outside Abyei town, NGOs were given a prominent role in providing for camps for the displaced. When MSF-France presented its project proposal for relief to the displaced in Meiram, according to its Sudan representative, the organization made it clear that this program would be ineffective without an adequate general distribution. MSF-France therefore proposed a role for itself in logistical support of the general distribution. But the agency was told this was the RRC's responsibility (interview with Christopher Carr, MSF-France, Khartoum, November 20, 1988). If so, it was certainly one that the RRC subsequently failed to fulfill. In the absence of adequate general distributions, the work of MSF-France and other NGOs in southern Kordofan was severely undermined.

To some extent, the lack of resources directed at the RRC by donors appears to have reflected an assumption that "emergencies" could be neatly delineated and that once emergencies were over, donors' priorities should lie in longer-term development work. This appears to have been seen as an either/or issue. The huge setback to economic development effected by the famine, together with the great variety of Sudanese emergencies following one another in quick succession, suggest that such conceptions were inappropriate.[40]

In the case of the EC, pressure from the EC Commission in Brussels had led the EC office in Khartoum to switch resources from dealing with emergencies to development initiatives, as well as encouraging a scaling down of support to the RRC (EC 1989a, 4). The EC Commission's Sudan desk officer warned in March 1986:

> The 1985 emergency operations claimed a disproportionately large slice of the time of highly qualified specialist staff. This diverted attention and effort from monitoring and evaluation of certain key ongoing projects and preparatory work for Lome III (a 1985 agreement governing aid and trade between EC and selected poor countries). This imbalance is being corrected but more must be done to subcontract responsibility to the more competent NGOs and consultants. Otherwise the most valuable initiatives in smallholder development strategy in rainfed agriculture, food self-reliance, and institutional strengthening could be lost or poached by others.[41]

Meanwhile, it became increasingly difficult for donor staff themselves to keep track of the growing numbers of emergencies in Sudan, something that increased the need for adequate support for the RRC (EC 1989a, 4).[42]

It is clear that the RRC, depending on donors for continued support and answerable to the Sudanese prime minister, had a vested interest in presenting a positive impression of relief operations that were under way. This may have been especially so, since donors were perceived as likely to respond to difficulties in distribution by holding back from allocations.[43]

An EC-funded official noted in the spring of 1988 that Western Relief Operation supplies had been acceptable and "adequate supplies will be in place in areas of need prior to the rains" (RRC/EC 1988c). A general ration had been provided for displaced southern Sudanese, and "because numbers are much larger than had been expected further food has been put into the area." (RRC/EC 1988k). Such discourses in effect assumed that because relief had been dispatched or was in the process of being dispatched, it could be assumed to be meeting the relevant needs—an assumption that had "informed" favorable accounts of relief during the Sahel famine of the early 1970s (Sheets and Morris 1974, 46–47). Yet the inadequacy of relief actually received by famine victims reflected such neat equivalences still less than it had in the Sahel.

Further, the official noted in the course of the Western Relief Operation: "Despite the slowness of the Western Relief Operation it has been a success. The programme was primarily devised to provide a strong training element to Regional Government."[44] Meanwhile, in Darfur, "the fact [that] there has not been massive movements of people, [and] malnutrition rates although increasing are not as high as predicted, indicate that WRO has been beneficial to the region."[45]

Subsequent evaluations revealed that the WRO had made little impact in Darfur, with very small quantities distributed (Oxfam-UK 1988b; Ministry of Finance and Economic Planning/EEC/Masdar (UK) 1988, 6–7; interview with el Hadi Ahmed, Sudanese Red Crescent, El Fasher, December 10, 1988; interview with Dr. Abdel Gabbar, Agricultural Planning Unit (APU), El Fasher, December 8, 1988).

A third manifestation of donors' tendency to avoid responsibility for "implementation" was their unwillingness publicly to highlight government obstruction of relief. In public, donors tended to excuse or play down obstruction of relief by elements of the Sudanese government. Sudan's close relations with the United States appeared to underpin—and indeed were used as justification for—donor quietude on relief, something that contrasted with U.S. public protests over Ethiopian policies in relation to famine (U.S. Congress 1988b, 10).

The government's repeated reneging on promises of substantial train deliveries to Aweil drew little public criticism from donors, although USAID was less reticent than the others in pointing to the RRC's relief failings (Oxfam-UK 1987b, 5–6). The UNDP resident representative later observed: "From when I arrived [April 1987], the donors were not focusing on Aweil. . . . The primary focus in 1987 was on getting food to Darfur. There wasn't much attention to Aweil before the flood [of August 1988]."[46] Yet donors knew that relief to Aweil was minimal and that only a minority of freight cars were being used for relief.[47]

The ineffectiveness of various behind-the-scenes protests was privately recognized by the donors themselves. This was clear from donors' description of a visit to the Sudanese minister of state for defense by the ambassadors of the United Kingdom, the United States, and West Germany, the chargé d'affaires of the Netherlands, the WFP representative, and the EC delegate in February 1988:

> [We] expressed distress at the lack of progress made since a demarche of last May [1987] when virtually [the] same issues were raised, i.e. food by road from Raga to Wau, by train from Babanousa to Aweil, by barge from Kosti to Malakal, and airlift as required into Juba. We expressed regret at [the] inability of government to coordinate provision of transport and military escorts in timely fashion to carry food made available by donors.[48]

A further demarche was made to the Sudanese prime minister in March 1988. Subsequently, after a rush of three trains in March, there were no further trains to Aweil until January 1989.

In public, the Sudanese government's record on relief was defended by donors through most of 1988. Senior USAID and U.S. State Department officials, addressing a House Select Committee on Hunger in July 1988, blamed relief failures on a wide variety of logistical factors but made no mention of the attitude of government officials to relief for the south (U.S. Congress 1988b, 53–54). A distinction was drawn between actions on the ground and government "policy." Kenneth Brown, deputy assistant secretary of state for Africa, U.S. Department of State, noted: "I think certainly there have been abuses in the south. . . . What I am saying is that it is not government policy to do that" (ibid., 10).

The Sudanese government was again exempted from blame in a State Department statement in October.[49] Even as late as February 1989, USAID officials said they were unable to conclude that the government (or the SPLA) was deliberately using food as a weapon (U.S. Congress 1989a, 45).

The UN's role in obscuring government obstruction was a significant one. The UN appeal document of November 1988 claimed to address the problem of the displaced. Noting the importance of Babanousa as the fulcrum of efforts to deliver relief to Bahr el Ghazal and to southern Darfur and southern Kordofan, the UN recommended a major upgrading of technical facilities at the railway yard: more trains, trucks, workshops, radios, housing, and staff, costing more than $6 million. Yet there was no mention of the central political problem with deliveries, namely, how these facilities might be used, and how facilities at Babanousa had been used in the past (UNOEA 1988, 39–46). Trains from Babanousa continued to be used for military purposes in the winter of 1988–1989.

For the most part, donors did not have their own representatives in the south. Such representatives might have provided information—for example, on government obstruction of relief—that threatened to create conflict between donors and the Sudanese government. There was also a risk that they might be expelled from the country, something likely to have more far-reaching diplomatic implications than the expulsion of NGO staff.

In the rare instances when donors did have their own representatives in the south, information reflecting badly on the government was sometimes simply ignored. Donor representative Paul Symonds's report on theft of relief grain at Raga makes clear that the stolen grain was dispersed thereafter—used as payment in the army compound, or sold to a number of merchants for sale in Wau. Clearly, this grain was lost to the relief operation. Yet John Davison, director of the Office of East African Affairs, U.S. Department of State, commented in July 1988: "There was food that was misplaced, but we understand that it has been found now by someone so that the deficit at Raga has been made up. The food has been accounted for."[50]

The speed and efficacy of relief were often exaggerated, and not just by the EC and the RRC. In June 1988—when famine conditions in Abyei were extremely severe—U.S. State Department officials told U.S. reporters that needs there were being met by the regional government, and the situation was under control (*Atlanta Journal and Atlanta Constitution*, June 27, 1988). In February 1989, a senior USAID official described the relief operation to Aweil (along with other operations) as "somewhat successful" (U.S. Congress 1989a, 30). The so-called paired-village schemes, in which the UN, in November 1988, proposed to integrate those who had fled into northern Sudan, were said by the UN to "maintain traditional rural life patterns" (UNOEA 1988, 48). For families that had been forcibly split up, and whose culture and economy to a large extent revolved around livestock they had lost, this seriously exaggerated the advantages of the proposed relief. The UN made clear that provision of land for the displaced would be only a secondary priority, and that they could generally be expected to work for northern Sudanese or on public work schemes (ibid., 144–47).

A fourth manifestation of donors' lack of concern with pushing through relief was their apparent unwillingness to take precautionary measures that might have smoothed the path for relief. In line with a tendency in bureaucratic decisionmaking highlighted by Clay and Schaffer, donors tended to proceed on overoptimistic assumptions, giving inadequate consideration to what were conceived as "implementation problems" when designing policy.

Delivering very substantial quantities of WRO grain in late 1987 would have helped ensure adequate supplies in southern Kordofan and southern Darfur, while at the same time diminishing the political difficulties involved in channeling relief to those displaced from the south. Yet the system of delivering WRO relief in four separate "tranches" meant that substantial delays in delivery were actually scheduled.[51] When delivery problems arose, these imposed additional delays. The "tranching" system also created the possibility that only some of the allocated grain would be dispatched: in the event, the third and fourth "tranches" of WRO grain were never delivered (Ministry of Finance and Economic Planning/EEC/Masdar (UK) 1988, 4).

A second useful precaution would have been to allocate amounts of relief to the displaced on the assumption that a portion of it would "leak away" from the target groups. This was not done. Even where such "leakage" was officially sanctioned, as in the RRC/town authorities agreement that 20 percent of relief grain arriving in Meiram should go to the town, it was not built into donor calculations on the requirements of the displaced. Indeed, rather than allocating more than a full ration for each displaced person, there is evidence that at least some donor officials favored allocating significantly *less* than a full ration to these famine victims. One official, urging a cautious relief response in the spring of 1988, argued that famine migrants coming north from Bahr el Ghazal would, according to guidelines in an unnamed Centers for Disease Control (CDC) report, require an average of only 150 grams of grain per person per day (RRC/EC 1988b).[52] This, he said, was less than half of what he had been pushing for. He added, "It is very easy to think of a number of displaced and then regard everyone as being totally dependent. Populations always require less than calculated." This argument appeared to be linked with the concern with avoiding "dependency," discussed above. CDC officials later told me that these "guidelines" appear to have been taken out of context.[53]

Finally, donors took insufficient precautions against the diversion of relief at the local level. The army's theft of grain in Wau in December 1986 did not prevent donors from relying on the army in Raga to store grain targeted at famine victims in Wau. The donors' own monitor in Raga noted that previous experience of the army and relief operations in Wau, Aweil, Malakal, and Babanousa "should have warned against relying on the army to protect the dura [sorghum]." The political difficulties in channeling grain to groups identified with the SPLA from a town, Raga, where people had themselves suffered at SPLA hands had not been properly taken into account (Symonds 1987, 4–15).

## DONORS' UNWILLINGNESS TO ADDRESS
## THE CONFLICT UNDERPINNING THE FAMINE

A third major limitation in donors' agendas and actions in relation to the famine was the neglect of the underlying causes of famine, notably militia raiding and, more broadly, the civil war. As with the near-silence on the government's failure to provide food to famine victims, the lack of public criticism of the government's prosecution of the civil war was acknowledged by U.S. diplomats to be linked with a desire not to push Prime Minister el Mahdi toward Libya (*New York Times*, March 14, 1989). As Allison (1971, 178) noted in his seminal analysis of policymaking in another context, "Reticence in one game reduces leaks that would be harmful in higher priority games." Meanwhile, the idea of linking aid with progress on peace was not taken up until 1989.

Donors' public statements commonly referred to "insecurity" and "civil strife" (see, e.g., UNOEA 1988, 5). But they gave minimal attention to the government's role in promoting it. Although the Famine Early Warning System reports put out by USAID described one of the system's aims as being to isolate the "proximate causes" of nutritional emergencies (USAID 1987a, i), they nevertheless generally omitted any mention of the critical importance of the government-sponsored militias. USAID staff in Khartoum later recalled that the organization had required (from NGOs) information on "the numbers of displaced, their location, where they were from, their nutritional status, local food availability, external assistance already in place, and the relationship between the displaced and the local residents."[54] There was no mention of a need for information on *why* people had been displaced.

As late as November 1988, the key UN document purporting to address the issue of the displaced made only one reference to militias in 164 pages (UNOEA 1988). In a book on the war that was widely circulated in the West in late 1988, senior UNICEF staff made no mention of northern militias, but noted: "It is not only a war between army and SPLA but southern militia have also been armed to assist the army in *defending civilian populations*" (my emphasis) (Twose and Pogrund 1988, 51). It is true that government-linked southern militias could serve a protective function in areas where the SPLA was abusing civilian populations (for example, parts of Equatoria). What was missing was any reference to the extremely destructive government-supported militias that attacked civilian populations (notably the Baggara militias).

In line with Wood's observation that in the field of welfare official discourse typically focuses on cases rather than on people with stories, donors' discussions of the famine (particularly in public) made extensive use of the term "the displaced," without explaining the causes of this "displacement" (Interdonor Memo. 1988; UNOEA 1988, 6). This helped to give a technical gloss to what was fundamentally a political process, obscuring the government's role in creating the famine it claimed to be relieving. When the militias were mentioned, their links with the government were for a long time denied,[55] and their role was generally portrayed as defensive. Kenneth Brown, of the Bureau of African Affairs, U.S. State Department, noted at a July 1988 congressional hearing that militias had been armed by the government "for the purpose of protecting [population unspecified] against the SPLA" (U.S. Congress 1988b, 26). The UNDP representative later told me: "I thought the major reason for arming the militias was as a defense force. . . . It was a good idea that went wrong" (interview with Bryan Wannop, UNDP, New York, September 6, 1988). Meanwhile, the resurgence of slavery, resulting largely from militia raids, was masked by the U.S. Department of State. In July 1988, Kenneth Brown said in response to reports of slavery: "Slavery is apparently a problem that has been a problem for generations in that area and it is a problem which the British tried to combat when they were in control of Sudan. It is against the law in Sudan and it is opposed by the Sudanese Government, but there are probably instances which continue."[56]

Donors, and the Sudanese government, frequently referred to the lack of information coming out of the south. Allegedly, this was a famine about which little was known or knowable.[57] It is not plausible, however, that donors were ignorant of the importance of militia raiding, or the role of the government in sponsoring it. As noted, the prime minister had publicly admitted arming tribal militias. Mahmud and Baldo (1987) published their report on slavery and the militias in July 1987, in which they detailed the government's role in supporting the Messiriya and Rizeigat militias. Donors received regular briefings from NGO staff and others (including priests) returning from the south (interview with Bryan Wannop, UNDP, New York, September 6, 1990). And donors' confidential analyses of the causes of famine were very different from their public statements, both in content and in tone. Thus, one restricted joint donors' report noted in April 1988 that a key cause of the northward exodus from Bahr el Ghazal had been "[h]arassment, killings and torturings by armed militia groups and proximity to areas of military conflict; stealing of cattle and household goods" (Interdonor Memo. 1988, 1).

To the extent that there were gaps in donors' information, these could have been filled to a large extent by talking to displaced people in the capital, Khartoum, where large numbers of southern Sudanese had fled from militia attacks (and many from the SPLA). In line with patterns of behavior discerned during the Ethiopian famine of 1984–1985 (when there was little systematic attempt to ask famine victims about the causes of famine), donors' "science" of relief was a very particular one, a science that in effect disqualified certain speaking subjects (Clay, Steingraber, and Niggli 1988, 1; Foucault 1980, 85). Limited definitions of "what was to be known" (including who was to be consulted) helped to underpin a narrow definition of "what was to be done" (Foucault 1981, 5).

Donors argued that the Sudanese government was actively pursuing an end to the civil war, and went so far as to imply that this was part of the government's antifamine strategy (U.S. Congress 1988b, 6). As with the issue of pressuring the government to improve relief performance, donors maintained that pressure to settle the war would constitute unwarranted interference with Sudanese sovereignty.

In fact, in the context of a struggle for control over populations through the use of food, donors were already interfering in political processes by directing aid at the northern government areas and Ethiopia (and limited supplies to government garrison towns), while assisting in the blocking of relief to rebel-held areas.

The benefits of aid, for the government, did not arise simply from appropriating relief supplies or controlling populations. Foreign currency for relief was often exchanged at rates very favorable to the government, providing a substantial income. And in addition to the politically important flows of program aid, U.S. military assistance to Sudan was over $17 million dollars in financial year 1986 (U.S. Congress 1988b, 88). Although it was trimmed to just under $6 million in 1987 and again to $900,000 in 1988, it remains the case that the Sudanese government's civil war campaign was greatly assisted by military resources from the United States. U.S. tanks came into Sudan in 1986 to help a hard-pressed national army, and the United States continued to supply spare parts for its military supplies (Alier 1990, 250).

In the context of continued economic assistance and U.S. protests over the obstruction of relief in Ethiopia, donors' silence can itself be seen as a form of political action: inevitably, it lent a degree of legitimacy to the Sudanese government. So, too, did the simple existence of donor/government operations apparently aimed at remedying famine: in late October of 1988, the Sudanese minister of social affairs, Ahmed el Radi Gubara, stated publicly that the recent UN delegation to the Sudan (examining the problem of the displaced) provided proof that the government was not using food as a weapon in the war against the south (*Sudan Times*, October 28, 1988). The physical manipulation of donor-sponsored "relief" efforts for the transport of military supplies to government garrison towns has been mentioned.

## BROADER AGENDAS AND MORE EFFECTIVE
## RELIEF IN 1989

Donors' actions and agendas in relation to the famine were greatly influenced by the nature and extent of publicity surrounding the famine. To a large extent, it was this publicity and the threat of public exposure of donors' ineffective relief policies, rather than information available to donors through private channels, that eventually prompted—for a time, at least—a more vigorous response from donors across a broader relief agenda.

A dependence on the press in shaping the actions and agendas of donors was acknowledged by a senior U.S. State Department official, when he explained that the State Department was not responsible for the minimal international attention given to Sudan up until the summer of 1988: "We respond to what's in the press. We don't drive the process" (*Atlanta Journal and Atlanta Constitution*, June 26, 1988).

Yet, up until September 1988, although there were periodic articles on the evolving famine, the famine in southern Sudan had not received mass coverage (Bonner 1989, 93), particularly in relation to a much less severe famine in Ethiopia. Journalists faced major obstacles in covering the Sudanese famine, including arrest, destruction of notes and photographs by government officials, and death threats, as well as lack of access to key famine areas (*Atlanta Journal and Atlanta Constitution*, June 27, 1988). Television journalists found that the Sudanese government would not allow them to film in famine camps (Bonner 1989, 93). The lack of sympathy for the south in most of the Sudanese press has been mentioned. According to a detailed and influential article in the *New Yorker* (Bonner 1989), donors had helped to create the shortage of press coverage at a critical stage in August 1988: MSF had considered alerting the press to famine in Meiram at the end of July, but was dissuaded, with UNICEF and EC prominent in the discussions. It was not until a month later that MSF "went public," with information in Meiram, after earlier statements to the press on the situation in Meiram by Oxfam staff. Such public statements were a critical catalyst for more vigorous action. U.S. diplomats subsequently complained that as the famine evolved, the press had not been asking them sufficient questions (ibid., 93–94).

Information on the developing famine received through private channels had included reports from CART, from NPA in Equatoria, and from various NGOs reporting on the situation in Bahr el Ghazal and on the displaced populations in southern Kordofan and southern Darfur. Yet such information had not been sufficient to prompt a vigorous response.

When famine mortality was reaching extremely high levels in Meiram in July–August, donors gave it little attention. The August flooding in Khartoum—which was easily accessible to, and widely covered by, the international media, and which constituted the primary relief concern of the government in the capital—took the bulk of donors' attention at this time. "In August, everyone was thinking about Khartoum, and a possible evacuation with the rising Nile," the UNDP resident representative, Bryan Wannop, later told me (interview with Bryan Wannop, UNDP, New York, August 24, 1990). Wannop added: "We in the comfort of Khartoum were not really aware until August–September [1988] of the situation in the south." The EC official in charge of emergency operations in Sudan said that the donors' focus in August had been on Khartoum, and that only in September had it switched back to the south. Out in the field, in the midst of what local aid workers described as a "wholesale slaughter" in Meiram, one MSF-France aid worker was lamenting: "With all the homeless of Khartoum, it is difficult to imagine that we will be able to obtain any help whatsoever for our faraway village" (MSF-France 1988f, 1988k).

The large-scale press coverage of famine in autumn 1988 was largely an accidental by-product of the August 1988 flooding in Khartoum. Press coverage of the famine increased dramatically when large numbers of journalists came to Sudan to cover the floods of August 1988. Finding that the

disaster was not as severe as some had anticipated, journalists started looking for stories on the famine further south. "We were very fortunate in having the floods," one senior MSF official commented (interview with Christopher Carr, MSF-France, Khartoum, November 17, 1988). He added that
Western ambassadors were spurred into urgent action by a BBC radio report
from Mike Wooldridge.

Even before the wave of press coverage of famine mortality in southern
Kordofan in particular, donors were clearly anxious about the possibility of
such coverage, taking this possibility into account when deciding what action to take on the developing famine. Thus, the agenda for a meeting of the
Heads of Mission Donor Group on August 30, 1988, began: "Serious food
situation in El Meiram; mortality rate higher than in Ethiopia at height of
drought; means to move food technically available; *international press attention most likely*" (my emphasis).[58]

The importance of widespread press coverage in prompting a major improvement in relief responses was emphasized by the UNDP's resident representative. He told me: "The press blew the whistle. If it hadn't been for
this international public exposure, nothing would have happened" (interview with Bryan Wannop, UNDP, New York, August 24, 1990). Noting that
the publics of North America and Europe became very aware of starvation
in the summer and fall of 1988, Wannop commented: "This started a tremendous pressure. There was a feeling that the world would condemn the
UN if there was a repetition. This led to the March meeting [a high-level
meeting of donors and government relief that launched Operation Lifeline]"
(ibid.).

Donors were now asking themselves, " 'Are you going to be able to get
away with public opinion saying we left it to ICRC?' The answer was obvi-
ously no" (ibid.). In the United States, a congressional delegation to Sudan
in October–November 1988 added to pressure for a change of policy in
relation to Sudan, and the new Bush administration, with James Baker as
secretary of state, began to adopt a position less deferential to the Sudanese
government (Africa Watch 1990, 113, 164).

Another important factor was propelling change. In the autumn of 1988,
Oxfam and SCF began to pressure donors for a changed stance on relief. The
NGOs had been frustrated by government obstruction of their attempts to
get access to Abyei, seen as the latest in a long line of actions impeding relief.
Further, they had been angered by the UN's November appeal, which did
not substantially address the issue of human rights violations despite NGO
briefings and documentation, and which did not give substantial attention to
how relief operations were to be made accountable (that is, how to ensure
that relief reached the intended beneficiaries). Oxfam and SCF threatened
publicly to criticize donors' lack of attention to human rights and accountability, and the British ambassador told the other donors that he would con-

sider breaking ranks with them if the NGOs' proposals were not taken up (Oxfam-UK 1988f). Other agencies, notably CARE—which had a close relationship with USAID and the Kordofan authorities—were more reticent on the issue of accountability (SCF-UK 1989, 3). The British NGOs' stance led to the setting up, despite resistance from the UN (Oxfam-UK 1988i), of a Steering Committee composed of donor representatives at the ambassadorial level to resolve difficulties in implementing the UN appeal.[59] This brought donors into regular contact with the Sudanese government in relation to NGO concerns (Oxfam-UK 1989, 2). Donors' broader agendas in 1989 appeared to reflect the combination of this NGO initiative and increased media coverage of famine/government obstruction. It was now risky not to act. The prime minister's evident intransigence in blocking the SPLA/ DUP peace accord also contributed to the donors' growing impatience with the government.

In 1989, under Operation Lifeline, greatly increased quantities of relief were delivered to the south on unescorted shipments designed for relief only. Operation Lifeline included deliveries to areas previously deemed inaccessible (notably rebel-held areas, as well as Aweil and Wau). Both the SPLA and the government had the right to inspect supplies passing through areas under their control (Wannop 1989, 5). Donors began to assume a greater degree of responsibility for pushing relief through to famine victims. There was also a degree of donor interest in tackling the processes (notably conflict) underpinning the famine and in geographical areas previously deemed "inaccessible." Such interventions came to be seen as legitimate after the worst of the famine. However, donors' willingness to pressure the Sudanese government remained limited,[60] and the pattern of allocations continued to give significantly greater relief to government-held areas (Minear 1991, 42).

An early example of successful interventions by donors to push through relief came on September 6, 1988, when a visit to Babanousa by the EC delegate, accompanied by the new governor of Kordofan, set in motion a long-delayed train with ten wagonloads of EC food aid (300 metric tons of sorghum), which arrived in Meiram on the following day. The EC delegate, as representative of all the donors, traveled with the train (EC 1988e). There were airlifts to Abyei, Meiram, and Aweil, and ICRC relief flights finally took off in December.

Increased pressure for peace and for reaching "inaccessible" areas came hand in hand. In December 1988, the Dutch government cut its aid budget to Sudan by $2.5 million, demanding resumption of peace talks, and warned of further cuts unless the government pursued peace talks (*Sudan Times*, January 30, 1989). On January 23, 1989, under the new Bush administration, the United States proposed that SPLA-held areas receive international aid. The UN echoed these proposals within a week. On February 8, the United

States called for a removal of obstacles to relief and progress toward peace (Africa Watch 1990, 113, 164–65). It threatened to withhold aid to Sudan. In March, the Canadian government said it would consider cutting off nonhumanitarian aid in the absence of a peace settlement (Minear 1991, 127). Perhaps most significantly, Prime Minister Sadiq el Mahdi was placed under pressure to provide relief by the prospect of having his authority further undermined if the United States carried through its stated intention to provide relief to SPLA-held areas, unilaterally if necessary (*Sudan Democratic Gazette*, December 1990, 2).

These new international pressures were exerted in the context of increasing pressure within Sudan for an agreement with the SPLA and for improved relief. This changing domestic political climate meant that for donors and the UN, at the same time as the risks of inaction were increasing, the risks of vigorous action on relief (of operations failing, and of government recriminations) were diminishing somewhat.

Meanwhile, the strategic risks of vigorous action were also diminishing in the context of a significant shift in the geopolitical alignments of the Sudan government. In late 1988 and early 1989, the Umma Party and NIF were moving closer to Libya in an attempt to secure military supplies and to counterbalance what they saw as the Egypt-inspired DUP peace initiative (Alier 1990, 272). In January, the U.S. government warned that the Sudan government's relationship with Libya was "inappropriate." And on March 14, the *New York Times* reported that the prime minister "has visited Iran, apparently in search of arms, and in the last several weeks he has been contemptuously dismissed by the Egyptians." Meanwhile, an easing of superpower tensions may have encouraged the United States to attach less importance to the idea of supporting a strategic ally against Communism (Minear 1991, 76).

Together, the new international and domestic pressures forced Prime Minister el Mahdi to allow free passage of relief under Operation Lifeline in April 1989 (Africa Watch 1990, 113–114). A "period of tranquillity" (initially a month, later extended) was agreed upon with the SPLA and the government, facilitating substantial relief deliveries to both government- and SPLA-held areas. New patterns of relief were accompanied by new patterns of discourse. In June 1989, USAID's Famine Early Warning System report gave a full tabulation of food aid requirements for the displaced in government- and SPLA-held areas (USAID 1989, 6). With people in rebel-held areas now deemed to be accessible, these people now figured in donor definitions of the relief problem.

The large number of monitors under Operation Lifeline appears to have reduced "leakage" (Minear 1991, 42, 52). UN representatives took direct personal responsibility for getting relief trains moving to Aweil and traveled with the trains (Wannop 1989). Wannop himself undertook this dangerous journey. Substantial payments were made to rail workers accompanying the trains (ibid., 7). According to John Garang, UN payments to railway workers had the effect of outbalancing the bribes merchants were paying for nondelivery (*Africa Report*, July–August 1989, 47). Relief in 1989 was still not fully accountable, however: the final destination of food often remained unknown to donors (Oxfam-UK 1989, 2).

The new relief operation helped mitigate the political and economic processes creating famine, just as earlier relief failures had allowed these processes to proceed virtually unhindered. Operation Lifeline helped to reduce conflict in the south, to reduce economic exploitation, and to produce a more normal pattern of trade and production. The new relief corridors were offlimits to military operations. The SPLA declared a ceasefire that lasted from May 1989 through mid-June, and the government declared a unilateral truce for July, extended through August and then September. Zones of peace became established around the corridors. In difficult peace negotiations between the government and the SPLM/SPLA, Operation Lifeline was reported to have helped maintain communication when other issues were deeply divisive (ibid., 128–35). Meanwhile, the heavy expatriate presence during Operation Lifeline appeared to deter violence on the part of military personnel (ibid., 37). Accompanying Operation Lifeline and the associated ceasefires was a fall in human rights violations and a partial revival in trade and rural production (ibid., 137; Deng and Minear 1992, 85). Larry Minear wrote in his evaluation of Operation Lifeline that "the protection of relief activities became a step toward a broader de-escalation of the conflict" (Minear 1991, 129). Meanwhile, merchant and army monopolies were partially undermined, and food prices fell sharply.

## OBSTRUCTION OF RELIEF AFTER MID-1989

Many of the dynamics that had blocked relief were soon to make themselves felt once again, however. The glare of international attention faded as 1989 wore on. And the military government of Lieutenant-General Omer el Beshir, which took power on June 30, 1989, reintroduced the blatant obstruction of relief.

While famine reached a peak in 1988, the south continued to suffer as the ongoing civil war was compounded by drought, by flooding, by disruption of trade, by the return of refugees from Ethiopia and northern Sudan, and by raiding among rival factions within the south. The needs of southern Sudanese—including a pressing need for rehabilitating the economy and infrastructure—continued to be neglected by the Sudanese government and, to a large extent, by international donors.

Relief operations were once more manipulated for military purposes. Although many of the relief shipments under Operation Lifeline in 1989 were for relief only, some of the relief corridors used in Operation Lifeline Sudan (OLS) in 1989 were reported to have been used to deliver government military supplies (*Christian Science Monitor*, November 1, 1989). An evaluation of the 1989 Operation Lifeline operation noted that "[t]he warring parties also used the tranquillity associated with Lifeline to prepare for renewed combat" (Deng and Minear 1992, 100).

In October 1989, the SPLA retook the town of Kirmuk, and this was quickly followed by government bombardment of the SPLA-held town of Yirol. The Sudanese government's attitude to the SPLA was clearly hardening once again, and in November 1989, it declared that it would rid the country of the SPLA within two months (Alier, 292–93). Moreover, by the autumn of 1989, OLS was running into major government obstruction: the government had halted relief flights and was failing to move supplies to the south (U.S. Congress 1990a, 44).

Despite this, the habitual optimism of the U.S. State Department was again in evidence. In March 1990, Herman Cohen, assistant secretary of state for African affairs, briefed a congressional committee on the situation in southern Sudan. Putting the main responsibility for the failure of peace talks on the SPLA, he gave a long list of signs that indicated that government cooperation with relief efforts was likely, concluding: "So I think the major diplomatic initiatives we have taken, especially led by President Bush's communication [to General el Beshir], are beginning to bear fruit."[61] Other, more skeptical observers pointed out that the government wanted the overwhelming majority of relief under the new OLS to be directed at government-held areas.[62]

The level of need in the south was still being minimized by the State Department in important respects. One senior USAID official stressed that the Dinka could be expected to meet most of their needs from wild foods, even in normal times. He added, "[I]f all the crops failed in the Dinka areas, they still have 70 percent of their dietary intake intact from cattle." This last statement not only contradicted the assertion that wild food was the primary source of nutrition but also assumed away much of the devastation of Dinka cattle through raiding and disease (U.S. Congress 1990a, 27).

By October 1989, some State Department officials appeared surprised that the promised cooperation of the Sudan government in providing relief had not been forthcoming. Jeff Davidow, deputy assistant secretary of state, Africa Bureau, observed that although 70,000 metric tons of food had been moved to the south in 1990, "[t]he indications that General Beshir gave us in March that his government would cooperate fully on OLS have not come to pass" (U.S. Congress 1990b, 18).

Andrew Natsios, director of the Office of Foreign Disaster Assistance, USAID, noted in more world-weary tones:

> The government of Khartoum has been increasingly indifferent, if not overtly hostile, to the relief effort. The recent bombing of OLS-sanctioned relief sites [for example, Torit and Bor] by the Sudanese air force is only the most extreme example of this. The litany of actions taken by the Government of Sudan to block relief efforts is beginning to sound like a broken record: the failure to move trains and barges loaded with relief food, interference with relief flights, unwillingness to allow ICRC to have access to areas of need, the harassment of private voluntary agencies, and the glacial pace with which even the most routine bureaucratic actions are taken.[63]

It was one thing to note these repeated failures in retrospect. But it is reasonable to ask why, if government obstruction was sounding like a "broken record," the State Department had been so optimistic in early 1990. Roger Winter, director of the U.S. Committee for Refugees, told a Senate subcommittee in November 1990:

> In the case of Sudan, government representatives made clear early on that there would be no OLS unless it comported with the government's military strategy. For example, Brigadier Dominic Cassiano said this plainly in his meeting with me and with John Prendergast of the Center of Concern in the fall of 1989. As a result, a clear pattern of government action emerged in which relief trains didn't move, relief barges remained moored at the docks, flights by the International Committee of the Red Cross were increasingly curtailed. This pattern was evident throughout last year, but culminated with the bombing of OLS relief sites in southern Sudan last month. Some of these bombings occurred while UN and Red Cross planes and personnel were on site.[64]

Overland distributions to SPLA-held areas were particularly subject to obstruction when passing through government-held areas. For its part, the SPLA had also again interfered with some relief operations, although its transgressions were on a smaller scale[65] and it gave a blanket permission for overland operations.

The lament of Thomas R. Getman, World Vision's director of government relations, had a familiar ring to those following relief operations from 1986 onwards: "In Kordofan Province, a train loaded with American grain has been waiting for more than a year for permission to leave on its route south into Bahr el Ghazal" (U.S. Congress 1990c, 41). Once again, donors had allowed relief operations to be manipulated by the Sudanese government. As Roger Winter commented in November 1990: "We didn't call a spade a spade as Lifeline deteriorated. It took Sudan's alliance with Saddam Hussein [over Iraq's invasion of Kuwait] to stiffen our position" (U.S. Congress 1990c, 61).

It is true that Western support for (and influence over) the Sudanese government was considerably less under Lieutenant-General el Beshir than under Sadiq el Mahdi. Indeed, military and development aid given directly by the United States to Sudan, having been reduced in large part because of dissatisfaction with Sudan's economic policies (Kilgour 1990, 642–43), was shut down altogether when the military regime seized power—something compelled by U.S. law when military rule replaces democratic government. It remains the case that the West held back from applying the full range of possible pressures against the el Beshir military regime. The United States continued to provide aid through multilateral institutions (U.S. Congress 1990c, 62). Program food aid was also still being provided. Other forms of leverage that could have been more vigorously explored were a major expansion of cross-border relief operations independently of the Sudanese government's consent, a drive for the complete diplomatic isolation of Sudan (on the lines of the isolation of Iraq), and a concerted campaign to highlight the continuing human rights abuses and the obstruction of relief in Sudan. Winter commented in November 1990: "Human rights conditions in Sudan deteriorated rapidly and massively, but US criticism was muffled at best; the Bureau for Human Rights and Humanitarian Affairs was absent. Operation Lifeline Sudan was manipulated into impotence, but the United States (and the UN, for that matter) was not aggressive about preserving Lifeline's effectiveness and humanitarian neutrality. Until Saddam."[66] Even at the end of November 1990, the State Department continued to argue that the Sudanese government would "come round and agree to cooperate with the international community" (U.S. Congress 1990c, 18).

Yet obstruction continued. Douglas Johnson observed:

> The UN Operation Lifeline Sudan was pledged to an impartial distribution of relief supplies to civilians on both sides of the civil war. Unfortunately, in my experience as a consultant for the World Food Programme in southern Sudan in 1990 and 1991, WFP rarely met these standards of impartiality. . . . Throughout the early part of 1991, the WFP office in Khartoum placed restrictions not only on convoys going into southern Sudan, but on the distribution of food already positioned in areas of need.[67]

At one point in 1991, UN relief flights were able to reach eighteen destinations in SPLA-controlled territory. But overland relief operations continued to be obstructed. And renewed obstruction of flights helped shrink the area that could be reached to only a fraction of that reached at this high point. Relief oriented toward rehabilitating the economy of the south was largely blocked by Khartoum: the possibilities for using relief to promote the reopening of schools and clinics, to support the reclaiming of land, and to encourage cooperatives to improve distribution of food remained largely unfulfilled (Douglas Johnson, personal communication, 1993). There was also a danger that tonnages of relief food that were supplied at this stage would encourage manipulation of displaced populations by both sides in the conflict.

In 1992, despite substantial relief needs identified by the UN, Bahr el Ghazal was deemed "inaccessible" and excluded from OLS/WFP operations on the ground that flight clearance for Akon could not be obtained from Khartoum. Of the relief needs that were assessed by the UN in southern Sudan, only a fraction of the allocated relief was getting through. In August 1992, in a context where WFP had canceled or suspended all food shipments to SPLA zones, the SPLA threatened to shoot down any aircraft bringing relief supplies to the city of Juba: it appeared that the lack of impartiality of relief operations was continuing, as in 1986–1988, to reinforce "security obstacles" to relief. Relief workers and human rights activists continued to express alarm at the inaction and "quiet diplomacy" of the UN.

In September 1992, relief operations were further undermined by the temporary withdrawal of UN and NGO staff after three relief workers and a journalist were killed in mainstream SPLA territory. After resuming relief activities, the UN scaled down its operations in late March 1993, after mainstream SPLA forces took Kongor from the Nasir faction and attacked a WFP expatriate there. The Kongor/Ayod/Waat area was particularly badly hit by the resultant reduction in aid (*News from Africa Watch*, April 15, 1993, 5–8). A perception that the UN was favoring the Nasir faction of the SPLA (which had become established in this area) combined with a continued feeling that the UN was too close to Khartoum to fuel hostility toward the UN on the part of many in the mainstream SPLA. Under the UN's Operation Lifeline in 1993, the neglect of relief needs in Bahr el Ghazal seemed to be continuing, and many were angered by the fact that the UN had not brought the needs in the Nuba Mountains within the purview of Operation Lifeline (see, e.g., *Sudan Democratic Gazette*, May 1993, 3–6; ibid., August 1993, 4–8). International donors continued to exhibit insufficient interest in breaking the vicious circle of neglect of relief, deteriorating security, and further neglect of relief.

Meanwhile, in southern Kordofan, the pattern of withholding food from famine victims was continuing. A classified cable from the U.S. Embassy in Khartoum, declassified at the request of Congressman Frank Wolf and presented to the Senate Foreign Relations Committee in June 1993, noted: "There are reports that thousands died of starvation in Meiram displaced camp last year, while local authorities would not release donated relief food stored in Babanusa. The PDF [Popular Defense Forces] routinely steals large amounts of relief food donated for the displaced" (U.S. Embassy Sudan/U.S. State Department internal cable, May 11, 1993).

This obstruction and diversion of relief was matched by a continuation of other human rights abuses. In late 1992 and February–March 1993, the U.S. Embassy reported, two military trains took a total of some three thousand troops (some from the army but most members of the new, militia-based PDF) from Babanousa to Wau.

> The first train advanced preceded by foot soldiers who killed or captured the civilians on their path. They burned houses, fields, and granaries, and stole thousands of cattle. Hundreds are estimated to have died. The March 1993 train carried horses that extended the soldiers' range. In five days, they reportedly killed almost a thousand persons between Manwal station and Aweil and captured 300 women and children. The burning of granaries and fields and theft of cattle caused many who escaped the troops to die later of starvation. . . . Credible sources say that when the March military train to Wau reached Meiram, soldiers raped scores of displaced women. (ibid., 1–2)

Despite the Baggara/SPLA agreement providing for the return of many captured Dinka, practices amounting to slavery were continuing:

> Credible sources say GOS [Government of Sudan] forces, especially the PDF, routinely steal women and children in the Bahr el Ghazal. Some women and girls are kept as wives; the others perform forced labor on Kordofan farms or are exported, notably to Libya. Many Dinka are reported to be performing forced labor in the areas of Meiram and Abyei. Others are said to be on farms throughout Kordofan. (ibid., 2)

The U.S. Embassy added:

> There are also credible reports of kidnappings in Kordofan. In March 1993 hundreds of Nuer displaced reached northern Kordofan, saying that Arab militias between Abyei and Muglad had taken children by force, killing the adults who resisted. The town of Hamarat el Sheikh, northwest of Sodiri in north Kordofan, is reported to be a transport point for Dinka and Nuba children who are then trucked to Libya. (ibid., 2)

The Embassy cable also noted that in some cases GOS authorities (including the army and police) secured the release of women and children captured by PDF forces (ibid.).

In October 1992, spurred by the execution of two local USAID staff in Juba, the U.S. Congress passed a strongly worded resolution condemning human rights abuses in Sudan. On December 2, UN General Assembly Resolution L.77 expressed alarm and concern about a number of abuses in Sudan, including detention without trial, torture, summary execution, forced displacement of populations, and the obstruction of humanitarian assistance. Reports of human rights abuses in the Nuba Mountains contributed to this climate of condemnation. While Western influence in Sudan had dwindled significantly since the 1989 military coup, with Iran in particular having stepped up its support of Khartoum, increasing numbers of observers were advocating a concerted bid to isolate Khartoum diplomatically, to conduct proper independent investigations of human rights abuses (including those in the Nuba Mountains region), and to undertake an effective program of relief to the south.

## CHAPTER 6

# Discussion and Conclusions

THE FAMINE was actively promoted by a number of powerful interests who stood to gain from it in important respects. One way famine was promoted was through obstructing relief, something that offered the prospect of maximizing the benefits extracted from famine and minimizing famine's unwanted side effects. The widespread conception of famine as simply a "disaster," and the emphasis placed by Sen and Drèze on the "negligence" of certain types of government, are unhelpful in understanding why this famine happened. So, too, is the idea of "policy failure": relief outcomes were actively shaped by local and international actors, who appear to have fulfilled many of their most important goals, famine notwithstanding.

## REFLECTIONS ON THE FAMINE

What is most striking about the victims of the famine is not that they were poor, although those who were still alive were certainly extremely poor once famine had run its course. Most evident is their near-total lack of rights or political muscle within the institutions of the Sudanese state. It was this that exposed them to the complex processes of famine, leaving them with no redress against violence and little or no access to famine relief. This political powerlessness was not a new phenomenon: in the nineteenth and early twentieth centuries, the people of southern Sudan had lacked significant political representation, and had as a result been exposed to widespread violence and famine. After independence, and more particularly from the mid-1970s on, this extreme powerlessness reemerged, as the forces of government were once again turned unambiguously against the south, and against the Dinka in particular. The partial incorporation of the Dinka into wider Sudanese political structures had tended to erode local systems of protection against exploitation and famine, without providing any secure protection at the center. As in the nineteenth and early twentieth centuries, particular groups were once again able to use their superior access to political power (including the direct use of force) in order to extract economic benefits from politically weaker groups.

By the early 1980s, the processes of famine offered the prospect of important benefits for both central and local interests. For successive governments in Khartoum, these processes held out the prospect of defeating rebellion in the south, gaining access to coveted resources in the south (notably oil), defusing the threat of Islamic fundamentalism with a "holy war," and deflecting the resentment of Baggara groups at their economic and political marginalization by turning them against even more politically marginalized groups in the south. Lacking the means to impose its authority, the central government sought instead to manipulate civil society for its own purposes. At the local level—for some Baggara, for army officers, and for merchants—processes of famine offered a number of significant economic benefits. Important elements of "conspiracy" have been highlighted: the initial concentration of raiding on oil-rich areas, the coordination between militias and the army, and the involvement of merchants and the army in restricting relief. However, the interests of politically powerful groups in relation to famine were quite diverse, and they were susceptible to change over time as famine developed its own dynamic and its own, sometimes unforeseen, consequences.

The democratic government of Sadiq el Mahdi was among those that promoted famine most vigorously. While Sen (1990) has suggested a close link between famine prevention and democracy, this study suggests a need to investigate precisely how particular democracies function and which groups they may fail to protect. This point is underlined by the way Western governments soft-pedaled in relation to the el Mahdi regime, in part because it was seen as "democratic."

This study has suggested that it was not simply "war" that created terrible famine in the 1980s. Processes of famine were fueled by long-standing conflicts over economic resources, exacerbated by a particular pattern of uneven development that generated growing pressures not only in the south but also, perhaps more importantly, in the north. Conflicts over resources were exacerbated by the discovery of oil in 1978: the desire to extract the oil encouraged a government policy of depopulating oil-rich areas of the south, while the SPLA directed intense military efforts toward preventing the extraction of oil.

Struggles over economic resources found their most extreme expression in war, which served also to legitimize the fiercer forms of struggle, but they were not simply generated by war. Once famine spilled over from the south into the north, resource conflicts grew more intense, and the desire to prevent famine migrants from straining scarce resources still further discouraged the provision of relief to them.

The common assertion that war creates famine fails to illuminate, at least in this case, the precise relationship between military and economic purposes. To some extent, as Duffield has stressed, controlling subsistence resources was a goal of conflict rather than simply a weapon (Duffield 1991, 8–9). Indeed, economic purposes ran the risk of conflicting with broader strategic goals. The widespread northern militia raiding on areas not at that time sympathetic to the SPLA has been noted, as has the part this played in boosting sympathy for the SPLA in these areas. The government's obstruction of relief even to government-held areas of the south also suggests the importance of economic goals (including army profits from the grain trade), when optimum military strategy might have urged the attraction of as many people as possible into government-held areas.

In the wake of Sen's work, it is often said that market forces create famine, as those unable to obtain food through the market prove vulnerable to starvation. It is true that price movements played a role in this famine. But this was not so much a reflection of market forces as of what I have called forced markets—that is, of market transactions that were actively shaped by the use of various kinds of force, including raiding, collusion, and intimidation in the marketplace; the restriction of nonmarket survival strategies; and finally, the restriction of relief. In addition, force was employed directly to rob people of their assets. Giving proper weight to the role of force can help to explain how even peoples who are relatively rich in natural resources (and perhaps relatively protected from natural shocks) can suffer severe famine. Indeed, the study suggests that it may be the wealth of a particular group, as much as its poverty, that exposes it to famine—as politically powerful groups resort to the use of various kinds of force in order to transfer wealth from victim groups to themselves. A by-product of the transfer of land in particular, as in South African apartheid, may be increased opportunities to exploit the labor of the dispossessed.

The real roots of famine may lie less in a lack of purchasing power within the market (although this will be one of the mechanisms of famine) than in a lack of lobbying power within national (and international) institutions. Sen has emphasized how poverty can lead to famine as people's access to market goods collapses, usually from already low levels; it may be equally, or more, important to investigate how powerlessness leads to famine, as people's access to the means of force and to political representation collapses, again usually from already low levels. This was precisely what happened with the Dinka, exposing them to raiding without redress and to famine without relief. Indeed, the Dinka's medium-term disenfranchisement within government institutions from the late 1970s on was compounded by an additional short-term disenfranchisement as thousands moved into areas of the north where they lacked local representation. An additional parallel with, and modification of, Sen's approach is worth noting: just as Sen has emphasized how an increase in one group's entitlements may contribute to famine in another group (for example, as rising incomes propel prices higher), so, too, an increase in one group's access to force may contribute to famine in another group. This was what happened as the Baggara became increasingly well-armed and increasingly influential in Khartoum from the mid-1970s on.

The relationship between markets and violence has another important, and often neglected, aspect. It is clear that the development of an increasingly market-oriented economy in nineteenth- and twentieth-century Sudan created losers as well as winners, and that these losers repeatedly resorted to violence in order to survive the harsh realities of market economies and uneven development. Often this violence was directed at people in southern Sudan who were showing some resistance to participation in the market economy on terms dictated by northerners. In the nineteenth century, the spread of a cash economy and the rise of production for export encouraged a resort to looting and exploitative trading in the south on the part of those northern Sudanese, notably the jellaba, who were marginalized by increasing land concentration in the north. Meanwhile, by the 1860s, the large merchants operating in the south were increasingly resorting to violence as competition intensified and their supplies of southern ivory began to dry up. In the twentieth century, Sudan's pattern of uneven development—with the bulk of resources directed at agricultural exports from central-eastern Sudan—played a major role in prompting elements of the Baggara herders to seek solutions to their growing economic problems by inflicting violence and famine on the Dinka in particular. Meanwhile, by the 1980s, the growing threat to the south-north cattle trade had encouraged an increasing resort to violence on the part of merchants and army officers seeking to defend and promote exploitative trading. The market economy also created losers on an international level, and the marginalization of a heavily indebted Sudan within the world economy encouraged a desperate government to resort to force and famine in a bid to gain access to contested oil reserves in the south.

From the point of view of those in the south, a growing dependence on marketed grain from the north after independence created a new kind of vulnerability because supplies from the north could easily be cut off. Moreover, the exploitative south-north cattle trade could quickly become still more exploitative in the context of wartime raiding and intimidation. Nor was the sale of labor any defense against famine in a context where force was used to make people work for nothing. The market, while it proved capable of reducing the damage from local drought in times of peace, created new forms of dependence for southern Sudanese and new incentives for violence on the part of groups in the north.

As political integration proceeded alongside economic integration, local sources of famine relief were not replaced by adequate access to state or international relief (the latter being mediated through state institutions in which the Dinka were poorly represented).[1] Given that groups affected by the famine lacked significant representation within Sudan, there was a pressing need for international donors to use their influence in an advocacy role on their behalf. However, the major international donors (including the

UN, as a special case) pursued their own strategic and bureaucratic agendas, and largely failed to counter the priorities of Sudanese groups who stood to benefit from famine. Donors failed to take vigorous action on relief until after the worst of the famine had been given widespread publicity. Their focus on "updates" and "the current situation" (numbers of displaced in particular areas, and so on) tended to neglect the processes of famine and their historical context, compounding the silence of the Sudanese government on these issues. To the extent that donors were trapped in an eternal present, it was difficult for them to take account of the past or to predict (or shape) the future. Like other groups addressing issues of public welfare (the police, doctors),[2] donors appear to have seen their task to a large extent as responding to a measurable emergency once it has been allowed to happen, rather than preventing it. And donors tended to equate the emergency of "famine" with famine's final stage, that of mass mortality. As later in the Kurdish emergencies of 1987–91, donors responded not so much to disaster itself but to particular, highly visible patterns of migration (Keen 1993). In Sudan, as in Guatemala and El Salvador, concentrating relief on government-controlled areas tended to reinforce the government's attempts to "pacify" rural areas through depopulation and the manipulation of hunger (cf. Barry 1987, 170–72; Garst and Barry 1990, 150–65). Concentrating the limited relief effort on urban areas also increased people's exposure to disease in overcrowded, insanitary environments.

In the meantime, unhelpful relief policies in Sudan were presented in such a way as to make them seem remarkably unobjectionable. Like the Sudanese government itself, donors remained almost entirely unaccountable to the victims of famine: the donors had a moral duty to help but few specific responsibilities. The lack of redress within the institutions of both the government and the international aid community goes a long way toward explaining why the famine occurred.

## THE DISINTEGRATION OF SUDAN?

Some of the limitations of analyzing Sudanese famine and war in terms of a north/south conflict have been emphasized. The events of the late 1980s and early 1990s have underlined this point, as well as suggesting the continuing importance of economic conditions in generating conflict in Sudan. As of early 1993, the situation was as follows.

The destruction and extraction of southern resources noted in this study had encouraged the beneficiaries of famine to turn their violence to new groups in the north, while economic hardship in the south had encouraged increasing divisions among the southern Sudanese. The raids on the Fur in Darfur by Baggara militias from mid-1988 on have been noted, as has the

Fur's support for the Umma party in 1986 and the primarily economic motivation for these Baggara raids. The benefits of exploiting the Dinka had been
reduced by this time—not only by the denuding of Dinka resources but also
by the Dinka's increasing ability, in conjunction with the SPLA, to offer
military resistance. Conflict in the Nuba Mountains region of southern Kordofan gathered force from 1989 on, yet the SPLA had only a weak presence
there. Again, Baggara raiding on the Nuba had important economic motives.

As with attacks on the Ngok Dinka in southern Kordofan and on the Uduk
and other groups in Blue Nile (Wendy James, personal communication,
1993), sympathy for the SPLA was as much a consequence as a cause of
attacks on the Nuba, while the alleged threat of the SPLA served to justify
the violence and exploitation. This pattern of exploitative violence, with
raiders moving from one victimized ethnic group to another in search of
scarce economic resources, could be expected to exacerbate internal divisions, even within the north of Sudan.

Meanwhile, divisions within the south had become more marked, with
the SPLA subject to increasing infighting. Again, these conflicts suggest the
limitations of a north/south military paradigm. A proper analysis of these
internal divisions cannot be attempted here. But their existence points to an
important benefit that Khartoum had gained from its strategy of starving the
south: it was not simply that southern Sudanese could be killed, weakened,
and driven from their lands; they could also be divided against one another.[3]
In the continued absence of proper international assistance, there appeared
to be a growing temptation for some groups within the south to use their
access to arms to secure economic resources from other southern Sudanese.

If the civil war in Sudan had been a straightforward military battle, it
would simply have been fought out until one side gave up. However, in large
part because it was a war fought by economic means for economic ends, it
had acquired a very different dynamic, tending to spread the conflict to new
areas, while also deepening internal conflicts within areas of devastation and
deprivation.

In conjunction with continuing intransigence from Khartoum, the southern infighting had added to the problems faced by relief agencies, while
some southern Sudanese frustration had been directed at the relief agencies
themselves. These developments underline a lesson that had emerged from
the famine in Somalia: when areas of famine are prematurely deemed to be
inaccessible (notably by the UN), they may become increasingly inaccessible
as poverty breeds violence, which in turn breeds more poverty in an increasingly vicious circle; providing proper assistance at an early stage offers the
prospect of checking this process before it spirals out of control. Aid agencies were increasingly expressing the fear that Sudan would become "another Somalia," with decentralized violence among different factions making
relief increasingly difficult. A related danger was that the international com-

munity (having in part created the problem through its own inaction and lack of impartiality) would be tempted to withhold aid from southern Sudan on the ground that it lacked stable and accountable administrative structures through which to channel relief.

### The Nuba

Although famine among the Nuba had not reached the levels of the famine documented in this study, nevertheless the plight of the Nuba exhibited important parallels with that of the Dinka. The Nuba's subjection to raiding and forced relocation was preceded, as with the Dinka, by a weakening in their political representation and their means of redress against such abuses. Like the Dinka, the Nuba had been subject to the manipulation of relief by Khartoum. And their plight had been similarly neglected by the international community, notably the UN. Any southern breakaway from the rest of Sudan could be expected to exacerbate the Nuba's isolation.

The Nuba are mostly farmers living in the Nuba Mountains region. Some 40 to 50 percent are Muslims. The long-running, low-level conflict pitting elements of the Nuba against elements of the Baggara and those involved in mechanized farming was noted in Chapter 2. This conflict had been allayed to some degree by important elements of cooperation, including trading and intermarriage. Long-standing competition over resources intensified, and violence was increasingly used to appropriate Nuba resources and to eject the Nuba from their fertile land. Both the Baggara militias and wealthy mechanized farmers stood to gain from these processes. Responding to an SPLA attack in the region in 1985, the Khartoum government armed local Baggara tribes, notably the Messiriya Zurug and the Hawazma. One aim appeared to have been to guard the Nuba, whose loyalty was considered suspect, not least because of their support for the Sudan National Party and their drift from the traditional religiously based parties.

Progressively, ethnic Nuba had been removed from judicial, administrative, and security posts in the Nuba Mountains region and elsewhere. This left all the major positions of authority in the Nuba Mountains region in the hands of Sudanese Arab groups in conflict with the Nuba. Like the neighboring Ngok Dinka, the Nuba were deprived of their means of redress within the institutions of the Sudanese state.[4] Meanwhile, as in the case of famine among the Dinka, foreign humanitarian agencies were kept out of the Nuba Mountains, and this impeded not only relief but also the monitoring of human rights. The UN in particular was slow to protest against the abuses inflicted on the Nuba.

Nuba attitudes toward the SPLA were ambivalent: many Nuba community leaders felt the SPLA would bring only trouble to the area. Africa Watch reported that when an SPLA unit infiltrated the eastern part of the Nuba Mountains in 1987, it "systematically assassinated and kidnapped community leaders who refused to cooperate"; thousands of farmers fled to the towns (*News from Africa Watch*, December 10, 1991, 5).

In 1989 attacks by Baggara militias became more frequent and more severe, with bands of Baggara searching aggressively for pasture and many more villagers forcibly displaced. Meetings in October 1989 between Kordofan militia leaders and members of the el Beshir's ruling Revolutionary Command Council led to the Popular Defense Act, which effectively legitimized the militias. Further Baggara raiding took place in 1990 and 1991.[5] The SPLA also raided for food, intimidated villagers, and engaged in forced recruitment. Appropriations were particularly marked when local units faced problems of supply. From 1990 on, there were signs of famine in the Nuba Mountains—but relief was very limited.

In September 1992, Africa Watch reported: "[A] large-scale campaign of forcible relocation has begun, with the apparent aim of removing the ethnic Nuba population from their ancestral lands, and scattering them in small camps throughout Northern Kordofan. This appears to amount to a systematic attempt to eradicate the identity of the Nuba. Since June, tens of thousands of Nuba have been moved each month."[6]

People were taken to transit camps within the Nuba Mountains, and then trucked north to camps, where conditions were often very bad. Meanwhile, more villages were burned and more people killed. Some villages were reported to have been bulldozed after attacks (*Sudan Human Rights Voice*, May 1993, 4). The relocation of over seven hundred thousand squatters and displaced people from around Khartoum demonstrated that the Sudanese government was willing and able to contemplate forced movements of populations on a very large scale.[7]

In January 1992, the Kordofan provincial government declared a *jihad* in the Nuba Mountains. The commander of the regional PDF, Colonel Ismail Ahmad Adam, said that his forces were "ready to cleanse every stretch of territory sullied by the outlaws" and that the PDF had "ensured the safety of the routes used by the nomadic Arabs." As with the deepening oppression of the Dinka, there were significant pockets of opposition; for example, opposition to the jihad campaign came from some military and police commanders, as well as from the commissioner of southern Kordofan, Mohamed el Tayib. But opponents were seen as unlikely to prevail without strong external pressure.

Kordofan government sources told Africa Watch in 1992 that a screening system was about to be introduced, whereby "productive" people (mostly young men) would be taken to large farms owned by wealthy merchants and made to work, with women and children sent to stay with "hospitable" families in northern Kordofan. The scheme, which followed the forced relocation of southern Sudanese in Khartoum to large farms near Renk in Upper Nile, had prompted some opposition in northern Kordofan, partly out of principle and partly because of fears that the region's already scarce resources would be further stretched.[8] The exploitation of migrant Dinka labor and the resurgence of slavery documented in this study were giving major cause for concern about the fate of Nuba forcibly displaced in this way.

Survival International noted in March 1993: "An extra 45,000 government troops, including tank battalions, reportedly entered the [Nuba] region in January 1993."[9]

## Divisions in the South

Some of the divisions within the south have been touched on already: government support for Anyanya 2 and the Ferteet militias; SPLA attacks on elements of the Nuer and the Ferteet; and the SPLA's forced requisitioning from civilians in parts of the south, including Bahr el Ghazal. While the SPLA's role in relation to the Bahr el Ghazal Dinka had been primarily a protective one (albeit belated), many groups in southern Sudan had regarded the SPLA as an enemy. This hostility among groups in the south was one of the reasons that the "Nasir faction" broke away from the main SPLA in August 1991. It is important to recognize the part played by the SPLA in inflicting hardship on southern Sudanese civilians, and to understand some of the reasons for this.

The Sudanese government had given encouragement and support to a number of tribal militias in the south, even before the fall of Nimeiri. These had included the Murle, the Toposa, and the Mundari. These militias had targeted civilian populations deemed to be supporters of the SPLA. The government had also supported Anyanya 2, recruited from various Nuer groups. The SPLA had a deliberate policy of retaliating against civilian populations with whom these militias were associated.

The SPLA's advance into Equatoria from late 1984 to 1986 had been particularly problematic. The SPLA met strong resistance from government-supported militias, and armed its own militias in response. The SPLA's distribution of arms to militias encouraged human rights abuses, and there were also abuses by SPLA units. Significantly, and contrary to the SPLA's expressed policy, these were not local Equatorian units at this time (Africa Watch 1990, 153). Accusations leveled by rival SPLA factions at one another should be treated with great caution. However, there is no doubting the legacy of bitterness against the SPLA for some of its actions, notably in Equatoria: the Nasir faction journal *Southern Sudan Vision* stated bluntly: "In Equatorial region Garang came not as liberator, but an occupier" (December 15, 1992, 6).

Significant resistance to the SPLA came from the Mundari, among whom the Sudan government had encouraged the formation of anti-SPLA militias. The Mundari had a history of conflict with the Bor Dinka, a strong force in the SPLA. After the capture of the government-held Mundari town of Tere-keka in September 1985, the SPLA carried out brutal reprisals on civilians (mainly on the eastern part of the Mundari tribe). There were further SPLA attacks in July of 1986, this time on eastern and western sections of the Mundari (Africa Watch 1990, 154).[10]

The government-supported Anyanya 2 was another source of opposition to the SPLA. Africa Watch reported that the SPLA used counterinsurgency tactics, including scorched-earth tactics and "possibly including forced re-moval of populations," in Upper Nile (Africa Watch 1990, 132, 153). The dissident journal *Southern Sudan Vision* accused Garang of having waged "a war of genocide against the Nuers of Gajack and Gajok and part of Lou Nuer with the help of the Ethiopians"; Garang was also charged in the journal with extending his war against Anyanya 2 into attacks on Nuer civilians.

SPLA bases in western Ethiopia have been mentioned. The SPLA distrib-uted weapons to groups in this area, who used them for raiding and settling old scores (Africa Watch 1990, 153–54). The SPLA also used raids to secure cattle for itself and to "punish" civilian groups associated with opposition to the Ethiopian government (Africa Watch 1991, 325–27). In February 1987, SPLA units, together with militiamen from the Toposa, Nyangatom, and Turkana tribes, were implicated in a massacre of more than five hundred Mursi living in southwestern Ethiopia (Africa Watch 1990, 159; Duffield, 1990b, 19). The Toposa and Nyangatom, it should be noted, had both re-ceived military support from the Sudan government, illustrating the com-plexity of the conflict in this area.

In areas it controlled, the SPLA sometimes used forced labor (for exam-ple, for portering) and confiscated food and other vital resources, including animals (Africa Watch 1990, 159–60). It was also accused of forcible con-scription into its military forces, mistreatment of boy soldiers, and appropri-ation of relief supplies (Duffield, 1990b, 20; *Sudan Monitor*, December 1991, January 1992). The abuse of civilian populations (including forced requisitioning) was encouraged by cutoffs in supply routes from Ethiopia, especially during the period 1984–1987, when Anyanya 2 in particular was able to impede such supplies to SPLA forces in Bahr el Ghazal.

To the extent that local conflicts were manipulated by the SPLA in its attempts to consolidate its hold on the south, the rebels were following not only in the footsteps of the Sudanese government but also in those of the British during the late nineteenth and early twentieth centuries.

From late 1987 on, the SPLA adopted a rather different policy toward government-supported militias and the groups from which they were re-cruited. This change of policy was encouraged by the reconciliation with

Anyanya 2 in late 1987 and by the increasing SPLA military control of the south. Wavering civilian populations were encouraged to side with the SPLA by its increasing military control and the (related) drying up of government support.[11] This in turn facilitated SPLA military successes in Equatoria in 1989. Soldiers who had been recruited from, and taken away from, eastern Equatoria by the SPLA were sent back to their home areas. The SPLA's changing behavior made itself felt among the Mundari; SPLA conduct improved in 1987, and the Mundari became increasingly receptive to the rebels. The SPLA's second campaign in Equatoria, in 1988–1989, was, for the most part more orderly than the first (Africa Watch 1990, 98, 153).

Increased SPLA control even persuaded some elements of the Baggara to reach an accommodation with the SPLA, underlining the continuing danger of Baggara "disloyalty" toward Khartoum, a danger that had helped generate the government's militia strategy in the first place. Following the army coup in June 1989, the military government of Omer el Beshir attempted to control and legitimize the Baggara militias by incorporating them into the new Popular Defense Forces. However, many among the Baggara were swayed against the military government of el Beshir—by resentment at this incorporation, by heavy taxation, by losses at the hands of the SPLA, and by a pressing need (in the context of severe drought in the north in 1991) to gain access to Bahr el Ghazal grazing land controlled by the SPLA (Gary Jones, personal communication, 1992). The outlawed Umma Party called on the Baggara in Darfur and Kordofan to "stop hostilities against the SPLA and to fight against the common enemy"—that is, the government (*Sudan Monitor*, July 1, 1990, 6–7). The SPLA reported in March 1992 that five thousand Messiriya youths in the government's Popular Defense Forces had defected to the rebels. Some Baggara were living permanently in SPLA-held areas of Bahr el Ghazal. Many enslaved Dinka had been returned by the Baggara, in return for access to grazing. While the Khartoum government continued to co-opt elements of the Baggara into the PDF, in March 1993, the Ansar issued a call to the army and the NIF "to revive democracy or face a campaign of civil struggle" (*Guardian*, June 1993).

If the SPLA was able to consolidate its support in many ways, the rebel army went on to suffer a series of reversals, beginning in 1991. The SPLA was gravely weakened by its expulsion from Ethiopia following the fall of the Mengistu regime in Ethiopia in May of that year. Sudanese refugee camps in Ethiopia were evacuated, and the Sudanese government blocked relief for people returning from Ethiopia.

The removal of the protection from Ethiopia (and the possibility of active cooperation between the Ethiopian and Sudanese governments) posed particular dangers for SPLA forces and commanders near the Ethiopian border. These new dangers came on top of a range of grievances against the military excesses of the SPLA and a growing dissatisfaction with the slow progress towards democratizing the SPLA as it consolidated its administration of much of southern Sudan. On August 28, 1991, three commanders at Nasir (Riek Mashar, Lam Akol, and Gordon Kong) announced the "overthrow" of Garang, denouncing him for human rights abuses and personal dictatorship. They also called for the separation of the south, an idea made more attractive to many by the continuing distance between the SPLA and the northern opposition.

Fighting followed between what became known as the Nasir and Torit (Garang) factions of the SPLA around Kongor and Bor. Attacks on civilian Dinka by elements of the Nasir faction (together with Anyanya 2 forces and some disgruntled Nuer) led to large-scale displacement and a severe food crisis. Cattle and other property were raided (WFP/FAO/UNICEF 1991). The Anyanya 2 forces in particular were widely suspected of having renewed links with the government in Khartoum. The Torit faction retaliated against these attacks.

The importance of scarcity and relief inadequacy in generating violence was illustrated by the raiding on the Dinka around Kongor and Bor (WFP/FAO/UNICEF 1991, 47–50). Many of those recruited into these attacks were Nuer from Ayod. The Nuer in this area felt they had been neglected in relief operations (for example, in the fields of health, water, and cattle vaccination), and saw this as an extension of their neglect in development before the war in relation to Kongor and Bor. Resentment at this lack of relief appeared to have encouraged them to join the Nasir faction in this raiding, from which they acquired cattle and grain.

It has been stressed that international relief for the south was often channeled through Sudanese government structures that were far from politically neutral. Of course, SPLA makeshift government structures had not been politically neutral either, although it is difficult accurately to assess allegations of "bias" and "corruption." What is clear is that by the early 1990s the inadequacy of international assistance to the south had created a fertile breeding ground for resentments that, in the absence of proper (and properly supported) democratic structures, were increasingly being channeled along ethnic lines. There are parallels here with the way that hardship among the Baggara had encouraged a hardening of ethnic conflict with the Dinka.

In addition to the raids on Kongor and Bor, from September 1991 on, there was also significant raiding on the Bahr el Ghazal Dinka by Nuer. The raiding was roughly along the Bahr el Ghazal/Upper Nile boundary. The split in the SPLA had apparently removed some of the previous restraint on the Nuer that had come with the Anyanya 2–SPLA pact of 1987.

The Nasir faction of the SPLA was accused not only of sponsoring large-scale violence against the Dinka but of seeking to control and exploit non-

Nuer civilian populations in the Ethiopian borderlands. The latter charge was to a large extent confirmed by an independent study (James 1992, 18–21, 37–39). The economic exploitation of the Uduk and the Meban (both from Blue Nile) by the SPLA in Nasir included the appropriation of fish and grain and the exploitation of labor. James reported that the movement of the Uduk was strictly controlled by the Nasir faction, and she registered the strong suspicion that the faction was seeking to use and maintain the deprivation of the Uduk in order to attract international assistance. In a similar vein, Douglas Johnson (personal communication, 1993) reported that local Nasir faction commanders, harboring a legitimate resentment at the failure of the UN's Operation Lifeline Sudan to fulfil commitments of assistance to local people, frequently opposed targeting international assistance to the most needy (largely non-Nuer) population in the area. Aid workers have accused both the breakaway Nasir faction and the Garang faction of appropriating aid intended for civilians (see, e.g., *Times* [London], February 5, 1992).

The divisions within the south underlined the importance of providing large-scale relief over a wide geographical area. Having largely blocked relief to the south, Khartoum was now able to exploit the divisions that had arisen partly as a result of this deprivation.

Divisions within the SPLA have inevitably helped the Khartoum government, and may have been actively encouraged by Khartoum to some extent.[12] In 1992, the Sudanese army retook Pochalla, Bor, Yirol, Pibor, Shambe, Kapoeta, and Torit, causing relief agencies to flee. The SPLA hit back with an attack on Juba in June–July 1992. In September, the SPLA suffered a further split, when deputy leader William Nyuon Bany declared his opposition to Garang. In late October and early November 1992, Nasir faction and former Anyanya 2 forces had attacked and regained Malakal (apparently helped by the defection of southern Sudanese from the Sudan government army).

As in Somalia, there were signs of human rights abuses' being used as a reason not to give aid;[13] in reality, adequate and properly directed aid, including aid for rehabilitation, could be expected to play (and could earlier have played) a key role in minimizing these abuses. Humanitarian and political problems were not separate, and the continued absence of proper humanitarian aid continued to encourage the more authoritarian and violent means of political and personal survival, with Khartoum taking advantage of southern deprivation and division. The UN has been particularly poorly adapted to dealing with such factional conflicts.

Nor was it enough to hope for the fall of the military regime in Khartoum: the devastation that had followed the demise of Siad Barre in Somalia had shown that the fall of an authoritarian government was no panacea for violence; its local causes must also be tackled.

## BENEFITS OF FAMINE: BEYOND THE CASE STUDY

It is dangerous to generalize about famines: there are probably as many causes of famine as there are famines. Nevertheless, many of the dynamics discerned in Sudan have been present, in some form, elsewhere.

Consider Ethiopia. Even though the "explanations" of most aid organizations and the Ethiopian government stressed that the 1983–1985 famine in Ethiopia was the result of drought, environmental decline, and/or overpopulation, it is actually difficult to analyze the causes of this famine without looking closely at its functions.[14] At least as important as drought in creating the famine were the government policies of sponsoring raids (by militias and the army) on rural areas where rebel support was strong, and of blocking relief to these areas. Tigray, with around one-third of Ethiopia's famine-affected population, received around one-twentieth of the total relief food. Relief was manipulated to encourage population shifts away from rural Tigray and Eritrea towards government towns and "protected" villages in those provinces and towards provinces further south, where workers were needed on state farms. Some six hundred thousand people were resettled from north to south in an operation described by the Ethiopian government as its famine relief effort. Yet the accompanying use of force, together with the cramped conditions for the people transported, led to an escalation in deaths during the famine. Meanwhile, the large-scale movements of people tended to spread famine conditions from the north to the south.

As in Sudan, those involved in planning relief operations largely failed to come to grips with the local processes of force and exploitation that were creating famine. And they failed to anticipate opposition from those with a vested interest in blocking relief. The UN and most Western governments (the main partial exception was that of the United States) did not speak out about the government's role in creating famine and blocking relief. The UN declined to back relief efforts undertaken by rebel groups. It endorsed erroneous government assessments of the relief needs in different areas, and it greatly exaggerated the number of people whom relief was reaching. It also declined to condemn the government's use of relief food to pay its militias in Tigray and Eritrea.

Peter Cutler reported in his detailed study of the 1983–1985 famine that the UN Emergency Office for Ethiopia (UNEOE) was denying press reports on misallocation of food aid even though these were based on figures collected by its own monitors. He suggested: "UNEOE's main function was to act as a 'screening device,' giving the appearance of competent action in response to famine but not compromising its actual position in Addis Ababa by unduly antagonising the host government . . . it would have been as embarrassing for the donors who had entrusted resources to the Ethiopian government as it was for the government itself to have aid misallocation exposed."[15] Such dynamics were to be repeated in Sudan—witness, for example, the donors' (and in particular the U.S. State Department's) dismissal of their own monitor's report on the theft of relief grain at Raga in Bahr el Ghazal.

In the Ethiopian case, as in Sudan, it appears to have been widespread media coverage of the final stages of famine that transformed donors' perception of the risk of taking vigorous action (Cutler 1989, 454). Again, the transformation came only after people were dying en masse.

A failure to ensure that grain was pushed through to famine victims has also been noted in relation to the Nigerian civil war. John Stremlau's study pointed to a lack of international monitors as contributing to the widespread diversion of aid in Biafra; as in Sudan, the diversion was largely obscured as international relief organizations repeatedly denied feeding anyone but the most desperate (Stremlau 1977, 247–50).

Nor is it only in war-related famines that such concerns are relevant. In the Sudanese drought-led famine of 1983–1985, relief supplies for Darfur that had been targeted by international donors to "the poorest and most needy" largely failed to reach the hardest-hit groups. Towns were able to secure a large share of the grain distributions, and suspicion of migrants discouraged distributions to them (Keen 1991, 191–206). It is clear that precisely those groups who suffered most severely from the famine (rural people, nomads, migrants) were also those who were least well placed to stake a claim to international relief that was channeled through local political institutions and power relationships. More politically influential groups, such as merchants and prominent officials, were able to secure some benefits from famine, notably from the purchase of livestock at low prices and from the acquisition of relief food intended for the most needy. Meanwhile, aid officials and evaluations tended seriously to exaggerate the efficacy of relief.[16]

Another drought-related famine was the Sahel famine of 1968–1973. In their study of the response to this famine, Sheets and Morris (1974) noted that in 1973 malnutrition (even within particular camps) was significantly more severe and persistent among nomadic groups than among sedentary groups; meanwhile, there was widespread discrimination against nomadic groups in relief distributions. Sheets and Morris explained this discrimination as stemming from traditional hostilities between the nomadic and sedentary peoples, adding that the latter were themselves suffering the effects of famine. They went on to argue that international donors had made no proper provision for observing or ensuring equitable relief distributions at the local level, facilitating the widespread discrimination against nomads. Indeed, such discrimination was played down in official discourse because of the likely disastrous impact on donor (notably U.S.) relations with host governments. As later in Ethiopia, Sudan, and Somalia, donors failed to intervene until the crisis had reached catastrophic proportions. Meanwhile, relief distributions were presented as having been effective (Sheets and Morris 1974, 38–48). Thus, the bureaucratic goal of appearing to be successful was reconciled with the strategic goal of not upsetting host governments. The feeling in some donor circles that the passing of nomadic lifestyles was a sign of progress has been mentioned.

A third example of a famine not related to war is the Great Starvation in Ireland in 1845–1849. Affecting people under the direct responsibility of an elected and wealthy government in London, this famine shows that there is no reason to assume that exploitative famine and host government neglect are confined to "the Third World." The Irish famine appears to have conferred significant benefits on some landlords—themselves under significant economic pressures—by clearing large sections of the peasantry and tenant farmers from the land through evictions, emigration, and outright mortality. This allowed the consolidation of larger landholdings, and at the same time created a significant group of landless people willing to work as day laborers (Nowlan 1956, 177–79; McDowell 1956, 8; Regan 1983, 112–16; O'Neill 1956, 254). For many years before the famine, landlords had used assisted emigration in an attempt to solve what they saw as the overpopulation of their estates. Such schemes, and still more the famine itself, facilitated the widespread replacement of tillage with livestock rearing, allowing landlords to meet a growing market for animal products in an increasingly urban England (MacDonagh 1956, 332). There was great resentment of landlords' actions on the part of famine victims (McHugh 1956).

Local landlords played down the severity of the potato disease appearing in 1845; later, the British reliance on local organization of relief foundered on landlords' indifference. The lack of action by landlords in either drawing attention to or relieving the famine appears to have sprung from a desire not only to avoid the cost of relief but also to clear land wherever possible (Regan 1983, 112–13; McHugh 1956, 428–30; Nowlan 1954, 177–79; O'Neill 1956, 252–54). Such "benefits" of famine were also perceived in London, where the assistant secretary at the Treasury and chief famine administrator, Charles Trevelyan, interpreted the famine as a God-sent opportunity to rid Ireland of an idle, unproductive peasantry, replacing it with educated landlord proprietors on the English model (Arnold 1988, 111).

It is striking that in a number of famines, a degree of wealth (in the absence of political power) has not provided immunity to famine; indeed, it may have actively encouraged it. A claim to some form of wealth—whether the land of Irish smallholders in the 1840s or the oil resources claimed by the Biafrans prior to and during the Nigerian civil war—can create vulnerability to processes of famine that are actively promoted by groups seeking to gain access to these resources.

The terrible famine of 1932–1934 in the Ukraine—an area rich in agricultural and mineral resources, harboring strong nationalist ambitions, and only weakly represented in Moscow—may provide a closer parallel to the Sudanese famine than do the famines highlighted by Sen. From his personal observation of the Soviet Union in the early 1930s, William Chamberlin noted: "The worst famine regions in 1932–33 were in many cases the most fertile and prosperous districts of pre-war Russia." Further, within particular areas, the more wealthy peasants were apparently particularly subject to expropriation (Chamberlin 1935, 66, 76–77, 88; Oleskiw 1983, 10–11). It appears to have been precisely the resources of the Ukraine, combined with a resistance to the Soviet regime's attempt to exploit them for its own industrialization, that fueled the processes of state-sponsored forcible expropriation that led to famine.

One of the few serious attempts to analyze the political and economic processes accompanying famine in Somalia has been made by Alexander de Waal and Rakiya Omaar, co-directors of African Rights and both formerly of Africa Watch. The discussion that follows draws largely on their work, and attempts to bring out some of the similarities between the dynamics to which they have drawn attention and those highlighted in this study.

The context of famine in Somalia is different from that in Sudan in a number of respects. In Somalia, the peak of the famine in 1992 did not coincide with the existence of a rebel movement as such; rather, the leaders of a number of different clans and subclans were competing for power after the fall of Siad Barre, while armed bands often resorted to raiding and looting simply to survive. By 1992, the disintegration of government had progressed much further in Somalia than in Sudan, and the central government in Mogadishu was unable to manipulate famine (or to do anything else) in the relatively calculating manner of its counterpart in Khartoum.

The parallels with the Sudanese famine are very striking, however. As in Sudan, the famine was driven to a large extent by raiding on politically marginal groups, which resulted in the transfer of assets from the victims to the raiders. As in Sudan, the use of violence became increasingly central to the extractive commercial strategies of elite groups. As in Sudan, the varying degree of access to arms helped determine which groups would benefit from raiding and which groups would suffer. (In the Somali case, the Hawiye clan inherited substantial arms from Siad Barre because they controlled the capital, Mogadishu, while the Darod retained considerable arms from their period in power under Barre.) As in Sudan, the blocking and looting of relief, as well as raiding itself, was sponsored by merchants with an economic interest in famine. As in Sudan, it proved extremely difficult to target relief food at groups whose politically marginal position had helped expose them to famine in the first place. As in Sudan, the designation of large areas as "inaccessible" helped render them increasingly so. And, finally, as in Sudan, the international community's unwillingness to come to grips with the political and economic processes generating famine played a significant role in deepening the suffering, while a vigorous international response came only once the final stages of famine had been widely publicized in the international media. A frequent failure to consult Somalis, notably by UN/US military forces, made it much more difficult to attack the root causes of famine and encouraged the neglect of many Somalis' desire for disarmament and economic rehabilitation (African Rights 1993; Stevenson 1993). There was insufficient "flow of words" to accompany (and guide) the "flow of grain." The continuing lack of accountability within the international relief system was shown by the resignation in late 1992 of the UN Secretary General's very able special representative in Somalia, Mohamed Sahnoun, after he was cautioned for criticizing the UN.

The three groups hardest hit by the Somali famine were the Rahanweyn clan, the Digil, and the Bantu, who were all outside Somalia's clan system. These groups were politically marginalized, but the Rahanweyn in particular were not economically marginalized. Indeed, they occupied some of Somalia's most fertile land, along the Juba and Shebelle rivers.

Attempts to appropriate the economic resources of the Rahanweyn, the Digil, and the Bantu were significant under the Siad Barre regime. The Gabaweyn subclan of the Rahanweyn (living on the fertile banks of the upper Juba River) were subject to dispossession at the hands of Siad Barre's neighboring Marehan clan in the mid-1980s. Marehan clansmen used relatives in the Somali Ministry of Agriculture to register Gabaweyn land in their name; some Rahanweyn were also forcibly ejected from land at gunpoint. Meanwhile, many Bantu had land taken for sugar and banana plantations. Renewed pillaging of the farmers of southern and central Somalia (including the Rahanweyn) took place with the collapse of the Barre regime in 1991. Fighting between rival clans and subclans encouraged such pillaging, and the Rahanweyn, Digil, and Bantu lacked the access to arms that would have allowed them to resist the heavily armed pastoral groups who raided them (de Waal and Omaar 1992, 62–63). These pastoral groups, like those in Sudan and much of Africa, had incidentally tended to be neglected in development spending.

In the lower Juba River area, farmers were attacked and cultivation severely disrupted by battles between the United Somali Congress (Hawiye) and the Somali Patriotic Movement (Darod) in the spring and summer of 1991.[17] As one Bantu man from the Juba valley put it when his property and crops were stolen, "When two bulls fight, it's the grass that suffers" (*Guardian*, August 22, 1992). Siad Barre's forces, retreating from Mogadishu, left a trail of destruction (Stevenson 1993, 143). Devastation in southwestern Somalia was renewed during March–May 1992, as Barre's troops gathered with the intention of marching on Mogadishu, and again during October–November, when the area was occupied by troops following Barre's son-in-law, General "Morgan" Mohamed Hersi.

Faced with a deepening famine, the UN was profoundly inactive, holding onto the "need to work through the government" in Mogadishu and citing security obstacles as the reason for its lack of relief activities, most notably in 1991. Yet such organizations as the ICRC and Save the Children Fund were able to carry out substantial relief operations, albeit at some risk to local and international staff.

While many donors favored targeting relief to the most needy (the U.S. Marines were eventually brought in to do so), and while the UN special envoy, James Jonah, tried to use the threat of a cutoff of relief food to control the violence (Stevenson 1993, 144), de Waal and Omaar at Africa Watch emphasized the importance of injecting large quantities of relief grain into Somalia at an early stage. Even if the grain were looted, they stressed, it would help bring down prices. This could reduce levels of raiding and looting, since militiamen would not have to steal to survive, while merchants' incentives for paying militiamen to steal food or fire at relief ships would be reduced, as would their incentives for hoarding. In the meantime, while a degree of targeting was possible through careful local negotiations, attempts to target the most needy would face important political obstacles: "Relief agencies negotiate with clan elders to do the food distribution; the practicalities of security and access mean that powerful clans are first in line for negotiating such deals. This means that members of clans such as the Hawiye are fed first. Less powerful clans are fed next, and groups outside the clan system altogether, such as the Bantu groups and Ethiopian refugees, are fed last or not at all."[18]

Targeting, moreover, held out the danger of inciting the wrath of groups left out (*Guardian*, August 14, 1992). Red Cross officials emphasized the importance of their distributing food through eighteen different entry points, in contrast to the UN's concentration on the capital. Red Cross staff said rival clans would be less likely to raid one another for food if distributions were more even from the start (*Guardian*, August 5, 1992), a point also emphasized by Save the Children Fund.[19] Relevant here is the fact that in conditions of general scarcity, it is often the food resources in particular geographical areas that expose the inhabitants to raiding and famine in the first place.

The Red Cross concentrated on distributing food through clan elders, something that de Waal and Omaar saw as strengthening the hand of the elders in relation to more belligerent elements in Somali society.[20] The latter included the major warlords, el Mahdi and Aidid, and ordinary militiamen.

One clan leader in the southern town of Haddur, near the Ethiopian border, was reported to have kept Aidid out of his territory by using his own relief at an early stage to "nourish local gunmen into obedience" (Stevenson 1993, 143). As in Sudan, the proliferation of arms in Somalia had encouraged a weakening of the authority of elders; realistic ways of shoring up this authority nevertheless existed (and were frequently neglected).

When it became apparent that targeting the neediest was proving extremely difficult, this was seen in the United States as necessitating a U.S.-led military intervention.[21] In a sense, as in Sudan, problems of targeting had been noted in retrospect (and once the famine had passed its peak), rather than allowed for in advance. Limited attempts at disarmament were focused on urban areas and prompted many militiamen to flee to the surrounding countryside with their arms. Some reports observed that militiamen had brought violence, and impediments to relief, to new areas after leaving areas occupied by the U.S.-led forces (*Guardian*, February 9, 1993; Smolowe 1992, 30–31; Stevenson 1993, 139–40). By increasing insecurity in some rural areas and encouraging people to remain concentrated in urban areas (with improved food supplies), the military intervention may have added to public health problems and slowed economic rehabilitation (African Rights 1993, 6–27). It also took resources away from economic rehabilitation and fueled hostilities toward international aid organizations (African Rights 1993; *Guardian*, July 9, 1993).

## POLICY IMPLICATIONS

One of the implications of this study for those seeking to prevent future famine in Sudan is that this is likely to be impossible without an adequate political settlement in the country, and adequate representation for all groups. In the absence of political safeguards, even the economic rehabilitation of the south would provide little lasting protection against famine, just as the rehabilitation of the south after the first civil war did not prevent renewed famine and raiding in the second civil war. Indeed, such rehabilitation might even attract raiding and famine if political safeguards are not in place. While it is well beyond the bounds of this study to suggest a solution for conflict, the study does show that the local causes of violence and exploitation will have to be addressed—not just broader issues, such *shari'a* law. Local, economic grievances would have to be addressed even if the south were to break away from the rest of Sudan.

One of the principal policy implications of this study for international donors is the need to understand, to engage with, and to take account of the political and economic processes creating famine, rather than simply (and optimistically) allocating relief to some of the poorest groups once they have descended into destitution. On an immediate level, a major injection of relief and, perhaps more important, development resources into the south is needed if long-standing deprivation is not to lead to further factional violence, thereby deepening famine and adding to the security obstacles impeding relief. This study has stressed some of the economic roots of conflict. It is emphasized that violence, which has been used in Sudan and Somalia as a reason for not giving relief, should instead be seen as something that can be reduced by effective and impartial relief operations. The international community should try to tackle the causes and not just the effects of violence.

The conventional practice in international relief operations, whether in wartime or peacetime, is to isolate the "poorest and neediest" group, to "target" relief to this group, and then to dispatch a quantity of relief sufficient for its needs, perhaps with relatively small resources allocated to monitoring the fate of the relief. This, in government-held areas at least, was the practice adopted in relation to the Sudanese famine. Now, if the Sen and Drèze model of famines were correct—if poverty and "market forces" were at the root of famines, and if governments were either well disposed or indifferent to famine victims—this approach might be expected to meet with some success.[22] However, in Sudan this approach proved seriously flawed even within the government-held areas, as politically weaker groups failed to gain access to relief, and the small quantities of relief received failed to counterbalance the active creation of famine. The study suggests a pressing need for international donors to adopt a more holistic approach to the famine process—a need to move beyond simply allocating relief to conveniently accessible areas once famine mortality occurs, and toward a concern with pushing relief through to all areas of need in a bid to halt the extended processes of famine before the final stage of mass mortality is reached. The study suggests that where relief operations are allowed to be manipulated for political and military purposes, where they are perceived as intrinsically biased, problems of security and access are likely to be greatly augmented. Just as the study stresses the need to tackle the causes of violence (whether the violence is directed at famine victims or at relief shipments), it also emphasizes the need to address the causes of famine, not only the most visible symptoms. This means monitoring and tackling a range of human rights abuses and not focusing exclusively on shifting quantities of grain to particular locations.[23]

The need for this kind of holistic approach is most obvious in the context of civil war—when normal power inequalities are likely to be exacerbated and when the active creation of famine is particularly likely. But peacetime famines are also likely to involve an extended process of exploiting politically powerless groups, with relief channeled through institutions in which famine victims have minimal representation. Various forms of official and unofficial violence may also be wielded, even in peacetime. The need for a holistic approach is therefore not confined to wartime famines.

Those who wish to prevent famine need to face up to the major problems involved in targeting needy groups who lack political muscle within their own societies. More often than not, it is the political weakness of victim groups that has exposed them to famine in the first place. This was certainly true of the Dinka. Even in the case of government garrison towns in the south, economic motives limited government authorities' desire to provide relief: some NGO staff felt that donors had seriously overestimated the determination of the Sudanese government to channel relief to these towns (interview with Melvyn Almond, Oxfam-UK, Khartoum, November 10, 1988). Problems of targeting should be allowed for in advance, rather than simply noted in retrospect. The more general advice to policymakers given by Pressman and Wildavsky in 1973 should be heeded in relation to famine relief: "The great problem, as we understand it, is to make the difficulties of implementation a part of the initial formulation of policy. Implementation must not be conceived as a process that takes place after, and independent of, the design of policy."[24]

The interests of a variety of relatively powerful groups in promoting processes of famine need to be taken into account when designing policy, rather than simply noted (or covered up) after the event. This involves obtaining some understanding of the strategies and needs of "oppressor" groups, as well as the more traditional "liberal" and "anthropological" focus on the strategies and needs of the victims.

The degree to which assistance should be provided beyond a target group will depend on the context: in the case of Somalia, such a strategy appears to have much merit, since hunger has been helping to drive the violence; in the case of Mozambique, where the renowned brutality of the rebel Renamo movement has been supplemented by government abuses, Wilson has argued for the use of aid to support government structures and salaries, thereby reducing the need of government forces to resort to seeking tribute from civilian populations (Wilson 1993, 1). On the other hand, benefits extracted by powerful groups from relief operations may in some circumstances create incentives for perpetuating the crisis. In northeastern Brazil, wealthy landlords have been able to appropriate much of the relief provided during recent droughts, and this has helped to undermine their willingness to back development schemes that might make famine less likely (*Guardian*, February 20, 1993). In the case of Sudan, Duffield (1992) has emphasized the dangers of a permanent emergency, the benefits of which may include prolonged appropriation of relief resources, not least through the manipulation of exchange rates.

It is worth looking at this question of targeting in the context of broader discussions on economic development in Sudan and elsewhere. A wide range of academic work on many poor countries, including Sudan, suggests that even in peacetime, policy has fairly consistently been shaped by a narrow range of interests, whether these are taken to be class, ethnic, or urban interests, or some combination of these.[25] It is worth asking why one should expect that such states, in the course of an emergency (and even more so, in the course of a civil war), should suddenly be transformed and begin to devote themselves to serving those most in need. Dominant groups might even be expected to be particularly self-serving during famines (Greenough 1982).

If existing analyses of development policies can inform our understanding of relief policies, the reverse may also be the case. It has become common, in World Bank circles and elsewhere, to suggest that poor countries should attempt to boost growth and exports, while providing a "safety net" to protect the entitlements of the most vulnerable groups.[26] While this study is an analysis of famine rather than of "structural adjustment," it does suggest that targeting resources to particularly needy groups may be difficult to achieve in practice, since aid will be channeled through local institutions in which the intended recipients are unlikely to be influential. Insofar as the growth strategy requires the cheap labor of marginal groups, such targeting may be doubly difficult.

The study suggests a further problem with the prescription of growth plus targeting. In addition to the two groups envisaged in this model—the beneficiaries of growth, and the residual group of particularly vulnerable people to be supported with a "safety net"—there may also be a third group, excluded from and perhaps even damaged by growth, but seeking to solve its own economic problems by actively exploiting the resources of the most politically marginal groups, perhaps by force. The coming of Sudan's second civil war should be seen not so much as a senseless outbreak of violence interrupting processes of development, but rather as the most extreme expression of the resource conflicts, exploitation, and resistance bred by a pattern of uneven development that has created losers in the north as well as the south. This pattern of development was sponsored by the British, and reinforced by multilateral institutions like the World Bank. It is one thing to condemn violence; it is another, and more useful, exercise to sponsor a pattern of development that makes violence less likely.

While this study has concentrated on forces promoting famine within Sudan, it was Sudan's marginal role in the world economy that created the context for this violence and exploitation. In particular, the lack of development in much of the country, the extreme vulnerability to drought, and Sudan's escalating international debt helped drive the processes of raiding and depopulation that created the famine. The international community cannot escape some responsibility for these processes. Any peaceful, demo-cratic government in Sudan would require major debt relief to help ensure against a similar recourse to violence.

So far, the discussion has centered largely on the problems of targeting, and brief reference has been made to the need to engage with the processes creating famine in the first place. What does such engagement mean in prac-tice? Three main areas of action may be appropriate.

The first is exerting diplomatic and economic pressures on governments and other influential groups that are promoting famine. Clearly, there are difficult moral and practical problems to be faced when the sovereignty of a country is seen as coming under threat. This study does not offer a blueprint for solving these problems. However, in documenting the lengths to which a government may go in abusing and starving its own civilians, the study adds weight to the growing body of opinion holding that unquestioning re-spect for a government's sovereignty may be a license for oppression.[27] While the UN Charter upholds the sovereignty of nation-states (and many of the nation-states that vote at the UN have an interest in preserving this priority), the UN Charter also upholds a range of individual human rights, which may be threatened by nation-states. In showing how donors were keen to influence Sudanese foreign and economic policy even as they turned a blind eye to human rights abuses, the study also casts doubt on donors' sincerity when they made the sovereignty argument.

The second (closely related) way of engaging with processes creating fam-ine is by speaking out against human rights abuses and pushing for improved access for journalists and human rights monitors. We have seen the impor-tance attached by Dinka elders to maintaining the "flow of words" from areas where the Dinka were vulnerable to exploitation and human rights abuses. In practice, Western governments and multilateral organizations did more to block this flow of words than to promote it: their silence compounded that of the Sudanese government. Donors' discourses often centered on flows of grain to the exclusion of almost everything else; but even grain flows are likely to be impeded without a proper flow of words in the opposite direc-tion—if only in the form of reports on the diversion and obstruction of relief. When the UN in particular is silent about abuses, this silence can be, and has been, used by governments seeking to downplay such abuses.

The third way of engaging with processes creating famine is by attempt-ing to use relief itself to support the political and economic strategies of victimized groups (and more broadly of those with an interest in preventing famine), and to undermining the economic and political strategies of those seeking to promote famine. Relief is important not just as a nutritional inter-vention, but also for its effects on a wider set of economic and political rela-tionships. Very often, those who are trying to promote famine realize this all too well, while those charged with preventing famine hold on to the old idea that relief should occupy a "humanitarian" sphere that is separate from "politics" and "economics." The widespread belief that relief should not interfere either with "sovereignty" or with "the free market" reflects and reinforces this desire to separate relief (and therefore famine itself) from the rest of society. This case study shows how such ideas can play into the hands of local groups manipulating famine for their own purposes. Withholding of relief is likely to assist the strategies of those benefiting from the price changes and the movements of population that accompany famine. Provision of relief is likely to assist those attempting to stave off starvation through sale of assets or through maintaining productive activities in their home areas. Withholding of relief from rebel-held areas will help government forces at the expense of the rebels. Patterns of relief, in short, inevitably affect political and economic processes. The important questions are how they affect those processes, and to whose benefit.

If donors do not address themselves to the underlying processes creating famine and to the local power structures that shape famine and famine relief, their interventions may actually reinforce these power structures, deepen inequalities, and exacerbate famine. The importance of Western aid in propping up and legitimizing the el Mahdi government has been emphasized, as has the manipulation of "relief" trains for delivering military goods. Meanwhile, donors' attention to "the displaced" and "numbers in need" tended to divert attention from the causes of displacement and the processes by which people became needy. The "target group" was very narrowly defined: the extent of "need" was minimized by a focus on government-held areas, on "numbers in need and reachable," and on the alleged dependency-inducing effects of providing relief to those not absolutely without assets. Defining the purpose of famine relief as helping those who have nothing served in many ways to legitimize and facilitate the transfer of assets to beneficiary groups from those undergoing the process of famine (but not yet completely destitute).[28]

Engaging with the use of force during famine means reforming famine "Early Warning" systems so that they no longer concentrate only on drought or even market prices but also give an indication of political developments likely to create famine. Dinka elders were profoundly aware of the political trends determining their vulnerability to famine and exploitation. There is no reason why the international community should not acquaint itself with such understandings. The experiences of Sudan and Somalia show that fertile regions may even be particularly vulnerable to famine, because of the raiding they attract.

After the Sahel famine of the early 1970s, Sheets and Morris pointed to a pressing need for a political advisory system for international relief operations, a system that would draw attention to political or social problems that might hinder relief (Sheets and Morris 1974, 63–64). This study suggests that such factors are still poorly understood, and poorly integrated into relief programs, let alone into Early Warning systems.

This study has emphasized the interaction between local processes of famine and the actions and discourses of donors. In understanding responses to famine, it is important for Westerners in particular to examine the belief systems not just of "other people" but also of international NGOs and other donors (Moore 1990, 2). It is also important to look at the hidden functions served by particular, limiting types of official discourse. In Sudan, a focus on famine as starvation helped to legitimize late interventions, and to confine relief to a stage when loss of assets had already progressed very far. Ignoring the economic processes of famine fitted well with the idea—favored by British colonial officials and now fashionable once more—that relief should avoid interfering in "local economies" and creating "dependency" (Morren 1983; Fraser 1988, 229–30; Jackson with Eade 1982, 22).[29]

With aid to Africa being threatened by economic stagnation in the West and by the demands of the former Eastern bloc, the danger that human rights abuses and diversion of aid will be used to justify withholding of aid is an increasingly acute one, as Duffield (1992) has argued. Yet providing the right kind of aid through the right channels can be the key to improving the observance of human rights, supporting democratic elements in a society, and stopping the vicious circle in which poverty breeds violence, which breeds further poverty. The recent neglect of assistance to the Kurdish democracy in Iraq suggests that the international community may prefer spectacular emergency interventions (and the punishment of "bad government") to the painstaking work of rewarding "good government" (Keen 1993). Many southern Sudanese have pointed out that (belated) Western condemnation of the Khartoum government has not been matched by a sustained effort at rehabilitating the south, just as many in the self-declared state of Somaliland have pointed out that for all the talk of rehabilitating Somalia, their own relatively peaceful and democratic structures have received scant international support.

This study has emphasized that the way we should respond to famines is by no means self-evident. We need to think carefully about the nature of famines, before we assume that we know how to react to them. When Foucault was highlighting the possible functions of the Soviet Gulag, he stressed that it should not be seen simply as a "disease," an "infection," a "dsyfunctioning." But of course even an infectious disease may have its functions—most notably for the germs that flourish (perhaps temporarily) as the patient dies. When it was recognized that disease had beneficiaries, that disease was often a complicated process of struggle among competing organisms rather than simply a set of symptoms, this realization opened the way to important medical advances in the treatment of disease. The parallel with famines is, of course, far from exact: for one thing, those who benefit from processes of famine should not be dehumanized, any more than famine's victims should, and this study has tried to suggest that preventing famine depends on considering the needs of beneficiary groups as well as the more obvious needs of those suffering from famine. Even so, recognizing that famine, like disease, is a process with beneficiaries as well as victims may constitute an important advance toward a remedy.

# Notes

## Chapter 1
## Overview

1. The cattle-keeping Dinka people traditionally live in an arc around the swamps of the central Nile basin in southern Sudan. The largest linguistic group in the south, they speak Dinka and possess a striking cultural homogeneity (Lienhardt 1961).

2. This is de Waal's (1989a, 3) characterization of the common Western conception.

3. Independent Commission on International Humanitarian Issues 1985, 25; de Waal 1989a, 9–32.

4. McAlpin (1983) is among those who have emphasized the weather.

5. For example, some in England attributed the Irish Great Starvation to Irish sloth or to divine punishment for Catholicism (Hilton 1988, 11).

6. A significant exception is the Malthusian idea that famine acted as a check on population growth. See Woodham-Smith 1962, 375–76.

7. Clay, Steingraber, and Niggli (1988, 1) note a focus on drought as opposed to conflict or government policy in relation to recent famine in Ethiopia.

8. Sen: "The entitlement approach to starvation and famines concentrates on the ability of people to command food through the legal means available in a society." (1981, 45).

9. Strictly, as Sen and Drèze (1989, 20) later made explicit, charitable (as opposed to legally institutionalized) relief falls outside the entitlement framework, since it is not a matter of right.

10. Raikes 1988, 89; Cathie 1982, 4; Brown et al. 1987; Kent 1987, 55.

11. Rangasami 1985, 1748; see also Copans 1983, 91.

12. See also Vaughan 1987, 108.

13. Sen (1981, 40) defines famine as a virulent manifestation of starvation (going without food) causing widespread death.

14. Cf. Jodha 1975.

15. Possible modes of intervention in this economic process are many and are well described by Jodha (1975, 1614–16). They include supply of fodder, mobile marketing facilities for distress sales, "scarcity loans," and facilities for outmigration (including protection against harassment by villagers).

16. O'Neill (1956, 223) notes the impact of merchants' lobbying on the British government's determination not to import food into famine-stricken Ireland in the 1840s. Vaughan (1987, 108–10) records lobbying by grain merchants in Malawi against relief in 1949.

17. On international wars, see, e.g., Burger, Drummond, and Standstead (1948), who record German tactics in the Netherlands during World War II. In 1918, Lenin described what he saw as the interaction of commercial and counterrevolutionary forces in sabotaging the nascent Soviet state through the creation, and manipulation, of famine ([1918] 1945, 39–46, 60–80).

18. See Wiseberg (1974) and Okpoko (1986) on the Nigerian civil war.

19. See, e.g., de Schweinitz (1961, 39) on eighteenth-century England; Vaughan (1987, 111) on Malawi in the 1940s; and Karadawi (1983, 539) on Ethiopian refugees in Khartoum in the late 1970s.

20. Mollat 1986, 8–9.

21. Bauer 1976, 116; see also Bauer 1971.

22. Stremlau has suggested that international relief played a key role in funding Biafra's military and civilian elite during the Nigerian civil war and in sustaining the Biafran war effort (1977, 238–52).

23. Schaffer 1984, 188–89.

24. Griffin 1974, 176; cf. Bates 1983, 120–25.

25. Foucault 1980, 135.

26. See also Barrett and Fudge (1981, 276) on policy as "a substitute for action"; and Smith and Clarke (1985, 173), on policy as "posture" with "symbolic purposes."

27. Cf. Foucault 1978, 13; Foucault 1975. Allison (1971) stressed that existing organizational procedures shape the production of data upon which decisions are based.

28. Cf. Max Weber, reprinted in Gerth and Wright Mills 1948, 233; Schaffer 1984.

29. This has been noted by de Waal (1990c, 743–44) and by Duffield (1991, 11).

30. John Prendergast of Washington's Center of Concern has pointed out how this view has been commonly espoused by the U.S. and Sudanese governments, and how failing to address the causes of war can inhibit progress towards peace (U.S. Congress 1989a, 56–57).

31. See, e.g., Panos Institute (1988), on Sudan.

32. On ahistoricity, see Hewitt (1983, 10) and Rangasami (1985). On ignoring the beneficiaries, see Rangasami (1985), who makes this criticism of Sen.

33. See, e.g., Kent 1987, 118.


## Chapter 2
### Famine and Exploitation in Historical Perspective

1. A number of famines that were not directly human-made nevertheless remained largely unrelieved by the Condominium government, which gave priority to relieving urban areas and excluded the south and west from the purview of famine regulations (de Waal 1989b, 45–46).

2. The Baggara are a group of Arabic-speaking tribes traditionally concentrating on cattle herding. The Messiriya Baggara settled in southern Kordofan after escaping tribute payable to the sultan of Wadai, to the west (Henderson 1939, 61). Among the other Baggara tribes are the Rizeigat of Darfur.

3. In the 1920s, the British official Major Titherington reported, "When times were bad, the rains a failure and the cattle all lost, they [the Raik Dinka] preferred to enter a cattle-house fifty at a time, bar the door, and lie down to die, rather than seeking a living abroad" (Titherington 1927, 164). Titherington also mentions the Raik Dinka's "indifference to food, which they will go without, if need be, for three or four days without concern" (178). The Dinka's willingness to die for their cattle has been well documented (Lienhardt 1961), and Schweinfurth (1873) commented, "Indescribable is the grief when either death or rapine has robbed a Dinka of his cattle"

(164). Indeed, it is a measure of the Dinka's attachment to cattle that it can be accompanied by a kind of resentment. Dinka legend tells that humans hunted and killed the mother of the buffalo and the cow. These animals decided on revenge: the buffalo would stay in the forest and kill any man who came into sight; the cow would become domesticated so that men should labor and kill themselves for her (Deng 1971, 242). Similar attitudes are mentioned by Francis Deng, who describes how many chose not to migrate during the first civil war, preferring to remain in their home areas, "perhaps to die and lie in the graves of the ancestral land they love" (Deng 1972, 152).

4. Cf. de Waal 1989a.

5. Deng 1971, 3. The first civil war had made a major dent in this cattle-wealth, however.

6. Deng 1971, 360; Alier 1990, 217.

7. Even famines precipitated by natural disasters may be subsequently shaped by exploitative processes (Rangasami 1985, 1747–52, and 1797–1801; Copans 1983).

8. The Ngok numbered some twenty thousand to twenty-five thousand in 1951. Some had come to their present position (Map 2) from the east in the nineteenth century, fleeing Nuer raiding (Howell 1951a).

9. The Messiriya of southern Kordofan consist of two tribes: the Humr and the Zurug. These were administratively merged in 1942 under a common chief, or *nazir*, but retained separate identities in important respects.

10. Following Howell (1951a), the tribe is taken to be a group within those Dinka (or Baggara) peoples who have formed a tradition of common action in defense or offense and who trace some common descent, at least among the dominant lineage. Particularly in the case of the Dinka, among whom whole segments of tribes were forced to take refuge with other tribes following Nuer raiding in the nineteenth century, the attempt to trace common descent may be rather strained. Tribal identity is only one of many that may be adopted, and the term should be used with caution.

11. Similarly, Rizeigat/Dinka relations were not inevitably hostile. Garang Anai, leader of a group of Dinka from the Aweil area displaced to a settlement at Adila, in southern Darfur, told me in 1988 that he had last been in southern Darfur in 1974, when he had earned enough money to buy cattle and get married (interview with Garang Anai, acting chief, Adila, December 3, 1988). Some of those who came and raided his village of Majak Bai, Aweil District, had been friends during this earlier period.

12. For example, in 1981 there was conflict over grazing near Lake Keilak, in southern Kordofan (El Sammani 1985, 86).

13. Gordon estimated that some eighty thousand to one hundred thousand slaves were exported from Bahr el Ghazal during 1874–1879 (Gray 1961, 127).

14. This was also the case among the Baggara. The Humr loaned cattle for milk to lineage or clan members during famines (Saeed 1982, 139).

15. Deng 1978, 134–35.

16. Cf. Rangasami 1985, 1749.

17. Western attention to human rights abuses in the south is still seen in some quarters as justifying an interventionist attitude that smacks of imperialism.

18. Nevertheless, Fluehr-Lobban (1990, 612) points out, there are many references to proper conduct regarding slaves as members of households.

19. The Malwal Dinka also sought refuge from flooding among the Twic (Deng

1972, 110). Despite protection offered, the Ngok had also, on occasion, enslaved other Dinka (Deng 1971, 152).

20. Deng 1971, 91, citing Sudan Intelligence Report, no. 147, October 1906. Sanderson and Sanderson (1981, 112) discuss the suppression of the Aliab Dinka in 1920.

21. Quoted in Warburg 1971, 153–55.

22. See, e.g., Wilson (1977, 498–99), on the Baggara's drive to rebuild herds, and de Waal (1989a, 62–66), on the devastation of the Rizeigat in successive famines.

23. From the Dinka's point of view, this was an improvement on the 40-mile boundary. The continued precedence of Rizeigat grazing near the river appeared to reflect Rizeigat loyalty in a 1921 uprising in Darfur.

24. On this break, see Niblock (1987, 249–56).

25. Army ties with the Unionists had never been entirely severed by Nimeiri. The DUP, formed in 1967 from a merger of the old National Unionist Party and the People's Democratic Party, was closely linked with the Khatmiyya sect. Many army officers came from the geographical stronghold of the Khatmiyya, north of Khartoum, where educational opportunities were relatively abundant. Khatmiyya officers had been important supporters of the previous military regime (1958–1964) under General Abboud.

26. The adherents of the Ansar movement were estimated at 5–8 million in 1988, mostly from the rural populations of western and central Sudan (Vincent 1988, 228).

27. See also Saeed (1982) on Ngok resentments of chiefly power.

28. A "generation gap" among the Dinka was to lead to some bemusement among the elders. After the raiding and famine of the 1980s, one Malwal chief recalled in 1990: "There was a quarrel between our educated sons and the Arabs in the town (Madhal). Because of that quarrel, our educated sons began to be killed and rebelled. Then the Arabs came to this area and took cattle, goats etc., and started killing us. Our sons in the SPLA should know that their parents are being killed" (UN/SRRA 1990, field notes, interviews with Malwal chiefs, May 11).

29. Mawson (1989, 85) notes the destruction of Agar Dinka villages and crops by army raids.

30. Deng 1972, 150.

31. Deng 1971, 66.

32. Notably, the Ngok politician Francis Deng was in the cabinet.

33. Deng 1980, 296.

34. Deng 1986, 266.

35. Deng 1980, 343.

36. Alier 1990, 89.

37. See, e.g., Titherington (1927, 176) on the Raik Dinka in the 1920s.

38. From a song sung by a Dinka urban laborer (quoted in Deng 1971, 309).

39. Deng 1972, 162. De Waal notes a strong continuing suspicion of wage labor in contemporary Darfur (1989a, 57).

40. Somewhat similarly, Johnson (1989b) noted that British attempts to keep the Nuer and the Dinka apart were damaging to food security in the south in some respects.

41. One example was an Anyanya attack in September 1964 on Gogiryal village, in northern Bahr el Ghazal, where some Messiriya had settled as merchants (Saeed 1982, 214); similar attacks were made by Anyanya 2 almost twenty years later, in 1983 (Ryle 1989a, 9).

42. For example, attacks on Aweil merchants in 1983 precipitated Rizeigat raids (Ryle 1989a, 9).

43. Watts (1983, 311) suggested that a somewhat similar "function" was served by the 1927 famine in Hausaland.

44. Relief targeted to victims of looting leaked to others, including Messiriya notables.

45. General Lagu, the Anyanya 2 commander in chief, reported some one hundred thousand head of cattle killed or captured in Bahr el Ghazal during April–August 1970 (Eprile 1974, 52). Crumbling veterinary services also reduced cattle numbers (Johnson 1989b, 482).

46. Deng (1972, 162) notes that migrants often failed to earn enough to get married. Shepherd (1988, 45–46) argues that the still-small scale of labor migration from the south helped make the region more vulnerable to famine than other areas.

47. Deng and Oduho (1963, 50) note increasing northern control of rice lands near Aweil. In southern Kordofan, Nuba groups attacked mechanized farming schemes (Mohamed Salih 1990, 127).

48. See, e.g., Almond (n.d., 18), on the British barring of the Beja nomads from the increasingly cotton-oriented Tokar Delta, in eastern Sudan.

49. Ibrahim 1988, 109.

50. Ibrahim (1985) notes outsider dominance of trade in western Sudan. Abdel-Aziz (1979, 71–73) records monopolistic grain trading in Sudan's principal production areas.

51. In Darfur, Hales (1978) notes similar trends among the Meidob, and Abdul-Jalil (1979) notes similar trends among the Fur and Zaghawa.

52. There was only one representative from western Sudan on this council (Ibrahim 1985, 336).

53. Many Ngok perceived that the Abboud takeover had put them on an even footing with the Humr (Deng 1973, 59).

54. See also ODA/Republic of Sudan (1986, annex 2, 10) on courts' discrimination against Baggara in southern Darfur.

55. The partial reconciliation between the Baggara and the SPLA after the famine of the late 1980s showed the continuing danger to the central government of Baggara unrest, particularly when allied with unrest from marginalized southern Sudanese (UN/SRRA field notes, May 10, 12, 1990; Sudan Democratic Gazette, May, 1991, 2).

56. These included Khartoum shantytowns, where displaced Baggara could be found alongside displaced Dinka (Ryle 1989a, 20).

57. Alier has argued that these perceptions were inaccurate (1990, 193–214).

58. Most of the seats in Equatoria were won by the People's Progressive Party and the Sudan African People's Congress. In Upper Nile, the SSPA and Sudan African Congress (which was sympathetic to the SPLM) each won two seats (Chiriyankandath 1987, 98–99).

59. This dynamic is discussed further in Chapter 3.

60. Woodward 1990, 212.

61. A similar removal of the means of political redress, this time from the Nuba, is noted in Chapter 6.

62. Certainly, the NIF won most of its seats in tight geographical clusters, suggesting an effective deployment of resources in particular areas (Chiriyankandath 1987, 100).

## Chapter 3
### Victims and Beneficiaries

1. Calculated from mortality figures (2,553 deaths) and camp population figures (rising from 2,000 to 6,000) in MSF-France (1988f).

2. Calculated from King (1986, 28–30).

3. The *Sudan Times* on November 4, 1988, quoted local officials as saying that at least six thousand people had died in Abyei since June.

4. Mortality figure from Aweil relief committee (in UNDP 1988, annex 2, 2); population estimates given below.

5. See an important discussion of this issue in de Waal (1989a); (see also Sen 1981, 195–216)

6. For example, the deaths in Aweil were attributed by the local relief committee to a shortage of food and medicines and to accompanying diseases, particularly diarrhea, dysentery, and giardia (UNDP, 1988b, annex 2). A measles epidemic also killed large numbers, abetted by the absence of vaccination programs (ibid., 5).

7. An estimated 1,445,500 had settled in northern Sudan, and some 290,000 in Ethiopia (USAID 1988b, 3).

8. Some of the cattle losses were from disease, but despite the emphasis put on disease as the root cause of the crisis by USAID (U.S. Congress 1990a, 27), disease was in large part a reflection of unusual movements of cattle due to raiding.

9. Interagency Situation Report 1988, 6.

10. de Waal 1990a, 2; Ryle 1989a, 6; and John Ryle, personal communication, 1989. See also Chapter 2.

11. UN/SRRA 1990, 47, 49, 51.

12. Letter from representatives of the Twic community to H. E. The Chairman, Transitional Military Council, Khartoum, January 25, 1986, "Subject: Destruction of Northern Gogrial (Twic Area) by the Messiriya (Baggara) tribesmen of southern Kordofan province."

13. These report more than two hundred thousand cattle stolen during November 1985–February 1986 (Duffield 1990a, 26–27).

14. Letter from representatives of the Twic community to H. E. The Chairman, January 25, 1986. This is probably an exaggeration.

15. See, e.g., de Waal, n.d., 104; Symonds 1987. Republic of Sudan/UNDP/ODA (1984, 56) refers to drought in 1982 and 1983.

16. Fighting between Anyanya 2 and the SPLA caused widespread destruction in Upper Nile, particularly in late 1986 and early 1987.

17. Rinderpest was reported around Aweil in 1988. Milk from Aweil cattle appeared contaminated and unfit for human consumption (UNDP 1988b, 6).

18. Letter from Norman Anderson, Ambassador of USA, Bryan Wannop, WFP Rep., UNDP, Adri Van Loopik, Chargé d'Affaires a.i. Royal Netherlands Embassy, R. G. Smit, Acting Delegate, EC, to Kamil Shawki, Commissioner, RRC, undated.

19. Central government rainfall records for the south are only for Malakal, showing no drought in 1986. The RRC Early Warning System Bulletin of November 15, 1988 records heavy rainfall in western Bahr el Ghazal in 1986.

20. Government production statistics, while unreliable, especially in wartime, give some indication of broad trends.

NOTES TO CHAPTER 3 **245**

21. Government figures reported that the area of grain cultivated fell from 845,000 feddans in 1981–1985 to 485,000 in 1986, while yields (despite the reported decline in crop tending) rose to 287 kilograms per feddan in 1986, from an average of 166 in 1981–1985 (Ministry of Agriculture and Natural Resources 1987a, 4–5).

22. A Swedish missionary who worked in camps in Ethiopia put the proportion at one-third (*Sudan Times*, May 11, 1988). Another estimate was 20 percent (*New York Times*, May 1, 1988).

23. Sudanaid said there was an influx of twenty thousand people in May–June (TCC meeting minutes, September 5, 1988, 3). The governor of Bahr el Ghazal put the figure higher (*Sudan Times*, November 10, 1988).

24. Wau's camp population rose from fifteen thousand to one hundred thousand between early April and early May of 1989. As in Darfur in 1984–1985 (de Waal 1989a), migration to camps had a strong seasonal element. Given improved security, the camp at Wau (like those at Meiram and Abyei) shrank dramatically during May 1989, as people left to farm. At Juba, however, minefields continued to hem people in (USAID 1989, 9–11).

25. Lack of food was cited as the main reason for leaving Bahr el Ghazal by 91 percent of respondents in an MSF-France survey of displaced people in Babanousa in mid-May 1988 (Interagency Situation Report 1988, 4).

26. A survey of 223 children aged one–five in early March reported that 74 percent were severely malnourished (weight/height) (UNICEF 1988).

27. An NGO survey of displaced people in Safaha in early March of 1988 found 67 percent severely malnourished (TCC meeting minutes, March 7, 1988, 3–4).

28. See also letter from representatives of the Twic community to H. E. The Chairman, January 25, 1980.

29. See also ibid.

30. See Interagency Situation Report (1988, 2, 4) on migrants in southern Kordofan; see Sudanaid (1988, 4) on Safaha, southern Darfur.

31. These included attacks by wolves and hyenas as well as by militiamen (Sudanaid 1988, 4).

32. I am grateful to Douglas Johnson for pointing up this dynamic.

33. From estimates just before 1987 harvest (Ministry of Agriculture and Natural Resources 1987a, 4–5; Ministry of Agriculture and Natural Resources 1987b, 5–6).

34. In 1987 rainfall was slightly below normal in Malakal and Kadugli, in southern Kordofan (EWSB, November 15, 1988).

35. One aid official (name withheld) involved in relieving famine migrants in Darfur told me that some 70 percent said they had left Bahr el Ghazal because of theft of cattle; 30 percent gave another reason (most frequently, drought).

36. This was notably the case in Aweil District (UNDP 1988b, 8 and annex 2, 1).

37. For example, the army depopulated stretches of countryside around Wau (Duffield 1990a, 27).

38. See, e.g., Johnson 1988a, 10; Hutchinson 1988, viii. In late 1988, a Ministry of Energy and Mining official told me the government was ready to move supplies to major oil fields to begin extraction. I said there would be resistance. He replied, "Yes, but there is the resettlement to Ethiopia."

39. Africa Watch 1990, 78; de Waal 1990a, 8. Anyanya 2 received equipment and formal training from the government. See also Alier 1990, 252–54. The use of

scorched-earth tactics, for example, in Shilluk areas in the vicinity of Malakal in 1986–1987 (Africa Watch 1990, 78), was apparently intended not only to deter support of the SPLA but also to make it more difficult for the SPLA to operate in areas surrounding government towns (Woodward 1990, 211; de Waal 1990a, 9).

40. Government figures indicate that the army suffered less than two thousand fatalities in 1983–1988—a remarkably low figure, even allowing for some underestimation (Africa Watch 1990, 65–66).

41. When the Ottoman government armed Kurdish militias in the late nineteenth century and gave them a "license to raid," this appears to have served a similar dual function in appeasing the Kurds, while at the same time offering a way of suppressing dissent (in this case, among the Armenians) (van Bruinessen 1992, 185–86).

42. Indeed, the Baggara militias were to be accused of being "party militias" by the DUP in late 1988.

43. Letter from representatives of the Twic community to H. E. The Chairman, January 25, 1986.

44. On el Mahdi's struggle to become Imam of the movement, see *New York Times*, March 14, 1989.

45. As Warburg (1978, 60–64) noted in relation to the period between the two world wars, traditional religious affiliations retained a hold over many Sudanese. The British had been mistaken in believing that the Mahdi family's religious role could be separated from its political aims.

46. Similar sentiments are noted by Warburg (1990, 636) in Sadiq el Mahdi's 1985 publication, "Islam and the South Sudan Problem."

47. DUP Working Paper on the South, Ramadan, 1986, signed Ad Hoc Committee for the Working Paper on the Southern Problem, General Secretariat.

48. Compare McHugh (1956, 10) on proselytizing and relief during the Great Starvation in Ireland.

49. Widespread theft of Dinka cattle by Messiriya militias and the army in and around Abyei is noted in Interagency Situation Report (1988, 6). Officers' gains from "famine" prices are dealt with below.

50. Ryle (1989a, 24). Uprooted Dinka spoke of militia attacks on Safaha.

51. The army was apparently fearful that people would go back to the south with information of use to the rebels (interview with Garang Anai, settlement leader, Adila, southern Darfur, December 1988).

52. Nuer migrant laborers were expelled in large numbers from Khartoum in 1981 and 1982, and many were recruited into the militias (de Waal 1990b, 9; de Waal, personal communication, 1989).

53. Letter from representatives of the Twic community to H. E. The Chairman, January 25, 1986.

54. Johnson 1988a, 10.

55. Similar perceptions among the Dinka are noted in UN/SRRA (1990, 51).

56. Letter from representatives of the Twic community to H. E. The Chairman, January 25, 1986.

57. These groups were also to be plundered by the army and militias when they began to return to Bahr el Ghazal from 1989 (UN/SRRA 1990, 58).

58. Adults were often simply killed.

59. These are the results of an informal survey of displaced people in Abu Ajura settlement (MSF-Belgium 1988). Among those arriving in El Lait rural council, Darfur, during 1988, more than half said that they or members of their immediate family had been captured in Kordofan (SCF-UK/Oxfam-UK 1988b, 4).

60. Full testimonies are in Keen (1991b).

61. Interview with Ushari Mahmud, Khartoum, December 20, 1988.

62. See also *Wall Street Journal*, September 12, 1989. UN/SRRA field notes for May 12, 1990, mention a ransom of Sud. £3,000.

63. Information from Ushari Mahmud and directly from Dinka held as slaves.

64. The Ngok Dinka had remained largely aloof prior to the raids on them during the 1985–1986 dry season (Oxfam-UK 1986e, 1).

65. Testimonies collected by the writer (Keen 1991b). John Ryle, who visited southern Kordofan and southern Darfur in late 1988, reported that accounts of rape of women and castration of men were common (Ryle 1989b, 63). See also Mahmud and Baldo (1987); letter from representatives of the Twic community to H. E. The Chairman, January 25, 1986.

66. Testimonies of enslaved Dinka (see Keen 1991b, app. 1).

67. Holt 1958, 133.

68. "I Am Not Heathen," poem by Aboud Suliman, *Heritage*, October 31, 1988.

69. Of course, even where "market forces" are apparently working unaffected by the exertion of force, the distribution of commodities arising from "market forces" (for example, the convention that I can sell what you produce from "my" field) will ultimately be underpinned by the threat of force embodied in law.

70. Rangasami (1985, 1749), citing conceptualization of famine among the Akamba, Kenya.

71. The Meiram relief committee reported the following sorghum prices (Sud. £/sack) in Meiram: November 1987, 80; December, 80: January 1988, 90; February, 90; March, 110; April, 110; May, 115; June, 200; July, 250; August, 600. Gradual increases prior to June suggest that monitoring of sorghum prices alone would have given little "early warning" of famine. Sharp price rises in June and July corresponded with the major influx of famine migrants. Normal seasonal rises were exaggerated.

72. Ramze Mony-Ping Chier, acting governor of Bahr el Ghazal province, quoted in *Toronto Star*, March 25, 1989.

73. EC 1987a.

74. Letter from Darious Beshir, acting governor of Bahr el Ghazal, to Sadiq el Mahdi, Prime Minister, January 15, 1988.

75. September 1988: Sud. £1,200 per sack (Technical Donor Committee on Relief 1988, 1).

76. The SPLA further contributed to suffering in Juba by placing a ring of antipersonnel mines around the city in October 1988 (Africa Watch 1990, 156), and by launching a series of shell attacks.

77. At the same time, certain restrictions were imposed at the village and regional levels on merchants seeking to buy grain in Darfur or Kordofan in late 1986 to sell further south (de Waal 1990a, 16).

78. There were also profitable opportunities in coffee and household items.

79. Merchants and army staff collaborated to boost prices in Juba, although army involvement threatened certain established merchant interests. The army delayed commercial convoys to Upper Nile and Juba (de Waal 1990a, 20).

80. The Sudan military regularly flew food to Wau, Juba, and Malakal to feed its troops, while civilians went hungry (*Sudan Times,* December 16, 1988).

81. Official sorghum price, Abyei, May 1988: Sud. £45–75/sack. Actual price: Sud. £250–300/sack (Interagency Situation Report 1988, 7).

82. Low official salaries helped merchants influence officials. See, e.g., Ryle 1989b, 76.

83. This involvement is discussed in the section on cattle markets and in Chapter 4.

84. Similar concerns appear to have contributed to the ejection of many famine migrants from Aweil in the autumn of 1988, after high mortality among residents.

85. Calculated using grain/cattle price ratio of Sud. £275/sack, noted above.

86. Some merchants with established trading links with Bahr el Ghazal were undercut by raiding. Moreover, traders and soldiers buying cattle at Safaha and Abyei were sometimes undercut by murahaleen raids on Dinka bringing cattle north to market. This led to the "reclaiming" of the cattle by army personnel. Competition between potential beneficiaries of famine became more intense as the numbers of cattle leaving Bahr el Ghazal diminished in 1988 (de Waal 1990a, 17).

87. Calculated from data in Ministry of Agriculture (1987b, 27, 33).

88. May 1988 prices, El Obeid: sorghum, Sud. £120.7/sack; cattle, average, Sud. £1,717/head (EWSB, June 15, 1988, 4).

89. Abyei price calculated as mean of 0.8 and 2.4 (1.6) times grain price 275, that is, 440.

90. Ed Daien merchants were also heavily involved in the grain trade (Mahmud and Baldo 1987, 2), benefiting from "famine" prices and from aid agency purchases.

91. One agency predicted the sharecroppers' portion of the next year's harvest would be mortgaged in advance as these migrants fell deep into debt (UNICEF 1987b).

92. One aid official said northern women and farmers were paying starving women about this sum for a teenage boy, to buy a ride to safety for the rest of their families (*Sudan Times,* May 11, 1988).

93. Interviews with farmers in Meiram market, November 24, 1988. Farmers from Migeinis and Agarib projects contacted the Ministry of Social Affairs, expressing their desire to use migratory labor for harvesting amid reports of a labor shortage (*Sudan Times,* November 4, 1988, January 11, 1989; USAID 1988c, 3).

94. Noted in Muglad by Concern (1988f).

95. See, in particular, Sen's discussion of the 1974 Bangladesh famine (1981, 131–53).

96. Dinka in Meiram reported a train fare of Sud. £20 for Meiram–Muglad in the summer of 1988. This compares with a standard fare of Sud. £6 for Babanousa–Ed Daien (significantly further). Africa Watch (1989, 129) notes unusually high rail and truck fares during the famine. By contrast, Dinka traveled free by train from Khartoum to Babanousa in 1990 when the government was seeking to remove displaced people from Khartoum (UN/SRRA field notes, May 12, 1990).

97. Amnesty (1989, sec. 2.2); interviews with uprooted Dinka, November–December 1988. One Twic family from Gogrial sold its two remaining cattle in Abyei to buy places on a merchant's Bedford truck to Muglad in May 1988 (Interagency Situation Report 1988, 6).

98. Similar restrictions were reported in Malakal (TCC meeting minutes, February 15, 1988, 4).

99. In 1949, by contrast, the government had issued cheap rail tickets to drought-stricken Beja during famine in Kassala, allowing travel to work on the Gash scheme (de Waal 1989b, 45).

100. The massacre of thousands of Dinka at Ed Daien in 1987 had been partly in retaliation for the SPLA's killing of some Rizeigat civilians in Safaha. The SPLA was also reported to have held some Rizeigat civilians hostage (Africa Watch 1990, 159).

101. During the 1983–1985 drought-led famine, official restriction of movement into wetter zones (including some areas demarcated for future mechanized farming) had exacerbated famine (Mohamed Salih 1990, 124).

## Chapter 4
## The Inadequacy of Relief

1. This study focuses on emergency food aid, the main type of relief attempted. Other types of relief (for example, livestock support) were only rarely attempted, although they could have been extremely valuable.

2. On the reduced severity of famine and mortality in 1989, see, e.g., USAID (1989, 3).

3. There had, however, been significant provision of relief from within Bahr el Ghazal in 1982–1983 (Republic of Sudan/UNDP/ODA 1984, 57).

4. Before government pressure intensified, very limited relief distributions were administered by CART to rural parts of Bahr el Ghazal in 1986 (see Chapter 5).

5. Details are in Keen (1991b).

6. This team consisted of the NGO consortium CART (Combined Agencies Relief Team), Sudan Council of Churches, Sudanaid, and UNOEOS.

7. Reasons cited were the need for large quantities and the unsuitability of the runway in Aweil for large planes such as Buffaloes (EC 1987b, 1).

8. Details are in Keen (1991b). Even this figure ignores needs in surrounding rural areas.

9. This involved the European Community (EC), U.S. Agency for International Development (USAID), and World Food Programme (WFP).

10. The last Ministry of Health drug supply had been in February 1987.

11. In addition, in the absence of significant veterinary services or livestock-oriented relief, cattle disease became rife, making milk unfit for human consumption.

12. "Report on Emergency Relief Situation in Bahr el Ghazal Region, Presented by the Committee Assigned to Raise Local Donations for the Displaced and Destitutes in Wau," September 18, 1988, 2.

13. There was also a donor airlift from Meiram and Muglad to Aweil, beginning on a small scale in December 1988, and delivering 43 per day by April 1989 (Wannop 1989, 5).

14. Minutes of a meeting held at Concern offices, May 27, 1988: briefing by A. Shepherd, UNICEF, on mission to southern Kordofan.

15. Based on a figure of twenty thousand displaced people in Abyei.

16. Minutes of a meeting held at Concern offices, May 27, 1988: briefing on mission to southern Kordofan by A. Shepherd, UNICEF.

17. *Sudan Times*, October 20, 1988, citing population estimates from Sudanese Red Crescent.

18. *Guiding Star*, November 3, 1988, quoting Mohammed Beshir, of Sudanese Red Crescent.

19. Distribution figures from MSF-France (1988c, 1988h, 1988k); full figures in Keen (1991b, 401–3).

20. As late as the end of October, people in the camp at Meiram were receiving only some 1.7 liters of clean water each (MSF-France 1988j).

21. The rains peaked at the end of July (and strongly again in late September), bringing problems of cold and heightening problems of sanitation.

22. The seven settlement sites in South Darfur had an average mortality rate of 35.3 per 1,000 per month for the last eight days of April 1988, falling to 14 in May and to 6.2 in June. Malnutrition (percentage of children below 80 percent of normal weight for height) fell from an average of 41 percent in May to 21 percent in July (MSF-Belgium 1988).

23. Substantial supplies became available only when Oxfam carried out local purchases (interview with Pierre Poivre, MSF-Belgium, Khartoum, November 10, 1988).

24. Letter from Prime Minister Sadiq el Mahdi to UN Secretary General, June 13, 1988, in UNOEA (1988, 162–63); RRC (1987, 1).

25. Clark (1987, 87). Bickersteth (1990, 224) notes that the export of five hundred thousand metric tons of sorghum from Sudan into Europe in 1987–1988 depressed sales of EC-produced animal feeds.

26. The abandonment of the Condominium policy of national and provincial "strategic sorghum reserves" had permitted a large rise in exports beginning in the late 1970s (Ahmed 1987, 332; Shepherd 1988, 60–63).

27. Expressed in wheat flour equivalents (Bickersteth 1988, 36).

28. A detailed comparison can be found in Keen (1991b, 405). These differences cannot be explained by the rather small amounts of relief received by individual households in the north (discussed later in this chapter and in Chapter 5).

29. UN Fund for Population Activities 1986; Otor 1984.

30. UNOEOS estimates in December 1986 suggested that Bahr el Ghazal had 59 percent of those "at risk" in southern Sudan (USAID 1987a, 7–8). CART's estimates of needs gave Bahr el Ghazal 54 percent of the needs in the south (EC 1987f). A fuller comparison is in Keen (1991b, 406).

31. U.S. Congress 1988b, 53.

32. The locomotives for the May 1989 relief train constituted a significant percentage of the Sudan Railways Corporation fleet (Wannop 1989, 8).

33. In September 1986, the local NGO group, Sudanaid/Sudan Council of Churches (1986, 4), assessed the grain needs of Bahr el Ghazal alone for six months at 146,700 metric tons.

34. By contrast, northern Sudan was declared a disaster area after the floods of August 1988 (*Sudan Times*, September 8, 1990).

35. The government chose Wau, Malakal, and Juba for relief; the latter was already accessible. If it had chosen Aweil and Bentiu, hundreds of thousands of extremely needy people in surrounding areas might have secured relief (*Sudan Times*, June 6, 1988).

36. Letter from UNDP Resident Representative Joachim von Braunmuhl to Prime Minister Sadiq el Mahdi, June 24, 1987, referring to donor meeting with General Fadlalla Burma Nasser, Minister of State for Defense, May 27, 1987: "During the meeting we were informed by the Minister of State that it had been agreed with the Sudan Railways Corporation that trains going to Aweil were intended primarily for the transport of relief goods. More specifically we understood that each month three trains with 108 wagons each would be directed from Babanousa to Aweil. . . . However, 3 weeks later at a meeting of the Steering Committee of the Sudan Railways Corporation on 17 June 1987 we were informed that out of the 108 wagons only seven would actually carry supplies for the relief operation. . . . "

37. Letter from Joachim von Braunmuhl, Resident Representative a. i., UNDP, to Prime Minister Sadiq el Mahdi, June 24, 1987, citing the meeting with General Fadlalla Burma Nasser, Minister of State for Defense, May 27, 1987.

38. Even assuming that there was a misunderstanding on the donors' part and that the three trains were supposed to carry a total of 108 wagons, the proportion is still only 3.6 percent.

39. Letter from von Braunmuhl to el Mahdi, May 27, 1987.

40. A full breakdown of the contents of the freight cars found is given in Keen (1991b, 400).

41. Of an anticipated 108 wagons leaving for Aweil at the beginning of March, only 20 were expected to carry relief (TCC meeting minutes, February 27, 1988).

42. Full breakdown in Keen (1991b, 395).

43. A train arriving in Aweil in August 1986 with no relief food was thought to be carrying food for the army and traders (Oxfam 1986m).

44. A similar imbalance affected the "relief" barges sent down the Nile to Malakal (RRC/EC 1988a); details in Keen (1991b, 408).

45. Relief channeled to the garrison town in Terekeka, Equatoria, suggests that diversionary tactics could allow the passage of relief when the army made this a priority (Africa Watch 1990, 136).

46. One RTU worker told me in December 1988 that RTU's fleet of around 150 trucks was being used by the army to fight the war in the south: "The army say they're for an emergency—the emergency of the war in the south."

47. RTU 1987.

48. Letter from Norman Anderson, Ambassador of the USA, Joachim von Braunmuhl, Resident Representative a.i., UNDP, Adi Van Loopik, Acting Chargé d'Affaires, Royal Netherlands Embassy, G. D. Gwyer, Acting Delegate, Commission of the European Communities, to Kamil Shawki, RRC, July 19, 1987, 1; TCC meeting minutes, February 15, 1988.

49. This perception has been noted by Roger Winter, among others. Director of the U.S. Committee for Refugees, Winter worked in the SPLA zone in 1988.

50. In early 1986, the local SPLA command in Wau told a Bandaid representative to keep food flowing into Wau, saying the SPLA would not hinder the movement of food aid (Oxfam 1986c, 1). Local understandings between governmental bodies and the SPLA in Bahr el Ghazal are noted below. There were unconfirmed reports that

such a local understanding with the SPLA had helped get relief through to Terekeka (Africa Watch 1990, 136).

51. Captain el Geneid, the commander in Muglad, in the last days before the departure of the first Operation Lifeline train on May 20, began obstructing the train by closing it off to all persons, including the UN monitors (Wannop 1989, 8). UNDP's Bryan Wannop feared that arms were being put aboard, feeling that this would wreck the train (interview with Bryan Wannop, UNDP, New York, September 6, 1990).

52. Although CART did not distribute to rebel areas, which at that time occupied only a small proportion of Equatoria, its neutrality did offer a possible springboard for relief to both sides in the conflict.

53. Oxfam 1987c.

54. A similar dynamic had encouraged the Biafran administration to mix relief and military flights during Nigeria's civil war (Stremlau 1977, 246; Edgell 1975, 51).

55. In May 1989, UN officials were told in the SPLA-held town of Makeir that people had been planning to move north into southern Kordofan and had dropped this plan only when told a relief train was imminent (Wannop 1989, 22).

56. These high prices were sometimes boosted by the purchase of grain for relief purposes from local merchants, when significant relief had failed to arrive.

57. Food relief brought sorghum prices down from Sud. £240/sack to 140/sack in the late spring of 1986 (Oxfam 1986h, 2). See also Minear (1991, 42, 69) on relief's breaking garrison town monopolies and lowering grain prices in 1989.

58. *Toronto Star*, March 25, 1989, citing information from Peter Winkler, the Red Cross delegate in Wau.

59. Juba merchants sold stocks on the arrival of food aid consigned to CART (interview with Bryan Wannop, UNDP, New York, September 6, 1990). Similar examples from northern Sudan are noted below. Release of trader stocks upon the arrival of relief had been noted as long ago as 1866 in India (Government of India 1867, vol. 2, 58).

60. Wannop 1989, 9.

61. Ibid.

62. The relative abundance of NGOs in Equatoria was also important in creating its relatively privileged position (see Chapter 5), as was the importance for the Sudan government of cultivating Equatorian support.

63. In the summer of 1988, the chairman of the Council of the South, Angelo Beda, came from Equatoria, as did the southern member of the Council of State, Dr. Pacifico Lolik, and the government minister, Richard Makebe.

64. Letter from Peter Ring Ajing, Director, Office of Bahr el Ghazal Administrative Area, Khartoum, to Samir Basta, UNICEF Representative, Khartoum, February 25, 1986.

65. "While foreign relief officials said that 250,000 have died this year from starvation or inadequate medical care, Sadiq El Mahdi claimed the estimate was 20 times the actual figure" (*Sudan Times*, October 28, 1988).

66. Symonds 1987, 7, citing information from the head of the Raga Chamber of Commerce.

67. The rate was 15–30 kilograms of sorghum/day (Symonds 1987, 10).

68. *Toronto Star*, March 25, 1989, citing information from the military commander of Bahr el Ghazal, Major-General A. A. Mohammed Fatih.

69. Ibrahim (1988, 293–94) notes such fears in southern Kordofan during the 1983–1985 famine.

70. See, e.g., *Le Monde*, November 3, 1988.

71. Minutes of aid coordination meeting held at Concern offices, Khartoum, May 27, 1988.

72. Interview with Marc Lejars, MSF-France, Khartoum, October 25, 1988. At the end of August, Babanousa officials told aid workers there was a weekly supply train to Meiram, although it does not seem to have run every week, at least in August (minutes of aid coordination meeting at Kordofan Regional Offices, El Obeid, August 25, 1988, 2).

73. RRC/EC 1988e; letter from Peter Jobber, Director of Operations, WFP, to Kamil Shawki, Commissioner, RRC, April 24, 1988.

74. Letter from Peter Jobber, Director of Operations, WFP, to Dr El Hag El Tayeb, Acting Commissioner, RRC, May 3, 1988.

75. Keen (1991b, 409) has a fuller discussion.

76. Minutes of aid coordination meeting with RRC, ABS, and donors, Khartoum, May 4, 1988, 1.

77. Another cause of delay had been a strike at ABS (ibid.).

78. On ABS support for large farmers, encouraging grain export, and speculation at the expense of consumers, see Ibrahim (1988, 115–16); El Hassan (1985, 311–12); and Duffield (1990a, 21).

79. Memo. entitled "Discussion Paper on Western Relief Operation for March 14," presented at Heads of Mission meeting, 1988.

80. Letter from Heads of Mission to Dr Beshir Omer Fadlallah, Minister of Finance and Economy, undated.

81. TCC meeting minutes, April 12, 1988, 2–3.

82. Some details on the diversion of relief en route are given in Keen (1991b, 412).

83. In Raga, prior to Symonds's September 1987 report on the relief grain theft, no government employer had been paid for six months (Symonds 1987, 4).

84. Also significant were the initiative of the local army commander (Africa Watch 1990, 131) and the influence exerted by NGOs, which had established development programs in the area and reasonable relations with local authorities, something that was largely missing in southern Kordofan (interview with Wim Van Damme, MSF-Belgium, Nyala, December 7, 1988).

85. These migrants were also subject to discrimination in relief distributions (Keen 1991b, 383–84).

86. Thompson noted this criticism in relation to Darfur; there was also criticism of NGOs from the governor of Darfur (Oxfam 1988g).

87. See, e.g., Ministry of Social Welfare, Zakat and the Displaced (1988, 2).

88. Islamic agendas may have played a role. In July 1988, the new minister of social welfare, Ahmed Abdel Rahman Mohammed—one of the leaders of the National Islamic Front—called for the gradual replacement of all Western relief agencies by Arab and Islamic agencies (*Sudan Times*, July 8, 1988).

89. Letter from A. Scott-Villiers, Bandaid, to T. Alcedo, CARE, July 3, 1986, 2.

90. Minutes of a meeting held at Concern offices, Khartoum, May 27, 1988.

91. SCF-UK/Oxfam (1988a).

92. These can be compared with blocks on those fleeing famine in the Ukraine in 1932–1934 (Oleskiw 1983, 34).

93. Report from deputy commissioner of South Darfur at coordination meeting on the displaced, August 8, 1988.

94. See de Waal (1989a, 139) on the perception in Darfur that water is perhaps the major problem people face.

95. U.S. Congress 1988b, 144.

96. One southern Sudanese expressed his amazement at such accusations in a poem about the displaced: "They are nude, helpless / Yet they call them Garang's advance guard / Where can guns be concealed! / On nude and bare skins!" (from "Sodom and Gomorrah," by M. Angoldit, *Guiding Star*, October 20, 1988).

97. It is arguable also that many of the most significant economic benefits of famine had, to a large extent, been reaped by this time, with Dinka assets (notably livestock) having been severely depleted and SPLA control over Bahr el Ghazal now significantly increased. It is possible that this influenced the new stance of both the army and the DUP (whose strong trading links reflected its geographical base in northern riverain areas). Profiteering, however, certainly did not come to a stop in 1989.

98. Wannop 1989, 10, citing information from the DUP foreign minister, the chairman of the Peace Committee in charge of negotiations with the SPLA.

99. Wannop 1989, 2, 8.

100. Indeed, during the 1988 floods, opposition leaders accused the government of manipulating relief by channeling relief, including tents, to planned areas only in order to destroy the Khartoum shantytowns (statement by leader of the opposition, Eliaba Surur, in *Sudan Times*, August 26, 1988).

101. Letter from Prof. Hassan A. Rahman Musnad, for Acting Commissioner of RRC, to Commissioner of South Kordofan, Kadugli, October 5, 1988, 1.

## Chapter 5
## The Inadequacy of Relief

1. Other donors involved in relief discussions were the Netherlands, the United Kingdom (these two were particularly influential), the Federal Republic of Germany, Switzerland, and Japan. UNICEF often had separate representation from other UN organizations.

2. This pattern was also seen during the Nigerian civil war (Wiseberg 1974, 70–73).

3. Kenneth Brown, the U.S. deputy assistant secretary for African Affairs, testified: "The Soviets, of course, are the primary supporters of Ethiopia. The Ethiopians are the primary supporters of the SPLA" (U.S. Congress 1989a, 51). Peter Bechtold, a Sudan specialist at the United States's Foreign Service Institute wrote in 1990: "There remains a deeply held conviction by many in and out of government that Garang's alleged communist leanings explain his intransigence [in peace negotiations]" (1990, 594).

4. U.S. Ambassador Anderson argued that aid cuts had reduced leverage (Minear 1991, 79–80), but this was still clearly substantial.

5. *New York Times*, March 14, 1989.

6. Bonner (1989, 88), citing interview with Mark Duffield, country representative of Oxfam in the Sudan. Problems with accountability within rebel areas were another drawback.

7. In fairness, some areas were more insecure than the area where NPA was working.

8. Indeed, when negotiations over Operation Lifeline began in early 1989, UN officials did not feel able even to mention SPLA-controlled areas (interview with Bryan Wannop, UNDP, New York, August 24, 1990).

9. One such was Roger Winter, the director of the U.S. Committee for Refugees.

10. Commenting on the closing of UNICEF's Nairobi office after pressure from Prime Minister el Mahdi, the regional director of UNICEF, Mary Rancelis, explained that the government might stop the organization's various projects in the north if the UN continued sending relief to the south. Because Sudan was a member of the UN and on the board of UNICEF, she added, "We have no choice" but to stop sending relief supplies (*New York Times*, October 28, 1988).

11. The U.S. ambassador, Norman Anderson, said that if the United States had soft-pedaled on humanitarian concerns in the south, it was to protect humanitarian activities in the north (Minear 1991, 78).

12. Letter from CART chairman Nick Roberts, endorsed by Archbishop Paulino Lokudu, Catholic Church, Juba, and Bishop Benjamin Yugusuk, Episcopal Church, Juba, to George Gwyer, EC Delegate, January 12, 1987. The six months' funding was needed to get trucks, and staff, as well as to give donors some assurance their food would be distributed, CART argued.

13. As the Sudan Council of Churches (1986) had earlier reported, the situation in the south did "not even allow making a precise, detailed needs assessment, and any emergency preparedness and/or actions [had] to be planned on the basis of guestimates."

14. Letter from CART Steering Committee to donors, May 14, 1987.

15. While it was true that many southern Sudanese secured much of their consumption needs from livestock, so, too, did many in western and eastern Sudan. In any case, livestock in the south had been severely depleted.

16. One EC report stated: "In no way did the EC let CART down at a time when CART was having difficulties with the Regional authorities. To the contrary, the EC put pressure on the Equatoria Government through its relations with the then Governor Cirillo and the then Minister of Finance, Mr Samson Kwaje, to enable CART to continue its operation" (EC 1989a, 2).

17. Africa Watch 1990, 111.

18. The U.S. ambassador, Norman Anderson, stressed his pressure on the prime minister to let relief go to both sides (Minear 1991, 79).

19. U.S. Congress 1988b, 6.

20. Ibid., 12.

21. The Safaha trucking operation, organized by NGOs and partially funded by donors, was an exception to the general inadequacy of relief.

22. RRC/EC 1988l.

23. Personal communication.

24. USAID 1988a, 24.

25. Sudan Council of Churches 1986.

26. U.S. Congress 1989b, 109.

27. Donors predicted that there would be little or nothing to sustain those in Meiram in 1987 after harvest work ran out (UNICEF 1987b).

28. Oxfam-UK 1987b, 7.

29. Copans 1983, 88.

30. EWSB, September 5, 1988, 5. Actual commitments did not fully match these, as funding for some "tranches" was not forthcoming. RRC worked closely with donors in formulating these figures.

31. Interdonor Memo. 1988, 6.

32. A USAID spokesman said: "I did not give details of famine in Sudan in my testimony because we do not have hard evidence. . . . We do not have people in that area (the south)" (U.S. Congress 1988b, 11–12).

33. This was sometimes echoed by the RRC (RRC 1987, 1).

34. This was in line with a broader faith in the market as the route to development (see, e.g., D'Silva, 1985).

35. See, e.g., Minear (1991, 115) on the importance attached by donors to this argument.

36. An extended extract from this letter is in Keen (1991b, 412).

37. For example, parts of southern Darfur were surveyed by MSF-Belgium.

38. Another source is British Embassy, Khartoum (1988), citing views of representatives of Concern, SCF, Oxfam, WFP, and UNICEF on southern Kordofan relief.

39. In Abyei, for a short period, distribution was in association with the Catholic Comboni Fathers.

40. Cf. Sen and Drèze (1989, 67) and Jodha (1975, 1614–16) on the probability that relief will assist production/development.

41. EC 1989a, 4.

42. The EC delegate in Khartoum subsequently noted: "One consequence of these directives [in 1986 from the Commission in Brussels] was that the emergency aid work burden, which had earlier been shared amongst some other advisers of the Delegation staff, became concentrated on the desk of the Economic Adviser . . . " (EC 1989a, 4).

43. One donor official noted that poor relief performance, to Aweil and Wau in particular, had led to "a much more cautious approach" by donors, and that positive press releases by RRC "could provide the key to positive donor response" (RRC/EC 1988d, 2).

44. RRC/EC 1988e.

45. Ibid., 1.

46. Interview with Bryan Wannop, UNDP, New York, September 6, 1990.

47. The TCC meeting minutes (February 29, 1988, 3) make this explicit in relation to the March 1988 trains to Aweil.

48. UNDP 1988a.

49. Bonner 1989, 95.

50. U.S. Congress 1988b, 13.

51. A fuller analysis of the disadvantages of "tranching" can be found in Keen (1991b, 413).

52. The relevant section of the unnamed report was cited by the official: "The following standards were developed by the US Center[s] for Disease Control of the US Public Health Service for calculating rations for short periods of time, based on experience in Nigeria, Sahel and Bangladesh: 100 will require a full ration by free distribution; 200 will require half ration; 400 will require quarter ration; 300 will

require no feeding" (RRC/EC 1989b). The full ration was given as 500 grams/person/day.

53. The report had arisen in the context of famine in Biafra, where many had some access to food and would have been used for overall needs, a CDC official said, adding that CDC officials visiting southern Kordofan in October and November 1988 had recommended full rations for the displaced (letter from Michael J. Toole, Technical Support Division, International Health Program Office, CDC, Atlanta, to the author, September 21, 1990).

54. Curtis 1991, 14.

55. State Department Country Reports for 1986 and 1987 referred to militias and slavery but made no mention of government involvement (Africa Watch 1990, 164).

56. U.S. Congress 1988b, 26.

57. See, e.g., the testimony of USAID officials in U.S. Congress (1988b, 7).

58. Agenda for Heads of Mission Donor Group meeting, Khartoum, August 30, 1988.

59. Letter from D. I. Lewty, Chargé d'Affaires, Netherlands, to Dr. El Hag El Tayeb, Acting Commissioner, RRC, December 7, 1988.

60. OFDA's Taft complained: "There was no international entity or donor willing to try to use Lifeline as an opportunity for public diplomatic efforts. There was never energy placed on the peace side that I saw" (Minear 1991, 148). Meanwhile, State Department officials were complaining that criticism of the Sudanese government was restricting U.S. access to the government (Africa Watch 1990, 165).

61. U.S. Congress 1990a, 24.

62. See, e.g., the testimony of Roger Winter, director of the U.S. Committee for Refugees, in U.S. Congress (1990a, 44).

63. U.S. Congress 1990b, 31–33.

64. U.S. Congress 1990c, 60.

65. See, e.g., the testimony of Thomas R. Getman, director of government relations, World Vision, in U.S. Congress 1990c, 40.

66. U.S. Congress 1990c, 62.

67. Letter to *The Independent*, August 24, 1992.


## Chapter 6
### Discussion and Conclusion

1. Cf. Swift 1983, 14.

2. Beetham (1987, 35) has argued that one of the reasons for the widespread neglect of prevention is that performance cannot easily be measured.

3. The strategy of Saddam Hussein in blockading and selectively attacking the Kurds exhibits important similarities (Keen, 1993).

4. "Sudan: Destroying Ethnic Identity—the Secret War against the Nuba," *News from Africa Watch*, December 10, 1991, 1–12.

5. See also letter from Suleiman Musa Rahhal, Nuba Mountains Solidarity Abroad Organization to UN Under Secretary General for Humanitarian Affairs, Charles la Munière, November 11, 1992.

6. "Sudan: Eradicating the Nuba," *News from Africa Watch*, September 9, 1992, 1–7. The process has also been noted by Survival International.

7. "Sudan: Refugees in Their Own Country—the Forced Relocation of Squatters and Displaced People from Khartoum," *News from Africa Watch*, July 10, 1992.

8. "Sudan: Eradicating the Nuba," *News from Africa Watch*, September 9, 1992, 1–7.

9. "Human Rights Abuses and Mass Deportations in Central Sudan" (report, Survival International, 1993).

10. See also the discussion of SPLA abuses in Gonda and Mogga (1988, 73), Wani (1988, 103–4), Jada (1988, 125–38), and Africa Watch (1990, 158).

11. A revealing exception as the Toposa, to whom the government was still able to channel supplies and even soldiers. This helped perpetuate divisions among the Toposa, and conflict between some sections and the SPLA continued.

12. There are a great number of accusations and counteraccusations on these lines.

13. One element of this problem is the danger of internal divisions' creating the impression abroad that southern Sudanese are not capable of governing themselves (*Southern Sudan Vision* [Interim National Executive Committee of the SPLM], December 15, 1992, 7). See also Duffield 1992; *Guardian*, September 12, 1992. A *Daily Telegraph* article of January 26, 1992, emphasized reports that armed Nuer attacking Bor and Kongor were "naked" and intent on making the Dinka "drink their own blood"; a perceived descent into "tribalism" could be used to legitimate international inaction.

14. The information on Ethiopia in this chapter is drawn from the excellent Africa Watch (1991) account, written by Alexander de Waal. See also Clay, Steingraber, and Niggli 1988.

15. Cutler 1989, 407–8.

16. This is clear from a comparison of Brown et al. (1987) and Deng and Minear (1992, 6, 72) with more detailed information on receipt of relief in de Waal (1989a) and Keen (1991a).

17. "Somalia: A Fight to the Death? Leaving Civilians at the Mercy of Terror and Starvation," *News from Africa Watch*, February 13, 1992, 17.

18. de Waal and Omaar 1992, 63.

19. See also Omaar 1992. Omaar puts UN distributions at 22,000 metric tons and ICRC distributions at 70,000 metric tons.

20. The importance of directing aid through clan elders was underlined by S. Samatar in an interesting article, "How to Save Starving Somalia," *Guardian*, December 3, 1992.

21. Africa Watch and Save the Children Fund pointed to the dangers of exaggerating the looting. See also African Rights 1993, 2–4.

22. The difficulties of targeting relief grain have been acknowledged by Sen and Drèze, who draw on work by the current writer, among others, in support of their advocacy of cash relief (Drèze and Sen 1989). However, the practice of "targeting" relief without giving adequate consideration to how, or indeed whether, this is likely to be achieved remains widespread. Also widespread is a continuing neglect of the local politics of relief. Cash relief and relief-for-work schemes can also be derailed by local political inequalities (O'Neill 1956, 233; Jackson with Eade 1982, 28; Jodha 1975, 1611).

23. Neglecting human rights abuses on the pretext that humanitarian aid should

not be jeopardized presents particular dangers, as the recent example of the former Yugoslavia has underlined. Humanitarian relief again distracted attention from the underlying conflict and the need to resolve it.

24. Pressman and Wildavsky 1973, 139–43.

25. On Sudan, see Mahmoud (1984); Barnett and Abdelkarim (1988); Johnson (1986); Niblock (1987); and Ibrahim (1985).

26. See, e.g., World Bank (1986), which draws heavily on Sen.

27. The Kurdish disaster has clearly helped put this question on the international agenda. J. K. Galbraith (1991) is among those who have suggested that existing UN procedures in particular have proved inadequate in relation to governments' abuse of sovereignty and the continuing horrors of internal conflict. He stresses that to avoid the use of the UN for bilateral purposes, real sovereignty should be conceded to it by all countries, including the United States.

28. During the Great Starvation in Ireland, it was precisely a form of "targeting" relief to the poorest—the 1847 Poor Law amendment clause prohibiting relief to those holding more than a quarter-acre of land—that allowed landlord Poor Law guardians to manipulate relief to clear smallholders from their estates (O'Neill 1956, 253).

29. A common argument in favor of targeted interventions is that they are likely to minimize "disincentives," notably in labor markets (see, e.g., World Bank 1986, 29–30).

# Bibliography

## Primary Sources

Abyei Dinka Association. 1987. "The Current Situation in Abyei Area." Public statement, March 19.

Action Internationale Contre la Faim. *See* AICF.

Agricultural Planning Unit, Darfur Regional Government. 1987. "Proposals for Relief Grain Distribution in Darfur." Memo. to Governor of Darfur and Darfur Technical Committee for Relief and Rehabilitation.

AICF. 1988. "Nutritional Survey for Displaced People in South Kordofan." May 6.

Akol, A. A. 1986. "Famine Situation in the Bahr el Ghazal Administrative Area." Memo. from the Governor, November.

Anti-Slavery Society for the Protection of Human Rights. 1988. "Slavery in Sudan." Report to the UN Working Group on Slavery, London.

Aweil Rice Development Project. 1987. "Report on the Food Situation in Aweil." April 25.

Bickersteth, J. S. 1988. "Sudan Food Security Situation." EC, June.

British Embassy, Khartoum. 1988. Memo. to members of the Donor Group (United States, Federal Republic of Germany, Netherlands, Japan, European Community, and Switzerland) and UNICEF.

CARE. 1988. Internal memo., by M. Ebrahim and A. Fadul, CARE International in Sudan, El Obeid, August 18.

Concern. 1988a. "Report on Grain Situation." June 28.

————. 1988b. "Situation Report on Relief Operations."

————. 1988c. "Report for July 1988."

————. 1988d. "Report on ECEP1, Babanousa/Muglad."

————. 1988e. "Grain Report." August 2.

————. 1988f. Untitled internal memo., November 24.

————. *See also* Minutes.

Davey, K., G. Glentworth, M. O. Khalifa, and M. S. Idris, eds. 1976. "Local Government and Development in the Sudan: The Experience of Southern Darfur Province." Vol. 1. Ministry of People's Local Government, Sudan, and Development Administration Group, Birmingham University.

Deloitte, Haskins, and Sells Consultants. 1985. "Emergency Food Relief Programme: Final Report on Development of an Accountability System and Other Related Tasks." USAID/Sudan.

EC. 1986a. "Note to the Delegate." From H. Rook, Resident Adviser, February 14.

————. 1986b. Telex from D. Frisch, Director-General, Development, COMEUR, Brussels, to Delegation, Khartoum, May 29.

————. 1987a. Internal telex, Khartoum to DG VIII, Brussels, March 26.

————. 1987b. "Report on the Food Situation in Aweil." April 25.

————. 1987c. "Southern Relief Operation." Telex from R. G. Smit, Acting Delegate, EC, Khartoum, to G. Molinier, DGVIII, EC, Brussels, August 16.

EC. 1987d. "Emergency Aid—Shelter for Displaced People around Khartoum." Memo. from D. McLure to the Delegate, EC, Khartoum, October.

———. 1987e. Internal memo., Khartoum, November 3.

———. 1987f. "Preliminary Estimates of Given Needs for Period 1st Nov 87/31st Aug 88." Internal memo., undated.

———. 1988a. Internal memo, spring.

———. 1988b. Internal memo., April 24.

———. 1988c. "Note for the Record, Southern Kordofan Situation." June 11.

———. 1988d. Telex from G. Gwyer, Acting Delegate, EC, Khartoum, to Molinier, DGVIII, EC, Brussels, June 29.

———. 1988e. "Emergency Aid Sudan: Situation in South Kordofan." Note from the Delegate, Khartoum, to the Directorate-General, Development, EC, Brussels, October 13.

———. 1988f. Report on visit to Raga, from Economic Adviser, EC, Khartoum, November 19.

———. 1989a. "Evaluation of EC Emergency Rehabilitation and Food Aid to Sudan, 1985–88." Note to the Directorate-General, Development, April 10.

———. 1989b. "Evaluation of EEC Emergency, Rehabilitation and Food Aid to Sudan, 1985–88," Note to Mr. Klinkenbergh, Director, from Soubestre, Director, DGVIII, May 3.

———. See also Minutes.

EWSB (Early Warning System Bulletins, RRC). Various dates.

FAO. 1989a. Production Yearbook. Rome.

———. 1989b. Trade Yearbook. Rome.

Father Deng Rudolf. 1988. Memo. from former Chairman, Aweil Relief Committee, to Sudanaid, Khartoum, spring.

Food and Agricultural Organization. See FAO.

Food Aid Administration, Kordofan Region. 1988a. "Distribution Plan for 20,000 mt of Dura (Second Tranche)" (amended). El Obeid.

———. 1988b. "Distribution of 11,790 Tons of Dura Donated by the Ministry of Finance." El Obeid.

Government of India. 1867. "Report, Commissioners Appointed to Enquire into the Famine in Bengal and Orissa, 1866." Vols. 1 and 2.

———. 1901. "Report of the Indian Famine Commission." Nainital, NWP, and Oudh Government Press.

Hassabo and Co. 1988. "Preliminary Evaluation of the Western Relief Operation." USAID contract, October 28.

Heads of Mission. 1988. Internal notes, Meeting of Heads of Mission, British Embassy, July 5.

———. n.d. "Situation Assessment: Darfur." Letter to Dr. Bashir Omer Fadlallah, Minister of Finance and Economy.

India, Government of. See Government.

Interagency Situation Report. 1988. "South Kordofan, June 1988."

Interdonor Memo. 1988. "Displaced Persons in Sudan: Food Needs and Related Issues." April 29.

Médecins Sans Frontières. See MSF.

Ministry of Agriculture. 1974. "Yearbook of Agricultural Statistics." Government of Sudan, June.

Ministry of Agriculture and Natural Resources. 1987a. "Situation Outlook," vol. 1, no. 3. April report, Department of Agricultural Economics.

———. 1987b. "Agricultural Situation and Outlook," vol. 3, no. 5. August report, Department of Agricultural Economics.

Ministry of Finance and Economic Planning. 1988. "Food Aid Administration, Kordofan Region: Distribution Plan." February 11.

Ministry of Finance and Economic Planning/EEC/Masdar (UK). 1988. "Evaluation of the Western Relief Operation, 1987/88." October.

Ministry of Social Welfare, Zakat and the Displaced. 1988. "A Draft Provided by the Ministry of Social Welfare, Zakat and the Displaced Regarding the Government's General Policy towards the Displaced." September 22.

Minutes of aid coordination meeting held at Concern office. 1988. Khartoum, May 27. Concern, Khartoum.

Minutes of aid coordination meeting held at Kordofan Regional Offices. 1988. El Obeid, August 25. EC, Khartoum.

MSF-Belgium. 1988. "Summary Report: Emergency Programme MSF-Belgium for Displaced People of the Dinka Tribe in Southern Darfur." July 27.

MSF-France. 1988a. "Situation Brief." Meiram, June 4.

———. 1988b. "Meiram Situation Brief." July 4.

———. 1988c. Internal memo., Meiram, July 26.

———. 1988d. Internal memo, Meiram, August 2.

———. 1988e. "Nutritional Situation in El Meiram." August 4.

———. 1988f. "Details des differentes pathologies rencontrées dans les consultations feeding du 7 au 20/8/88." Meiram, August 18.

———. 1988g. "Memorandum for Record." Meiram, August 27.

———. 1988h. "Situation Brief, El Meiram, III." September 6.

———. 1988i. "Rapport, Mission El Meiram." September 8.

———. 1988j. "El Meiram, Situation Brief, IV." September 22.

———. 1988k. "Rapport du mission du 31 aout au 25 sept." Meiram, September 25.

———. 1988l. "Report for 14/10 to 15/11." Meiram, November 16.

———. 1988m. "Premier rapport, mission El Meiram." Undated.

Overseas Development Administration. See ODA.

ODA Republic of Sudan. 1986. "Strategy for Development of Rainfed Agriculture." Khartoum, March.

Otor, S. C-J. 1984. "The 1983 Population Census, Administrative Report for the Southern Sudan." Juba, June.

Oxfam-UK. 1986a. "South Sudan, Tour Report, Wau, Bahr el Ghazal, 20th to 25th February 1986."

———. 1986b. "Food Distribution in Bahr el Ghazal." March 21.

———. 1986c. "Note on the Food and Security Situation in Wau." March 23.

———. 1986d. "Wau Tour Report 25th/26th March 1986."

———. 1986e. "Political Situation in Abyei." March 29.

———. 1986f. "Aweil Tour Report." May.

Oxfam-UK. 1986g. "Preliminary Report, Aweil." Spring.

———. 1986h. "Tour Report, Wau, 18–22 May 1986." June 6.

———. 1986i. "The Economic War against the Dinka of Bahr el Ghazal." June 4.

———. 1986j. "Ed Daien Tour Report." June 18.

———. 1986k. "A Statement from Juba." June 20.

———. 1986l. "Tour Report, Abu Zaba, El Fula, Babanousa, En Nahud, Kadugli, 17th–27th June 1986." July 1.

———. 1986m. "Aweil Update." August 24.

———. 1986n. Memo. from Country Representative, Khartoum, to Oxfam House, Oxford, August 31.

———. 1986o. "Establishing CART's Independence." October 13.

———. 1986p. "Policy Situation Report number 4." December 16.

———. 1986q. "CART and the EEC." Memo. from Country Representative, Khartoum, to Oxfam House, Oxford, December 23.

———. 1987a. Oxfam notes of meeting with EC, Khartoum office, January 20.

———. 1987b. "Policy Situation Report no. 6." March 1.

———. 1987c. Memo. from Melvyn Almond to Country Representative Mark Duffield, August 31.

———. 1987d. "Report on Meeting about Harassment of Displaced Southerners in Arkaweat." December 3.

———. 1988a. "Darfur Tour Report, 21/2/88–12/3/88."

———. 1988b. Memo. from Oxfam Nutritional Coordinator, to El Hadi Ahmed, Director, Sudanese Red Crescent, May 31.

———. 1988c. "Situation Report no. 3." July 3.

———. 1988d. "Tour Report, South Kordofan, 6–12 September 1988." September 13.

———. 1988e. "Tour Report, Visit to Kordofan with the Prime Minister, 17–19 September 1988."

———. 1988f. Telexes from Country Representative Mark Duffield, Khartoum, to Oxfam, Oxford, November 6, 7, 8, 9.

———. 1988g. Memo. from Nyala, Darfur, November 7.

———. 1988h. "Present Uncertainties and Difficulties: Donors and the South." Mark Duffield, Country Representative, Khartoum, to Oxfam House, Oxford, December 14.

———. 1988i. Telex from Mark Duffield, Country Representative, Khartoum, to Oxfam House, Oxford, December 20.

———. 1989. "The Changing Political Scene: Implications for Relief Work." Khartoum, February 1.

———. 1991. "Situation Report." Khartoum, September 8.

Relief and Rehabilitation Commission. *See* RRC.

Republic of Sudan/UNDP/ODA. 1984. "Decentralization: Management and Development Issues. Report of the Inter-Regional Seminar held in Juba, 21–23 Nov 1984."

Road Transport Unit. *See* RTU.

RRC. 1987. "Comments made by GOS during Meeting of Commissioner of Relief and Rehabilitation, Minister of Finance, Commissioner of Khartoum and ABS with Donors in RRC on 9 December 1987." Undated.

RRC/donors. 1987. "The 1988 Relief Food Assistance Program for Sudan. Inactive Plan for Western Sudan, Dec. 1987–Sept. 30, 1988." December 11.

———. 1988. Report of meeting at RRC on May 4 on progress of WRO.

RRC/EC. 1987. Memo. from Adviser to Acting Delegate, EC, October 19.

———. 1988a. Memo. from Adviser to RRC Commissioner, January 18.

———. 1988b. Memo., March 11.

———. 1988c. "Summary of Attached Tour Reports." April 3.

———. 1988d. Radio message from Adviser to APU, Darfur, April 26.

———. 1988e. "Handover Notes." Adviser to Deputy Commissioner, RRC, May 28.

———. 1988f. "Report on Visit to Food Aid Administration, el Obeid." May 29.

———. 1988g. "South Kordofan and Abyei Area Council." Spring.

———. 1988h. "Note to the Acting Delegate." From Adviser, June 10.

———. 1988i. "Chronology of RRC/Donor/GOS Actions 1987/88."

———. 1988j. "South Darfur Programme for Displaced." Memo. to RRC Commissioner Dr. el Hag el Tayeb el Tahir, September 18.

———. 1988k. "Note on Displaced."

———. 1988l. Internal memo. from RRC/EC adviser, spring.

RTU, 1987. "To Whom It May Concern, re: Road Transport Unit/Khartoum." Memo. from Aldo Barone, Road Transport Unit Director, June 16.

Save the Children Fund. *See* SCF.

SCF-UK. 1988. "Report on Visit to Abu Karenka, Darfur." August 23.

———. 1989. Memo. from A. Timpson, London, to J. Patel, Khartoum, January 5.

SCF-UK/Oxfam-UK. 1988a. "Confidential Report on Visit to Meiram, 4.9.88 to 9.9.88."

———. 1988b. "A Rapid Assessment and Nutrition Survey of the Displaced Dinka in El Lait Rural Council, Umm Keddada Area Council, N. Darfur, Sudan, 6.12–11.12.88."

Sudanaid. 1988. "Field Trips and Relief Activities in S. Darfur." March 24.

Sudanaid/Sudan Council of Churches. 1986. "Emergency Assistance Needs [in] Bahr el Ghazal and Upper Nile." September 28.

Sudan Council of Churches. 1986. "Regional Situations: Especial Report on South Sudan." February.

Sudan, Government of. *See* Ministry; Republic.

Symonds, P. 1987. "A Report on the Situation in Raga, Western Bahr el Ghazal Province, June–August 1987." Khartoum, September.

TCC. *See* Technical Coordination Committee.

Technical Committee for Relief and Rehabilitation. n.d. Memo., El Fasher, Darfur.

Technical Coordination Committee (TCC). 1987. Notes on meeting, recorded by T. J. Bos, August 10.

———. Various dates. Minutes of meetings.

Technical Donor Committee on Relief. 1988. "Agreements." Record of weekly meeting at WFP, September 25.

UNDP. 1988a. "Food Situation in South Sudan." Telex, Khartoum, February 8.

———. 1988b. "Report of the Multi-Agency Survey Mission to Aweil, 30 November–1 December, 1988." Khartoum.

UN Fund for Population Activities (with Democratic Republic of Sudan). 1986.

"Sudan: Report of Second Mission on Needs Assessment for Population Assistance." Report no. 84, New York, July.

UNICEF. 1987a. "Situation in El Meiram, Abyei District, South Kordofan." Khartoum, September 10.

———. 1987b. "Note for the Record, Visit to El Meiram, 27–28 October 1987." Khartoum.

———. 1988. "Note for the Record, Situation Update: Abyei, March 14th 1988."

United Nations. *See* UN.

United Nations. *See* U.S.

UNOEA. 1988. "The Emergency Situation in Sudan: Urgent Humanitarian Requirements." November.

UNOEOS. 1986. "Southern Sudan Emergency Operation, Weekly Status Report no. 8, as of 21st Aug. 1986."

UN/SRRA. 1990. "Lifeline Sudan: An Investigation into Production Capability in the Rural Southern Sudan: A Report on Food Sources and Needs"; also field notes for this report.

USAID. 1987a. "Country Report: Sudan." Famine Early Warning System (FEWS), January.

———. 1987b. "Country Report: Sudan." FEWS, June.

———. 1988a. "Sudan: Vulnerability Assessment." FEWS Country Report, June.

———. 1988b. "Sudan: A Good Start to the Rainy Season." FEWS.

———. 1988c. "Record Harvest in the North, Famine Continues in the South." FEWS.

———. 1989. "Sudan: Vulnerability Assessment." FEWS Country Report, June.

U.S. Congress. 1988a. *U.S. Response to Relief Efforts in Sudan, Ethiopia, Angola, and Mozambique: Joint Hearings before the Select Committee on Hunger and the Subcommittee on Africa of the House Committee on Foreign Affairs.* 100th Cong., 2d sess., March 10.

———. 1988b. *Ethiopia and Sudan: Warfare, Politics and Famine: Hearings before the House Select Committee on Hunger.* 100th Cong., 2d sess., July 14.

———. 1989a. *War and Famine in Sudan: Hearings before the Subcommittee on African Affairs of the Senate Committee on Foreign Relations.* 101st Cong., 1st sess., February 23.

———. 1989b. *Politics of Hunger in the Sudan: Joint Hearings before the Select Committee on Hunger and the Subcommittee on Africa of the House Committee on Foreign Affairs.* 101st Cong., 1st sess., March 2.

———. 1990a. *War and Famine in the Sudan: Joint Hearings before the Subcommittee on Africa of the House Committee on Foreign Affairs and the International Task Force of the House Select Committee on Hunger.* 101st Cong., 2d sess., March 15.

———. 1990b. *Impending Famine and Recent Political Developments in the Sudan: Hearings before the Subcommittee on Africa of the House Committee on Foreign Affairs.* 101st Cong., 2d sess., October 25.

———. 1990c. *Emergency Situations in Sudan and Liberia: Hearings before the Subcommittee on African Affairs of the Senate Committee on Foreign Relations.* 101st Cong., 2d sess., November 27.

U.S. Department of State. 1985. "Background Notes: Sudan." Washington, D.C., August.

Wannop, B. 1989. "Report on the First Muglad-Aweil Relief Train, May 20 to May 28." UNDP, Khartoum, June.

WFP. 1988. "Khartoum Population and Vulnerable Population Estimates, Affected Areas and Food Distribution Quantities." Undated report.

WFP/FAO/UNICEF. 1991. "Crop, Food and Emergency Needs Assessment Mission, Southern Sudan." October–December.

World Food Programme. *See* WFP.

## Secondary Sources

Abakr, A. R., and D. Pool. 1980. "The Development Process in Its Political-Administrative Context." In *Problems of Savannah Development: the Sudan Case*, edited by G. Haaland. African Savannah Studies, Occasional Paper no. 19. University of Bergen.

Abd-al Ghaffar, M. A. 1974. *Shaykhs and Followers: Political Struggle in the Rufa'a al Hoi Nazirate in the Sudan*. Khartoum: Khartoum University Press.

Abdel-Aziz, O. E. 1979. "*Production and Marketing of Sorghum and Sesame in the Eastern Central Rainlands of the Sudan: The Contrast between the Public and Private Sectors*." Ph.D. diss., Leeds University.

Abdel-Rahim, M. 1968. *The Development of British Policy in the Southern Sudan, 1899–1947*. Khartoum: Khartoum University Press.

Abdul-Jalil, M. A. 1979. "The Dynamics of Ethnic Identification and Ethnic Group Relations among the People of 'Dor,' Northern Darfur, Sudan." Ph.D. diss., Edinburgh University.

Abdul-Jalil, M. A., and S. U. Rabih. 1986. "Problems and Prospects of Horticulture in a Subsistence Economy: The Case of Wadi Kutum (Northern Darfur)." In *Perspectives on Development in the Sudan*, edited by P. van der Wel and A.G.M. Ahmed. The Hague: ISS; Khartoum: DSRC.

Affan, K. 1981. "Effect on Aggregate Peasant Labour Supply of Rural-Rural Migration to Mechanised Farming: A Case Study in Southern Kordofan, Sudan." Ph.D. diss., Sussex University.

African Rights. 1993. *Somalia—Operation Restore Hope: A Preliminary Assessment*. London: African Rights.

Africa Watch. 1990. *Denying the "Honor of Living": Sudan, a Human Rights Disaster*. New York, Washington, D.C., and London: Africa Watch.

———. 1991. *Evil Days: 30 Years of War and Famine in Ethiopia*. New York, Washington, D.C., Los Angeles, and London: Africa Watch.

Ahmed, M. B. 1987. "Agrarian Change in Dar Hamar: A Study in the Development of Crop Production and Desertification from Western Sudan." Ph.D. diss., Hull University.

Ali, T.M.A. 1988. "The State and Agricultural Policy: In Quest of a Framework for Analysis of Development Strategies." In *Sudan: State, Capital and Transformation*, edited by T. Barnett, T. Abdelkarim, and A. Abdelkarim. London, New York, and Sydney: Croon Helm.

Alier, A. 1990. *Southern Sudan: Too Many Agreements Dishonoured*. Exeter: Ithaca Press.

Allen, T. 1986. *Full Circle? An Overview of Sudan's "Southern Problem" since Inde-*

*pendence*. Manchester Discussion Papers in Development Studies, no. 8604. University of Manchester.

Allison, G. 1971. *Essence of Decision: Explaining the Cuban Missile Crisis*. Boston: Little, Brown and Co.

Almond, M. n.d. *Pastoral Development and Oxfam in the Sudan*. Oxford: Oxfam.

Ambiranjan, S. 1978. *Classical Political Economy and British Policy in India*. Cambridge: Cambridge University Press.

Amnesty International. 1989. *Sudan: Human Rights Violations in the Context of Civil War*. London: Amnesty International.

Appadurai, A. 1984. "How Moral Is South Asia's Economy?—A Review Article." *Journal of Asian Studies* 43(3):481–97.

Arnold, D. 1988. *Famine: Social Crisis and Historical Change*. Oxford: Blackwell.

Article 19. 1990. *Starving in Silence: A Report on Famine and Censorship*. London: Article 19.

Ateeg, A.I.H. 1983. "A Critical Analysis of Livestock and Meat Marketing in Sudan." Ph.D. diss., University of London.

Barnett, T., and A. Abdelkarim, eds. 1988. *Sudan: State, Capital and Transformation*. London, New York, and Sydney: Croon Helm.

Barrett, S., and C. Fudge. 1981. *Policy and Action: Essays on the Implementation of Public Policy*. London and New York: Methuen.

Barry, T. 1987. *Roots of Rebellion: Land and Hunger in Central America*. Boston: South End Press.

Bates, R. H. 1981. *Markets and States in Tropical Africa: The Political Basis of Agricultural Policies*. Berkeley: University of California Press.

———. 1983. *Essays on the Political Economy of Rural Africa*. Cambridge: Cambridge University Press.

Bauer, P. [1971] 1976. *Dissent on Development*. London: Wiedenfeld and Nicolson.

———. 1984. *Reality and Rhetoric*. London: Wiedenfeld and Nicolson.

Bechtold, P. K. 1990. "More Turbulence in Sudan: A New Politics This Time?" *Middle East Journal* 44(4): 579–95.

Beetham, D. 1987. *Bureaucracy*. Milton Keynes, England: Open University Press.

Bickersteth, J. S. 1990. "Donor Dilemmas in Food Aid: The Case of Wheat in Sudan." *Food Policy* 15(3): 218–26.

Bonner, R. 1989. "A Reporter at Large: Famine." *New Yorker*, March 13, 85–100.

Borton, J., and J. Shoham. 1989. "Experiences of Non-Governmental Organisations in the Targeting of Emergency Food Aid." Report on a Workshop on Emergency Food Aid Targeting at the London School of Hygiene and Tropical Medicine, London, January 4–6.

Bowbrick, P. 1986. "The Causes of Famine: A Refutation of Professor Sen's Theory." *Food Policy* 11(2): 105–24.

Brown, R.P.C. 1988. "A Background Note on the Final Round of Economic Austerity Measures Imposed by the Numeiry Regime: June 1984–March 1985." In *Sudan: State, Capital and Transformation*, edited by T. Barnett, T. Abdelkarim, and A. Abdelkarim. London, New York, and Sydney: Croon Helm.

———. 1992. *Public Debt and Private Wealth: Debt, Capital Flight and the IMF in Sudan*. Basingstoke: Macmillan.

Brown, V. W., S. S. Stolba, R. C. Walker, and D. H. Wood. 1987. *An Evaluation of the*

*African Emergency Food Assistance Program in Sudan, 1984–1985*. Washington, D.C.: U.S. Agency for International Development.

Burger, G., J. Drummond, and H. Standstead. 1948. *Malnutrition and Starvation in Western Netherlands, September 1944–July 1945*. The Hague: General State Printing Office.

Cathie, J. 1982. *The Political Economy of Food Aid*. Aldershot: Gower.

Chamberlin, W. H. 1935. *Russia's Iron Age*. London: Duckworth.

Chiriyankandath, J. L. 1987. "1986 Elections in the Sudan: Tradition, Ideology, Ethnicity—and Class?" *Review of African Political Economy*, no. 38, 96–102.

Clark, C. 1987. "The Vanishing Famine." *Africa Report*, January–February, 68–70.

Clark, J. 1991. *Democratizing Development: The Role of Voluntary Organizations*. London: Earthscan.

Clay, E. J., and B. B. Schaffer, eds. 1984. *Room for Manoeuvre: An Exploration of Public Policy in Agriculture and Rural Development*. London: Heinemann Educational Books.

Clay, J. W., S. Steingraber, and P. Niggli. 1988. *The Spoils of Famine: Ethiopian Famine Policy and Peasant Agriculture*. Cambridge, Mass.: Cultural Survival, Inc.

Collins, R. O. 1971. *Land Beyond the Rivers: The Southern Sudan, 1889–1918*. New Haven and London: Yale University Press.

————. 1983. *Shadows in the Grass: Britain in the Southern Sudan, 1918–1956*. New Haven and London: Yale University Press.

Copans, J. 1983. "Sahel Drought: Science and Underdevelopment." In *Interpretations of Calamity*, edited by K. Hewitt. Winchester, Mass.: Allen and Unwin.

Cordell, D. D. 1985. *Dar al-Kuti and the Last Years of the Trans-Saharan Slave Trade*. Madison: University of Wisconsin Press.

Cunnison, I. 1954. "The Humr and their Land." *Sudan Notes and Records* 35, pt. 2: 50–68

————. 1966. *Baggara Arabs: Power and Lineage in a Sudanese Nomad Tribe*. Oxford: Clarendon Press.

Curtis, P. 1991. "Towards an Understanding of NGO-Donor Relationships during Crisis Management." Paper presented at International Symposium, Refugee Studies Programme, Oxford University, Oxford, March 17–20.

Cutler, P. 1984. "Famine Forecasting: Prices and Peasant Behaviour in Northern Ethiopia." *Disasters* 8(1): 48–56.

————. 1985. *The Use of Economic and Social Information in Famine Prediction and Response*. London: Overseas Development Administration.

————. 1989. "The Development of the 1983–85 Famine in Northern Ethiopia." Ph.D. diss., University of London.

Davis, M. 1974. "Some Political Dimensions of International Relief: Two Cases." *International Organization* 28(1): 127–40.

————. 1975. *Civil Wars and the Politics of International Relief: Africa, South Asia and the Caribbean*. New York: Praeger.

Deng, F. M. 1971. *Tradition and Modernization: A Challenge for Law among the Dinka of the Sudan*. New Haven and London: Yale University Press.

————. 1972. *The Dinka of the Sudan*. New York: Holt, Rinehart and Winston.

————. 1973. *Dynamics of Identification: A Basis for National Integration in the Sudan*. Khartoum: Khartoum University Press.

Deng, F. M. 1978. *Africans of Two Worlds: The Dinka in Afro-Arab Sudan*. New Haven and London: Yale University Press.

———. 1980. *Dinka Cosmology*. London: Ithaca Press.

———. 1982. *Recollections of Babo Nimir*. London: Ithaca Press.

———. 1986. *The Man Called Deng Majok: A Biography of Power, Polygyny and Change*. New Haven and London: Yale University Press.

———. 1990. "War of Visions for the Nation." *Middle East Journal* 44(4): 596–609.

Deng, F. M., and L. Minear. 1992. *The Challenges of Famine Relief: Emergency Operations in the Sudan*. Washington, D.C.: The Brookings Institution.

Deng, W., and J. Oduho. 1963. *The Problem of the Southern Sudan*. London: Institute of Race Relations; London, Karachi, and Nairobi: Oxford University Press.

de Schweinitz, K. [1943] 1961. *England's Road to Social Security: From the Statute of Laborers in 1349 to the Beveridge Report of 1942*. New York: Perpetua.

de Waal, A.W.L., 1989a. *Famine That Kills: Darfur, Sudan, 1984–1985*. Oxford: Clarendon Press.

———. 1989b. *The Sudan Famine Code of 1920: Successes and Failures of the Indian Model of Famine Relief in Colonial Sudan*. London: Action Aid; Oxford: Nuffield College.

———. 1990a. "Starving Out the South: Famine, War and Famine, 1983–9." Mimeo.

———. 1990b. "Armed Militias in Contemporary Sudan." Mimeo.

———. 1990c. "A Conquerable Ill." *Times Literary Supplement*, July 13–19.

———. n.d. *Famine That Kills: Darfur 1984–85*. London: Save the Children Fund.

de Waal, A.W.L., and R. Omaar. 1992. "The Lessons of Famine." *Africa Report*, November/December, 62–65.

Dreyfus, H., and Rabinow P. 1982. *Michel Foucault: Beyond Structuralism and Hermeneutics*. Brighton: Harvester Press.

Drèze, J., and A. Sen. 1989. *Hunger and Public Action*. Oxford: Clarendon Press.

D'Silva, B. C. 1985. *Sudan: Policy Reforms and Prospects for Agricultural Recovery after the Drought*. Washington, D.C.: U.S. Department of Agriculture.

Duffield, M. 1990a. "Sudan at the Crossroads: From Emergency Preparedness to Social Security." Institute of Development Studies paper, no. DP275. May.

———. 1990b. "War and Famine in Africa." Oxfam Research Paper, no. 5. Oxford.

———. 1991. "The Internationalisation of Public Welfare: Conflict and the Reform of the Donor/NGO Safety Net." Paper presented at Workshop on the Prospects for Peace, Recovery and Development in the Horn of Africa, Institute of Social Studies, The Hague, February 19–23.

———. 1992. "NGOs, Disaster Relief and Asset Transfer in the Horn: Political Survival in a Permanent Emergency." Paper presented at 1992 Annual Conference of the Development Studies Association, University of Nottingham, September 16–18.

Edgell, A. G. 1975. "Nigeria/Biafra." in *Civil Wars and the Politics of International Relief: Africa, South Asia and the Caribbean*, edited by M. Davis. New York: Praeger.

Edwards, R. D., and T. D. Williams, eds. 1956 *The Great Famine: Studies in Irish History, 1845–52*. Dublin: Irish Committee of Historical Sciences and Browne and Nolan.

El Hassan, A. M. 1985. "The State and the Development of Capitalism in Agriculture in Sudan: the Case of the Savannah Rainland." Ph.D. diss., University of East Anglia.

El Khalifa, E., R. Ford, and M. M. Khogali. 1985. *Sudan's Southern Stock Route: An Environmental Impact Assessment.* Khartoum and Worcester, Mass.: Institute of Environmental Studies.

El Sammani, M. O. 1986. *Kordofan Rehabilitation Development Strategy.* Vol. 1. Khartoum: Sudanese Ministry of Finance and Economic Planning, UNDP, and Khartoum University.

————, ed. 1985. "El Khuwei-Mazroub-Tinna Study Area, North Central Kordofan and Messeriya Study Area, Southern Kordofan." Project no. 698–0427. Institute of Environmental Studies, Khartoum University, and USAID.

Eprile, C. 1974. *War and Peace in the Sudan, 1955–1972.* London: Newton Abbot.

Firth, R. 1959. *Social Change in Tikopia,* New York: Macmillan.

Fluehr-Lobban, C. 1990. "Islamization in Sudan: A critical Assessment." *Middle East Journal* 44(4): 610–23.

Foreign Affairs Committee, House of Commons. 1988. *Famine in the Horn of Africa.* London: HMSO.

Foucault, M. 1975. *I, Pierre Riviere.* Harmondsworth: Penguin.

————. 1977. *Discipline and Punish: The Birth of the Prison.* Harmondsworth: Penguin.

————. 1978. "Politics and the Study of Discourse." *Ideology and Consciousness,* no. 3, 7–26.

————. 1981. "Questions of Method: An Interview with Michel Foucault." *Ideology and Consciousness,* no. 8: 3–14.

————. 1988. *Power/Knowledge: Selected Interviews and Other Writings, 1972–1977.* Edited by C. Gordon. Brighton: Harvester Press.

Fraser, C. 1988. *Lifelines: For Africa Still in Peril and Distress.* London: Hutchinson.

Galbraith, J. K. 1991. "The Call of Arms and the Poor Man." *Guardian,* March 27.

Garang, J. 1987. *John Garang Speaks.* London: KPI Ltd.

Garst, R. and T. Barry. 1990. *Feeding the Crisis: U.S. Food Aid and Farm Policy in Central America.* Lincoln and London: University of Nebraska Press.

Gerth, H. H., and C. Wright Mills, eds. 1948. *From Max Weber: Essays in Sociology.* London, Henley, and Boston: Routledge and Kegan Paul.

Ghosh, K. C. 1944. *Famine in Bengal, 1770–1943,* Calcutta: Indian Associated Publishing Co.

Gittinger, J. P. 1982. *Economic Analysis of Agricultural Projects.* Baltimore: Johns Hopkins University Press.

Gonda, S., and W. Mogga. 1988. "Loss of the Revered cattle." In *War Wounds: Sudanese People Report on Their War,* edited by N. Twose and B. Pogrund. London: Panos Institute.

Gray, J. R. 1961. *A History of the Southern Sudan, 1839–1889.* London: Oxford University Press.

Greenough, P. R. 1982. *Prosperity and Misery in Modern Bengal: The Famine of 1943–44.* New York: Oxford University Press.

Griffin, K. 1974. *The Political Economy of Agrarian Change: An Essay on the Green Revolution.* London: Macmillan.

Gurdon, C. 1984. *Sudan at the Crossroads*. Wisbech, England: Menas Press.

Hales, J. M. 1978. "The Pastoral System of the Meidob." Ph.D. diss., University of Cambridge.

Hancock, G. 1989. *Lords of Poverty*. London: Macmillan.

Hargey, T. 1981. "The Suppression of Slavery in the Sudan, 1898–1939." D. Phil., Oxford University.

Harrell-Bond, B. E. 1986. *Imposing Aid: Emergency Assistance to Refugees*. Oxford, New York, and Nairobi: Oxford University Press.

Hartmann B., and J. Boyce. 1979. *Needless Hunger: Voices from a Bangladesh Village*. San Francisco: Institute for Food and Development Policy.

Henderson, K.D.D. 1939. "A Note on the Migration of the Messiria Tribe into South West Kordofan." *Sudan Notes and Records* 32, pt. 1: 49–77.

Hilton, B. 1988. *The Age of Atonement: The Influence of Evangelicalism on Social and Economic Thought, 1785–1865*. Oxford: Clarendon Press.

Holt, P. M. 1958. *The Mahdist State in the Sudan, 1881–1898: A Study of Its Origins, Development and Overthrow*, Oxford: Oxford University Press.

Holt, P. M., and M. W. Daly. 1988. *A History of the Sudan: From the Coming of Islam to the Present Day*. London and New York: Longman.

Howell, P. P. 1951a. "Notes on the Ngok Dinka of Western Kordofan." *Sudan Notes and Records* 32: 239–93.

———. 1951b. *A Comparative Study of Customary Law among Cattle-Owning Tribes in the Southern Sudan*. Vol. 2. D. Phil., University of Oxford.

Hunting Technical Services. 1974. *Southern Darfur Land Use Planning Survey, Sudan*. Borehamwood, England: Hunting Technical Services.

Hutchinson, S. 1988. "The Nuer in Crisis: Coping with Money, War, and the State." 2 vols. Ph.D. diss., University of Chicago.

Ibrahim, A.R.A. 1985. "Regional Inequality and Underdevelopment in Western Sudan," Ph.D. diss., Sussex University.

Ibrahim, F. N. 1984. *Ecological Imbalance in the Republic of the Sudan—with Reference to Desertification in Darfur*. Bayreuth: Bayreuther Goewissenschaftliche Arbeiten.

Ibrahim, H. 1988. "Agricultural Development Policy, Ethnicity and Socio-political Change in the Nuba Mountains, Sudan." Ph.D. diss., University of Connecticut.

Illife, J. 1987. *The African Poor*. Cambridge, New York, and Melbourne: Cambridge University Press.

ILO/UNDP Employment Mission. 1976. *Growth, Employment, and Equity: A Comprehensive Strategy for the Sudan*. Geneva: ILO/UNDP.

Independent Commission on International Humanitarian Issues. 1985. *Famine: A Man-Made Disaster*. London and Sydney: Pan Books.

Jackson, T., with D. Eade. 1982. *Against the Grain: The Dilemma of Project Food Aid*. Oxford: Oxfam.

Jada, M. L. 1988. "The Four Enemies." In *War Wounds: Sudanese People Report on Their War*, edited by N. Twose and B. Pogrund. London: Panos Institute.

Jamal, S. 1990. "Sudan at War–and Slavery Flourishes." *Panoscope* (Panos Institute), no. 17, 3.

James, W. 1988. "Perceptions from an African Slaving Frontier." In *Slavery and*

*Other Forms of Unfree Labour*, edited by L. Archer. London: Routledge and Kegan Paul.

———. 1992. "Uduk Asylum Seekers in Gambela, 1992: Community Report and Options for Resettlement." UNHCR, October.

Jodha, N. S. 1975. "Famine and Famine Policies: Some Empirical Evidence." *Economic and Political Weekly* 10(2): 1609–23.

Johnson, D. H. 1986. "North-South Issues." In *Sudan since Nimeiri*, edited by P. Woodward. London: School of Oriental and African Studies, University of London.

———. 1988a. "The Southern Sudan." Report no. 78. Minority Rights Group, London.

———. 1988b. "Sudanese Military Slavery from the 18th to the 20th Century." In *Slavery and Other Forms of Unfree Labour*, edited by L. Archer. London: Routledge and Kegan Paul.

———. 1989a. "Political Ecology in the Upper Nile." *Journal of African History* 30(3): 463–86.

———. 1989b. "The Structure of a Legacy: Military Slavery in Northeast Africa." *Ethnohistory* 36(1): 72–88.

Karadawi, A. 1983. "Constraints on Assistance to Refugees: Some Observations from the Sudan." *World Development* 11(6): 537–47.

Karam, K. M. 1980. "Dispute Settlement among Pastoral Nomads in the Sudan." Master's thesis, University of Birmingham.

Keen, D. P. 1986. "The Incidence and Origins of Food Crises in Darfur, Sudan, since the Second World War." Master's thesis, London School of Economics and Political Science.

———. 1991a. "Targeting Emergency Food Aid: The Case of Darfur in 1985." In *To Cure All Hunger: Food Policy and Food Security in Sudan*, edited by S. Maxwell. London: Intermediate Technology Publications.

———. 1991b. "Benefits of Famine: A Political Economy of Famine and Relief in South-west Sudan, 1983–89." D.Phil, Oxford University.

———. 1991c. "A Disaster for Whom? Local Interests and International Donors during Famine among the Dinka of Sudan." *Disasters* 15(2): 150–65.

———. 1992. *Refugees: Rationing the Right to Life—the Crisis in Emergency Relief*. London: Zed Books.

———. 1993. *The Kurds in Iraq: How Safe Is Their Haven Now?* London: Save the Children Fund.

Kent, R. C. 1987. *Anatomy of Disaster Relief: The International Network in Action*, London and New York: Pinter Publishers.

Khalid, M. 1990. *The Government They Deserve: The Role of the Elite in Sudan's Political Evolution*. London and New York: Kegan Paul International.

Kilgour, M. C. 1990. "Refugees and Development: Dissonance in Sudan." *Middle East Journal* 44(4): 638–48.

King, P. 1986. *An African Winter*. Harmondsworth: Penguin.

Kovel, J. [1970] 1988. *White Racism: A Psychohistory*. Reprint, London: Free Association Books.

Kuper, L. 1981. *Genocide: Its Political Use in the Twentieth Century*. Harmondsworth: Penguin.

Lenin, V. I. [1917] 1939. "Imperializm, kak vîsshaya stadiya kapitalizma." Reprinted in *New Data for V. I. Lenin's Imperialism, the Highest State of Capitalism*, edited by E. Varga and L. Mendelsohn. London: Lawrence and Wishart.

————. [1918] 1945. "Letter to Petrograd Workers, May 22, 1918" and "Report to Joint Meeting of Central Executive Committee, Moscow Soviet and Trade Union Representatives, June 4, 1918." Reprinted in *Articles and Speeches, 1918–1919*. Vol. 23 of *Collected Works*. London: Lawrence and Wishart.

Lesch, A. M. 1991. "Sudan's Foreign Policy: In Search of Arms, Aid and Allies." In *Sudan: State and Society in Crisis*, edited by J. O. Voll. Bloomington: Indiana University Press.

Lienhardt, G. 1961. *Divinity and Experience: The Religion of the Dinka*. Oxford: Clarendon Press.

McAlpin, M. B. 1983. *Subject to Famine: Food Crises and Economic Change in Western India, 1860–1920*. Princeton, N.J.: Princeton University Press.

MacDonagh, C. 1956. "Irish Emigration to the USA and the British Colonies during the Famine." In *The Great Famine*, edited by R. D. Edwards and T. D. Williams. Dublin: Irish Committee of Historical Sciences and Browne and Nolan.

McDowell, R. B. 1956. "Ireland on the Eve of the Famine." In *The Great Famine*, edited by R. D. Edwards and T. D. Williams. Dublin: Irish Committee of Historical Sciences and Browne and Nolan.

McHugh, R. J. 1956. "The Famine in Irish Oral Tradition." In *The Great Famine*, edited by R. D. Edwards and T. D. Williams. Dublin: Irish Committee of Historical Sciences and Browne and Nolan.

McKerrow, R. J. 1979. "Inside the Agencies." *Disasters* 3(2): 131–33.

McLoughlin, P.F.M. 1962. "Economic Development and the Heritage of Slavery in the Sudan Republic." *Africa* 32(4): 355–91.

MacMichael, H. A. 1967. *The Tribes of Northern and Central Kordofan*. London: Frank Cass and Co.

Mahmoud, F. B. 1984. *The Sudanese Bourgeoisie: Vanguard of Development?* London: Zed Books; Khartoum: Khartoum University Press.

Mahmud, U. A., and S. A. Baldo. 1987. *Al Daien Massacre: Slavery in the Sudan*. Khartoum: Human Rights Violations in the Sudan.

Malwal, B. 1985. *The Sudan: A Second Challenge to Nationhood*. New York: Thornton Books.

Mawson, A.M.M. 1984. "Southern Sudan: A Growing Conflict." *The World Today*, December, 520–27.

————. 1989. "The Triumph of Life: Political Dispute and Religious Ceremonial among the Agar Dinka of the Southern Sudan." Ph.D. diss., University of Cambridge.

Meillassoux, C. 1974. "Development or Exploitation: Is the Sahel Famine Good Business?" *Review of African Political Economy*, no. 1, 27–33.

Minear, L. 1991. *Humanitarianism under Siege: A Critical Review of Operation Lifeline Sudan*. Trenton, N.J.: Red Sea Press; Washington, D.C.: Bread for the World.

Mohamed Salih, M. A. 1990. "Ecological Stress and Political Coercion in the Sudan." *Disasters* 14(2): 123–31.

————. 1993. "Pastoralists and the War in Southern Sudan: The Ngok Dinka/Humr

Conflict in South Kordofan." In *Conflict and the Decline of Pastoralism in the Horn of Africa*, edited by J. Markakis. Basingstoke: Macmillan and Institute of Social Studies, The Hague.

Mollat, M. [1978] 1986. *The Poor in the Middle Ages: An Essay in Social History*. Reprint, New Haven and London: Yale University Press.

Moore, H. 1990. "When Is a Famine Not a Famine?" *Anthropology Today* 6(1): 1–3.

Morren, G.E.B. 1983. "A General Approach to the Identification of Hazards and Responses." in *Interpretations of Calamity*, edited by K. Hewitt. Winchester, Mass.: Allen and Unwin.

*News from Africa Watch*. Various dates. Africa Watch, London.

Niamir, M., R. Huntington, and D. C. Cole. 1983. *Ngok Dinka Cattle Migrations and Marketings: A Missing Piece of the Sudan Mosaic*. Development Discussion Paper, no. 155, Harvard Institute for International Development, Cambridge, Mass.

Niblock, T. 1987. *Class and Power in Sudan: The Dynamics of Sudanese Politics, 1898–1985*, Basingstoke: Macmillan.

Nowlan, K. B. 1956. "Political Background." In *The Great Famine*, edited by R. D. Edwards and T. D. Williams. Dublin: Irish Committee of Historical Sciences and Browne and Nolan.

O'Fahey, R. S. 1973. "Slavery and the Slave Trade in Dar Fur." *Journal of African History* 14(1): 29–43.

―――. 1980. *State and Society in Dar Fur*. London: C. Hurst and Co.

Okpoko, J. 1986. *The Biafran Nightmare: The Controversial Role of International Relief Agencies in a War of Genocide*. Enugu, Nigeria: Delta.

Oleskiw, S. 1983. *The Agony of a Nation: The Great Man-made Famine in Ukraine, 1932–33*. London: The National Committee to Commemorate the 50th Anniversary of the Artificial Famine in Ukraine 1932–33.

Omaar, R. 1992. "Somalia's Nightmare." *West Africa*, August 17–23, 1382–83.

O'Neill, T. P. 1956. "The Organisation and Administration of Relief, 1845–52." In *The Great Famine*, edited by R. D. Edwards and T. D. Williams. Dublin: Irish Committee of Historical Sciences and Browne and Nolan.

Philp, M. 1985. "Michel Foucault." In *The Return of Grand Theory in the Human Sciences*, edited by Q. Skinner. Cambridge: Cambridge University Press.

Pressman, J., and A. Wildavsky, eds. 1973. *Implementation: How Great Expectations in Washington Are Dashed in Oakland*. Berkeley, Los Angeles, and London: University of California Press.

Prunier, G. 1986. *From Peace to War: The Southern Sudan 1972–1984*. Occasional Paper, no. 3, Department of Sociology and Social Anthropology, Hull University.

Raikes, P. 1988. *Modernising Hunger*. London: Catholic Institute for International Relations.

Rangasami, A. 1985. "'Failure of Exchange Entitlements' Theory of Famine: A Response." *Economic and Political Weekly* 20(41, 42): 1747–52, 1797–1801.

Ravallion, M. 1987. *Markets and Famines*. Oxford: Clarendon Press.

Regan, C. 1983. "Underdevelopment and Hazards in Historical Perspective: An Irish Case-study." In *Interpretations of Calamity*, edited by J. Hewitt. Winchester, Mass.: Allen and Unwin.

Ryle, J. 1982. *Warriors of the White Nile*. Amsterdam: Time Life Books.

Ryle, J. 1989a. "Displaced Southern Sudanese in Northern Sudan with Special Reference to Southern Darfur and Kordofan." February. Mimeo.

———. 1989b. "The Road to Abyei." *Granta* (Cambridge) 26 (spring): 41–104.

Saeed, A. 1982. "The State and Socioeconomic Transformation in the Sudan: The Case of Social Conflict in Southwest Kordofan." Ph.D. diss., University of Connecticut.

Sanderson, L. P., and Sanderson, N. 1981. *Education, Religion and Politics in Southern Sudan, 1899–1964*, London: Ithaca Press; Khartoum: Khartoum University Press.

Schaffer, B. B. 1984. "Towards Responsibility: Public Policy in Concept and Practice." In *Room for Manoeuvre*, edited by E. J. Clay and B. B. Schaffer. London: Heinemann Educational Books.

Schweinfurth, G. 1873. *The Heart of Africa*. Vol. 2. London: Sampson Low, Marston, Low and Searle.

Sen, A. K. 1981. *Poverty and Famines: An Essay on Entitlement and Deprivation*. Oxford: Clarendon Press.

Sen, A. K. 1990. "Individual Freedom as a Social Commitment." *New York Review of Books*, June 14, 49-54.

Sheets, H., and R. Morris. 1974. "Disaster in the Desert: Failures of International Relief in the West Africa Drought." Special Report. Humanitarian Policy Studies, Carnegie Endowment for International Peace.

Shepherd, A. W. 1984. "Nomads, Farmers, and Merchants: Old Strategies in a changing Sudan." In *Life before the Drought*, edited by E. Scott. Boston: Allen and Unwin.

———. 1988. "Case Studies of Famine: Sudan." In *Preventing Famine: Policies and Prospects for Africa*, edited by D. Curtis, M. Hubbard, and A. Shepherd. London and New York: Routledge.

Sikainga, A.A.M. 1986. "British Policy in Western Bahr el Ghazal (Sudan), 1904–1946." Ph.D. diss., University of California, Santa Barbara.

Smart, B. [1985] 1988. *Michel Foucault*. London and New York: Routledge.

Smith, S., and M. Clarke, eds. 1985. *Foreign Policy Implementation*. London: Allen and Unwin.

Smolowe, J. 1992. "Great Expectations." *Time*, December 21, 29–31.

Sobhan, R. 1979. "Politics of Food and Famine in Bangladesh." *Economic and Political Weekly* 14(48): 1973–80.

Spaulding, J. 1982. "Slavery, Land Tenure and Social Class in the Northern Turkish Sudan." *International Journal of African Historical Studies* 15(1): 1–20.

Stevenson, J. 1993. "Hope Restored in Somalia?" *Foreign Policy*, no. 91, 138–54.

Stremlau, J. 1977. *The International Politics of the Nigerian Civil War, 1967–1970*. Princeton, N.J.: Princeton University Press.

Swift, J. 1989. "Why are Rural People Vulnerable to Famine?" *IDS Bulletin* 20(2): 8–15.

Titherington, Major G. W. 1927. "The Raik of Bahr el Ghazal Province." *Sudan Notes and Records* 10: 159–209.

Tosh, J. 1981. "The Economy of the Southern Sudan under the British, 1889–1955." *Journal of Imperial and Commonwealth History* 9(3): 275–88.

Twose, N., and B. Pogrund, eds. 1988. *War Wounds: Sudanese People Report on Their War*. London: Panos Institute.

United Kingdom. *See* Foreign Affairs Committee.

U.S. Committee for Refugees. 1990. *Khartoum's Displaced Persons: A Decade of Despair*. Washington, D.C.: U.S. Committee for Refugees.

U.S. Committee for Refugees. 1993. *Quantifying Genocide in the Southern Sudan 1983–1993* (M. Burr).

van Bruinessen, M. 1992. *Agha, Shaikh and State: The Social and Political Structures of Kurdistan*. London: Zed Books.

van Voorhis, B. 1989. "Food as a Weapon for Peace." Centre for Concern, July. Mimeo.

Vaughan, M. 1987. *The Story of an African Famine: Gender and Famine in Twentieth Century Malawi*. Cambridge: Cambridge University Press.

Vincent, A. W. 1988. "Religion and Nation in a Traditional Society: Ideology, Leadership and the Role of the Umma Party as a Force for Social Change in Northern Sudan." Ph.D. diss., University of Pennsylvania.

Wai, D. 1973. *The Southern Sudan: The Problem of National Integration*. London: Frank Cass and Co.

Wani, M. 1988. "Women—Now the Sole Breadwinners." In *War Wounds: Sudanese People Report on Their War*, edited by N. Twose and B. Pogrund. London: Panos Institute.

Warburg, G. 1971. *The Sudan under Wingate: Administration in the Anglo-Egyptian Sudan, 1899–1916*. London: Frank Cass and Co.

―――――. 1978. *Islam, Nationalism and Communism in a Traditional Society: The Case of Sudan*. London: Frank Cass and Co.

―――――. 1990. "The *Sharia* in Sudan: Implementation and Repercussions, 1983–89." *Middle East Journal* 44(4): 624–37.

―――――. 1992. *Historical Discord in the Nile Valley*. London: Hurst and Co.

Watts, M. 1983. *Silent Violence: Food, Famine, and Peasantry in Northern Nigeria*. Berkeley, Los Angeles, and London: University of California Press.

Whittaker, A. 1988. "Slavery in Sudan." *The Reporter and Aborigines' Friend*, 7th ser. 13(4): 64–71.

Wilson, K. 1989. "Towards Understanding the War." *Africa Events*, April, 27–29.

―――――. 1991. "Ecological Dynamics and Human Welfare: A Case-Study of Population, Health and Nutrition in Southern Zimbabwe." Ph.D diss., University College, London.

―――――. 1993. "Relief and Livelihoods in War Zones in Africa." In *Development Research Insights for Policymakers*. Brighton, England: Overseas Development Administration/Institute of Development Studies.

Wilson, R. T. 1977. "Temporal Changes in Livestock Numbers and Patterns of Transhumance in Southern Darfur, Sudan." *Journal of Developing Areas*, July, 493–508.

Wiseberg, L. S. 1974. "Humanitarian Intervention: Lessons from the Nigerian Civil War." *Revue des droits de l'homme*, March, 61–98.

Woldegabriel, B. 1991. "Red Tape and Refugees: Food Distribution Problems in Host Countries." Paper read at International Symposium, Refugee Studies Programme, Oxford University, March 17–20.

# Index